Reading
Dream of the Red Chamber

Also by Ronald R. Gray
and from McFarland

American Gadfly: The Intellectual Odyssey of Paul Fussell (2019)

Reading
Dream of the Red Chamber
A Companion to Cao Xueqin's Masterpiece

Ronald R. Gray

McFarland & Company, Inc., Publishers
Jefferson, North Carolina

LIBRARY OF CONGRESS CATALOGUING-IN-PUBLICATION DATA

Names: Gray, Ronald R., author.
Title: Reading Dream of the red chamber : a companion to Cao Xueqin's masterpiece / Ronald R. Gray.
Description: Jefferson, North Carolina : McFarland & Company, Inc., Publishers, 2022 | Includes bibliographical references and index.
Identifiers: LCCN 2022037087 |
ISBN 9781476681146 (paperback : acid free paper) ∞
ISBN 9781476645827 (ebook)
Subjects: LCSH: Cao, Xueqin, approximately 1717-1763. Hong lou meng. | BISAC: LITERARY CRITICISM / Asian / General | LCGFT: Literary criticism. | Encyclopedias
Classification: LCC PL2727.S2 G73 2022 | DDC 895.13/48—dc23
LC record available at https://lccn.loc.gov/2022037087

BRITISH LIBRARY CATALOGUING DATA ARE AVAILABLE

ISBN (print) 978-1-4766-8114-6
ISBN (ebook) 978-1-4766-4582-7

© 2022 Ronald R. Gray. All rights reserved

No part of this book may be reproduced or transmitted in any form or by any means, electronic or mechanical, including photocopying or recording, or by any information storage and retrieval system, without permission in writing from the publisher.

Front cover: (left) One of the *Twelve Beauties of Jinling* by an anonymous artist of the Qing dynasty (Posner Center Collection, Carnegie Mellon University); (right) dragon from the flag of the Plain White Banner Group of the Cao family

Printed in the United States of America

McFarland & Company, Inc., Publishers
Box 611, Jefferson, North Carolina 28640
www.mcfarlandpub.com

To
Zhou Ruchang 周汝昌 (1918–2012)
Scholar, Teacher, Mentor, Friend

Table of Contents

Acknowledgments viii

Preface 1

Introduction 7

A Brief Biography of Cao Xueqin 11

Tips on Reading
Dream of the Red Chamber 19

The Companion 23

Recommended Reading 255

Index 269

Acknowledgments

I would like to thank my former Beijing Language and Culture University student Li Li, who now teaches at Central University of Finance and Economics, for her help with the bibliography and the entry on spitting. In addition, great thanks to Terence Allred, who diligently and carefully edited the text. Although we have vastly different views concerning the aesthetic value of reading translated literary texts, his extensive corrections made my argument for reading *Dream of the Red Chamber* clearer. Thanks also to my former Ohio University colleague Robert Wyss for his editing and positive feedback. *Komapsumnida* again to my wife Kyongsook Park for her constant support and help with the Chinese characters. Finally, my greatest thanks to the late Chinese scholar Zhou Ruchang, whose personal kindness and infectious enthusiasm for and great knowledge of *Honglou meng* kept me motivated while researching, writing, and talking about this novel for the last 20 years.

Preface

One of the hallmarks of a great work of literature is that after a person reads it, they long remember where and when they did and why it made such a strong impact on them. Literary masterpieces have a tendency to influence our lives in unexpected ways, as has certainly been the case for me on reading *Dream of the Red Chamber*.

Beijing in January 2002 was bitterly cold. I was teaching at Beijing Language and Culture University in the capital's Haidan district, and it was winter vacation. My wife, who was studying Chinese in the university's graduate program, had gone back to South Korea to visit her family for the break, and I was looking forward to a quiet period and getting some reading done. The university's library was a short walk from the foreign faculty's apartments, and I soon found myself browsing reading material in its English section. I came across translations of the famous four classics of traditional Chinese fiction: *Outlaws of the Marsh, Journey to the West, Three Kingdoms,* and *Dream of the Red Chamber,* and, having recently heard about the latter, I decided to give it a try. The translation I selected was done by the well-known husband and wife team of Yang Hsien-Yi and Gladys Yang and was published in 1978.

I began reading the first volume that afternoon and was instantly transfixed by the story. Few books have emotionally and intellectually affected me so strongly. After three days of intensive reading, I completed the novel and then did something that I have rarely done with a book: I immediately read it again. I next tried to find as much information as I could about the work and its mysterious author, Cao Xueqin. Unfortunately, no comprehensive reader's guide to the novel existed in English at that time, but there were numerous scholarly studies and articles. I also decided that I would one day try to write one on this work.

Nearly 21 years later, I can still easily recall why I was so taken with this book. First of all, I found the story, for a novel that was written in the 18th century and that took place in a very different society from today's, remarkably realistic and riveting. The story's characters were believable, and many were interesting, finely drawn, and spoke realistically. They were also often relatable as they dealt with real-life dilemmas and concerns. What's more, I was surprised to find in the story several characteristics frequently associated with many modern novels, such as skepticism, irony, and an open-text nature and ending. In addition, I was also captivated by the book's encyclopedic nature and the way in which virtually all aspects of traditional Chinese culture were captured as well as all strata of Qing dynasty society. Before coming to China in 2000, I had spent more than ten years teaching in Japan and South Korea and hence was familiar with some of the cultural beliefs held in *Dream of the Red Chamber*, but the novel's cultural scope really stood out. I was also impressed by the philosophical content and subtext of the work. My undergraduate and graduate degrees are in philosophy, and, although I did not have an extensive knowledge of Chinese philosophy, I knew enough to appreciate the philosophical sophistication and richness of the work and was struck by Cao Xueqin's fascination with perennial philosophical issues like the status and validity of an individual's epistemological, moral, and ontological claims about the self and world.

Furthermore, the novel fundamentally touched on all the core events of life itself: birth, family, youth, career, love, systems of belief, and death. With each reading, I have also been amazed by how tightly woven the novel is and the multilayered levels on which it operates (the realistic, mythological, supernatural, autobiographical, narrative, allegorical, and philosophical).

Several months later, I came across a notice about an upcoming lecture on *Dream of the Red Chamber* in a weekly English magazine for expats in Beijing. The announcement said the talk was to be delivered by one of China's premier experts on the work, Zhou Ruchang. Zhou had written over 70 books on all aspects of the novel and had uncovered important historical information about Cao Xueqin's life and family background. He was also a controversial figure in academic circles in China because of several of his theories about the novel. I knew little about him at the time other than he was a prominent scholar whose research was frequently cited by Western scholars. The talk was to be held at the Cha Jia Tea House in the Houhai lake area of Beijing, which was an ideal venue for many experts on the novel believe the Jia family mansions had been located in this area. Moreover, Zhou had argued in a best selling book that the small but elegant garden in nearby Prince Gong's mansion served as the model for the story's celebrated Prospect Garden. Because of my newfound interest in the novel, I decided to attend the event.

On the day of the lecture, the small teahouse where it was held was full with about 30 foreigners and Chinese. Zhou, who was then 85, began the lecture by stating that his message was that reading *Dream of the Red Chamber* was an excellent and entertaining way to understand Chinese culture and society. Among the many intriguing points he made during the talk was the importance of viewing Cao Xueqin not only as a great novelist but also as a gifted poet and a remarkable philosopher. He also maintained that the high status Cao Xueqin has enjoyed in China was comparable to the towering status accorded to Shakespeare in the West. In addition, he also underscored the significance of the concept of *qing* in the novel, which he translated as meaning "good will, a tender heart, a concern for others, the need to treat others well ... it means more than simply love or feeling."

Zhou spoke for over an hour, without notes and often in English, until a break was taken, which was remarkable because at this stage he was nearly blind and almost deaf. He then adeptly answered a wide variety of questions. The audience was spellbound by the talk, and Zhou's infectious enthusiasm about the novel quickly spread, and there were numerous questions for him after the break. I felt reluctant to talk to him because I had been so awed by his performance. Fortunately, Zhou gave another excellent lecture for foreigners at a small hotel in Beijing several months later, which I also attended. This time I resolved to speak to him, which I did, shortly before the lecture. Surprisingly, during the break, he got up from his chair and walked over to me and said, "Could I talk to you for a minute?" I was completely nonplussed and replied "Sure." He then told me in English, "Remember, when you speak or write about *Dream of the Red Chamber*, to talk about the differences." What he meant (for Zhou was very much a cultural essentialist) was that in order for Westerners to understand this massive and complex novel, it was essential that they have some understanding of the key cultural differences that exist between China and the West.

After the lecture, when my wife and I were leaving, we ran into Zhou and his daughter, who were waiting for a taxi at the entrance of the hotel. My wife asked his daughter if we could visit him sometime. She graciously agreed and gave us his telephone number. Less than a month later, we paid our first of many visits to his book-cluttered small apartment in the Chaoyang district of Beijing. During the next six years, until I moved to the U.S., I would meet him a total of ten times (all of which were recorded) and would attend several more of his lectures. From that time on, our relationship quickly became that of a teacher and student. Each visit, which usually lasted two to three hours, soon began to roughly follow the style of an Oxford-type tutorial. I would conduct extensive research and come armed with a list of questions (usually around ten) and my current thoughts about aspects of the novel. Zhou was always polite and attentive and would patiently answer each of my questions, no matter how foolish they were. (And, in retrospect, I fear some of them were.) Sometimes, he would give further thought to a question I had asked or a point I had raised on a previous visit and would expand on it when we met again. We also communicated by letters and e-mail, and, on one occasion, he phoned to recommend some books.

Zhou was a first-rate motivator. After each of these meetings, I felt even more riveted by the novel and more determined to write about it.

In 2005, I had the opportunity to guest co-edit a special issue devoted to *Dream of the Red Chamber* of the English international journal on Chinese literature, the *Tamkang Review*. This was the first journal in English to do this. My co-editor, Mark Ferrara, and I were happily able to get a number of famous Western scholars on the novel, including Andrew Plaks, Lucien Miller, Louise Edwards, Andrew Schonebaum, Haun Saussy, and Dore Levy, to contribute to it. I contributed an article on the Chinese philosopher Zhuangzi and the character Jia Bao-yu as well as a bibliography of English writings on the novel, and Zhou provided an insightful paper on Cao Xueqin's philosophy of *qing*. In 2009, much to Zhou's delight, Ferrara and I edited an English translation of one of Zhou's books, which was

Zhou Ruchang and the author in Zhou's apartment in Beijing in 2007 (photograph by Kyongsook Park).

published under the title *Between Noble and Humble: Cao Xueqin and the Dream of the Red Chamber*. My wife and Ferrara's translated the book, and I supplied most of the book's footnotes.

As I progressed in my study of the novel, further opportunities presented themselves. Thanks in no small part to the tremendous efforts of one of my undergraduate students, Li Li, who became an invaluable research assistant and would eventually write her doctoral thesis on *Dream of the Red Chamber*, I was able to meet many other noted Chinese scholars on the novel, such as Cai Yijiang, Zhang Qingshan, and Duan Jiangli, and have discussions with them. Conducting research in China at that time, even on *Dream of the Red Chamber*, was not that easy and often required a great deal of patience. Academic search engines and digital libraries were limited. However, this was offset by the fact that Beijing University and Tsinghua University, the top schools in China, had at that time the wonderful policy of allowing foreign teachers and students to use their libraries and make copies of books and articles. (But the items could not be checked out.) Moreover, major bookstores in the city were full of studies on the novel. Ditan Park, in the northern part of the capital, held an outstanding book fair several times a year where it was easy to pick up older and hard-to-get copies of books on the work. In addition, the National Library of China, with its impressive collection, and the Cao Xueqin museum in the suburbs of Beijing, which contained an informative exhibit on Cao's life and family, were also good sources of information. By the time I left China in 2008, I had amassed ten boxes of research material to ship to the U.S. that contained books, articles, notes, pictures, and tape recordings of interviews I had conducted with Zhou and other Chinese scholars.

At first, I became very interested in the topic of the history of how *Dream of the Red Chamber* was perceived in the West and its English translation history. I had several papers published in Chinese journals (including the *Honglou meng Xuekan*, which is devoted to the novel) and Western periodicals and gave a lecture on the subject at an international conference on the novel held in Chengdu, China, in 2011. I then branched out to writing about Cao's life and times. In 2014, my own biography of Cao Xueqin, *Wandering Between Two Worlds: The Formative Years of Cao Xueqin 1715–1745*, was published. The extensive research required for this book was greatly helped when I received a research grant from Ohio University, where I was then teaching, that enabled me to travel to Beijing and visit areas of the city associated with Cao's life. Zhou kindly took the time to write an introduction to it.

One of the things that made Zhou unique was his all-consuming devotion to the novel, a passion that was almost religious in its fervor. He personified the fact that people who are *interested* are interesting. Right up until the day he died in 2012, in spite of his failing condition, he was, at the age of 94, in the process of writing yet another book on the work. I quickly learned from Zhou the importance of simply getting the word out to Westerners that *Dream of the Red Chamber* is not just a grand work of Chinese literature but also of world literature and that the best way to accomplish this is by writing about it.

    This guide is written in that spirit. For many years I have wanted to write a book that would answer the questions I had when I first read *Dream of the Red Chamber*, provide much needed background information, and explain why this novel is so special and worth reading. This companion does not purport to give definite answers to many of the controversies that rage about the work (some of which will probably never be settled); rather it seeks to offer readers differing interpretations of it and lets them decide for themselves. I have also endeavored to follow, when I can, Zhou's recommendation "to talk about the differences."

Introduction

The 18th-century Chinese novel *Honglou meng* (*Dream of the Red Chamber*) by Cao Xueqin is China's greatest and most popular novel. It is difficult to overemphasize the cultural significance of this work for Chinese. John Minford, who collaborated with David Hawkes on the most widely used English translation of the novel, has stated, "more than any other work of traditional Chinese literature [it] captures what it means and still means to be Chinese, to live a Chinese life, to feel Chinese.... It has occupied a central—and always controversial—space in Chinese cultural life ever since it was written."* (Even today, it is not uncommon for Chinese, when criticizing or praising other people, to compare them to characters in the novel.) One American scholar on the novel has written, "To appreciate its position in Chinese literature, we should imagine a work with the critical cachet of James Joyce's *Ulysses* and the popular appeal of Margaret Mitchell's *Gone with the Wind*."† The novel has also been popular outside of China. It has been translated into more than 22 languages (two full English translations have been published as well as numerous partial ones), and it has been estimated that it is the seventh best-selling book of all time and that more than 100,000,000 copies of the book have been sold.

But for Western readers, taking on this novel in translation might initially seem to be a daunting endeavor. The standard English translation of the book consists of five volumes and is around 2,500 pages long. The story has over 400 characters, which is more than all the characters in Shakespeare's dramas. Moreover, it was written more than 250 years ago. But this would be a wrong impression. *Dream of the Red Chamber* is a surprisingly accessible novel that operates on several levels. On its most basic level, it is a deeply human story with an engaging plot and is chock-full of

---

* John Minford. Foreword, *The Dream of the Red Chamber* by Cao Xueqin. Translated by H. Bancroft Joly (Tokyo: Tuttle Publishing, 2010): xii.
† Dore Levy. *Ideal and Actual in The Story of the Stone* (New York: Columbia University Press, 1999): 2.

realistic "round" and interesting characters talking in realistic dialogues and confronting real situations. Like all great works of literature, it deals with universal themes like death, love, friendship, and conflicts over systems of beliefs. *Dream of the Red Chamber* is also a tragic love story, a *bildungsroman*, and an illuminating tale of the rise and sudden fall of an illustrious family. Moreover, the novel surprisingly has characteristics that are commonly associated with many modern novels: irony, skepticism, subversion, an interest in the question of fictional representation, and an open-text nature and ending. (When one compares it to the quality of many of the novels that were appearing during the same period in the West, its achievement becomes even more impressive.)

The book is also a remarkable cultural compendium and encyclopedia of upper-class Qing dynasty life. It describes in great detail such varied subjects as Chinese gardening; medical, educational, drinking, monetary, culinary, literary, sexual, and religious practices; clothing styles; the lives of servants, upper-class reading habits and pastimes; and contains a generous sampling of all the major Chinese literary genres and modes as well as philosophical schools. It also gives readers useful tips on managing a large household, writing good verse, cooking a tasty dish, elegantly decorating a room, painting a picture, and appreciating dramas. The distinguished Chinese scholar on the novel, Zhou Ruchang, has stated that *Dream of the Red Chamber* provides the easiest and most interesting way for Westerners to learn about traditional Chinese culture.

Finally, the book can also be read as a philosophical novel. It is deeply concerned with longstanding, troubling philosophical issues like the transitory and illusory nature of existence, the meaning of life, what constitutes personal identity, the nature of love, the ontological status of dreams, and the problematic relationship between truth/falsity and reality/illusion. It also asks hard questions about the Qing dynasty and traditional Chinese society, and some have argued that it offers a radical critique of the human condition. This philosophical bent can be seen in the novel's Chinese title, *Honglou meng*. *Hong* means "red," which, in Chinese culture, signifies happiness, fortune, prosperity, beauty, and youth. *Lou* is a two-story building and conveys images of a luxurious place where young women lived or stayed and suggests a feminine world. *Meng* is "dream" and carries strong philosophical meaning and signifies past happy or golden days that are vivid in one's memory but now seem like nothing more than an unreal or illusory dream. The novel also has a great deal of thematic indeterminacy and ambiguity, and there is still a great debate over what its major theme or overarching vision is or if it ultimately even has one.

Readers will also find the novel an eye-opening corrective to widely held Western exoticized images of traditional China, which sees the country as having been a land of Confucian harmony, wise scholar-officials, eccentric and learned religious sages, familial accord, unreflective filial obedience, passive and pliant but sexually alluring women, reserved and inscrutable males, and glamorous Daoist and Buddhist mysticism. They will find instead believable and often relatable characters who are attempting, like the reader, to deal with the warp and woof of everyday existence. Moreover, *Dream of the Red Chamber* graphically shows the conflict that existed between Confucianism and social beliefs and actual behavior.

The purpose of this companion is to provide general readers with a useful guide to this masterpiece. It aims to help them successfully navigate this massive novel. While both published complete English translations of the novel contain notes, the notes are very limited and fail to provide comprehensive information about important aspects of the story. This companion attempts to remedy this situation and covers topics ranging from information on the novel's main characters, themes, narrative techniques, naming system, significant events, important historical and literary allusions to its use of doubles, outsiders, and foreshadowing techniques. It also has entries on such subjects as Confucianism, Buddhism, Daoism, Chinese philosophy, the imperial examination system, the Qing legal system, government censorship, marriage practices, money, festivals, clothing, drama, food, Chinese garden design, poetry, medicine, riddles, the status of women, and Chinese and Western critical perceptions of the novel. Because of severe length restrictions, it was unfortunately impossible to cover all the allusions, references, and topics covered in this huge and dense work or to discuss the ones that are covered in the amount of detail they deserve. Chinese guides to *Dream of the Red Chamber* that use the form this guide takes are typically massive, but a deliberate attempt is made here to describe the important ones. Some of the entries are accompanied by a short list of further readings on the topic being discussed.

This book also contains a short biography of Cao Xueqin's life and practical tips on reading the novel. Finally, the appendix has a detailed bibliography of recommended books and articles for individuals who want more information on aspects of the story. All of these recommended readings and the references cited in this guide come from works in English because this guide is primarily intended for individuals who do not know the Chinese language. This companion will primarily rely upon the David Hawkes and John Minford English translation of *Honglou meng* (which is published under the title of *The Story of the Stone* by Penguin Books) for names and quotes. It will also occasionally quote passages from the Yang Xianyi and Gladys Yang translation, which is titled *A Dream of Red Mansions* and published by Beijing's Foreign Languages Press. The Hawkes/

Minford translation will be referred to as SS and the Yang as DRM, followed by the relevant volume and page number. For example: (SS, 1: 27). For the sake of continuity, the pinyin system will be used for the transliteration of Chinese names where needed, including in quotations from secondary material.

A Brief Biography of Cao Xueqin

Cao Xueqin's life is full of tragic ironies: his masterpiece *Dream of the Red Chamber* was not published until nearly 30 years after his death, and he was not formally recognized as the author of the novel until the early 20th century. Moreover, even today we know very little about his life, and what we do know would barely fill a page. But we do know much about his unusual family background.

There are many theories regarding Cao Xueqin's ancestors and the location of his ancestral home, but they remain unsubstantiated. It appears that in 1621, his great-great-grandfather, Cao Xiyuan, a Chinese colonist in Manchuria, was captured in Shenyang by Manchu forces under the command of the famous Jurchen chieftain Nurhaci. Xiyuan was subsequently made a bondservant and was eventually placed, along with his family, in the Plain White Banner of the famed Manchu Eight Banner system. The banner system was a very complicated Manchu social institution that performed numerous key economic, military, economic and political functions and over time became an essential part of Manchu identity. According to one noted historian, the Eight Banners can be thought of as a mixture of the American "Marine Corps, the Civil Service, the Veteran Administration, thickly overlaid with a combination of old-boy networks, political preferences, and partially articulated Affirmative Action Policies."*

Belonging to the Plain White Banner was a remarkable piece of luck and would greatly contribute to the rise of the Cao family in power and affluence for it was a very prestigious Upper Banner that eventually came under the direct control of the emperor himself. An added benefit was that bondservants of this banner later became attached to *Neiwufu,* the Imperial Household Department, which primarily catered to the needs of the emperor and his family in the Forbidden City.

---

* Mark C. Elliott. *The Manchu Way: The Eight Banners and Ethnic Identity in Late Imperial China* (Stanford: Stanford University Press, 2001): 41.

The flag of the Plain White Banner group to which the Cao family belonged.

Cao Xiyuan's son, Cao Zhenyan, was able to take advantage of belonging to this banner because Upper Banner bondservants could take the imperial civil service examination. He did and passed and, owing to his competency, was later elevated to the lucrative post of Salt Controller of Tang-che. During the early years of the Qing dynasty, the Manchu government needed to secure its control of the lower Yangtze region in the south and gain the support of and carefully monitor the behavior of Han Chinese in the region. In order to achieve this, emperors developed the policy of using competent Imperial Household Department bondservants to serve as Textile and Salt Commissioners in the important southern cities of Nanjing, Hangzhou, and Suzhou. Members of the Cao family for several generations would fulfill this role. But there always was a special condition that came with these high positions because imperial bondservants had the unique status of being both masters and slaves. While they wielded much power and could accrue a great deal of money, they were also slaves of the emperor, and their future was entirely dependent upon his whims, and they could be broken at any time by him.

Cao Zhenyuan's young son, Cao Xi, who was Cao Xueqin's great-grandfather, was the first member of the family to become one of these commissioners. He started out as a palace guard and was eventually appointed to the very high and respected position of Textile Commissioner for Nanjing. This position involved overseeing the city's large government-owned silk factories which employed thousands of workers, ensuring that yearly quotas were met and that the finished silk was safely transported to the imperial court in Beijing via the Grand Canal. In addition, Cao Xi's wife, nee Sun, served as a wet nurse to the future Kangxi emperor's children and formed a special relationship with him.

But the member of the Cao family who has most stood out and has had a great influence on Cao Xueqin was his grandfather Cao Yin. Talented in many fields, Yin was a government official, poet, dramatist, a devoted collector of books and Western objects, and skilled at archery and horsemanship. On the emperor's orders, he also supervised the printing of a massive collection of poetry of the Tang dynasty. Cao Yin was a well-liked and gregarious individual who developed close friendships with high-ranking officials, affluent salt merchants, and members of the literati. Moreover, he was also a confidant of the Kangxi emperor, hosting him on four occasions during Kangxi's famous southern tours, and both of his daughters married Manchu princes. (Cao Xueqin's pride in his grandfather's accomplishments can be seen in *Dream of the Red Chamber* in chapter 16, where Kangxi's visits to the Cao family are alluded to, and chapter 54, where Grandmother Jia references Cao Yin's drama *The Lute Player's Return,* which was a sequel to the very popular Ming dynasty play *The Story of the Lute* by Gao Ming.)

Like his father, Cao Xi, he also served as Textile Commissioner for Nanjing and was also Salt Censor for the Lianghuai Salt Monopoly. He also performed the vital role of interceding between the Manchu government and Chinese officials and literati. While he amassed a large private fortune, at the time of his death in 1712 he was deeply in debt. His passing marked the eventual decline of the Cao family. After Cao Yin's death, his only son, Cao Yong, took over the post of Textile Commissioner, but he unexpectedly died in 1715. Thanks to the intercession of Emperor Kangxi, the Cao family was able to adopt a paternal nephew, Cao Fu, to succeed Cao Yong. Evidence appears to support the conclusion that Cao Fu was Cao Xueqin's father.

While it is still unclear precisely when Cao Xueqin was born in Nanjing, it is now generally thought it was sometime in the spring of 1715. He had a pampered upbringing in the palatial official residence for the Textile Commissioner in Nanjing, which was built in 1662 and consisted of 483 rooms, a large beautiful garden that surrounded a mossy pond, an archery field, a theater where the family's theatrical group performed, and government offices. The middle section of the residence, which contained the family quarters, was five buildings deep with graceful, sloping roofs in the southern architectural style and a small elegant garden. The compound was staffed by an army of 114 servants. Cao's childhood was suddenly cut short in January 1728 when the Yongzheng Emperor ordered the confiscation of the Cao family properties officially because of Cao Fu's mismanagement of government funds and charges that he committed extortion. This traumatic event would haunt Xueqin for the rest of his life. After the confiscation, his impoverished family was forced to relocate to a 17-and-a-half-room courtyard house in the Outer City of Beijing.

The Cao family's situation appears to have briefly improved during the first years of their time in Beijing, but, in 1745, another political purge occurred during the reign of the Qianlong Emperor, and the Cao house may have been confiscated and some family members arrested. It is unclear what Cao did during much of his early years in the capital. There are unsubstantiated rumors that he worked as a tutor to several rich families and that he lived with Prince Ping, who had married one of Cao Yin's daughters, until Ping's death in 1748 and then stayed in a monastery in

Houhai, a lake in the center of Beijing. During the Qing dynasty, many members of the royal family and high officials lived in mansions in this area. It has been argued, based on clues in the novel, that the Jia family mansions would have been located here. Prince Gong's famous mansion, whose garden may have served as a model for the novel's Prospect Garden, is also nearby.

An old tree in the Xidan district of Beijing that would have "seen" Cao Xueqin because it grew on the grounds of the Right Wing Imperial Clan School where Cao worked at one time.

the city for a short time. It does appear that he worked as a clerk in the Right Wing Imperial Clan School founded by Yongzheng in 1724 to educate the children of noble families. At this school he met the Dun brothers, who were related to the royal family but whose family, like Xueqin's, had suffered from political persecution. The brothers became two of his closest friends, so we will provide what little information we have about him.

A Brief Biography of Cao Xueqin

Cao Xueqin began to write *Dream of the Red Chamber* around 1745. At first, he intended the work to be a drama but then decided to write it as a novel. He then spent years writing and rewriting the story and loaning versions of it to friends for comments. The most important of these commentators was the mysterious Zhiyanzhai (Red Inkstone), who was personally close to Cao, helped edit the novel, and provided illuminating comments on the story's themes, Cao's writing techniques, and real incidents on which parts of the novel were based. Many existing manuscript versions of the novel contain Red Inkstone's comments in red ink. The identity of Zhiyanzhai remains unknown. Another influential commentator was Odd Tablet, who also was close to Cao Xueqin and persuaded him to cut a section of the story dealing with the death of the female character Qin-shi. Cao was not able to put together a final, complete version of the novel before he died. Sadly, some of his manuscripts were lost or misplaced after being borrowed, so we have no manuscript copies of the novel that go beyond the first 80 chapters. According to accounts by his friends, Cao

The Western Hills outside Beijing where Cao Xueqin lived during the last years of his life.

A Brief Biography of Cao Xueqin

Xueqin was not only a gifted writer but also was well schooled in many areas, including the theater, painting, and music, and he sang and played the lute well. Cao was known for being a complex character. While he was an entertaining, witty, and humorous conversationalist and great storyteller, he was also noted for his unorthodox beliefs and behavior and love of drinking. (He was most probably an alcoholic.) He could also come off at times as proud, contentious, and cynical. Cao is described physically as being stocky, short in stature, swarthy, and heavy faced.

In the last years of his life, Cao lived a hardscrabble existence and struggled to support his family. Deeply frustrated about his situation, he moved to the countryside west of Beijing and settled in a small cottage near a Plain White Banner military camp. Details remain unclear about what he did during these difficult years. Some scholars have argued that he may have opened a tavern with his wife; others have conjectured that he made several trips to the Southern Yangzi region in search of work and that he tried to take the imperial exam. But the evidence for these theories remains weak. He might have received a small government stipend because he was a needy bannerman. We do know that he was gifted at painting rocks, which he sold as artwork, and that he probably made

Biyun Temple located in the Western Hills of Beijing near where Cao Xueqin lived after he moved out of the capital. He undoubtedly would have visited it.

some money loaning out manuscript versions of his novel. One friend, the Manchu poet Zhang Yiquan, who visited him during this time, wrote this about him:

> He loves to gratify his romantic ideas with pen and ink,
> The cottage he found in the western suburbs is uniquely quiet.
> Outside his door, hills and water offer themselves for his painting,
> In front of his hall flowers and birds come to his poems and song.*

Cao Xueqin was married twice. He had one son who tragically died in 1763, and Cao himself died from grief several months later on Chinese New Year's Eve in the same year. His burial place remains unknown. *Dream of the Red Chamber* would not be published until 1792 in a controversial 120-chapter edition that was edited by the Chinese poet, bannerman, and minor official Gao E. The novel was an immediate success and from that time on remained very popular in China (in spite of being banned on several occasions during the Qing dynasty and during the Cultural Revolution in the 1960s and early 1970s). It was not until 1921 with the publication of the essay "Proofs on *Dream of the Red Chamber*" by the Chinese scholar Hu Shih that Cao Xueqin was definitely acknowledged to be the author of the novel.

Further Reading

Gray, Ronald R. *Wandering Between Two Worlds: The Formative Years of Cao Xueqin 1715–1745* (New York: Peter Lang, 2014).

Huaiming, Miao, Guosheng Yang Chen, Trevor Hay, and Bo Ai. *Cao Xueqin* (Nanjing China, Nanjing University Press, 2010).

Wu, Shih-Ch'ang. *On the Red Chamber Dream: A Critical Study of Two Annotated Manuscripts of the XVIIIth Century* (Oxford University Press, 1961).

Zhou, Ruchang. *Between Noble and Humble: Cao Xueqin and the Dream of the Red Chamber*. Edited by Ronald R. Gray and Mark S. Ferrara (New York: Peter Lang, 2009).

---

* Wu Shih-Ch'ang. *On the Red Chamber Dream: A Critical Study of Two Annotated Manuscripts of the XVIIIth Century* (Oxford University Press, 1961): 127.

Tips on Reading
Dream of the Red Chamber

The first decision that first-time English readers of *Honglou meng* have to make concerns which translation to use. There exist two complete English translations of the novel, and both are readily available. The first was translated by the husband and wife team of Yang Xianyi and Gladys Yang and appears under the title of *A Dream of Red Mansions* and is published by Beijing's Foreign Languages Press. The second translation, which has the title *The Story of the Stone*, was completed by David Hawkes and John Minford and is published by Penguin. The Yangs' three-volume translation is considered competent and has been underrated by many critics, but the Hawkes/Minford five-volume work is thought to be the better translation and is the most widely read. Moreover, this translation is considered one of the finest English translations of Chinese literature ever published.

There are several important differences between these translations. The Yang translation is literal, sticks very closely to the original, and uses the Wade–Giles system to transliterate names and places in the story. The Hawkes/Minford translation is literary, and they use the pinyin system when transliterating names and places. In addition, both translations use different manuscript versions of the novel. Yang follows the *Jen-min* B version, and Hawkes principally relies upon *Jen-min* A, so the opening of the novel is slightly different as well as several other small scenes. While the Hawkes/Minford translation contains notes at the end of each volume covering topics like the Chinese imperial examination system, games in the novel, Chinese regulated verse, inconsistencies in the story concerning characters, the answers to certain riddles and the meaning of the song and dance suite in chapter 5, the Yang translation contains short notes on historical and literary personages, and Chinese cultural practices. For serious readers who want a more comprehensive and fuller feel for the novel, it is recommended that they read both translations of the novel.

There are several techniques first-time readers can use to help them get through the story. One of the first hurdles they encounter is the novel's large number of characters. (There are over 400.) Many of them come fast and furious in the initial chapters, and they often have similar-looking names, so keeping track of them all at first might seem quite overwhelming. Both translations provide readers with useful and detailed family trees that warrant study. Furthermore, Hawkes/Minford also give, at the back of each volume, a list of characters who have appeared in that volume and basic information about them. They also Romanize the names of the story's main characters and the members of the Jia family and transliterate the names of servants into English equivalents. This enables readers to differentiate between servants and the novel's main characters. As the reader proceeds deeper in the story, he will soon realize that the focus is on around ten central characters, and it will become progressively easier to remember them. Moreover, Cao Xueqin is so good at making each character unique, the reader should have a clear idea about who is who by the time the first volume has been finished.

It is strongly recommended that particular attention be paid to the first six chapters, for they are key, and where Cao brilliantly spells out the story's themes, topics, characters and concerns. (See this guide's entry on this topic: **The First Six and Other Key Chapters**.) In addition, the Hawkes appendix on the all-important chapter 5 is especially useful in explaining the meaning of the registers and the song and dance suite. Another tip is to carefully read the titles for each chapter. They take the form of antithetical couplets and give important information about what will occur in that chapter.

Several other points should also be kept in mind. *Dream of the Red Chamber* is an extremely sophisticated, tightly woven, and interconnected work of fiction, and Cao Xueqin has high expectations for his readers if they want to understand the gist of the novel. He uses several techniques to force them to be active readers, to read critically and, at times, skeptically and between the lines. Among these techniques he employs are the wide use of foreshadowing devices. Much of the novel's plot involves the working out of the "love *karma*" consequences of the fates of many of the central characters, mainly female, along with the story's protagonist. As a result, a wide variety of these devices, ranging from riddles, card games, and drinking songs to dramas and the connotations of character's names, subtly inform the reader what will happen to these people. (See **Foreshadowing**.) What's more, the novel is also a reflective work and often draws attention to its fictionality by shifting viewpoints, operating on several levels (including the mythological, realistic, allegorical), in the nontraditional role the narrator plays, its open-text nature, and by stressing the concepts of origins and originality. It is also very concerned with the interplay and relationship between the dualistic categories of truth and falsity, the real and unreal, and it does this through the contrasting worlds of the Land of Illusion (which is formally introduced in chapter 5) and the mundane human and underscoring the fact that the story is a work of fiction.

It is also useful to pay attention to the story's frequent use of doubles and doubling to further define characters, drive the plot, and compare and contrast scenes. Social events like funerals and family gatherings are often replicated; the first time they occur they show the affluence of the Jia family, and later, when they are repeated, they are intended to illustrate the family's decline, thereby reinforcing the traditional Chinese belief in the cyclical nature of human existence and of notions concerning prosperity and adversity. (See **Doubles and Doubling**.) Finally, the concept of *qing* (love, affection, desire, attachment) has a special prominence in the novel, and much attention is devoted to it. *Dream of the Red Chamber* attempts to provide a typology of the various forms of *qing* and tries to rank them in terms of their quality (primarily through the experiences of the main female characters). It also provides, on several occasions, warnings about its illusory and potentially destructive nature. (See **Qing**.)

Finally, many modern readers (including Chinese) have difficulties with the novel's extensive use of poetry. The question for them has been whether to read or simply skip them. To appreciate the verse (for Cao Xueqin was also considered a great poet) it is necessary to understand the role poetry plays in the tale. Cao deemed the subject important enough to offer concrete and detailed advice in the novel on how to write and appreciate the genre. Poetry formed an important part of many educated Chinese lives during this time and was written for a variety of social occasions, and the ability to compose it at social gatherings and celebrations was considered a mark of being an educated person. Furthermore, it was not unusual for the women in upper-class gentry families, especially in the southern part of China, like the members of the novel's Crab Flower Poetry Club, to compose verse and belong to poetry clubs during this time. Many of *Dream of the Red Chamber*'s most memorable scenes involve poetry writing contests; for example, the uproarious linked verse competition in chapter 50. These gatherings give the female members of Prospect Garden the opportunity to vent their feelings, display their talents, and exert some agency in their restricted lives. Pay particular attention to the characters who are considered the best poets: Lin Dai-yu, Xue Bao-chai, Shi Xiang-yun, and Xue Bao-qin for their poems reveal their often-hidden inner lives and abilities and sometimes foretell their and the Jia family's future, and augment themes. As the fortunes of the family change for the worse, the decline is often reflected in the poetry being written and quoted by characters. (See **Poetry**.)

So take a deep breath, remain calm, and jump right in (life vests are not required), and enjoy a masterwork of not just Asian but world literature.

The Companion

Abbot Zhang 张道士

Zhang is the 80-year-old Daoist chief priest of the Lunar Queen Temple outside of Beijing. Born poor, he was a proxy novice for Grandmother Jia's husband. These special novices were members of poor families who were paid by rich families to take their place as monks or priests to ward off evil spirits. Zhang is very well connected and was awarded special titles by a previous and the current emperor, and members of the aristocracy and high officials address him as His Holiness. In chapter 29, he is presented as an urbane, worldly, and canny operator. As with most of the clerics in the novel, he is also shown to be a bit corrupt. He receives Bao-yu's ire when Zhang attempts to arrange a marriage for him.

See also **Monks, Nuns, and Temples**

Adamantina 妙玉

Eighteen-year-old unshorn Buddhist nun who lives in Prospect Garden's Green Bower Hermitage. Born to a well-educated family of officials from Soochow, she was sickly when young. When her health did not improve, she became a lay sister, which meant she did not have to cut her hair. Her health then improved. Adamantina is her religious name, while her given name is Miao-yu, which means "Wonderful Jade." A telling near homonym to her name is "Absurd Desire." She is well educated, strikingly beautiful, and is friends with Xi-chun and Xiu-yan. A good poet, she also can use the planchette well, as shown in chapter 95 when she uses it to find the location of Bao-yu's missing jade. Adamantina is also haughty, eccentric, highly independent, and a great admirer of the philosopher Zhuangzi. Moreover, she is also fastidiously obsessed with physical cleanliness and spiritual purity. But her purity is upended when she becomes attracted to Jia Bao-yu, with the result that "a flood of passions allows evil spirits to disturb the serenity of Zen" (HLM, 4: 158). (The fact that she has not taken the final step to becoming a nun by shaving her head is revealing given that this step signifies the erasure of a physical sign of femininity.) In chapter 112, she is kidnapped, and though her eventual fate is not clearly stated, there are rumors in chapter 117 that she had been killed. In the end, as Zhou Yiqun has observed: "Nothing in her behavior betrays her as a Buddhist cleric, either in the stereotypical negative image or according to monastic ideal. If she is free of the greed and coarseness of other religious professionals, her obsession with her own superior taste and open contempt for the village woman [Grannie Liu] are decidedly at odds with the fundamental Buddhist belief in the vanity and emptiness of material existence and the equality of all creatures. Miao-yu is depicted less as Buddhist nun than as an eccentric literatus figure in her debut" (282).

Further Reading

Zhou, Yiqun. "Temples and Clerics in *Honglou meng.*" *Harvard Journal of Asiatic Studies* 71. 2 (2011): 263–309.

Analects

See **Confucianism, Education and the Examination System**

Archery

This sport was prized by the Chinese and especially the Manchus during the Qing dynasty. Cao Yin, Cao Xueqin's grandfather, was known for his archery skills. Because the Jia family are imperial bondservants and archery was a favorite pastime of this particular group, the sport is mentioned several times in the novel. In chapter 26, Jia Lan is shown practicing it in Prospect Garden. Later in the story, it serves as a further symbol of the moral decline of the Jia family. In chapter 75, Cousin Zhen uses competitive archery as an excuse to circumvent the Confucian ban on amusements that was being observed owing to the mourning period after Jia Jing's death because it was not a banned activity. This quickly leads to the establishment of an archery club that held illegal gambling and drinking parties by members of the club at the family's mansion.

See also **Mourning Practices**

Aroma 襲人

Jia Bao-yu's loyal chief maid. She was originally one of Grandmother Jia's maids, and her given name is Pearl. Her surname is Hua, which means "Flowers," but Bao-yu changed it to Aroma after seeing the name in a poem. Aroma is an indentured servant sold by her family for a certain number of years because they needed the money. But she decides to remain with the Jia family as a maid after this period. She is known and respected for her fidelity, competency, and good-heartedness and is one of the few characters in the novel whom Bao-yu listens to even though she is a stout defender of the Confucian orthodoxy. But Aroma also possesses, as Lady Wang notes, a determined and inflexible character. Moreover, she also has a scheming side, as seen in her *tête-à-têtes* with Lady Wang regarding Bao-yu's behavior toward and deep feelings about Dai-yu. After Bao-yu visits the Land of Illusion in chapter 5, he initiates a sexual relationship with her, and in chapter 36 Lady Wang and Xi-feng discuss whether to make her his chamber wife. But it is decided that the two are too young for this. When Bao-yu disappears at the end of the novel, Aroma considers committing suicide but eventually marries Bao-yu's friend, the actor-manager Jing Yu-han (which is highly ironic given her previously stated strong aversion to actors), thereby fulfilling the prophecy made about her in chapter 5.

The Art of War 孙子兵法

Famous Chinese military treatise written in the 5th century by the Chinese general, philosopher, and military strategist Sun Tzu. The book discusses such topics as strategy, tactics, weapons, and gives tips on how to maintain military discipline. Sun Tzu places particular emphasis on the importance of deception, intelligence gathering, and espionage. Lin Dai-yu humorously quotes from it in chapter 73.

Aunt Xue 薛姨妈

Fiftyish widowed mother of Bao-chai and Xue Pan and younger sister of Lady Wang. She is originally from Nanjing and comes from a cultured family. While she is good-natured and tolerant, she is also very weak willed. She has thoroughly spoiled Xue Pan and is unable to control his appalling behavior nor that of his shrewish wife. Aunt Xue takes pity on and establishes a close relationship with Dai-yu and becomes her godmother.

Aunt Zhao 赵姨妈

Jia Zheng's concubine and mother of Jia Huan and Tan-chun. She was originally a maid but was then selected by Zheng to be his chamber wife. Her name, Zhao Yiniang, is similar in sound to the Chinese word that means "bad." She is one of the novel's evil characters. Extremely jealous, vindictive, and paranoid, she is haunted by her precarious position as a concubine. Working with Mother Ma, Bao-yu's godmother, she attempts to kill Wang Xi-feng and

Bao-yu in chapter 25. She also treats Tan-chun badly throughout the story and in chapter 60 gets into a physical altercation with the Jia family's former actresses, much to Tan-chun's great embarrassment. But as is true of virtually all the characters in the novel, Cao Xueqin also provides glimpses of her humanity. She is loyal to Jia Huan, and, in a brilliantly described and poignant scene in chapter 67, she is shown brooding over presents given to Jia Huan by Bao-chai. Aunt Zhao dies a particularly agonizing death in chapter 112 after being possessed by an evil spirit.

Bao Er 鲍尔

Servant of Jia Zhen who was also used by Jia Lian. His name implies "Having Thoughts of Betrayal." He is installed by Lian to take care of Er-jie in her new house. Bao Er is married to the promiscuous Mattress with whom Lian had a torrid affair earlier in the novel. After Er-jie moves into Prospect Garden, he is reassigned to Jia Zhen. In chapter 88, Bao Er gets into a fight with Zhou Rui's troublesome adopted son He San and is dismissed.

Bao Yong 包勇

Former Zhen family servant who is employed by the Jia family after the Zhens run into trouble. He is a straightforward, hardworking, and loyal individual. But he also has a strong prejudice against Buddhist nuns and gets into trouble with Jia Zheng for his hostile treatment of several of them from the nunnery in Prospect Garden. As a result, he is demoted to caretaking duties in the garden. In chapter 111, armed only with a club, he valiantly takes on a gang of thieves robbing the Jia compound by climbing on the roof of the mansion and killing the former servant He San.

Bees

In China bees are used to symbolize a person who is hardworking, thrifty, and industrious. They are used to satirical effect in chapter 13 when the corrupt eunuch Dai Quan meets Jia Zhen in the mansion's Honey bee Gallery where he arranges the purchase of an official title for Jia Rong. The phrase "honey mixed with oil" is a euphemism in Chinese for a false friendship.

Beijing

Although the name of the "capital city" is never stated in *Dream of the Red Chamber*, it seems to be Beijing. Based upon references made in the story, the

Jia mansions appear to be located in the city's Houhai Lake area, possibly near Prince Gong's famous mansion, which some have argued is the model for the novel's Prospect Garden. At that time, Beijing was divided into three cities: (1) the Forbidden and Imperial City, which consisted of members of the imperial family and high-ranking officials, eunuchs, and bondservants; (2) the Inner or Tartar, which was exclusively Manchu and banner group territory and also contained government offices and was where the civil examination was held (in chapter 19 Bao-yu and Jia Lian would have taken their exam here); (3) the Outer or Chinese City, where the Chinese population lived (and where Cao Xueqin and his family were forced to live after they left Nanjing). The Houhai Lake area is in the Western Inner City, near the capital's Drum and Bell towers. Jia Zheng's office at the Board of Works, the ministry concerned with government projects like flood control and maintaining roads and canals, would have been located in the Imperial City, which would not have been far from the Jia mansions. In addition, members of the Jia family pay frequent visits to the Forbidden City to visit the Imperial Concubine Jia Yuan-chun. The palace was literally a city in itself and contained in the Inner Court the living quarters of the emperor, his concubines, and female members of the imperial family, the imperial garden, and ceremonial buildings like formal throne rooms. The Outer Court held the empire's grand public halls and administrative offices, like the Imperial Household Department, with which the Jia family would have had some contact given that they were imperial bondservants. Officials like Jia Zheng would have had their audiences with the emperor in the impressive Hall of Supreme Harmony in the Outer Court. Men (except for eunuchs and male members of the imperial family) were, as the novel shows, banned from the Inner Court. The Jia family's mansion is located not far from the palace. As the Imperial Concubine's health declines, members of the family often visit her, and Grandmother Jia and other female relatives are there when she dies.

In chapter 53, Bao-yu attends a party given by Feng Zi-yang at his house. The gathering has female entertainers and boy singers from an establishment called the "Budding Grove." This establishment would have been located in the capital's infamous entertainment district in the Outer City near Zhengyang Gate because these businesses were not allowed to be located in the Imperial and Inner City.

Big Jiao 焦大

Jiao is an outspoken but prescient Ning-guo House retainer. When he was young, he saved the life of Jia Dai-hua during a military campaign and because of this has received special treatment. In chapter 7, a drunk Jiao gets into an argument with Jia Yong and gives an early warning about the moral decline of the Jia family. Big Jiao reappears in chapter 105 during the Embroidered

Jacket raid and tells Jia Zheng that there is no longer anything to live for, and the "whole place has gone to the dogs" (SS, 5: 124).

See also "**Father-in-law Pokes in the Ashes, Aunties Has It Off with Nevvy**"

Bond of Gold and Jade

In the first song in the Dream Suite in chapter 5, it is stated, "Well matched all say, the gold and the jade" (DRM, 1: 80). Traditionally in China, gold and jade together are considered a metaphor for a happy marriage. In the story, gold signifies Bao-chai and jade Bao-yu, and the song foretells their eventual marriage. In chapter 8 it is revealed, much to Bao-chai's embarrassment, that a scabby monk wrote the words that appear on her locket and that he insisted that they be engraved in gold. The inscriptions on Bao-yu's jade are very similar to the writings that the monk wrote. Both objects warn the wearers not to mislay them and claim that they will protect them. Moreover, according to Lady Xue, the monk who gave the locket to Bao-chai predicted that she would marry a person with a corresponding piece of jade. This association becomes an ongoing and bitter point of contention between a jealous Dai-yu and an increasingly exasperated Bao-yu, with her frequently bringing the "bond" up in arguments. In chapter 95, she speculates about the bond's meaning. But it is important to also realize that the connection is only for *this* world, the world of illusion. For "The monk has placed the locket not so much to fulfill the destiny of gold and jade as to guarantee that the destiny of flower and stone [Dai-yu and Bao-yu] will be fulfilled.... The affinity of 'jade and gold' is the destiny of the present life: the affinity of 'stone and flower' is the prior attachment. When Bao-yu soothes Dai-yu's spasms of jealousy by reminding her that *theirs* is the earlier affection and *theirs* is the stronger bond, he unknowingly has the force of karmic history on his side" (Levy, 41). Moreover, Bao-yu's eventual marriage to Bao-chai contributes to his final realization of the illusory nature of emotional attachments and the need for transcendence.

FURTHER READING

Levy, Dore. *Ideal and Actual in* The Story of the Stone (New York: Columbia University Press, 1999).

Bond of Stone and Flower

It is mentioned in the first song of Fairy Disenchantment's song and dance suite. The bond signifies the special, karmic affinity between Bao-yu (Stone) and Dai-yu (Flower) that occurred in the Land of Illusion. While Bao-yu is fated to marry Bao-chai in the mundane world, his real bond is with Dai-yu.

The noted scholar Anthony Yu has observed what makes *Dream of the Red Chamber* so remarkable "is that a plant and a stone, objects noted by the Chinese for their proverbial lack of sentiency and feeling are made veterans of the most passionate attachments" (289).

FURTHER READING

Yu, Anthony. "Cao Xueqin's *Honglou meng*." In *Masterworks of Asian Literature in Comparative Perspective: A Guide to Teaching*. Edited by Barbara Stoler-Miller. (Armonk, New York: M.E. Sharpe, 1994): 285–298.

Bondservants

There remains some controversy over whether the Jia family, like Cao Xueqin's, are imperial bondservants attached to one of the Manchu Eight Banner groups. (For information on the Manchu banner system, see the biography of Cao Xueqin section in this book.) The novel seems to support the belief that they are. Much of the debate centers on whether the female members of the family have bounded feet. This is an important question considering both Manchu and Chinese women who belonged to the Eight Banners did not bind their feet. The Jia family is clearly Han Chinese, and based upon the quickness and ease with which female characters like Wang Xi-feng (especially when angry) can walk, it appears that the family's female members' feet are not bound. Moreover, as David Hawkes has noted, the family show the deep uneasiness a high-ranking Chinese bondservant family would have felt at the time. While bondservants in high positions, like the Jia's, could wield a great deal of power, they were also technically slaves of the emperor and were completely dependent upon his will and mood. Hawkes writes, "Consider the family's anxiety, amounting to panic, when Jia Zheng is summoned to the Palace in chapter 16 or the cavalier way they are treated by palace eunuchs" (SS, 1: 27). This can also be seen in their deep anxiety over the Imperial Concubine Yuan-chun's health. While this concern over her medical status might appear to be natural, a character in the novel remarks on how extreme it is with the Jias. This fear becomes understandable if the family are bondservants, for Yuan-chun would have been their protection in case of trouble. Furthermore, there is an indirect allusion in chapter 45 to Cao Xueqin's own ancestors who worked as slaves before he was lucky enough to be born into a rich family, when Mrs. Liu reminds her grandson of the hard times his forefathers had to endure as bondservants so that he can enjoy a pampered upbringing, by saying, "I doubt you know how the word 'bondservant' is written" (SS, 2: 390).

Additionally, in chapter 4, it is mentioned that the Xue family is traveling to Beijing in part so that Bao-chai can be presented to the Ministry for possible selection as a study companion for one of the royal princesses. The noted historian Mark C. Elliot has written that during this period all young banner women were ordered to present themselves in the capital for possible selection to serve as "elegant females" in the Forbidden City for five years. Elliot states that the purpose of this requirement "was to guarantee marriage partners for the imperial clan and other nobles" (253). (The fact that Yuan-chun was an Imperial Concubine implies that she was at one stage selected to be a study companion and hence was also a member of a banner group.) Elliot also notes that the "useless lout" behavior of Xue Pan is in several ways representative of the behavior of some bannermen. Further evidence for the Jias being imperial bondservants is that it appears, based upon several hints in the novel, that the Jia family residences are located in the Inner City of Beijing, which was restricted to only Manchus and members of the banner groups. (Cao Xueqin's own family had a residence in the Inner City, which they subsequently lost after their property was confiscated by the government.) Finally, it has been further argued by another noted historian that the Jias possess many of the same characteristics a typical upper-class bondservant family of that time would have had: they enjoy the same activities (like horseback riding and archery), eat the same food, belong to the same aristocratic social network, and also own slaves (Rawski, 148–153).

See also **Imperial Household Department**

FURTHER READING

Elliott, Mark C. *The Manchu Way: The Eight Banners and Ethnic Identity in Late Imperial China* (Sanford: Stanford University Press, 2001).

Rawksi, Evelyn S. "The Banner *Story of the Stone*." *Approaches to Teaching Cao Xueqin's Dream of the Red Chamber*. Edited by Andrew Schonebaum and Tina Liu (New York: Modern Language Association of America, 2012): 144–158.

Book of Changes 易经

A highly influential Chinese book of divination and philosophy, it is over 3,000 years old and continues to be consulted for guidance and understanding. The book is a complex work with numerous symbols, levels of meaning, and enigmatic language. Its cultural significance cannot be overstated. The historian Richard Smith has written that it "extended into virtually every area of traditional Chinese life. In the first place, it provides an inexhaustible repository of symbols with which to represent and explain nearly every realm of human experience, from artistic, musical, and literary criticism to science, medicine, and technology. Second, from the standpoint of philosophy, it established the conceptual underpinnings for much of traditional Chinese cosmogony and cosmology" (194). *The Book of Changes* is used in chapter 102 by a fortune teller named Half-Immortal Mao, an expert on the book, to help diagnosis You-shi's malady after she falls sick after walking in Prospect Garden. Mao concludes, after a lengthy analysis based upon the work, that her illness was caused by a white tiger spirit originating from a corpse.

FURTHER READING

Smith, Richard J. *The Qing Dynasty and Traditional Chinese Culture* (Lanham: Rowman & Littlefield, 2015).

Brightie 旺儿

Wang Xi-feng's most trusted servant. He is used by her for her most secretive and confidential missions. These include delivering a letter that led to a breaking off of an engagement (which leads to unexpected tragic results) in chapter 15. While he claims to an infuriated Xi-feng that he had no knowledge of Jia Lian's secret marriage to Er-jie, she orders him, in chapter 68, to find her former fiancé Zhang Hua, bribe him, and put his name on an indictment against Hua. But Brightie does have his limits. When Xi-feng orders him to kill Zhang Hua, he concocts the story that Hua had been murdered by a robber. Brightie and his wife are also involved in Xi-feng's illegal financial activities, like loaning money at high rates of interest.

Buddhism

Dream of the Red Chamber contains numerous allusions to Buddhist beliefs and practices, and several of its main characters become or are Buddhist monks and nuns. Buddhism is one of the three central Chinese religious traditions, along with Daoism and Confucianism. It originally came to China around the 1st century from northeastern India. The historic founder of the religion was the spiritual leader and philosopher Siddhartha Gautama who lived in what is now modern Nepal in the late 6th to early 5th century BC. The foundation of Buddhist teaching is based on what is known as the Four Noble or Holy Truths: (1) Life is suffering. (2) Suffering originates in attachment or desire and the craving for pleasure. (3) Suffering can be eliminated through the cessation of attachment. (4) This can occur by following a certain procedural way or path. This way involves the famous Eightfold Path, which lists the eight central teachings Buddhists should practice in their daily lives. This practical program is designed to help an individual overcome attachment, which causes suffering and involves an individual adopting: (1) Right Views, which refers to clear understanding of the Four Noble Truths; (2) Right Thought, which means seriously resolving to practice Buddhism; (3) Right Speech, which necessitates always speaking the truth and avoiding slander, gossip, frivolous, or false speech; (4) Right Conduct, which involves not stealing or committing any sexual misconduct; (5) Right Livelihood, which means living a correct lifestyle and not killing animals or praising yourself, and properly relating to others; (6) Right Effort, which refers to avoiding negative thoughts and emotions like anger, envy, jealousy, and hatred; (7) Right Mindfulness, which means being fully aware of and focused on the moment; it involves paying constant attention to your body and emotions. Through mindfulness the mind is anchored in the present. It is the foundation of meditation. (8) Right Concentration, which means using meditation to obtain total focus so that you can direct it.

A central tenet in Buddhism is the idea of no self. It is believed that human suffering is the result of people clinging to an erroneous conception of a self, that is, a substantial or permanent sense of identity. By "self," it is meant not only personality or ego but also our physical being, soul, or spiritual nature. This lack of understanding about the self produces egocentric desires that maintain the illusion of a self and, as a result, people suffer. These attachments in turn keep the wheel of rebirth (karma) turning. For Buddhists, the ultimate goal is to obtain enlightenment, the state where one has seen through the fantasy of self and severed one's attachments, thereby obtaining complete freedom from the cycle of rebirth. By Cao Xueqin's time, Buddhism and Daoism had significantly borrowed from each other with the result that they "and folk religious elements had fused into an almost ultimate undifferentiated popular religion" (Wright, 98). Furthermore, neo-Confucianism also appropriated ideas from Buddhism regarding the idea of self-cultivation, and the ethical systems of both Buddhism and Daoism were influenced by the Confucian ethical values of integrity, duty, loyalty, and filial piety. *Dream of the Red Chamber* clearly shows the daily result of this syncretism as well as the fact that the Chinese traditionally have been very practical concerning religious matters and have had no trouble using differing religious traditions for different purposes and occasions.

The Buddhism in *Honglou meng* has received a great deal of scholarly attention. Many have argued that the work should be viewed in large part as a Buddhist novel. Anthony Yu has posed and answered the question of whether it is "a grand parable of Buddhist quest and enlightenment? In view of the experience of the male protagonist and many of the other characters, three of the four titles supposedly given to their story [*Tale of Brother Amor, A Bejeweled Mirror of Romance,* and *Dream of the Red Chamber*], and the vast and vibrant network of echoes and allusions in Buddhist themes and rhetoric, it is virtually impossible not to consider seriously an affirmative answer to such a question" (136–137). Yu points out that Bao-yu's philosophical development tracks the Buddhist idea that it is through fully experiencing passion, desire, lust, and love and the eventual resulting disillusionment over these transitory gratifications that one will understand the vanity of life and awaken to its emptiness. He notes, "Not only do the final five chapters provide us with what is arguably a lengthy and vivid account of Bao-yu's last leg in his journey toward disillusionment, but in the final debate with his wife Bao-chai, he refers specifically to the Buddhist notion of four delusions [*klesas*] in reference to the ego [greed, anger, folly, and desire] to counter her desperate admonition to cultivate the virtues of the Confucian sage" (137).

Qiancheng Li has argued in an influential study that the novel clearly shows the structure, theme, and language of Buddhist soteriological (religious belief concerning salvation) models. Li, who calls *Honglou meng* a "secular scripture" (167), contends that its plot is generally patterned after the narratives of several famous Mahayana sutras concerning the quest for enlightenment, and that Buddhist concepts are woven into its structure, the result being that the book can be classified as belonging to a genre Li labels, "the fiction of enlightenment not only because of its decidedly Buddhist tenor—that is, the paradoxical enlightenment by way of involvement, or detachment by the way of attachment—but also because of the narrative techniques, mainly the doubling and mirroring devices, which correspond and contribute to the novel's concern with [the] character's psychological growth. The novel is about the self, which to Buddhists means the mind: the mind in its relationship with others and the mind turning against itself. In short, it is about reflection and reflexivity" (134–135). It has also been maintained that the popular Buddhist scripture, the *Heart Sutra*, which discusses the doctrine of the emptiness of self and all phenomena and how an understanding of this emptiness leads to wisdom, frames the first and last chapter of the novel. Karl-Heinz Pohl has posited, "The message of non-duality [in the sutra] is crucial to the understanding of *Dream of the Red Chamber*. There is no difference between 'emptiness' and 'form/lust,' no difference between 'true' [reality] and 'false' [fiction], no difference between Buddhist awakening and passion/love, no difference between Samsara and Nirvana" (9).

But there are also detractors who oppose this stress on Buddhism in the novel. They point, for example, to the negative portrayal of Buddhist monks and nuns, including clergy who are members of or close to the Jia family, like Xi-chun and Adamantina, and contend that the religion is often rendered as being conservative and repressive. Zuyan Zhou has suggested that Cao Xueqin is very critical of the Buddhist notion of purity, which is "the spiritual state purged of human cravings, free from the delusory attachment to the mundane" (260). He also believes the narrative satirically mocks "the non-religious motivations that lead some of the female characters to turn to Buddhism … the notion of the purging of sexuality essential to Buddhist purity through the lovemaking of Qing Zhong and Zhineng…[that an] unadulterated satire of the Buddhist value of purity is prominent in the characterization of Abbess Jingxu whose name 'purity and emptiness' contrast sharply with her personality" (270, 268). Moreover, Zhou also notes Bao-yu and Dai-yu's use of Buddhist rhetoric in their courtship. "While reflecting the secularization of Buddhism in late imperial China, these plots also poke fun at Buddhism to an extent bordering on sacrilege" (275). Finally, he observes that while the story "admittedly echoes the Buddhist imperative of sexual transgression early … this Buddhist caution against sexuality becomes less audible and more ambiguous and problematic" (273–274) and that even when Buddhism "serves as [an] outlet for romantic souls, a role designed by divinities at the outset of the narrative, the spiritual freedom it offers turns out to be highly questionable" (275).

Robert Hegel has taken aim at the way the novel depicts Buddhist enlightenment, saying that the value of cutting one's attachment to worldly concerns is actually shown to be of doubtful value and is intended to illustrate the drawbacks of established Buddhist beliefs. Tina Liu surmises, "The novel's uses of Buddhism in its narrative are more literary than religious ... actual Buddhist practice in it is not particularly sympathetic, and the content of Buddhist doctrine is relatively unimportant" (278). She concludes: "We are probably better off considering the structural influence on *Stone* of Buddhist teachings rather than the ideological content" (279). The question has also been raised by critics as to whether *Dream of the Red Chamber*, because of its Buddhist elements, should be taken "as a serious expedient to lead us to enlightenment, so that we in the end can throw the novel on the ground and laughingly float away?" (Bech, 20). One scholar has written in response: "It seems to me that more than 200 years of interest in *Honglou meng* so far has sent few readers floating and if this was the author's purpose, he has failed.... While the novel might not in itself be able to lead its readers to enlightenment, it can certainly lure the reader into taking the fictive for the real, which, according to the stories about both Kongkong Daoren and Bao-yu, is the necessary first step towards enlightenment" (Bech, 20-21). Finally, it has also been asserted by Chinese scholars like Zhou Ruchang that the Buddhism in the story is a mere formality and that it was a common narrative structural feature of traditional Chinese fiction and a reflection of the encyclopedic form of the work, and it does not have any ideological significance. It does seem clear that Cao Xueqin possessed, as he did with Daoism, a good understanding of Buddhism as well as an abiding interest. Whether he personally believed in the religion will probably remain unsettled.

See also **Chinese Philosophy: Characteristics and Syncretism, Zhuangzi, Enlightenment, Themes and Indeterminacy**

FURTHER READING

Bech, Lene. "Fiction That Leads to Truth: *The Story of the Stone* as Skillful Means." *Chinese Literature: Essays, Articles, Reviews* 26 (2004): 1–21.

Hegel, Robert. "Unpredictability and Meaning in Mid-Qing Literati Novels." In *Paradoxes of Traditional Chinese Literature*. Edited by Eva Hung (Hong Kong: The Chinese University Press, 1994): 147–166.

Li, Qiancheng. *Fictions of Enlightenment:* Journey to the West, Tower of the Myriad Mirrors, *and* Dream of the Red Chamber (Honolulu: University of Hawaii Press, 2003).

Lu, Tina. "Dreams, Subjectivity, and Identity in *Stone*." *Approaches to Teaching Cao Xueqin's* Dream of the Red Chamber. Edited by Andrew Schonebaum and Tina Liu (New York: Modern Language Association of America, 2012): 274–282.

Pohl, Karl-Heinz. "The Role of the *Heart Sutra* in *Dream of the Red Chamber*." *European Journal of Sinology*, 5 (2014): 9–20.

Wright, Arthur F. *Buddhism in Chinese History* (New York: Atheneum, 1968).

Yu, Anthony. *Rereading the Stone: Desire and the Making of Fiction in* Dream of the Red Chamber (Princeton: Princeton University Press, 1997).

Zhou, Zuyan. *Daoist Philosophy and Literati Writings in Late Imperial China: A Case Study of* The Story of the Stone (Hong Kong: Hong Kong University Press, 2013).

Butterfly

Traditionally, in China, it is a symbol of beauty, elegance, and long life. Bao-chai is directly associated with the colorful insect in chapter 27 where she spots a pair of large turquoise-colored butterflies in Prospect Garden and plays a game with them using her fan.

Calligraphy

A decorative art form that has long been practiced in China. Calligraphy has been used as a means of personal disclosure, self-expression, and cultivation. It is also thought to reveal personality for it is held that the form is an index of an individual's morality, learning, and philosophy, hence the old Chinese adage, "If the heart is right, the brush is right." Moreover, calligraphy was traditionally considered the supreme art form, even more so than painting. Its cultural and social importance can easily be seen in *Dream of the Red Chamber* where most of the allusions to it relate to Bao-yu. For example, in chapter 70, he frantically attempts to compile, with the help of Bao-chai, Dai-yu, and Tan-chun, a sizeable number of calligraphy sheets in case his father inquires how his studies are progressing when he returns from his current post. There are six basic styles of calligraphy, and the novel alludes to regular script (*kaishu*), where each stroke is clear, separate, and straight (Bao-yu uses this style when writing his Skybright's elegy and when copying poems during the Imperial Concubine's visit), grass characters (which is on the wooden cup from which Grannie Liu drinks in chapter 41), "pearl drop" seal script, and *li-shu* characters (which are on Adamantina's cups in the same chapter).

Caltrop 香菱

The ill-fated daughter of Zhen Shi-yin, she is kidnapped when she is a young girl and is later sold to Xue Pan, who mistreats her, and, after much turmoil, she becomes his chamber wife. Her name, Zhen Ying-lian, which literally means "Heroic Lotus," evokes her brave and ethical behavior and beauty. Her name also connotes "Ought to Be Pitied." Caltrop is gentle natured, highly intelligent, and deeply loyal. She also has a passion and talent for writing poetry, and the novel details her education in writing verse under the mentorship of Dai-yu. Later in the story, in an elaborate plot, Xue Pan's malicious wife, Xia Jin-gui, attempts to kill her. But the plan backfires, and Jin-gui dies by accident. At the end of the novel, she is rewarded for her faithfulness and is made Pan's proper wife but dies in childbirth. She does, however, deliver a son who will carry on the Xue family name.

Cao Cao 曹操 (155–220)

Famous Chinese general and politician during the Eastern Han dynasty. He is considered a cruel, cunning but efficient ruler. Cao is a prominent character in the popular 14th-century Chinese historical novel *Three Kingdoms*. Jia Yu-cun references him as an example of exceptional wickedness in support of his theory of good and evil.

Censorship

The 18th century in China was a period of strong literary censorship and an infamous literary inquisition. While earlier dynasties like the Song, Yuan, and Ming attempted to monitor and control the publishing business and prevent the publication of unorthodox and questionable texts, the literary inquisitions and state censorship during the rule of emperors Yongzheng and Qianlong that encompassed Cao Xueqin's life were especially harsh and prolonged. Because the Manchu emperors felt deeply insecure about their status as foreign rulers and had doubts about the loyalty of their Chinese subjects (especially intellectuals), individuals were vigorously prosecuted for writings that officials deemed to contain political messages that were directly or indirectly against the regime, were anti–Manchu or pro–Ming dynasty. This concern was so strong that Chinese writers were prosecuted for writing innocuous words or phrases that were wrongly interpreted as being covertly seditious. Writers of literature could get into trouble if officials thought their works were obscene, exceeded the boundaries of correct morality, or even possessed "poor literary style." Unfortunately, these categories were sufficiently vague so that an ambitious official could take advantage of them to prosecute people in order to curry favor with his superiors—which is what frequently occurred. Consequently, writers like Cao Xueqin had to be very careful about what they put in their works. In fact, Cao had to be more cautious than the usual author because of his problematic family background and unstable social status. He also had to make sure that his story of the Jia family's decline did not hew too closely to what had happened to his own family lest it catch the attention of the emperor. He also undoubtedly would have understood the importance of steering clear not only of overzealous officials looking to advance their careers by turning in suspicious literati but also of ambitious scholars trying to advance by informing on other writers. This toxic environment was especially true of Beijing, where writers had to be more cautious about what they wrote than any other city in China at that time.

Cao covered himself in *Dream of the Red Chamber* by using several methods. He was careful not to set the story in any clear dynastic period and mixed together aspects of Ming and Qing society. For example, the imperial guards that raid the Jia compound are referred to using a Ming dynasty and not Qing dynasty name, and the titles of some government officials are based on different dynasties. Furthermore, all the allusions to the emperor in the novel are extremely positive and supportive of the Imperial Concubine, and she is even granted the special favor of visiting her family. Even Bao-yu, who is highly critical of the examination system, the existing Confucian orthodoxy, and officialdom in general, buckles down and ends up taking the imperial exam and even does well. In addition, he is shown in chapter 37 acknowledging that emperors are granted their power from heaven, which would bestow it only upon a worthy individual. Moreover, the confiscation raid, while terrifying and disastrous for the family, could have been much worse (when compared, for example, with what happened to Cao's own family and others) and, on a certain level, even justified. Members of the royal family, like the Prince of Beijing, are shown to be fair minded and supportive of the family. Finally, and tellingly, at the end of the story, a judicious and understanding emperor graciously restores the Jia family to its former status, restores their hereditary titles, pardons Jia She and Cousin Zhen, returns all confiscated goods, and honors Bao-yu.

Although the sexuality in the novel is restrained (especially when compared with the infamous Ming dynasty novel *Jin Ping Mei*), it was considered in some quarters during the Qing dynasty obscene and, as a result, was formally banned by the government on several occasions. Matthew Sommer has noted that this was due to objections to Bao-yu's behavior and his overt violations of the moral code of that time. Sommer writes, "It is easy for modern readers to be so captivated by the work's beauty that they miss its obscenity. By the normative standards of elite society in eighteenth and nineteenth century China, this novel was unquestionably obscene.... [Its] entire magnificent and complex edifice depends on the collective abdication of responsibility by the novel's men and on the collective conspiracy of the novel's women to pretend that a sexually mature young man is an innocent little boy. Thus, the segregation of sexes is waived and Bao-yu moves into the garden. Everything that follows constitutes a gross violation of Confucian moral order, prefiguring the household's ultimate crisis" (206).

FURTHER READING

Sommer, Matthew H. "Scandal in the Garden: *The Story of the Stone* as a Licentious Novel." *Approaches to Teaching Cao Xueqin's* Dream of the Red Chamber. Edited by Andrew Schonebaum and Tina Liu (New York: Modern Languages Association of America, 2012): 186–207.

Chamber Wives and Concubines

A chamber wife is a type of concubinage. When the personal maid of a male was believed to be a good enough match, she was promoted from servant to third or second wife. She thereby became the male's chamber wife but was ranked lower than his principal wife. At one stage in the story, Lady Wang considered making Aroma Bao-yu's chamber wife but decided against it because she thought he was too young and Aroma would be less likely to tell him what she thinks when he is misbehaving and because Jia Zheng objected to the idea. She does, though, plan on making Aroma his chamber wife in two or three years, but this never occurs. The formal reason why concubinage was traditionally practiced in China was because of the filial obligation to produce sons to continue a family's male line. Most concubines were from poor families and were bought by wealthy ones. They also did not have the same status as the principal wife and the daughters of concubines because of their mother's lower status and, as Xi-feng tells Patience about Tan-chun, were frequently hampered in their attempts to find a marriage partner. Moreover, "unlike principal spouses, concubines were usually chosen by the husband rather than his parents, and they often were selected for their beauty or their artistic, literary, and musical talents rather than their moral character and/or family connections. Although ostensibly brought into the household for the purpose of producing sons to assure continuation of the line, concubines served as little more than symbols of elite conspicuous consumption. Despite their social inferiority to the principal wife, they were often the primary object of the husband's sexual attention and thus a potential source of jealousy" (Smith, 360). These acrimonious feelings clearly can be seen in the vindictive behavior of Xi-feng toward Er-jie and Xue Pan's vicious wife Xia Jin-gui.

FURTHER READING

Smith, Richard J. *The Qing Dynasty and Traditional Chinese Culture* (Lanham: Rowman & Littlefield, 2015).

Chang E 嫦娥

The Chinese goddess of the moon. She fled to the moon when her partner, the Lord of the Archer Hou Yi, found out that she had stolen the elixir of immortality that he had received from the gods. Dai-yu is strongly associated with Chang E throughout the novel. In chapter 85, for her birthday party she dresses like Chang E descending to earth, and the celebration includes a performance of a scene from the play *The Palace of Pearls*, where the Goddess of Mercy opens Chang E's eyes to the vanity of mortal love, and she dies before her marriage to her mortal lover, thereby foreshadowing Dai-yu's own tragic death. Moreover, in chapter 89, it is stated that she has a painting of Chang E in her dwelling; in chapter 99, Li Wan compares Dai-yu to Chang E; and in chapter 100, Bao-yu, when thinking about Dai-yu, concludes that she and Chang E had the "same ethereal beauty, the same otherworldly charm" (SS, 5: 43).

Chapter Endings

Each chapter ends with a sentence stating that what has just occurred will be explained in the next or in following chapters. This is based on a technique that was commonly used by professional storytellers at a point of suspense or uncertainty in the story to advance the plot and keep the interest of their audience.

Character Description

Although *Dream of the Red Chamber* introduces over 400 characters, Cao Xueqin is a master of making virtually all of them believable and unique, whether they are major, minor, or make only a single appearance. The noted scholar C.T. Hsia has written, "*Dream of the Red Chamber* is to be distinguished from all other classic Chinese novels for its fascination with characters: even characters of minor consequence are presented as real individuals and not as stereotypes" (258). Moreover, unlike the characters in traditional Chinese novels, which are depicted as being either good or evil, Cao often portrays them as psychologically complex, nuanced, and on the spectrum between black and white, as most people are. As the insightful commentator, Red Inkstone noted, from "this book, I have learned a secret … the nice thing about it is that the author himself never made any comment or annotation saying, 'So and so is such and such a person.' He merely employs occasional remarks by the characters in the book; therefore, there are no unclosed seams to be discovered by the reader. His pen is really tricky" (quoted in Wang, 217–218). Many of the characters that readers encounter are similar to people we encounter in our own lives. The novel's character descriptions are often relational in nature, that is, dependent upon their contextual relations with others. Thus, the contrast, similarity, and parallelism among individual characters become important in discerning what a character is like.

In addition, Cao is also brilliant at providing small yet meaningful details that disclose key aspects of characters' personalities, whether through their clothes, residence, the objects they own, actions, or even eating habits. Xia Jin-gui's love of gnawing fried chicken bones and loudly swearing when she has difficulty eating them is a striking image that shows her rapacious and crude nature. In chapter 54, Musk and Ripple carelessly throw down the lids of two food boxes held out by women servants for their inspection, which reveals not only their impatience but also their sense of entitlement, considering they outrank the women in status. In the same chapter, Aroma and Faithful have a short but intimate heart-to-heart talk about the deaths of their mothers, which shows their feelings of being outsiders. In chapter 42, Xiang-yun laughs so hard that the rickety chair on which she is sitting collapses during a discussion, and in chapter 50, she is so convulsed with laughter during a linked verse contest that she cannot be understood by others when she talks. Both scenes neatly highlight her vivacious and fun-loving character. Bao-yu's intense feelings of standing in the middle of a massive, sparkling bowl made of crystal after a night's snowstorm emphasize his special, otherworldly nature. The description of the maids happily eating from their food boxes on the rockery and grass in Prospect Garden in chapter 41 concisely shows their humanity. Perhaps the best example of this technique at work is Cao's telling description in chapter 91 of Xue Ke's reaction to a poem he has just composed. At first, he takes a certain pride in it and sticks it on the wall above his desk, but he then feels a bit self-conscious and takes it down. He then rereads the poem, concludes that no one would care if he put it up, and places it back on the wall so he can see it if he feels he is in need of some cheering up. Ke then rereads the poem for a third time and decides to just place it in the pages of a book. The short scene simply but effectively reveals Ke's humility and self-awareness.

A final example of Cao's versatile skill at character depiction that is worth mentioning is the straightforwardly written but painterly way in which he describes in chapter 38 members of the poetry club ruminating about the poems they are going to compose and how their actions subtly reflect, in part, their characters. In the scene, Dai-yu is quietly fishing by herself, Bao-chai is dropping cassia in the garden's lake and watching fish nibble at them, Tan-chun is watching waterfowl, Xiang-yun is peacefully musing, and Bao-yu is walking about, observing Dai-yu, talking to Bao-chai, and drinking wine with the maids. Lastly, it should be noted that when there is a full description of a character in the story, it usually takes a certain form. First, it begins with the individual's external trappings and ends with their internal qualities. In other words, things like clothing and jewelry are initially described, usually starting with the head and moving down. Then their physical appearances are discussed, starting with the body, then the head, and after that the face. Finally, the person's character is described.

Further Reading

Hsia, C.T. *"Dream of the Red Chamber."* In *The Classic Chinese Novel: A Critical Introduction* (New York: Columbia University Press, 1968): 245–297.

Wang, John. C.Y. "The Chih-yen chai Commentary and the *Dream of the Red Chamber*: A Literary Study." *Chinese Approaches to Literature.* Edited by Adele Rickett (Princeton: Princeton University Press, 1978): 189–220.

Chess 司棋

Ying-chun's headstrong and hot-tempered principal maid. A homonym for her Chinese name, Siqi, means "Expecting Death." We are introduced to her in chapter 61 when she leads a raucous raid on the kitchen of Prospect Garden's cook because Mrs. Liu refused to cook a dish she ordered. (According to Bao-chai, Ying-chun's maids have a reputation for being spiteful and mean.) Ironically, when the garden itself is raided (under the leadership of Chess's grandmother), it is discovered that Chess illegally holds items of men's clothing and a love letter from her cousin. An earlier chapter relates that the two have long been carrying on a clandestine relationship. In chapter 71, a shocked Faithful accidentally comes across them cavorting in the garden, but she promises a frightened Chess that she will not report their illicit behavior. The erotic purse that is discovered in the garden appears to have belonged to the couple. After Chess is cashiered, she returns home and constantly broods over the relationship. In chapter 92, her cousin, who had suddenly disappeared, reappears and is now a wealthy man and wants to marry her. Chess's mother misinterprets his motive and refuses to let her marry him. Chess then kills herself by dashing her head against a wall in a fit of anger, and the cousin commits suicide soon after. When Xi-feng is told this story by one of Ying-chun's servants, she is impressed by Chess's determination and promises to help her mother, who is under investigation over what happened.

Chinese Philosophy: Characteristics and Syncretism

In addition to being a great work of fiction, *Dream of the Red Chamber* is also a philosophical novel. As Andrew Plaks has noted, it "takes up some of the central issues of seminal Chinese thinkers (Lao Zi, Zhuangzi, Confucius, Mencius, and Chan masters)" (11). It poses troubling questions about such philosophical issues as the status of dreams, fate, the differences between reality and illusions, truth and falsity, the transitory nature of existence and the meaning of life. It also takes a hard look in chapter 118 at the perennial Chinese philosophical debate over the claims of such virtues as sympathy, compassion, and loyalty versus the pull of personal transcendence, detachment, and withdrawal. The famed 20th-century literary critic, poet and historian Wang Guowei was impressed by the novel's philosophical insight regarding the will and suffering and by Cao Xueqin's relentless quest for the meaning of life. While *Honglou meng* ultimately does not offer definite answers or comprehensive doctrinal answers to these perennial questions, it can be characterized as a form of philosophical discourse, one which gave Cao the opportunity to offer some speculations through the vehicle of fiction about philosophical issues he was intrigued with and deemed important. As a result, it is important for readers to have a rudimentary and broad understanding of the role, focus, and style of traditional Chinese philosophy and Cao Xueqin's critical reaction to it in order to have some understanding of the philosophy in the novel.

Traditionally, in China, philosophy was very much part of the culture. Chinese were introduced to philosophy early in life as part of the educational process for it formed an essential part of the imperial examination system, and educated Chinese and the bureaucratic elite were expected to have good knowledge of it. The first primer children studied to learn Chinese characters was the *Three Character Classic* which is full of Confucian maxims and beliefs. Philosophy was not seen as a profession but as a subject with which all men should be acquainted. The noted historian of Chinese philosophy, Wing-tsit Chan, has written, "If one word could characterize the entire history of Chinese philosophy it would be humanism—not the humanism that denies or slights a Supreme Power, but one that professes the unity of man and Heaven" (3). It was believed that the purpose of philosophy was to make people great, to help them improve themselves and society. The philosophical problems with which most traditional Chinese philosophers dealt concerned practical subjects like order in society, the philosophical reasons for specific ways of living, and the development of theories regarding human nature. The final goal was to produce what was called an "Inner Sage and Outer King," that is, a person who has internalized virtue and displays it externally. As a result, Chinese philosophical theory was closely bound with practice, with the world being viewed as dynamic and relational in nature. Little speculation was done for speculation's sake about abstract philosophical issues. Consequently, Chinese philosophy predominately concentrated on ethical and political matters rather than metaphysical and epistemological theorizing (although there were some traditional philosophers who were interested in formal problems of logic and dealt with some basic epistemological issues). As Zhang Dainian has explained, "Chinese philosophers were not concerned with how knowledge was acquired but rather with what knowledge should be acquired and what ought to be the object of knowledge and research" (421).

The human world was considered central, and philosophy was intimately connected with daily life. Methodologically, it was inclusive and usually directed outward. Most of the Chinese philosophers whose works Cao Xueqin read and was influenced by believed, "We are all complex and changing constantly. [They maintained that] every person has many different and often contradictory dispositions, desires, and ways of responding to the world [and that] our emotional dispositions [are] developed by looking *outward*, not inward... [These dispositions] are formed in practice, through the things you do in your everyday life: the ways you interact with others and the activities you pursue. In other words, we aren't just who we are: we can make ourselves into better people all the time" (Puett, 12). Stylistically, traditional Chinese philosophical writings are commonly filled with aphorisms, allusions and illustrations, suggestive language, and seemingly disconnected remarks. During Cao's time, a certain amount of syncretism between the major philosophical and religious schools had occurred, and there was a blending and mutual appropriation of Confucian, Buddhist, and Daoist beliefs among them, especially in the realm of popular religion.

The Chinese have long had no problem mixing religious and philosophical practices and were very practical about them. Individuals commonly selected the practice that was most appropriate for the situation they were in. This easily can be seen in *Honglou meng*, where members of the Jia family follow Confucian precepts in their social and familial relationships with others, during birthday celebrations and important festivals. When performing ancestral rites and observing periods of mourning, they perform Buddhist and Daoist rites during funerals, consult fortune sticks, watch dramas, and make offerings to the Gods in Buddhist temples, compose Buddhist koans with each other, copy famous Buddhist sutras for special occasions, employ Daoist priests to exorcise Prospect Garden, and read Daoist texts in the privacy of their studios or while relaxing in their garden.

See also **Buddhism, Confucianism, Zhuangzi**

FURTHER READING

Chan, Wing-tsit. *A Source Book in Chinese Philosophy* (Princeton: Princeton University Press, 1963).

Plaks, Andrew. *Archetype and Allegory in the* Dream of the Red Chamber (Princeton: Princeton University Press, 1976).

Puett, Michael, and Christina Gross-Loh. *The Path: What Chinese Philosophers Can Teach Us About the Good Life* (New York: Simon & Schuster, 2016).

Zhang, Dainian. *Key Concepts in Chinese Philosophy*. Translated by Edmund Ryden (New Haven: Yale University Press, 2002).

Clothing

Much space in the novel is devoted to characters describing clothing as well as descriptions of the clothing they wear. It is estimated that 218 different articles of clothing are mentioned, and the costumes of 13 characters are described in detail, some only once or twice or at most four times (Sychovs, 288, 302). There are several reasons for this prominence and Cao Xueqin's interest in this subject. The first was personal, for his family had been deeply involved for several generations as Textile Commissioners, overseeing the production of clothing and the sending of them up the Grand Canal for use at the imperial court in Beijing. Consequently, he would naturally have had good knowledge and an appreciation of clothing in general. Secondly, this focus on clothing enabled him to concretely illustrate the high social position and affluence of the Jia family, along with their power, given that some of their clothing were expensive gifts from the Imperial Concubine. In addition, descriptions of the attire would have drawn the attention of his readers, who mostly came from a similar class. This attention is also in keeping with the encyclopedic nature of the novel. Furthermore, the clothes of specific characters give further information about aspects of their personalities. Finally, clothing descriptions reinforce certain themes in the story because a "costume is the most vivid embodiment of the material shell which covers up the human essence. What else can best symbolize the vicissitudes of human existence, its vain ups and sad downs, its colors and aroma? Yes, this is precisely the leit-motif of the novel" (Sychovs, 288).

All of these reasons are on display in the novel's descriptions of Bao-yu's clothing, which is discussed 16 times in the novel, the most of any character. The Russian sinologists L. and V. Sychov have perceptively analyzed the elaborate clothing Bao-yu wears when he makes his famous first appearance in chapter 3, which Cao Xueqin significantly describes in great detail (using 89 Chinese characters). Based upon a careful examination of his headband, gold coronet, and other head gear, his robe jacket, the black satin boots he wore, and the dragons and butterflies on items of his clothing and their coloring, they have concluded that a cluster of important meanings can be derived about Bao-yu and the novel's messages. They maintain that the items Bao-yu wears are intended to symbolize his celestial origin and incarnation, the Jia family's extreme indulgence, the transitory nature of the world, and the fleeting and dreamlike nature of life. In direct contrast, there are only two occasions where Dai-yu's clothes are described; both descriptions are limited, and her garments are characterized as being beyond any current fashion. She is also directly associated with the Moon Goddess Chang E and dressed like her for a family gathering. This lack of description signifies Dai-yu's otherworldly, pure, and ethereal character, unmarked by a worldly standard.

See also **Chang E**

FURTHER READING

Sychov, L. and V. "The Role of Costume in Ts'ao Hseuh-ch'in's Novel the *Dream of the Red Chamber.*" Translated by Cecelia Shickman. *Tamkang Review* 11.3 (1981): 287–305.

Coastal Defenses and Disturbances

Piracy and coastal disturbances in China were a major problem during Cao Xueqin's time. It was such a severe problem in the south of the country that people traveling from the south to the north would not go by sea but by land or would use the Grand Canal. These disturbances are alluded to on several occasions in the novel. Tan-chun's father-in-law is the commandant of the coastal region. In chapter 104, it is mentioned that the emperor was unhappy with the condition of coastal defenses. In chapter 114, Zhen Ying-jia tells Jia Zheng that he has been ordered to the south to quell an outbreak of piracy. Later, Jia Zheng states that piracy and coastal disturbances have prevented news about Tan-chun from reaching the Jia family. Finally, in chapter 118, Zheng encounters an army convoy on the Grand Canal that is returning to the capital after a successful campaign, possibly against pirates, and he also receives word from an official from the Coastal Defense headquarters that the commandant has also been recalled to Beijing and will be bringing Tan-chun with him.

Confucianism

Extremely influential system of thought developed by the Chinese philosopher and politician Confucius (551 BC–479 BC). He is also referred to as Kongzi or Kongfuzi (Master Kong) and is widely considered China's most important thinker. Confucius was born to a minor aristocratic family in Qufu in the small feudal state of Lu and lived during the Warring States period and the end of the Zhou dynasty. He established a school to teach political leadership, which attracted many students. He was noted for being an excellent and tolerant teacher and when selecting students made no distinctions based on their economic and social background. But he was also very serious and had high expectations of them. Confucius was frustrated during much of his life for he had little opportunity to put his political theories into actual practice and held only minor office, much to his regret. After his death and over time, his teachings gained popularity, and, during the Han dynasty (26 BC–220 AD), they were adopted by the imperial government and became the orthodoxy. This remained the case in China until the end of the Qing dynasty in 1911. Confucius left no writings, and his teachings were turned into a set of prescriptions and practices by his students and disciples. The major texts of Confucianism are nine books referred to as The Four Books and The Five Classics. These texts served as the basis for the examinations for the imperial bureaucracy, and all educated Chinese had studied them. The time in which Confucius lived was a period of political instability, social disintegration, violence, and a collapse of morality in China. As a consequence, he focused his attention on the subjects of social and political reform and became concerned with the question of how to create and maintain a well-ordered and benevolent society.

Confucius was an agnostic in most of his religious beliefs but also conservative and looked back to the early part of the Zhou period as a golden age where compassionate leaders ruled, and people lived in harmony with each other. He also contended that man's original nature was good and human nature malleable and that this golden age could be recreated through the internalization of a system of ethical beliefs and social conduct that were grounded in a humanistic social philosophy that was concerned with human beings and their relationships in society. Confucius premised that all human life occurred within the context of some type of a family and that it is this, and not the isolated individual, that is the basic component of humankind. He felt that there was no individual "self" but rather that a person was the sum total of the relationships they formed and the roles they played in life. In other words, an individual's very identity was defined by a system of relationships and depended upon the maintenance of their status or position within society and fulfilling the responsibilities this station entailed. Hence, the goal of life was to obtain a harmonious and happy relationship with others by behaving in a manner that is appropriate to the role one played. In Confucian thought, this imperative was famously called the rectification of names, the belief that for every situation and role there was an appropriate way to behave and that this way was dictated by social names (father, son, husband, wife, ruler, etc.) and making these names correspond to reality. Names were not considered passive labels but were thought of as prescriptions for proper behavior and correct thoughts. For example, being a father entailed a host of strict obligations and behavioral practices.

As one scholar has put it, Confucianism held, "Through studying ritual, history, the Five classics, and under Neo-Confucianism, the Four Books, the individual is able to learn the proper expression and response for every situation and, in doing so, train the self to embody the ideal. The Confucian self is a social being expressed through the 'Five relationships' [ruler and subject, father and son, husband and wife, older sibling and younger sibling, and elder and junior friends].... With the exception of friendship, these codified bonds are hierarchical and situationally contingent; everyone, even the emperor had at least one relationship in which he or she was ritually subordinate. At the core of ritual practice is the belief that the observance of distinctions is necessary to the maintenance of domestic and social order" (Epstein, 21). This ritualized hierarchy is brilliantly depicted at work in chapter 53 when the Jia family perform elaborate and precisely choreographed Confucian sacrifices in the Hall of the Ancestors during New Year's Eve, one of the key days on the Confucian calendar. It is important to underline that, contrary to some popular misconceptions, Confucius did not consider these relationships to be simply hierarchical and one sided, for he strongly held that they involved mutual bonds of responsibility and obligations.

For Confucius, the ideal person was the "superior or cultivated man," but he did not agree with the traditional notion that such a person had to be of noble birth. He controversially believed in man's natural equality and in the idea that any individual could become a superior person through self-cultivation and the internalization of these five core and interrelated virtues: humanity or human-heartedness (*ren*), which makes human beings distinctly human; propriety or proper behavior (*li*), which concerns the observance of rituals, customs, and relationships that have long been established by human practices, including the five relationships and the rectification of names; righteous (*yi*), which tells us the correct way to act in situations that accord with *jen*; moral wisdom (*zhi*), which is the knowledge of right and wrong; and finally, the most important virtue, filial piety (*xiao*), the virtue of respect and reverence for one's family and the obedience of children to their parents. The basis of jen is found in *hsiao*. Confucius was a traditionalist and patriarchal in his attitude toward the family and thought that the relationship between father and son was the basic model for society. Putting all of this together, Confucius felt that the sincere and diligent cultivation of jen through *li, yi, zhi* and *hsiao* would make a person a virtuous, morally cultivated and aware individual whose humanity was developed, and this would, in turn, contribute to the creation of a well-ordered, happy society, and good government.

During the period in which Cao Xueqin lived, Confucianism changed from its previous concentration on metaphysical questions, like the status of moral principles, to a focus on careful philological analysis of classical and historic texts. This occurred because Confucian scholars thought that using the tools of philology could establish the Confucian canon on a firmer scholarly basis. As a result, textual scholarship became the main task of Confucian scholars. At the same time, the Manchu government, seeking to legitimize their rule, adopted as official orthodoxy the conservative Cheng-Zhu school of Confucianism. The historian Richard Smith has characterized the general features of Confucian thought during this time as having: "(1). A comparative lack of interest in metaphysics; (2). A rationalistic outlook predicated on a belief in the intelligibility of the universe; (3). A great reverence for the past; (4). A humanistic concern with 'man in society'; (5). An emphasis on morality in government and a link between personal and political values; (6). A belief in the moral perfectibility of all human beings; (7). The supreme authority of fundamental Confucian principles, and (8). A general disesteem of law" (110). Confucian beliefs and practices are ubiquitous in the lives of the characters in *Dream of the Red Chamber*. They dictate behavior and etiquette, determine status and how individuals communicate, and explain most of the rituals the Jia family observes. They also structure the physical space and environment in which they dwell because traditional Chinese architecture both embodies and reinforces Confucian notions of hierarchy and gender relations.

This can easily be seen in the novel in the way the Jia family mansions are designed, with their segregated women's inner quarters; the fact that, traditionally, the main hall in the inner courtyard is reserved for the oldest member of the family and side halls in the outer courtyard for sons and daughters; the ceremonial rooms and ancestor halls where a strict hierarchy is observed in seating assignments and during the performances of rituals; and the sharp distinctions made in rooms between the inner and outer realm, as well as between the wall surrounding the mansions and the outer world. All of these elements, with their strong sense of order and formal spatial relationships, combine to reinforce Confucian hierarchical and status-related patterns. As two historians of Chinese architecture have noted, "Social status within *Honglou meng* is signaled by stylized forms or reception, seating arrangements, and a host of other matters [like clothing, standard forms of address, everyday objects used] bounded by formal rules.... One consequence is that Cao Xueqin may use the position of characters in the fictional space of the novel to denote their status. This is especially evident in relation to the structure of the mansion complex, composed of a series of courtyards ordered through an abstract notion of hierarchy, so that small changes in positions—top, bottom, left, right, inner, and outer—may determine their function. Such spaces also have a propensity for linear order, reflecting differences in status from top to bottom, outer to inner" (Li and Yeo, 55). This linear order runs from the inner real or private space and ends up in the outer realm or public space. (In direct contrast, Prospect Garden is depicted as being largely free of these formalities.) The novel is also good at showing the gap that existed between Confucian theory and actual social practices. Many of the male characters, in incident upon incident, glaringly fail to live up to their Confucian obligations to serve as moral models and follow the principle of the rectification of names. The result is that their bad conduct greatly contributes to a breakdown in the Jia family's social order. In chapter 106, Jia Zheng and Grandmother Jia acknowledge that they have been at fault because of their failure to properly instruct the younger generations in the principles of proper behavior.

Dream of the Red Chamber has often been viewed as an anti–Confucian work. This perception is in part based upon Bao-yu's highly critical attitude toward the philosophy's stress on hierarchy, achievement, filial piety, and officialdom, conservative beliefs regarding women, and its association with the imperial civil service examination system, which critics contend reflect Cao Xueqin's own beliefs. They point out that Bao-yu frequently uses the dismissive term "career worms" to describe ambitious, social-climbing, and self-serving individuals who use Confucian rhetoric and the imperial examination to cover and advance their naked ambition. And, in chapter 118, he tells Bao-chai that he considers Zhen Bao-yu to be an example of a career worm because he talks a lot but says nothing profound and uses terminology like "filial piety," "loyalty," and "management of affairs." But the novel's attitude toward Confucianism is much more nuanced than is commonly assumed. While Cao Xueqin is clearly very critical of large elements of Confucian teachings, he is also ambivalent about the philosophy. Bao-yu himself, on several occasions, defends what he deems to have been the original teachings of the philosopher before they were adopted by imperial governments and became the official orthodoxy and the basis for the examination system. He also tells Aroma in chapter 19 that, apart from the work *The Great Learning*, "all the rest are trash produced by fools of old who didn't understand the sage" (DRM, 1: 278), and he later notes that Confucius never argued for the use of the examination system. Furthermore, as one scholar has noted, "In novels, such as *Honglou meng*, which seem to celebrate anything but the orthodox, the performance of one's proper social role is treated as so foundational to order that unless the father acts like a father, the son as son, and the wife as wife, chaos will ensue no matter how much author(s) and readers might wish things were different" (Epstein, 24).

This key Confucian belief is prevalent in the story, so much so that some commentators have gone so far as to claim that the novel is actually on several levels a Confucian novel. One Qing dynasty commentator wrote that the novel's central purpose "is to elucidate the teachings of *The Great Learning* and *The Doctrine of the Mean*.... The entire text can be summed up in one phrase, 'condemnation for failure to instruct'.... Confucius composed *The Spring and Autumn Annals* ... with the purpose of edifying later generations so they might rectify their ways of thinking, restore moral order and the adherence to principle, and bring social interaction into a state of harmony. *Honglou meng* definitely borrows this idea" (Chang, 324, 326, 325). The renowned literary critic C.T. Hsia contended that the story endorses "Confucian morality for everyday conduct" (273). It has also been noted, "The fall of the Jia family can ultimately be attributed to its neglect of two fundamental Confucian virtues: frugality and moderation" (Egan and Hsien-Yung, xxii). Another commentator has argued that Cao Xueqin was attempting to bridge the long-standing conflict between feelings of sentiments and love (*qing*) and orthodox Confucianism by using the emotion to obtain a Confucian ideal (Xu, 443). And Maram Epstein has maintained that Cao Xueqin was attempting to show in the novel that the relaxation of hierarchical standards by the inhabitants of Prospect Garden and the failure to follow ritually determined identities in chapters 37 and 49 leads to a breakdown in the social order and that a *qing*-based view of the self must be checked and regulated by Confucian rituals or turmoil will ensue (168, 171, 173).

Many of the commentators who argue for a strong Confucian take on the novel hold that virtually all of the problems that occur in the story are not in the main caused by the malicious effects of Confucian ideas but because of the chronic inability of individuals to properly follow those tenets, meet their obligations, and serve as correct moral models. But in spite of these Confucian elements in the story, other critics have observed that the Confucianism in the novel is depicted as conservative, suppressive of the natural, and intellectually stifling. It is also argued that the story makes it plain that Confucianism at times places unreasonable demands on the individual, is frequently used for reasons of mercantile self-advancement, and is deeply suspicious of and incapable of understanding the significance of emotions like *qing*.

See also **Education and the Examination System, Qing**

Further Reading

Chan, Wing-tsit. Translator and Compiler. *A Source Book in Chinese Philosophy* (Princeton: Princeton University Press, 1963).

"Chang Hsin-chih on How to Read the *Hung-lou Meng (Dream of the Red Chamber)*." Translated and annotated by Andrew Plaks. In *How to Read the Chinese Novel*. Edited by David Ralston (Princeton: Princeton University Press, 1990): 316–322.

Egan, Susan Chan, and Pai Hsien-Yung. *A Companion to the* Story of the Stone: *A Chapter-By-Chapter Guide* (New York: Columbia University Press, 2021).

Epstein, Maram. "Reflections of Desire in *Honglou meng*." In *Competing Discourses: Orthodoxy, Authenticity, and Engendered Meanings in Late Imperial Chinese Fiction* (Cambridge: Harvard University Press, 2001): 150–197.

Hsia, C.T. "The Scholar-Novelist and Chinese Culture: A Reappraisal of *Ching-Hua Yuan*." In *Chinese Narrative: Critical and Theoretical Essays*. Edited by Andrew H. Plaks (Princeton: Princeton University Press, 1977): 266–305.

Li, Xiaodong, and Yeo Kang-shua. "The Propensity of Chinese Space: Architecture in the Novel *Dream of the Red Chamber*." *Traditional Dwellings and Settlements Review* 13.2 (2002): 49–62.

Smith, Richard J. *China's Cultural Heritage: The Ch'ing Dynasty, 1644–1912* (Boulder: Westview Press, 1983).

Xu, Ma. "Can Sentimentalism Survive? Revisiting the Negotiation Between *Qing* and Confucian Ideology in *Honglou meng*." *Tsing Hua Journal of Chinese Literature*, 14 (2015): 437–447.

Xue, Weihe. "How Humor Humanizes a Confucian Paragon: The Case of Xue Baochai in *Honglou meng*." *Humor in Chinese Life and Letters: Classical and Traditional Approaches*. Edited by Jocelyn Chen and Jessica Milner Davis (Hong Kong University Press, 2011): 139–168.

Corruption

Corruption—governmental, legal, social, and personal—is one of the important themes of the novel. Members of the Jia family often illegally subvert the judicial system and other governmental organizations to their advantage by bribing judges, censors, and eunuchs, stealing, extorting, and putting undue pressure on the police. They trade on their relationships with other officials, offer promotions for financial gain and illegally loan money at exorbitant rates of interest. Male members of the family violate central Confucian ethical precepts as a matter of course and fail to act as moral models and properly instruct others. Corruption by officials, in particular, was a serious and systematic problem during the Qing dynasty. Cao Xueqin had a personal interest in the subject because his family's fall and the confiscation of their properties were precipitated by corruption charges against his father, Cao Fu. He must have long thought about the reasons for this event and how it might have been prevented. Nancy E. Park, who has conducted extensive research on corruption in 18th-century China, has shown that the term had a fluid and situational-based meaning during this period. She demonstrates that, although the Qing government had formulated numerous objective and extremely detailed laws into the legal code governing official corruption, which covered such common forms as bribery, extortion, influence peddling, and customary fees, and that specific punishments for these crimes were instituted, the reality was that the enforcement of these laws was often very subjective. In most cases, practical, political, and social considerations played a more important role in judicial decision-making than the precepts of formal law. Individuals were sometimes not charged with crimes simply because the government could not afford to clamp down too hard on corruption because it would have wrecked the civil service, estranged the bureaucracy, and made the general population question the authority of the dynasty. Therefore, when officials were persecuted, in many cases it was due to political reasons. Park has concluded, "The laws concerning corruption were enforced only when the perceived benefits to the impeacher—whether emperor or official—outweighed the cost" (997).

The key reason for this widespread corruption was the simple fact that salaries for government officials were extremely low and failed to cover all their administrative costs. Local and provincial officials were commonly responsible for paying the salaries of most of their employees, including their private secretaries and clerks, along with basic administrative costs like food, water, and even ink, brushes, and writing paper. They were also expected to make contributions to high-ranking officials and offer imperial tribute on holidays and birthdays. Because all of these expenses could not be covered by their salaries, officials were forced to either rely upon their own private sources of income or to look for informal or even illegal sources of funding. But Park is also quick to point out, "Most 'corrupt' officials—in the restricted sense of individuals who engaged in acts that were prohibited under the corruption laws—were energetic and devoted public servants with a sincere desire to improve the common welfare. Although there were certainly examples of officials who used their positions primarily to enrich themselves, there were others who solicited only such funds as were necessary to fulfill their professional responsibilities" (997).

Numerous works of Chinese literature in the 17th and 18th centuries, most prominently in the famous short stories of Pu Songling and Wu Jingzi's *The Scholars* (which was published during Cao Xueqin's lifetime), dealt with the ubiquity of official corruption. But *Dream of the Red Chamber* goes further and concretely shows the troubling moral dilemmas in which officials were placed through the experiences of Jia Zheng and Jia Yu-cun. In chapter 99, Zheng is assigned the post of Grain Intendant for Jiangxi province. Although he is limited in ability, Zheng is personally honest and determined to run a clean administration. But he soon encounters the harsh reality of governing far from the capital. Soon after he arrives, the servants who accompanied him and borrowed money for their new jobs, and his staff who paid for their positions, all of whom banked on making profits from squeeze, begin grumbling about his refusal to take any bribes. As a result, when Zheng wants to make a visit to town, the attendants, chair bearers, insignia bearers, runners, and members of the ceremonial band who usually accompany him fail to show up in protest, and he is forced to cancel his trip. The next day, his cook asks for more money for food. Zheng's administrative costs quickly escalate, and he runs through most of the money he brought with him, and the provincial yamen (administrative headquarters) descends into chaos. A porter on his staff, Li Ten, then informs him about the unpleasant realities of running a yamen, saying in essence that making appeals to "family honor" and being honest means little if you get caught up in a scandal and that if Zhang wants to successfully perform his duties, he must adapt and play the game. He also tells him, "You've got to look at the common people.... If your ideas came into general fashion and the shire or district mandarins were strictly forbidden to take even the tiniest squeeze, why, nothing would *ever* get done in the provinces!" (SS, 5: 28). Li then recommends that Zheng concentrate on keeping things aboveboard on the outside while he takes care of things on the inside. Zheng grudgingly agrees but warns Li that he wants no part in what he is going to do. Ironically, Zheng's new approach fails to work. Although things return to normal, the administrative corruption gets out of hand, and Zheng is eventually impeached for gross mismanagement, demoted, and summarily sent back to the capital.

In chapter 4, Jia Yu-cun is met with a similar situation. While working as a magistrate in Ying-tian-fu, he faces a case involving the powerful Xue family. Xue Pan has ordered his servants to beat Feng Yuan in a dispute over to whom the kidnapped Caltrop belongs. Feng subsequently dies from his injuries. Yu-cun wants to charge Xue Pan with the crime, but a court usher, who knew Yu-cun when he was living in a temple, in chapter 1, strenuously warns him about doing this. The usher contends that the Xue family is too powerful and that it would be dangerous to do anything against them. Moreover, he states that not charging Xue Pan would be doing the Xues a favor, which could bring him some advantages in the future. He also makes the point, as was made to Jia Zheng, that the ability to adapt to situations is central to making decisions as an official, cautioning Yu-cun to "Remember the old sayings: 'A gentleman adapts himself to circumstances' and 'The superior man is one who pursues good fortune and avoids disaster'.... Better think it about carefully" (DRM, 1: 59–60). Yu-cun, unlike Jia Zheng, eventually agrees, and the two concoct a successful scheme whereby Xue Pan escapes punishment and Feng's family is satisfied. In short, Cao Xueqin appears to have had an ambivalent attitude toward official corruption. On the one hand, he is aware, probably in part based upon his family's experiences as high-ranking officials, that because official corruption is so systematic, a certain amount of formally illegal acts like bribery are necessary on occasion for things to operate efficiently or for certain worthwhile goals to be met. But he also understood that if these acts were not carefully controlled and monitored, the corruption could easily spiral, ethically warp the person who commits them, and result in unseen and terrible consequences. (It should be noted that while Jia Yu-cun's strategy worked well in Xue Pan's case, he eventually gets his comeuppance on several occasions for other corrupt acts [including extortion and avarice], and at the end of the novel he has been impeached yet again.)

Cao Xueqin is also very good at describing how the personal immorality of the Jia family underlies their numerous acts of official corruption. The family's strong sense of entitlement and power, avid love of affluence and obliviousness to its cost, and the refusal of many of its members to follow fundamental Confucian and social norms produces a dysfunctional family environment. Most importantly, the abject failure of male senior family members, like Jia She, Jia Zhen, and others, to act as moral models, their obsession with sensual pleasures and propensity to abuse their authority, results in the bad behavior of their offspring and their servants mimicking the bad behavior of their masters. As Cao shows, all of this ensues in a situation where the family members instinctively use, without any qualms, the methods of bribery, extortion, witness intimidation, robbery, and even murder when they encounter a problem. Even sympathetic and generally honest characters, like Xue Ke and Lady Xue, easily get swept up in forms of corruption.

See also **The Embroidered Jacket Raid**

FURTHER READING

Park, Nancy. "Corruption in Eighteenth-Century China." *The Journal of Asian Studies*. 56.4 (1997): 967–1005.

Cousin Zhen

See **Jia Zhen**

Crab Flower Club

The first name of the poetry club founded by Tan-chun in chapter 37. In a letter to Bao-yu, she writes that although poetry clubs have a long history in China, they should not be restricted to males, and "female versificators [should also be] allowed a voice in the tumble concert of the muses" (SS, 2: 214). Members include Li Wan (president), Dai-yu (pen name River Queen), Bao-chai (Lady Allspice), Bao-yu (Green Boy), Tan-chun (Plantain Lover), and Xiang-yun (Cloud Maiden). Ying-chun (Amaryllis Islander) and Xi-chun (Lotus Dweller) do not like writing poetry and are instead assistants who set rhymes, themes, and work as copyists. The club's first meeting occurs in Prospect Garden's Autumn Studio, and the topic is crab blossoms.

See also **Linked Verse, Poetry, Women**

Crab Tree Flowering

In chapter 94, the crab trees at Bao-yu's residence unexpectedly bloom. This is taken to be very mysterious because the trees were struck by blight for nearly a year, and crab trees usually blossom during the third month, but this blossoming occurs in the 11th month. Li Wan believes the occurrence is favorable and that it foretells good fortune for Bao-yu (namely, his secret upcoming marriage with Bao-chai). Grandmother Jia decides to hold a small party to celebrate the event and orders Bao-yu, Jia Lian, and Hua to write verse in honor of the occasion. But Tan-chun and Jia Zheng feel that the blossoming is a bad omen, as does Xi-feng, who directs that strips of red silk be hung from the trees in order to change the bad luck into good. The flowering is ironic for several reasons. Contrary to the feelings of most of the participants, it is not auspicious, and it does foreshadow bad luck for Bao-yu. Moreover, his and Dai-yu's reaction to it is especially ironic given they also greatly misinterpret it. Dai-yu, who is unaware of Bao-yu's upcoming nuptial, excitedly misunderstands Li Wan's allusion to this event and argues that the flowering has occurred because Bao-yu is finally seriously applying himself to his studies and Jia Zheng is pleased, and this, in turn, has caused the crab trees to be pleased.

The event initially depresses Bao-yu because it makes him recall Skybright's recent death, but his mood changes when he surmises that the budding might be foretelling the arrival of Fivey as his maid. Significantly, he loses his jade during this period, and the Imperial Concubine dies shortly after this event.

Crabs and Chrysanthemums

Crabs, along with chrysanthemums, have traditionally been symbols of autumn in China. Chinese writers have long written about the delights of eating crabs. Writers in ancient China would drink wine and eat crabs while composing poetry. Appropriately, in chapter 38, a cassia viewing party is held in autumn by the young female members of the Jia family and their maids, and participants write poems on chrysanthemum-related themes and happily eat huge crabs and drink wine in beautifully patterned cups.

Critical Reception—Chinese

When *Dream of the Red Chamber* was first published in 1792, it was an immediate bestseller. Readers were taken by its realistic depiction of upper-class Chinese life, its tragic central love story and encyclopedic scope, the vivid characters, and the lushness of the prose and imagery. Soon groups of dedicated enthusiasts of the novel began to write about it, and an appreciable body of criticism (called *Hongxue*, which literally means "Study of the Red") developed. This term was coined around 1875, and even today individuals who study the novel are referred to as Redologists. Broadly speaking, the 19th century was chiefly governed by the "Annotating School," which treated the book as a canonical work, with followers punctuating the text while making comments in its margins. This school also viewed the work as a roman à clef, so attempts were made to discern the real events and historical persons that were secretly represented in the story. For example, it was argued that Bao-yu was in reality the third Qing Emperor Shunzhi and Dai-yu his much-loved concubine Donggo, who died young, and that the novel describes their doomed relationship. Also popular during this period was the "Small Details School," which focused on complicated concepts and details in the text, for example, individual words like real and unreal, true and false, and pointed out discrepancies in the plot.

Hongxue took another turn in 1904 with the publication of the famous essay "Critical Discussion of *Dream of the Red Chamber*" by the versatile historian, literary critic, and poet Wang Guowei. In it, Wang takes a comparative literary approach to analyze the novel, uniting the pessimistic philosophy of the German thinker Arthur Schopenhauer and his notions of tragedy and aesthetics with Chinese Buddhist beliefs of life as suffering and Daoist beliefs concerning desire. Among the conclusions he makes is that *Honglou meng* is the first work of Chinese literature that can be properly called a tragedy. Wang's essay was considered revolutionary because it showed Chinese scholars that it was possible to use the techniques of Western literary theory and apply them to a Chinese novel. Moreover, during the early part of the 20th century, when Chinese nationalism was on the rise, devotees of the novel started to view it as an anti–Manchu work. This perception developed into the "Allegorical or Hidden Meaning School," which figured most prominently in the writings of the educator and first President of Beijing University Cai Yuanpei. This camp expanded on the ideas of the Annotating School and concentrated on political aspects of the novel. It contended that Cao Xueqin was expressing intense feelings of nationalism in his work and arguing for the restoration of the Ming dynasty, the dynasty which preceded the Qing. Cai, in particular, held that the novel was really about the court of Emperor Kangxi, and the men in it represented the ruling Manchu and the women native Han Chinese, and all of the main characters stood for historical figures. Bao-yu was thought to represent Yin Reng, Kangxi's crown prince, and Dai-yu the noted poet Zhu Yizun, whom Kangxi befriended.

The year 1922 saw another important turning point in *Hongxue* with the publication of the essay "*Dream of the Red Chamber* Philology" by the renowned scholar, philosopher, educator, and diplomat Hu Shih. Hu Shih had been educated at Cornell and wrote his doctoral thesis under the noted American philosopher John Dewey, whose theory of pragmaticism had a major influence upon his thinking. He began the essay by taking aim at previous attempts to find hidden historical or political messages in the story, saying that these approaches "have not sought facts from those verifiable materials such as *Honglou meng*'s authorship, its social milieu, its various editions etc., but have gathered lots of irrelevant fragmentary historical events and drawn lots of strained analogies to the plot of *Honglou meng*. They certainly did not know how to carry out textual research" (quoted in Edwards, 1994, 27). Hu Shih went on to make a plea for the use of a rigorous methodology of textual analysis based upon the principle of "boldly hypothesizing and carefully verifying" (quoted in Edwards, 27). Consequently, he focused his analysis of the novel not on attempting to discover the real identity of characters in the story but on finding through a close scrutiny of 18th-century memoirs, local almanacs, and government documents who the author of *Dream of the Red Chamber* was. He concluded that it was Cao Xueqin and that the novel was largely an intimate account of Cao's own family history. He also claimed that Bao-yu was based on Cao Xueqin himself. Hu Shih's discovery and methodology had an enormous influence upon *Hongxue* and led to the creation of the "Investigative School," which emphasized the collection and rigorous examination of historical resources and of the study of how the novel was composed. Yu Pingbo and Zhou Ruchang were the most prominent members of this approach, and both believed that since Cao Xueqin's authorship was established, it was essential to learn as much as possible about his background so that his work could be better understood. Zhou, in particular, uncovered a great deal of information about Cao and his ancestry. Yu collated and wrote about the novel's existing manuscripts and the mysterious Qing dynasty commentator Red Inkstone's insightful remarks about the book.

The next consequential development in Chinese *Hongxue* occurred in 1954. After the establishment of the People's Republic of China, Marxist literary theory slowly came to the fore among critics. These critics had become increasingly irritated by the way Hu Shih and Yu Pingbo had interpreted *Dream of the Red Chamber*. In 1954, several widely read articles by two college teachers appeared in the Beijing press and literary journals accusing the two of having "reactionary political motivation" and fostering in their writings an idealistic bourgeois take on the novel for more than 30 years, which had badly influenced the thinking of young people in literary circles. The Redologists were specifically castigated for failing to fit their analysis within a Marxian class structure framework and not treating the novel as a realistic depiction of feudal society and a critique of feudal landlordism, thinking, and the traditional extended Chinese family system. These pointed criticisms quickly led to an intense campaign against Yu Pingbo that lasted for nearly three months (Hu Shih was at that time living in the U.S.), which resulted in him being forced to admit that he had been deceived by Hu Shih and acknowledge that the novel was in a general sense "anti-feudal." One of the upshots of this campaign, which was launched with the approval of the then leader of China, Chairman Mao, was that Marxist literary criticism was formally recognized. It also resulted in Bao-yu and Dai-yu now being viewed as revolutionaries against feudalism and autocracy and Xi-feng being seen as an exploitive capitalist. Ironically, this campaign also made *Honglou meng* even more popular. From 1958 to 1962, 140,000 copies were sold in China. During the upheaval of the Cultural Revolution in China during the 1960s and early 1970s, it was banned by the government for political reasons.

Beginning in the late 1970s, Marxian *Hongxue* began to slowly fade, and the tenets of the Investigative School began to exert an increasingly strong presence. But there were also some detractors regarding *Hongxue*'s longstanding focus on the work as a historical record. In a famous 1974 article, the distinguished historian Yu Ying-shu complained that Redologists have wrongly exclusively concentrated on the realism of the novel and constantly treated it as a historical document or a "real world" instead of as a work of fiction that was the product of Cao Xueqin's imagination. Yu maintains that in order to comprehend the novel, one has to appreciate the significance of both the "real world" and the Land of Illusion, stating that during "the past fifty years the nature of Redology was such that its chief efforts were devoted to research on the historical aspect of the novel. Our Redologists being mostly historians or adherents to the historical method had naturally focused their attention on the world of reality which the novel described so much so that the other world in the novel—the ideal world, the castle in the air which the author had 'labored ten years' to create—was utterly neglected. In fact, the chief concern of these scholars had been to demolish this castle in the air and restore it to the bricks and stones that belonged to the world of reality. Under the influence of the 'autobiographical approach,' restoration efforts went even further with a shifting of emphasis from the world of reality in the novel to the world of reality in which the author once lived ... [consequently]. The ideal world in the book is blanked out and, if one may borrow the words of the author, 'It is a world wiped clean; only aspects of white remain'" (5–6).

Generally speaking, since that time, *Hongxue* has splintered into several specific areas of study. The first is Cao studies, which is concerned with Cao Xueqin's life and family history and how they relate to the novel. This area remains very popular, with numerous biographies and historical studies of Cao and his family being published in China every year. The second area is a study of the various manuscript versions of the novel and the extensive commentary (including by Red Inkstone) that has been written on it. Another topic that continues to receive much attention is translation studies of the novel (especially English) and the history of these translations. Studies of the material culture of the story and aspects associated with its encyclopedic nature, like food, horticultural, medical, and garden practices and clothing are also popular. Furthermore, dictionaries and encyclopedias that detail all aspects of the novel, with a heavy stress on cultural matters, frequently appear, and there are also several respected academic journals that are devoted to *Hongxue*. In addition, the philosophy and religion in the novel—Daoism, Buddhism, Confucianism, and *qing*—have started to receive some scholarly attention. Finally, another interesting topic that has generated some scholarly attention concerns whether it is correct for critics to apply studies of the Qing dynasty to the novel.

Moreover, publications containing elements of the Hidden Meaning School sporadically are published. In 2002 and several years after, the novelist Liu Xinwu came out with a series of books on *qinxue* (the study of the character Qin-shi). In them, he maintained that she was based on the illegitimate daughter of a crown prince whom Emperor Kangxi had disowned and the Cao family took her in with hopes that the prince would be restored and they would be recompensed, but the Imperial Concubine Yuan-chun betrayed her. While Liu's books were wildly popular in China, they were also panned by scholarly Redologists, but their popularity reveals there is still a deep interest by readers in the old question of whether the novel contains any hidden allusions to actual historical events and persons. Finally, studies of literary aspects of the novel, like its poetry, depictions of characters, and organization, occasionally appear. But even today, there are still, when compared to other studies of the book, relatively few publications that directly deal with *Honglou meng* purely as a work of fiction, but this situation is slowly beginning to change for the better. What's more, modern studies have often avoided discussions of Cao Xueqin's use of the fantastic and supernatural, mainly because these elements in the novel have been largely considered by modern critics to be irrelevant, having no special meaning or simply are uninteresting. (But this situation is also changing.) Chinese *Hongxue*, like the debates concerning Shakespeare and his works in the west, is often marked by fierce and sometimes highly personal battles among scholars of differing schools on how to interpret the novel and its meaning.

To give the reader a flavor of the range and content of contemporary *Hongxue* studies in China, the following is a list of the topics of 18 recently published books on *Dream of the Red Chamber* that were available in several large bookstores in Beijing: an analysis of the dramas in the story, a comparative examination of two English translations of 50 poems from the novel, and a biography of Cao Xueqin. There were also studies of Buddhism, Zen culture, Western objects, silk, classic cuisines, poems, and the traditional Chinese family material objects, in the story, and analyses of English translations from the perspective of rhetoric, and a discussion of construal equivalences in translating discourse markers. In addition, several books of essays on "hot topics" in *Hong* studies, like aesthetics, tea, love, the relationship between Buddhism, Daoism, and Confucianism, the concept of emptiness, Goddesses, and Bao-yu's relationship to feudal society, as well as a 200 year history of *Hongxue* were also available for purchase.

See also **Red Inkstone**

FURTHER READING

Bonner, Joey. "Yu P'ing-po and the Literary Dimensions of the Controversy Over *Hung lou Meng*." *The China Quarterly* 67 (1976): 546–581.
Edwards, Louise. *Men and Women in Qing China: Gender in the Red Chamber Dream* (Leiden: E.J. Brill, 1994).
Greider, Jerome B. "The Communist Critique of *Hong-lou Meng*." *Papers on China* 10 (1956): 142–168.
Saussy, Haun. "The Age of Attribution or How *Honglou meng* Finally Acquired an Author." *Chinese Literature: Essays, Articles, Reviews* 25 (2003): 119–132.
Wang, Xiaojue. "*Stone* in Modern China: Literature, Politics, and Culture." *Approaches to Teaching Cao Xueqin's Dream of the Red Chamber.* Edited by Andrew Schonebaum and Tina Liu (New York: Modern Language Association of America, 2012): 413–426.
Wei, Shang. "The *Stone* Phenomenon and Its Transformation from 1791 to 1919." *Approaches to Teaching Cao Xueqin's* Dream of the Red Chamber. Edited by Andrew Schonebaum and Tina Liu (New York: Modern Languages Association of America, 2012): 390–412.
Yu, Ying-shih. "The Two Worlds of *Hung-lou Meng*." Translated by Diana Yu. *Renditions* 2 (1974): 5–22.
Zhou, Ruchang. *Between Noble and Humble: Cao Xueqin and the* Dream of the Red Chamber. Edited by Ronald R. Gray and Mark S. Ferrara (New York: Peter Lang, 2009).

Cui Yingying 崔莺莺

Fictional female character in the Tang dynasty tale "The Story of Cui Yingying" by Yuan Zhen (779–831) and the famous Yuan dynasty drama *Dream of the Western Chamber* by Wang Shifu (1250–1337?). The first is the story of the tragic romance between Zhang Sheng, a scholar, and his cousin Cui Yingying.

Zhang falls for her when they first meet but is initially rebuffed by Cui. They soon fall in love but eventually break up because Zhang is intent on taking the civil service exam, and they end up marrying different partners. *Dream of the Western Chamber* has the same persons, and, while they encounter many difficulties during their romance, they do marry in the end. Cui's character has been so popular that more than 70 stories have been written about her. Some scholars have compared Lin Dai-yu to Cui, arguing that they are both beautiful, talented, passionate, and strong-willed women who defy traditional morality and select their mate on the basis of love and not obligation. It is also pointed out that when Dai-yu reads the *The Romance of the Western Chamber* for the first time, she is overwhelmed by the lyricism and emotion of the story. There are several other allusions to the character in the novel. In chapter 58, Musk jokingly tells Parfumee that she does not look like Cui but her faithful maid Reddie. And in chapter 120, Shi-yin tells Jia Yu-cun that Cui was a "fallen fairy [whose] celestial heart polluted the base desires of this world" (SS, 5: 372).

See also **Drama**, *The Romance of the Western Chamber*

Cutting Hair as Protest

The cutting of one's hair as an act of protest or rebellion was considered a shocking act in Imperial China. A person's hair, body and skin were believed to be a gift from one's parents, and damaging or removing them was thought to be extremely unfilial. *Dream of the Red Chamber* has several instances where aggrieved women threaten to cut their hair as a form of protest. In chapter 117, Xi-chun cuts off all her hair and threatens to kill herself if she is not allowed to become a Buddhist nun, and in chapter 46, Faithful manages to cut off a large piece of her hair in protest of Jia She's attempts to make her his concubine. This practice is not uncommon in East Asia even today. For example, South Koreans, especially men, occasionally publicly cut their hair off as a form of political protest.

Daoism

See **Zhuangzi**

Death by a Thousand Cuts 凌迟

A horrifying form of torture and execution used during China's imperial period as punishment for very serious crimes like treason. A knife would be used to remove parts of a charged person's body over a long interval of time. This punishment was also intended to be a form of humiliation after death. It is referred to in a proverb cited by Xi-feng in chapter 68, which says that a man sentenced to be punished by this technique is not afraid to drag the emperor off his horse.

Deva Kings

Buddhist religious beings who serve as guardian deities who protect people from evil spirits. They are usually located to the left or right of temple gates. Xue Pan, in chapter 34, sarcastically calls Bao-chai a Deva King when he is accused of causing Bao-yu's vicious beating by Jia Zheng. Bao-yu dislikes these temple guardians who frequently are depicted as ferocious looking.

Diagram of the Supreme Ultimate 太极图

A drawing or symbol used in Chinese philosophy to depict the cosmic process of the universe, it illustrates the universe's entire evolutionary sequence beginning with creation, "Non-Polarity," the mysterious source of all reality, then the development of the forces of *yin* and *yang*, to the Five Elements of water, fire, wood, metal, and earth, which make up the five seasons and lead to the myriad things of the world. The Diagram was first devised by the Song dynasty Neo-Confucian philosopher Zhou Dunyi (1017–1073), who also wrote a famous 256-page, 40-chapter explanation of it. On a basic level, the Diagram is an exposition of the book of divination, the *I Ching* (*Book of Changes*). The Diagram forms the cornerstone of Neo-Confucian cosmology and has exerted a strong influence on Daoist thought. In chapter 52 of the novel, Bao-chai jokingly states that one of the themes for the next poetry club meeting will be a 300-line poem on the Diagram. Intellectually irrepressible, Bao-qin immediately responds that it could be done but would involve "filling up the lines with phrases from the *Book of Changes*" (DRM, 2: 181).

See also **Five Elements**, *I Ching*, *Yin* **and** *Yang*

Ding

An ancient bronze cooking vessel. It has two looped handles and three or four legs. Dai-yu comes across a large *ding* covered with green patina the first time she visits the Rong mansion in chapter 3.

Door Gods

These guardian deities protect homes and buildings from evil spirits. A picture of them was customarily placed or painted on the doors to residences and buildings for protective purposes during imperial times. The doors of both Jia family mansions would have had them, especially during festivals like a New Year's celebration, as noted in chapter 53. This practice is also frequently observed in China even today.

Doubles

Dream of the Red Chamber is replete with doubles that serve a variety of purposes. Literary doubles are commonly divided into two types: latent and manifest. Latent doubles are cases in which doubles share personality characteristics but do not look alike. Manifest doubles are when a double looks exactly like the original person. Several of the main characters in the novel are latent doubles (for example, Xue Bao-chai and Aroma; and Lin Dai-yu and Skybright). But the most famous double in the story is Bao-yu's manifest double Zhen Bao-yu. The fact that Zhen Bao-yu is Jia Bao-yu's manifest double and that they actually meet both in a dream and in person makes *Dream of the Red Chamber* unique because manifest doubles are virtually unheard of in traditional Chinese literature. (There are only four examples in traditional Chinese literature of a character meeting his manifest double. They are in the novels *Journey to the West* and *The Tower of Myriad Mirrors*, the play *The Palace of Everlasting Life*, and the short story "Becoming an Immortal" by Pu Songling. It is interesting to note that doubles did not start appearing in Western literature until the 19th century.)

Not surprisingly, much attention has been devoted to explaining why Cao Xueqin created Bao-yu's manifest double. Among the explanations offered are these: he wanted to further explore the duality of and interplay between notions of truth (Zhen) and falsity (Jia)—namely, how the false is in the real and the real is in the false and to illustrate that truth and falsity are not dialectically opposed but rather are complementary elements of experience; Cao was interested in raising some central metaphysical questions about the concept of the self; Zhen's superficial conformity is used to represent Jia's fate, that is, if he had not had a supernatural background; Cao wished to demonstrate the theme that everything has its counterpart or becomes its opposite in the end; he was created to help give structure to the story; Zhen was intended to further highlight the novel's criticism of the existing Chinese social system; he was designed to act as a foil to Bao-yu's avid individualism; Cao wished to show Jia Bao-yu's divided self to offer a look into his warring psyche; he was employed to bring to the fore Bao-yu's long and arduous quest to discover who he was and his future plans; Zhen Bao-yu represents Jia Bao-yu's search for himself and his attempt at understanding himself; and that Cao meant for him to help Jia Bao-yu along on his difficult journey to enlightenment.

There is also another novel way of interpreting this character. Dore Levy has surmised that Zhen Bao-yu "represents the possibility of 'If only…' and incidentally reveals that only if Bao-yu had not been encumbered by his jade, or if he had not [had] his fundamental disability, he might not have been so interesting and sympathetic a character. Moreover, if his future had really been under his control, the pressure of his life would certainly have kept him from reaching enlightenment and blocked the reader also" (98). Surprisingly, a large number of Chinese experts on *Dream of the Red Chamber* find Zhen Bao-yu a problematic character, dismissing him as an unseemly and supernatural figure who was probably not created by Cao Xueqin but by the controversial Gao E. The famous scholar Yu Pingbo considered Zhen an uninteresting and meaningless character and felt that he should have been cut from the novel.

Jia Bao-yu's confrontation with his manifest double is for him, as it would be for anyone, a deeply disturbing, psychologically threatening and ontologically puzzling experience for it raises fundamental questions concerning the constitution of his personal identity. Moreover, Zhen Bao-yu would have concretely represented a potential alternative self, career path, and sensibility that Jia Bao-yu had consistently rejected. As a result, his comprehension of why he could not take the conventional path that Zhen Bao-yu has taken assists him in his own development and quest for a sense of self. By concretely knowing what he is *not* in the form of his manifest double, Jia Bao-yu is able to understand what he *is*. The connection between the meeting of the Bao-yus and Bao-chai's and Jia Bao-yu's philosophical debate regarding virtue and responsibility, which occurs soon after the two Bao-yus' meeting, has often been overlooked and touches on concerns Zhen Bao-yu's attitude has raised. During the discussion, Bao-chai takes the conventional Confucian position, a stance of which Zhen Bao-yu is illustrative, while Jia Bao-yu defends a philosophy that is Daoist in nature and emphasizes personal liberation and transcendence. Their debate, on one level, serves to mirror more fully the two Bao-yus' opposing beliefs about life and life choices that are represented in their discussion.

It is also quite possible that for Cao Xueqin personally this special meeting between the Bao-yus represented a psychological attempt by him to look at and deal with the choices he had made in his life and to reach some sort of understanding of why it had turned out the way it had. By writing about a character who confronts a potential self (the haunting unlived in a lived life), he might very well have been writing about a self (and life) that at one juncture in his own lifetime he could also very well have become (and might have reached some reconciliation with his inability to have done so), if the tragedy of his own family had not happened or if he had passed the imperial examination and not have become the outsider that he was. The novel also frequently uses doubling and mirroring techniques as structuring devices.

See also **The Last Forty Chapters, Narrative Patterns and Techniques**

FURTHER READING

Chan, Ping-leung. "Myth and Psyche in *Hung-lou Meng*." In Winston Yang and Curtis Atkins, eds., *Critical Essays on Chinese Fiction* (Hong Kong: Chinese University Press, 1980): 165–179.
Gray, Ronald R. *Wandering Between Two Worlds: The Formative Years of Cao Xueqin* (New York: Peter Lang, 2014): 120–124.
Levy, Dore. *Ideal and Actual in* The Story of the Stone (New York: Columbia University Press, 1999).
Liu, Joyce C.H. "The Doubling of the Stone: The Double Motif and the True Self in *Xiyou Ji* and *Honglou meng*." *East-West Comparative Literature: Cross-Cultural Discourse*. Edited by Tak-wai Wong (Hong Kong: Department of Comparative Literature, University of Hong Kong, 1993): 121–150.
Miller, Lucien. *Masks of Fiction in the "Dream of the Red Chamber": Myth, Mimesis and Persona* (Tucson: University of Arizona Press, 1975): 155–180.
Yu, Anthony. *Rereading the Stone: Desire and the Making of Fiction in* Dream of the Red Chamber (Princeton: Princeton University Press, 1997): 159–160, 163–164.

Dragons

In China, dragons are mythological creatures that are associated with power, strength, prosperity, and the emperor. They are considered the first among the famous four greatest creatures (the others are the tiger, tortoise, and phoenix). They are seen as auspicious, benevolent, and able to control the forces of nature, like life-giving rain. Dragons are also thought to bring wealth, virtue, and harmony and are the fifth animal in the traditional Chinese zodiac. During the Qing dynasty, the dragon was a symbol of the state, and its motif was used on the emperor's possessions and furnishings and on the silk robes of members of the imperial court. During important festivals, dragon dances were (and continue to be today) often performed, and the Dragon Boat festival associated with the poet and minister Qu Yuan is one of the most famous festivals in China. The image of a regal dragon flying amidst clouds is one of the most important design themes in Chinese crafts and arts. Dragons are frequently mentioned in *Dream of the Red Chamber* and are symbols of the Jia family's wealth, power, and connections to the throne. In chapter 3, when Dai-yu visits the Rong-guo mansion, it is mentioned that the Hall of Exalted Felicity has a large blue board that is framed in gold dragons, and above a huge *ding* is a vertical scroll of a black dragon among clouds and waves. Chapter 15 has both Bao-yu and the Prince of Beijing wearing clothing that contain images of dragons. In chapter 41, Bao-yu drinks from a cup that belongs to Adamantina that is shaped like a dragon. Chapter 47 contains an allusion to the Dragon King, the Chinese Water and Weather God and ruler of the ocean, and chapter 58 to his daughter. And chapter 53, which describes the Jia family celebrating the New Year, states that a board over the main entrance to the family's ancestral temple is framed by two dragons, and over the entrance to the temple's vestibule is a board that shows nine interlocking dragons. Both of these boards are inscribed with the calligraphy of both the late and current emperor.

Drama

Dramas are often performed in *Dream of the Red Chamber*, and they are frequently discussed, debated, quoted, and avidly read in secret by central characters. The story mentions over 30 dramas, including one that was written by Cao Xueqin's grandfather Cao Yin. Cao Xueqin had a long and deep interest in the genre, and the novel is loaded with scenes where characters are enthralled while watching dramas and overwhelmed reading them. When he was growing up in Nanjing, his family, like the Jia family and many elite families at the time, had their own dramatic troupe that periodically put on performances for his family and friends. And when his family was forced to move to Beijing after the government raid, they lived in an area that was a short walk from the capital's famous entertainment district where plays were performed. There have also been long-standing rumors that Cao might have developed a close friendship with an actor, as Bao-yu does in the story, or even briefly have been an actor. Moreover, Cao had initially planned to write *Dream of the Red Chamber* as a drama.

Traditional Chinese dramas were basically musical dramas. They contained arias to be sung, the lyrics often being first-rate poetry set to anteceding melodies, and the spoken parts were said using plain or mannered speech. Plots commonly were based on legendary events in stories and novels. The *Kunqu* style of Chinese theater was the most favored form of opera enjoyed by officials and literati in the southern region where Cao Xueqin grew up, and it, along with the Capital style, *Jingqiang* (an amalgamation of southern and northern tunes), was the most popular form of opera in Beijing. *Kunqu* was a mixture of singing, poetry, dancing, and drama. It also contained elements of the Chinese theatrical tradition such as acrobatics, mime, farce, and ballad recital. Actors' hand movements (there were seven basic types), use of fingers (there were more than 20 different pointing gestures) and other body movements (there were more than 12 just for leg movement) were highly stylized and tailored to the personalities of characters. Action was sparse, and the movement of performers was slow and coordinated to song and woodwind instrumental music. Costumes were extremely colorful and elaborate. The color of the actors' makeup revealed their characters' personalities: white meant that they were bad, stubborn, or hotheaded; red that they were loyal and brave; and black that they were good, wise, honest, and strong. Stages were small and bare, and no props were used; therefore, audiences had to use their imagination to fill in what was physically left out of the story. Because many *Kunqu* dramas were extremely long and could take several days to perform, usually only one or possibly more scenes were performed at a time, as occurs in *Dream of the Red Chamber*.

Besides being a favorite form of entertainment for the Jia family to celebrate festivals, job promotions, birthdays, weddings, births and other auspicious occasions and a way to socialize, dramas also perform an important role in *Honglou meng* as foreshadowing devices and help to more fully define characters. This foreshadowing function can be seen in several of the four sets of dramas that are performed on major festival occasions in the story and in some single operatic pieces. In chapter 18, selections from four popular plays of the time are selected by the Imperial Concubine Yuan-chun and staged in honor of her visit. The famous Qing dynasty commentator Red Inkstone has stated that each of these selections contains clues foretelling the eventual fall of the Jia house. The first is the scene "The Grand Feast" from the drama *The Handful of Snow*. In it, a powerful prime minister, Yan Shifan, holds a feast to demonstrate his wealth and costly treasures. The play is about a snow-white jade cup that is owned by Mo Huai-ku, who runs into trouble and whose family is eventually ruined because an unscrupulous, high-ranking official desires it. The story is based on a Ming dynasty general named Wang Yu, who was the proud owner of a Song dynasty picture titled "Spring Festival on the River." The painting was wanted by the son of a corrupt premier, Yan Shi-fan. After he finally obtained it, he was told by the villain Tang Biao-bei that it is a fake. As a result, Wang was executed, officially for incompetent military actions but really because Yen believed that Wang had fooled him. This reference has been taken as foreshadowing Jia She's coveting of Stony's antique fan collection and his illegal confiscation of it in chapter 98. Jia She's crime in large part leads to the Embroidered Jacket raid, as Mo's cup and Wang's picture led to the ruin of their families. Red Inkstone has claimed that the second play, *The Palace of Eternal Youth*, foretells the premature death of the Imperial Concubine. The scene performed, the "Secret Oath," refers to the pledge of love made between Emperor Tang Xuanzhong and the Imperial Concubine Yang Guei-fei. At the end of the play, Yang is forced to hang herself.

The next production, *The Handan Story*, comes from the well-known Tang dynasty short story "The World Inside a Pillow" by Shen Jiji, which is about the illusory and dreamlike nature of fame, affluence, and the vicissitudes of life, which is also one of the themes of *Dream of the Red Chamber*. Red Inkstone has argued that the scene refers to an incident that apparently was later cut from *Dream of the Red Chamber* where Zhen Bao-yu returns Jia Bao-yu's jade. Moreover, the protagonist in this play, who eventually realizes the vanity of human striving and ambition, might be taken to represent Jia Bao-yu, who becomes a Buddhist monk when he realizes that his pampered life is but a dream. The final scene performed, "The Return of the Soul," is from the Ming dynasty classic drama *The Peony Pavilion*. The scene poignantly depicts the death of the play's lovesick heroine Du Liniang, and Red Inkstone has said that it is intended to foreshadow the death of Dai-yu.

In chapter 29, members of the Jia family enjoy plays at the Buddhist Temple of the Lunar Goddess. The three dramas that are performed here respectively symbolize the family's ascent to power, present prosperity, and is a prophecy of their fall. The first is *The White Serpent*, which concerns the rise to power of the founder of the Han dynasty, which began when he killed a large white snake, which references the Duke of Rong-guo, who first brought fame and rank to the Jia family because of his wartime exploits. The next selection, *A Heap of Honors,* portrays the famous Tang dynasty General Guo Zi-yi's luxurious 60th birthday in which his seven sons and eight sons-in-laws, all of whom occupy high positions, participate. It has been taken to refer to the high status of the Jia family at that time. The last play mentioned is the Ming dynasty work *The Seventh Branch*, which is about discharged military officer Chunyu Fen, who has a dream in which he enters an ant hole, marries the daughter of the king of the ants, and becomes a high official for 20 years. After his wife dies, a powerful political rival causes his downfall, and he is arrested and exiled by the king. When Chunyu awakens from the dream, he realizes that human life, with all its glory and fortune, is as insignificant as the life of an ant, exclaiming, "I am really awakened this time. Isn't the hierarchy of royalty and subjects the same as that of ants? The ups and downs of life are no different than what happened in the Sophora [ant] Kingdom! All is a dream, even going up to heaven! I have been living in a dream until this very moment!" (Tang, 306). Chunyu's understanding results in him obtaining Buddhahood. This drama clearly foreshadows the eventual fall of the Jia family and Bao-yu becoming a Buddhist monk.

There are several other plays that also have special significance in the novel. In chapter 22, during her birthday celebration, Bao-chai recites to Bao-yu the "Cling Vine" aria from *Zhi-shen at the Monastery Gate*, which describes the lonely life of the monk Zhi-shen, and he is awed by the lyrics. The scene also foreshadows Bao-yu's later decision to become a Buddhist monk. In chapter 23, Bao-yu and Dai-yu are enthralled while reading the 13th-century play *The Romance of the Western Chamber* by Wang Shifu, which concerns the love story of the lovely and gifted Cui Yingying and the poor student Zhang Sheng. This play is one of China's most famous love stories, and the couple's turbulent romance is told with sophisticated psychological insight and realism. Another renowned drama to which Dai-yu and Bao-yu are directly linked is Tang Xianzu's masterpiece *The Peony Pavilion*. It is considered the greatest work of traditional Chinese theater and the best example of *Kunqu* drama. The drama describes the love affair between cloistered 16-year-old heroine Du Liniang, who dreams of romance, and her handsome suiter, the impoverished scholar Li Mengmei. As with *The Romance of the Western Chamber,* the couple's relationship encounters many setbacks, including a long separation, but they are eventually reunited and married in the end. *The Peony Pavilion* has been widely praised for its elegant language, psychological acumen, and philosophical depth. It was also a great influence upon Cao Xueqin. As Wong Kam-ming has perceptively observed, both works "are subtly woven into the fabric of Dai-yu and Bao-yu's romance. Not only do these two plays provide the lovers a means of communicating their love and desire for each other, but allusions to them allow the lovers to do so without transgressing for themselves the norms of propriety. In the eyes of society at large, however, the plays remain off-limits reading. So, no matter how discreetly the lovers draw on them for self-definition and expression, their very familiarity with such literature oppresses as a source of anxiety" (246).

Attentive readers of the story will be puzzled by this fact that, although it is acceptable for younger people to watch romantic plays and they are an important part of how the Jia family celebrates special occasions and socializes, their reading of the texts of these dramas is considered scandalous and is strictly forbidden. This was in large part because private readings were commonly thought to lead to an individual developing a sentimental and individual interiority that ran counter to the sense of community created by the aural experience of the performed play. It was also believed that this interiority could corrupt the reader and result in bad behavior. (Interestingly, Li Wan makes fun of this belief saying, "It could hardly be said that to have read a few lyrics from the *Western Chamber* or *The Soul's Return* is tantamount to reading pornography" [SS, 2: 515]). As one scholar has put it, *Dream of the Red Chamber* "is less about the repression and liberation of human desire than about the construction of interiority and its disconnect as mirrored by the rise and fall of Prospect Garden.... In the novel, sentimentality or sexuality is not what happens when we discover the existence of a secret desire but the result of our creation" (Lam, 397–398).

There is another characteristic of the theater during this period that the novel realistically captures: the upper-class and literati's cult of male beauty that focused on young male actors. Traditionally, actors in China had an ambiguous status. On the one hand, they formally occupied a very low social station, were looked down on by people, and were considered to be prostitutes or vagabonds. Actors were also associated with criminality because they moved around a lot. On the other hand, during the late Ming and Qing dynasties, the greatest actors were well read in areas that the literati, in particular, placed much value on—painting, history, poetry, philosophy, and literature—and, as a result, were respected and even admired by them. During this time, notions concerning sexual morality and aesthetic conceptions regarding gender were being reconsidered. One way literati manifested this redefinition was through an increasing fascination with the theater and actors. By Cao Xueqin's time, the popularity of actors rose to new heights, and Beijing became the hub of a refined aesthetic homosexual cult of male beauty that centered on young stage actors. The cultural historian Wu Cuncun, who has extensively studied the diaries, letters, and published writings of late imperial Chinese literati, has noted that starting in 1735, "The fashion for catamites was a pervasive part of literati life in Beijing. A large number of the literati, possibly even the majority [including those with and without official post] were caught up in the rage for charming actors who graced the stage of the capital city" (85).

This fascination focused on actors who were male *dan*, specialists in female roles. (According to the law, all stage actors had to be male.) Furthermore, during the late Ming and early Qing, an artistic vogue developed among the literati where actors were treated "like luxury goods traded among the elite.... Not only individual actors but entire troupes were sold, bestowed upon friends and relatives. Their circulation served to create and maintain networks of social exchange, in much the same manner as did gifts of fine ceramic ware, calligraphic scrolls and ancient bonzes. The cultural prestige of the actor as a luxury good, in turn, was predicated on a highly refined discourse of connoisseurship" (Volpp, 949). These conflicting attitudes toward actors are on display in *Dream of the Red Chamber*. Aroma's comment that actors are "low creatures" (DRM, 1: 417) was what women in particular felt at the time. (Her remark is heavily ironic given that at the end of the story she will have a successful marriage with the very actor with whom she is criticizing Bao-yu for associating.) Bao-yu's close (and possibly sexual) relationships with and deep admiration for several actors is indicative of the time and his class, as is the Prince of Zhong-shun's very proprietary and possessive reaction to the actor Bijou's sudden disappearance in chapter 33. (The Prince's chamberlain's statement that Bijou "is so skilled in anticipating the Prince's wishes and so essential to his peace of mind that it would be utterly impossible for him to dispense with his services" [SS, 2: 143] is revealing but not uncommon.)

Finally, the dramas in the novel help to further define certain characters and show their hidden emotional side. When Bao-chai chastises Dai-yu about reading this type of literature and lectures her about the duties of a young female, she admits she also read these types of plays when she was young, thereby disclosing her own romantic side. Dai-yu's reactions after reading *Romance of the Western Chamber* and accidentally overhearing a performance of *Return of the Soul* reveal her intense but tamped down feelings of romantic love. In addition, dramas enable Dai-yu and Bao-yu to experience what one writer has called "the double meaning of 'enlightenment through feeling': It is awakening to love and experiencing love enchantment ... but also acknowledges the inadequacy and the subjective nature of love" (Wu, 314).

See also **Homosexuality, *The Peony Pavilion*, Qing, *The Romance of the Western Chamber***

Further Reading

Lam, Ling Hon. "The Matriarch's Private Ear: Performance, Reading, Censorship, and the Fabrication of Interiority in *The Story of the Stone*." *Harvard Journal of Asiatic Studies* 65.2 (2005): 357–415.

Volpp, Sophie. "The Literary Circulation of Actors in Seventeenth-Century China." *The Journal of Asian Studies* 61.3 (2003): 949–984.

Wong, Kam-ming. "The Allure of Melancholy: The Anxiety of Illusion in *Honglou meng*." In Wolfgang Kubin, ed., *Symbols of Anguish: In Search of Melancholy in China* (Bern, Switzerland: Peter Lang, 2001): 213–261.

Wu, Cuncun. *Homoerotic Sensibilities in Late Imperial China* (New York: Rutledge, 2012).

Wu, I-Hsien. "'Enlightenment Through Feelings': Poetry, Music, and Drama in *The Story of the Stone*." *Approaches to Teaching Cao Xueqin's Dream of the Red Chamber*. Edited by Andrew Schonebaum and Tina Liu (New York: Modern Language Association of America, 2012): 296–316.

Dream of the Red Chamber as Encyclopedia

Readers of *Honglou meng* are commonly struck by the vast cultural scope and encyclopedic nature of the novel. The novel provides a wealth of information of virtually every aspect of Qing dynasty everyday life as well as enduring Chinese cultural practices. While the most famous traditional Chinese novels, *Outlaws of the Marsh, Journey to the West, The Three Kingdoms,* and *Jin Ping Mei*, were also long works of fiction, contained a broad range of practical knowledge, and assumed a certain encyclopedic form, *Dream of the Red Chamber* is different. Traditional Chinese fiction commonly focused on the family as a way of discussing society at large. *Dream of the Red Chamber* expands upon this and uses the trope of the family as a macrocosm to also represent Chinese civilization itself. The distinguished sinologist Andrew Plaks has called the novel "an encyclopedic vessel of culture...[it] provides in one volume a summation of the three-thousand-year span of Chinese literary civilization... [it is] an encyclopedic compendium of an entire tradition in a form that itself serves as a model against which to judge works of a less imposing nature" (11). John Smith states that the novel's range "in a very real sense represents the culmination of China's entire pre-modern literary tradition. The novel includes every major type of Chinese literature—including philosophy, history, poetry, and fiction.... In both its psychological realism and psychological scope, it is unparalleled in the history of traditional Chinese literature" (338-339). And Liu Zaifu has written that the work "sifts everything in Chinese culture and crystallizes its essence into a literary classic" (7).

Dream of the Red Chamber belongs to a rare and unique literary genre that the critic Edmund Mendelson has called an encyclopedic narrative. Among the characteristics of works in this genre are that they are a rich compendium of the core beliefs and knowledge of a national culture, have a defining place in their culture, rose in opposition to the respective cultures they represent, make use of all the literary styles and conventions used by that culture, and commonly view their cultures from the perspective of exile (1976). Examples of this type of fiction include Dante's *Commedia*, James Joyce's *Ulysses*, Herman Melville's *Moby Dick*, and Cervantes's *Don Quixote*. The intriguing question is why Cao Xueqin decided to write his novel in this form, considering this genre plainly involves a great deal more effort than the usual work of fiction. The most common explanation is that he simply wanted to fully memorize his previous life in Nanjing, and his family and this format were used as an extended exercise in nostalgia and a way for him to psychologically and philosophically deal with the fallout of what had happened to him. But it also can be argued that there are several additional reasons.

Writing the novel as an encyclopedic narrative enabled Cao to add depth to the realism of the story. By vividly grounding his tale in the minute, everyday details of his characters' experience and the material and cultural environment in which they dwelled helped him to construct a believable world. It also permitted him to display his vast knowledge and cultivation and show the playful side of his personality. In addition, the employment of this type of narrative served to concretely bring to the fore and underscore important themes in the novel, like the ultimately illusory nature of the things he so painstakingly describes, the fundamental difficulties inherent in making any hard distinctions between what is real and unreal, truth and falsity, and the often glaring gap between Chinese social theory and actual social practices. It also gave Cao the opportunity to indulge his great, aesthetic delight with things and indulge his wide-ranging curiosity about processes. Furthermore, he believed that Chinese readers would find this encyclopedic format interesting (e.g., the novel's depiction of luxury items and everyday upper-class life, the types of clothing characters wore, etc.), informative (e.g., the novel's descriptions of medical diagnostic techniques and medicines and discussions of the philosophy of garden design), and useful (e.g., the detailed advice given in the novel on how to write poetry, paint, cook certain foods, manage a large household, and tastefully decorate a room).

Finally, presenting the novel in this form provided Cao Xueqin with an extensive stage on which he could ask hard questions, criticize, subvert, and occasionally affirm the central tenets of the Chinese cultural tradition and society. For him to effectively accomplish this, he first had to comprehensively lay out the contours and details of the traditions and society to which he was reacting. As Wai-yee Li has concisely noted, "In its encyclopedic inclusiveness, *Stone* in a sense sums up Chinese culture, but the greatness of the book lies in the way it asks difficult questions of that culture" (655).

Some Western scholars have accused Chinese scholars of focusing too much on the encyclopedic nature of the novel and not enough on it as a work of fiction. Anthony Yu, for example, has complained about "the endless flow of secondary literature … [of] increasingly complex and minute reconstructions of the economic, social, intellectual, and cultural settings of the story…. Although the bulk of such lucubration does serve to confirm the encyclopedic scope of the narrative and provide illumination of isolated aspects of its copious content, it remains to be seen whether this kind of scholarship can enhance our perception and enjoyment of *Honglou meng* as verbal art beyond, say the assurance that the drinking of important port was indeed a coveted practice for aristocratic families in Qianlong's China" (18). While Yu raises a pertinent point, there is no doubt that the encyclopedic content of the novel is one of the elements that has attracted and continues to attract readers to the novel, and Cao Xueqin felt that incorporating it was important to the story for the reasons just noted.

FURTHER READING

Li, Wai-yee. "Full-Length Vernacular Fiction." In *The Columbia History of Chinese Literature*. Edited by Victor H. Mair (New York: Columbia University Press, 2001).
Mendelson, Edmund. "Encyclopedic Narrative: from Dante to Pynchon." *Modern Language Notes* 91 (1976): 1267–1275.

Plaks, Andrew. *Archetype and Allegory in the* Dream of the Red Chamber (Princeton: Princeton University Press, 1976).
Smith, Richard J. *The Qing Dynasty and Traditional Chinese Culture* (Lanham: Rowman & Littlefield, 2015).
Yu, Anthony. *Rereading the Stone: Desire and the Making of Fiction in* Dream of the Red Chamber (Princeton: Princeton University Press, 1997).
Zaifu, Liu. *Reflections on* Dream of the Red Chamber (Amherst: Cambria Press, 2008).

Dreams

The dream motif was extremely common in traditional Chinese literature. Literary dreams were customarily used to highlight Buddhist and Daoist beliefs about the illusory and transitory nature of human existence, the idea that life is a dream and reality an illusion, and the doctrine that the only solution to the problem of human desire is detachment through transcendence. Dreams were also often used in stories to foretell future events. Cao Xueqin uses dreams for both of these purposes, as can be seen in the novel's title, *Dream of the Red Chamber*, and in chapter 5 where Fairy Disenchantment's registers and song suite foreshadow the fate of the story's main female characters. But the novel also differs from the usual way dreams are depicted in traditional Chinese fiction by the large number (over 13) and types of dreams (ranging from Crimson's dream about Jia Yun finding her lost handkerchief to Bao-yu's extended dream of his trip to the Land of Illusion) in the story and their special significance.

Firstly, dreams in the novel further define characters. In chapter 82, Dai-yu's nightmare pointedly reveals her deep-rooted fears about being an orphan and an outsider in the Jia family, while Bao-yu's dream about his heart being pierced possibly shows his concerns over the future of his relationship with Dai-yu. Caltrop's dream in chapter 48 in which she composes a regulated verse reveals her strength of character and intelligence, and Crimson's dream about her lost handkerchief illustrates her attraction to Jia Yun. Dreams also provide a way in which Bao-yu is able to travel to the Land of Illusion. This is in keeping with the traditional Chinese belief that the act of dreaming was an out-of-body experience that involved "spirit-wandering," where one had communications with other people and even strange creatures like gods, ghosts, and demons. Bao-yu's famous dream in chapter 56 in which he meets his double, Zhen Bao-yu, is used to raise a host of intriguing issues and fits into the novel's narrative pattern of using doubles and counterpoise to define characters and drive the plot. *Honglou meng's* numerous dreams also allow Cao Xueqin to imaginatively explore the intriguing issue of the porous boundaries between truth and falsity and the real and unreal and the virtual impossibility of making distinctions between these categories (as exemplified in the famous couplets on the gateway to the entrance to the Land of Illusion). In doing so, he subtly underscores and reinforces the juxtaposition of real and ideal worlds and the ideas that the real and unreal together form a unitary reality and that people run into trouble when they treat the illusory and the unreal as truth. It has also been argued that Cao Xueqin deftly uses dream theory, of which it is believed he had considerable knowledge, as well as Buddhist philosophy to emphasize the novel's self-reflexive nature and concern with the question of its fictionality. Another reason for this inclusion of dreams in the narrative is that it fits into Cao's concerted attempt to produce a work that is a comprehensive cultural compendium. Chinese have long been fascinated with and have produced an extensive body of writings on the topics of dreams, what causes them and what they mean since the Shang dynasty, so it is natural that he would devote some space to the subject.

One scholar has gone so far as to claim that the *Dream of the Red Chamber* itself has "a dream-like feel. Although some aspects of everyday life with the Jias are treated with precision and scrupulous care, details are often withheld. Alone among all the plays and fictions of its day, the novel never situates itself in either time or space.... The Jia family lives neither in Beijing nor in Nanjing but in some unearthly, dreamy amalgamation of the two capitals.... We never find out the name of the emperor or his dynasty We never even have a clear sense of how old the cousins are for most of the novel; they are something like children, in the adult's treatment of them, but at the same time they are of marriageable age.... Whatever other purposes such indeterminacy serves—to rise above politics by not defining the Jia's [sic] ethnicity, to further narrative by not specifying the character's ages—it also contributes to the novel's oneiric feel" (Liu, 274, 275). Finally, frequently coloring the novel's dreamlike nature is a strong sense of nostalgia, the sad awareness that, like all dreams, happy moments must eventually end, that nothing endures because of the swift passage of time and therefore cannot ever be completely recaptured, and deep regrets over this situation. The fact that we know through hints the sad fates of many characters and that the scenes of joyous family gatherings in *Dream of the Red Chamber* are often punctuated by bad news and misfortunes makes this sense of wistfulness pronounced. (It is difficult not to think that these feelings of nostalgia and remorse are also the result of Cao Xueqin's emotions regarding his own family's tragic history.)

See also **Doubles**

FURTHER READING

Lu, Tina. "Dreams, Subjectivity, and Identity in *Stone*." *Approaches to Teaching Cao Xueqin's* Dream of the Red Chamber. Edited by Andrew Schonebaum and Tina Liu (New York: Modern Languages Association of America, 2012): 274–282.

Drenched Blossom Bridge and Pavilion

This area in Prospect Garden has special symbolic importance. First, it is where one of the most famous scenes in the novel occurs. In chapter 23, Bao-yu first reads the play *Western Chamber* while sitting on a rock under a peach tree while being covered by falling red flower petals beside Drenched Blossom Bridge. Dai-yu soon joins him there and also reads the drama and is completely overwhelmed by the beauty of the writing. Moreover, Dai-yu, with Bao-yu's help, notably buries the red flowers that have fallen behind the rockery near Drenched Blossom Bridge. In chapter 57, Nightingale discovers Bao-yu crying under a peach tree behind Drenched Blossom Pavilion because he erroneously believes that Dai-yu is leaving. Finally, in chapter 96, in an ironic turn of events, Dai-yu learns of Bao-yu's upcoming marriage to Bao-chai at the very spot where they had buried the flowers, knowledge which quickly leads to her death.

Du Fu 杜甫 (712–770)

Widely considered one of China's greatest poets, he lived during the Tang dynasty. Du Fu was a master of all the poetic genres of his time, and his dense, concentrated poetry was characterized by a love of the beauty of the natural world and a strong sense of moral engagement, as well as a sophisticated technical facility. He is mentioned on several occasions in *Dream of the Red Chamber* and is one of the first poets whom Dai-yu recommends Calthrop carefully study (namely, up to 100–200 of Du Fu's regulated verses) when she is learning how to write poetry. According to the scholar Zhou Ruchang, Du Fu had a significant influence on Cao Xueqin.

Duck and Drake Swords

These elegant swords are owned by Liu Xiang-lian, who gives them to Xue Pan as a pledge that he will marry San-jie. They are a family heirloom given to him by his grandfather and are encrusted with jewels and adorned with interlacing sea monsters and dragons. Their sharp blades are described as being cold and deadly in appearance. There is a special significance to these swords being duck and drake: mandarin ducks in China symbolize marital fidelity and happiness, and a drake is a mature male duck. Xue Pan gives the swords to San-jie, who proudly hangs them over her bed. Later, in chapter 66, when Xiang-lian abruptly retracts his proposal, San-jie slashes her throat with the duck sword. Soon after, Xiang-lian uses the drake sword to cut his queue and then disappears with a Daoist monk with a disabled leg. The fact that they used these auspiciously named swords, San-jie to commit suicide and Xiang-lian to sever his connections with the mundane world, ironically underscores one of the novel's central themes: the temporal and illusory nature of love. As one commentator has put it, "Only the mandarin-duck swords can kill the mandarin ducks, only people immersed in love can free themselves from the trap of love" (quoted in Zhou, 56).

FURTHER READING

Zhou, Zuyan. *Daoist Philosophy and Literati Writings in Late Imperial China: A Case Study of the* Story of the Stone (Hong Kong: Hong Kong University Press, 2013).

Education and the Examination System

Dream of the Red Chamber's jaundiced view of the Chinese educational system and the imperial civil service examination accurately reflects the contradictions of the age in which Cao Xueqin lived. Generally speaking, education had two purposes during this period. The first was Confucian and hence ethical: education was thought to perform the important function of instilling morality and moral improvement. In theory, a rudimentary education was considered critical for the moral and social development of everyone, including women. The second purpose was to prepare men to successfully enter the main gateway in China to high status, an official career, and prosperity—the imperial examination. For many elite families like the Jias, having an educated son who performed well on the examination in each generation was central to the family retaining status and power because they did not possess, in most cases, any viable source of wealth and influence that was independent of their official position. (Ironically, Confucius never argued for the use of an examination system.) As Simon Leys has pointed out, "Confucius considered education to be humanistic and universalist.... What matters is not to accumulate technical information and specialized expertise, but to develop one's humanity. Education is not about *having*, it is about *being*" (xxix). But by Cao Xueqin's time, this goal had eroded and been replaced by the idea that education was essentially a tool to obtain a good government position.

During their early years, males in upper-class families like Bao-yu were often initially educated by their mothers (in his case it was his older sister Yuan-chun) starting at the age of around three. At age seven, formal education would begin when a tutor was hired, and learning how to write Chinese characters would become a primary focus. Confucianism formed the basis for the entire educational process. Works like *Primer of One Thousand Characters, The Three Character Classic,* and *A Hundred Surnames* would be read first and then an increasing number of canonical Confucian texts. Instruction would mainly concentrate on what is called the famous Four Confucian Classics, which formed the heart of Confucian thought. These works were *The Analects* (a collection of Confucius's remarks on such topics as education, politics, ritual, and ethics); *The Great Learning* and *The Doctrine of the Mean* (which were written by Confucius's followers and discussed the importance of, and relationship among, self-cultivation and practical aims and ritual); and *Mencius* (the writings of the Warring States period philosopher Mencius). After this, students moved on to the Five Confucian Classics: *The Book of Songs* (an ancient poetry anthology); *The Book of Changes* (an extremely influential work of philosophy and divination); *The Spring and Autumn Annuals* (a history of important events in Confucius's home state of Lu); *The Book of Rites* (essays on propriety and the importance of ceremony); and *The Book of History* (speeches and announcements by high officials and rulers during China's first three dynasties). Students were expected to memorize these nine books in their entirety, as well as read detailed commentaries on them, and to answer questions about them. In addition to these works, students were also required to be familiar with other literary, classical, and historical writings. In theory, the method of learning was intense repetition, memorization, and reflection. The philosophy behind this, according to the neo-Confucian philosopher Zhu Xi, was, "In reading a book we must read and reread it, appreciating each and every paragraph, each and every sentence, each and every word. Furthermore, we must consult the various annotations, commentaries, and explanations so that our understanding is complete. In this way, moral principle and our own minds will be in perfect accord" (quoted in Hui, 35).

But for many overworked students, the reality was different. Learning this much material required an enormous amount of tedious (and at times, seemingly mindless) repetition and brute memorization. The total number of Chinese characters for the nine Confucian classics that needed to be memorized was over 400,000. (It should be noted that these were not over 400,000 different ideographs; rather many of these characters were frequently repeated in several of the books.) Nevertheless, the numbers are daunting. It has been estimated by one scholar that if a student memorized 200 characters every day, it would take him six years to finish the process (Miyazaki, 16). (One Qing dynasty private academy instructor estimated that students could memorize 200,000 characters in only 690 days if they were diligent [Elman, 267]). Bao-yu's own struggles to learn material reflects the difficulty of achieving this. The culmination of the educational process was learning how to write and then repeatedly practicing the notorious, highly structured Octopartite Composition (*zhiyi, baguwen*), popularly known as the Eight-Legged Essay, which was used in the imperial examinations. This series of tests required examinees to write an essay that was divided into eight sections (legs) on a topic from the Five Classics or Four Books using quotations and the appropriate rhetorical rubrics like balanced clauses and balanced pairs of characters. The essay also had to be composed within the framework of the Zhen-Zhu Neo-Confucian school and had a strict word limit. To prepare for this exam, individuals, like Bao-yu, would carefully study model examples of examination essays and Eight-Legged essays on subjects assigned to them by their teachers. (John Minford, in his English translation of the last 40 chapters of the novel, uses Latin rhetorical terms to describe terms for the essay because he sees a parallel between the language of rhetoric for the essay and Latin rhetoric. While this is a novel idea, Minford seemingly fails to understand that not all readers have the advantage he had of a British public school education, and many find the use of Latin to be uninformative and even confusing.)

The Chinese imperial civil service examination system consisted of a series of increasingly difficult tests. It began with the district or preliminary exams that were held twice every three years. Successful applicants were awarded the degree of government student and could progress to the next level. The next stage was the provincial and comprised three sessions. One session was on the Four Books, another on the Five Classics, and the last on the formation of policy. Individuals who passed this level received the "recommended man" degree, which meant that they were qualified for a low-level government position or could advance to the next exam, which was the coveted metropolitan (national). This exam also included three sessions that were similar, and those who passed were awarded the highest degree of "advanced scholar." (The three degrees roughly have been compared to a Western bachelor, master, and doctoral of arts degree.) The top three classes of the metropolitan exam would advance to the final stage, the pro forma palace exam, which was held in the Forbidden City. The emperor himself oversaw this exam, and those who performed well were employed at the prestigious Hanlin Academy in Beijing, China's top research institute. The competition for degrees was ferocious. There were firm quotas on the number of successful applicants for every level of the examination. The odds against passing were formidable. For the district level, it was one in 60, but for the all-important metropolitan, it was just one in 6,000. Consequently, many candidates took the exam numerous times, some even when they were elderly.

Of course, wealthy families like the Jias had many advantages that others lacked. They were able to invest in expensive education and hire competent tutors. Moreover, the vast majority of successful applicants during the 18th century came from families that had one or more degree holders. There was also an additional benefit the novel mentioned that gave wealthy examinees a marked head start over those who were not: the opportunity to purchase outright low-level "degrees" and even official positions. In chapter 118, a puzzled Old Mrs. Li asks how it was possible for Bao-yu and Jia Lan to take the provincial exam when they haven't obtained the first degree. Lady Wang matter-of-factly replies that Jia Zheng, when he was Grain Intendant, had bought the licentiate degree for them. This practice was shockingly very widespread during Cao Xueqin's time. The historian William T. Rowe has noted, "The sale of gentry rank to wealthy commoners for a 'contribution' of cash or grain was first systematically employed by the Kangxi emperor during the early years of his rule in the 1680's. Under his successor, Yongzheng, the sale of degrees became a regular method not only of financing the government's response to natural disasters or pressing military needs but also of restocking the expanding system of granaries" (113–114). Rowe states that by 1800, it has been estimated that there were 350,000 individuals in China who had bought degrees.

In spite of these advantages, even elite families were starting to have difficulties in retaining their positions via the examination system during this period. Greatly compounding the situation was China's rapidly growing population. At the start of the Ming dynasty, there were 65,000,000 people. By the beginning of the Qing, this number had grown to 100,000,000, and by the end of the 18th century, it had greatly increased to 300,000,000. In spite of this massive population increase, the number of official posts remained essentially the same. As a result, a person's chances of passing the examination became even lower. Furthermore, with this rise in population and China's economic growth, elite families were beginning to find themselves in competition for positions with wealthy merchant families who were commoners. With the development of this affluent merchant class came an interest by these families in raising their status by having sons who would be officials. Given these factors (along with the decline of the Jia family), it is easy to see why Jia Zheng was so strenuously pressing Bao-yu to properly prepare for the civil service examination. Bao-yu's strong resistance to this pressure, his hatred of studying, and constant complaints about "career worms," were not unusual for that time. (It seems probable that Bao-yu largely mirrored Cao Xueqin's own beliefs about the exam. It has been speculated that he took the exam himself but failed to pass.) The stress on individuals who took the examinations is difficult to overemphasize. Family expectations for individuals were often high, and much was riding on the results. The historian Benjamin Elman, who has documented the severe emotional anxiety they felt, has written, "For all, their emotional tensions, based upon years of preparation for young boys, and even more years of defeat for old men, were the human response to the dynasty's examination regime.... Emotional tensions, which brought a few fame and fortune, but left most dealing with despair or disappointment" (295).

Interestingly, most of Bao-yu's objections to the examination system rests upon Confucian grounds. He points out that Confucius himself never endorsed in his writings the idea of a government examination system and strongly objects to the imperial or state form Confucianism took when it was adopted by the government and used as a way to impose conformity. Though he acknowledges that taking the examinations and obtaining a degree and hence a job was not necessarily bad in and of itself, he feels that the attempt to "voice the views of the sages" (DRM, 3: 81) in the essays was ridiculous. Nevertheless, he decides in the end to take the exam for a Confucian reason—to repay his debt of appreciation for "Heaven's favor and our [ancestors'] virtue" (SS, 5: 330). Bao-yu's loathing of the entire examination system was also felt by many who took it at the time. The distinguished sinologist David Nivison has observed that these complaints were perfectly understandable given what was expected of applicants: "If one had to read and imitate such essays as if one's life depended on it for the years needed to acquire sufficient skill to satisfy the examiners, one would readily imagine that ennui would soon give way to intense distaste. The necessity of finding antithesis in the theme to carry the essay through was particularly galling, since it was a purely formal requirement which took precedence over whatever the classical passage might contain. Candidates had to be prepared to distort, or even invent, meaning in the assigned text, and had by long practice to learn this art thoroughly" (194).

Examinees also typically complained about the way it was scored, that the test fostered too much competition between candidates, that it conferred too-extravagant rewards on the successful, and that it undermined important Confucian values like humility, altruism, and self-cultivation. There were, though, defenders of the Eight-Legged Essay as a work of prose, and Cao Xueqin also captured this in the novel. While Bao-yu dismisses them as "nothing but a hotch-potch of classical tags, the most ludicrous ones are written by ignoramuses who drag in this, that, and the other to make up a monstrous mishmash, yet boast of their erudition!" (DRM, 3: 81), Dai-yu, to his disgust, declares that she has read a few, and "some of them showed good sense, some were quite subtle. Though I didn't altogether understand them, I thought highly of them" (DRM, 3: 81). Although complaints about the examination system continued to be expressed throughout the Qing dynasty, they were not abolished until 1905.

See also **Confucianism, Jia Bao-yu**

FURTHER READING

The Analects of Confucius. Translation and notes by Simon Leys (New York: W.W. Norton & Company, 1997).

Elman, Benjamin. *A Cultural History of Civil Examinations in Late Imperial China* (Berkeley: University of California Press, 2000).

Hui, Andrew. *A Theory of the Aphorism: From Confucius to Twitter* (Princeton: Princeton University Press, 2019).

Millward, James. "Bao-yu's Education." *Approaches to Teaching Cao Xueqin's* Dream of the Red Chamber. Edited by Andrew Schonebaum and Tina Liu (New York: Modern Language Association of America, 2012):159–163.

Miyazaki, Ichisada. *China's Examination Hell: The Civil Service Examinations of Imperial China.* Translated by Conrad Schirokauer (New Haven: Yale University Press, 1981).

Nivison, David S. "Protest Against Conventions and Conventions of Protest." In *The Confucian Persuasion.* Edited by Arthur F. Wright (Stanford: Stanford University Press, 1960): 177–201.

Rowe, William T. *China's Last Empire: The Great Qing* (Cambridge: Harvard University Press, 2009).

Eight Stems and Branches

A complex traditional Chinese calendric system. It is used to number days and years and is important in Chinese medicine, Feng Shui and astrology. Heavenly Stems use decimals, a numeral system using decimals, and Earthly Branches duodecimal, a numeral system based on the number 12. The stems and branches make up 60 stem-branches, each of which signifies a year along with months and days within that year. It was believed by Chinese at that time, "Individuals fit into the cosmic order according to their date of birth, which was always carefully recorded in the form of eight characters, two each for the year, month, day, and hour. In the popular mind—and among many members of the elite as well—birth in a certain year identified an individual with one of twelve symbolic animals associated with the system of 'earthly branches.' Each of these animals, which are from the Chinese Zodiac, in turn, was linked with certain character traits, the qualities of *yin* and *yang*, one of the five agents and certain stars or constellations. Quite naturally, such natal information had to be taken into account by both fortune tellers and matchmakers" (Smith, 214). In *Dream of the Red Chamber*, this system is used to devise a horoscope for the Imperial Concubine in chapter 86 based upon her birthdate, and, in chapter 97, the Stems and Branches of Bao-chai's birth are written on her betrothal card.

See also **Five Agents, Yin and Yang**

FURTHER READING

Smith, Richard J. *China's Cultural Heritage: The Ch'ing Dynasty 1644–1912* (Boulder: Westview Press, 1983).

The Embroidered Jacket Raid

One of the most memorable chapters in *Dream of the Red Chamber* is chapter 105 where the imperial guards raid the Jia mansions. The incident is clearly based upon Cao Xueqin's own experiences in 1728 when he was 13 and his family's residence in Nanjing was raided by order of the Yongzheng Emperor. Government confiscation of property, money, estates, and servants and the exile of family members of disgraced officials were common punitive practices employed by emperors during China's Qing dynasty, particularly during the reign of Emperor Yongzheng. It was also a good way of enriching the imperial coffers and was such a frequent practice that a separate department was set up by the government in 1721 to oversee it. These raids, as this chapter shows, would involve large numbers of the military or the imperial secret police suddenly and unexpectedly surrounding an official's dwelling. All the exits would be blocked and women and children forced into separate rooms and held under close guard. Senior servants and maids would be taken away for questioning and regular servants confined to rooms. The house would be sealed and no one allowed in or out, and the property would be ransacked from top to bottom. A detailed inventory would be taken by a clerk of all the items found, and confiscated goods were stored in designated rooms that were padlocked and sealed with strips of white paper stamped with official seals stating they were state property. Later, goods and properties would be sold according to current market values, and personal effects, including money and antiques, would be sent to Beijing. The accused would often be sentenced to penal service, as Jia She is, at military posts in the unhealthy border regions, or put in prison or even forced to commit suicide. Family members were frequently sent to Manchuria to work as hunters in remote regions or the border area or were even given away as slaves. Servants were sold or condemned to public service.

In *Dream of the Red Chamber*, the raid follows the pattern that many of these confiscations took. It occurs when the Jia family is quietly entertaining friends and relatives. Suddenly, members of the Embroidered Jackets, under the command of the officious Commissioner Zhao (whose name connotes "Bad, Confiscates Everything"), pour into the mansion. Guests are allowed to leave, and constables are placed at each doorway to prevent the movement of family members and servants. Next, an edict from the emperor is then read that lays out the numerous charges against Jia She and others. His and Jia Lian's residences are turned upside down, and chests and cupboards are pried open. Lady Xing's servants are locked inside rooms and the rooms sealed, and a detailed inventory is taken of items found. Female members of the family are in a panic and male members dumbfounded. Luckily, the Prince of Beijing appears bearing another imperial edict proclaiming that only Jia She is to be arrested and that Commissioner Zhao be replaced by the sympathetic Prince of Xi-Ping. When illegal promissory notes with high rates of interest are discovered, Jia Lian is detained. Later, the final imperial verdict would find Jia She guilty of abusing his personal authority in the case of Stony's fans. Cousin Zhen is found guilty of breaking the law by not reporting the burial of San-jie. Jia Rong is acquitted of any charges due to his young age. The Jia family is punished by losing both of their hereditary titles. Only Jia She's property is confiscated. (Other property is returned to the family.) She's domestic servants are taken into public service, and he is sentenced to penal servitude at a military post on the Mongolian frontier, while Cousin Zhen is sent to a maritime frontier region. In addition, Jia Lian is stripped of his position and Xi-feng's promissory notes kept. Late in the novel, She and Zhen are pardoned, their confiscated items returned, and the family's hereditary titles restored. As bad as the Jia family's experience was, it could have been considerably worse (as it was with Cao Xueqin's family).

See also **Corruption**

Embroidered Purse with Human Figures

The discovery of this erotic purse, which was found behind some rocks just inside the gate to Prospect Garden in chapter 73 by Simple and shown to Lady Xing, leads to the raid on the garden. Embroidered on one side of the cheap purse are two naked people embracing, and on the other side is some writing. It later appears that the purse belongs to Ying-chun's maid Chess and her cousin. The importance of this discovery and its damaging effect on the fortunes of the Jia family is hard to overemphasize for it means that sex has conspicuously entered the safe confines of peaceful Prospect Garden. Some critics have gone so far as to compare this incident to the entrance of the seductive serpent in the Garden of Eden in the Bible. The renowned scholar C.T. Hsia has written that for the young women in the garden the finding "precipitates their descent from the Garden ... to the elder Jia family ladies it means that the Serpent has entered the Garden, endangering the sheltered virtue of the young ladies.... Chapter 73-74, which contain the episodes of the purse and the search, mark the tragic turning point in the novel: from then on, the Jia family becomes largely plagued by unfortunate happenings and can no longer make a pretense of gaiety or merriment" (280).

FURTHER READING

Hsia, C.T. "Dream of the Red Chamber." In *The Classic Chinese Novel: A Critical Introduction* (New York: Columbia University Press, 1968): 245-297.

English Critical Reception and Translation History

English translations of *Dream of the Red Chamber* began to appear early in the 19th century, which was surprising since the novel was published in 1792, and continued to be published throughout the period. During most of this century, a handful of partial translations were done by a small collection of often young and eccentric British Consular and Imperial Customs officers and a missionary. These translators did not work with any sophisticated translation philosophy and were frequently helped by Chinese assistants. All of them were practical men who had onerous full-time jobs and did their translations during their free time, often under difficult circumstances while living in treaty ports in China, and they had little access to research materials like dictionaries and libraries. The first recorded translation, which was only recently discovered, was by the noted English Protestant missionary and sinologist Robert Morrison (1782-1834) who translated a section of chapter four of the novel concerning Feng Yuan's murder in 1812. Morrison's translation is very plain and line by line and was supposed to have appeared in a book of essays but was never published. Morrison intended the translation to serve as a warning to Westerners about China and to show the deplorable "state of society in China. The checks to oppression are few. Anything may be bought—almost any crime be committed with impunity if the offending party can and will pay for it" (Chan, 21). In 1816, Morrison published a Chinese language textbook entitled *Dialogues and Detached Sentences* which contained a translation of a conversation between Bao-yu and Aroma from chapter 31. Morrison also mentioned in the book that reading *Dream of the Red Chamber* is a great way to learn the Chinese language. In 1819 and 1830, the British diplomat and second Governor of Hong Kong, John Francis Davis, published, respectively, an excerpt from chapter three that describes the clothing of two of the novel's characters, and an essay on Chinese poetry which contained a poem from chapter three which describes Bao-yu.

The year 1846 saw the appearance of the book *The Chinese Speaker, or*

Excerpts from Works Written in the Mandarin Language as Spoken in Peking, Compiled for the Use of Students by China Consular Officer Robert Thom (1807–1846). Thom was noted for having a strong interest in the Chinese language and culture and had also translated *Aesop's Fables* into Chinese. His book contained a literal translation of an excerpt from chapter six which describes Grannie Liu's visit to the Rong-Guo mansion. Thom also provided notes to his translation. In 1868 and 1869, the Imperial Customs Service Officer Edward Charles Bowra (1841–1874) published a skillful and largely faithful translation of the first eight chapters complete with numerous informative footnotes. Bowra differed from the previous translators in that he primarily treated the novel as a work of literature and not simply as a tool to learn the Chinese language. Fifteen years later, the famous British sinologist and diplomat Herbert Allen Giles (1845–1935) published in *Gems of Chinese Literature* a two-paragraph extract from the story that deals with a doctor's visit to the Jia family mansion to examine Grandmother Jia. In the introduction to the excerpt, Giles wrote that *Dream of the Red Chamber* is one of the world's greatest novels primarily because of the originality of its plot. And in 1892–1893, Consular Service Officer H. Bencraft Joly (1857–1898) came out with a two-volume translation of the first 56 chapters of the novel. Joly had planned to translate the entire book but died in South Korea before he could finish it. In the translation's introduction, he writes "I shall feel satisfied with the result, if I succeed in affording a helping hand to present and future students of the Chinese language" (xxvi). His translation, while at times stilted, and too literal, coupled with the fact that he edited passages in the novel that he considered bawdy, in general still stands up quite well. All of these early translators felt that *Dream of the Red Chamber* was a valuable source for learning the Chinese language because it offered the best examples of the all-important Beijing Mandarin dialect. Some also thought it offered important information (usually negative) about Chinese culture and society. Only a few translated excerpts from the novel because they considered it a great work of literature or even commented upon its literary aspects.

As these partial translations began appearing in the 19th century, articles in journals like *Chinese Repository, The China Review,* and *Notes and Queries on China and Japan*, and entries in assorted books (virtually all of which were published in China or Hong Kong), also started to come out on the novel. These publications were penned by another odd group of British and German missionaries and two British diplomats, many of whom knew each other (and the early translators of the novel), and some of whom studied Chinese together. These articles gradually became more appreciative of the novel as time went on. In 1842, the notorious Prussian Lutheran missionary, buccaneer, and interpreter for British diplomatic missions Karl Gutzlaff (1803–1851) published "Hung Lau Mung, or *Dreams in the Red Chamber*," the first article written in English on the novel. Seven pages long, it gives a relatively detailed but often inaccurate overview of the work. In it, Gutzlaff strangely states that Bao-yu was female. Gutzlaff concluded the essay by stating that "in expressing our opinion about the literary merits of the performance, we must say that the style is without any art, being literally the spoken language of the high classes in the northern provinces…Whoever wishes to familiarize himself with the manner of speaking the Northern court dialect, may peruse the work with advantage" (273). In 1867, the British Protestant missionary Alexander Wylie (1815-1887) published *Notes on Chinese Literature* and said this about the novel, "There is said to be a framework of fact running through the narrative, but it is so enveloped in factitious decoration as to be discernible only to the initiated" (quoted in Gray, 34).

But in the same year, the pioneer sinologist W.F. Mayers (1831–1878) (whom Edward Bowra had studied under) and author of the classic *The Chinese Reader's Manual*, published the first appreciative article in English on the book, writing that it "is beyond possibility of cavil the work for which general admiration may be expressed.… Human character in its complex variety of shades, the intricacies of family relations, the force of passion and the torture of disappointed yearnings after love are portrayed with a degree of skill and knowledge such as in truth suggests a resemblance with the two great master-spirits of English romance" (quoted in Gray, 34). The years of 1878 and 1885 saw the appearance of two pieces by the British Consular Officer Herbert Giles, who was previously mentioned. In the first piece, Giles briefly but positively noted *Honglou meng* in his *A Glossary of Reference on Subjects Connected with the Far East*. His second article, which was published in the *Journal of the North China Branch of the Royal Asiatic Society*, provided a concise and highly accurate summary of the story. This article was later reprinted and expanded on in Giles's 1901 influential and popular work *A History of Chinese Literature*. In 1885, the British sinologist and Consular Officer William Henry Wilkinson (1858-1930) in his book *When Chinese Drive: English Student Life at Peking By a Student Interpreter* which describes his experiences learning Chinese, noted that *Dream of the Red Chamber* was one of several Chinese novels that young British Consular Service officers read at that time to learn the language. Wilkinson then describes the novel in negative terms, saying that "To the foreign student it usually appears as a succession of wearisome chapters—marriages, intrigues, funerals—strung together without any apparent purpose" (101). But he then suddenly changes tack and writes that "there are passages in the *Hung Lou Meng* of real beauty, which seem, it may be, all the more beautiful from their plain setting. Among the songs and versicles scattered throughout the book are some that are exceedingly beautiful" (101).

But not all of these old China hands were taken with the novel. In 1893, the conservative German Protestant missionary and lexicologist Ernest Johanna Eitel (1838–1908), in a virulent review of H. Bencraft Joly's partial translation, wrote that *Dream of the Red Chamber* does not "possess the general moral tendency of most other Chinese novels.… The author's mind is utterly devoid of any trace of Confucian ethics, and conscience to him is a factor absolutely of no account. His heroes have no intellect, no manliness, no conscience. His heroines are utterly devoid of delicacy, piety, virtue. He draws human nature neither as it ought to be nor, we hope in charity, as it really is in China. He works the complicated story of his book without a single lofty idea and without any moral purpose whatever" (quoted in Minford, 1999, 308). Finally, in 1898, two additional publications by Hebert Giles appeared which are worth noting. The first, which he edited, was *A Catalogue of the Wade Collection of Chinese and Manchu Books in the Library of the University of Cambridge*. Wade refers to Thomas Francis Wade (1818–1895) who was a British diplomat, sinologist, the first Professor of Chinese at Cambridge University, and the author of a widely used Chinese language textbook. His book collection contained an 1842 copy of the novel with illustrations. (Interestingly, several early British sinologists deemed *Dream of the Red Chamber* important enough to bring back to England when they returned from China. Sir George Staunton [1737–1801], who some consider the "father" of British sinology brought a 20-volume edition of it in 1817, and Robert Morrison when he took 10,000 volumes of Chinese books back to Britain in the hopes of finding a library to house them (he was unsuccessful), made sure to take three copies of the novel, three sequels, and a one volume adaptation using lyrics set to music of 16 scenes from the story). Giles's second book was his well-received *A Chinese Biographical Dictionary*. It contained a short entry on Cao Xueqin which said "17th century reputed author of the famous novel known as the *Dream of the Red Chamber*" (quoted in Gray, 35). This is the first reference in English to Cao Xueqin being the author of the novel.

Starting in the late 1920s, more comprehensive partial English translations slowly began to appear. They became more and more aimed for general audiences and not for Chinese language learning purposes. In 1929, Chi-chen Wang of Columbia University (1891–2001), published a popular 371 page translation adaptation which was rewritten and republished in 1958 with a special introduction by the famous critic Mark Van Doren. Van Doren stated "that the story is truly great, its essential features will be recognizable because they are features of the human mind and heart, which neither time nor place seem to alter … it transcends the ordinary novel of matters. It transcends it, indeed, to the point of tragedy" (vii, viii). In 1928 and 1927, short excerpts from the novel were published by Eldrida Wade in *The China Journal* and by Chia-Hua Yuan and Shih Ming in their book *Hung-lou Meng and Tuan-huan Ling-yen Chi: English Translations From Chinese Literature* which was published in Shanghai. The year of 1958 saw the appearance of Florence and Isabel Kuhn's 582-page English translation of Franz Kuhn's 1928 abridged German translation of the novel. This translation has generally not been well received.

The 1970s and 1980s marked an important milestone in the English translation history of the novel: for the first time during this period two complete English translations were finally published. Starting in 1973 and ending in 1986, the five-volume David Hawkes and John Minford translation, called *The Story of the Stone*, came on the market. This translation was very well received and is the most widely used of the two. In 1978–1980, the husband and wife team of Yang Xinyi and Gladys Yang published their three-volume work, which is entitled *A Dream of Red Mansions*. There are significant differences between the two translations. While the Yangs translation is a literal one and relies upon one manuscript version of the novel, the Hawkes relied on several versions of the novel. Moreover, the Hawkes/Minford use British English in conversations between characters and the *pinyin* romanization system when translating Chinese (the Yang uses Wade Giles), and characters' names are usually given their equivalent meaning in English (for example Xi-ren is Aroma), while the Yangs simply transliterate names. There have also been several other attempts at comprehensive translations of the novel that were never translated. Recently, an unpublished English translation by the noted Chinese novelist and writer Lin Yutang was discovered in Japan. This translation is not literal and comprises around half the length of the novel. Finally, it has been revealed that sinologist Dr. B.S. Bonsall completed a full translation in the 1950s but it also was never published.

In the early part of the 20th century, the novel started to be included in widely read reference books on China. In 1906, the missionary James Dyer Ball (1847–1919) mentioned it in his popular *Things Chinese or Notes Connected with China* which was published by the prestigious publishing house Charles Scribner's and Sons. In it, Ball writes that *Honglou meng* is a popular novel that is primarily concerned with domestic activities but that the work is not moral in tone. In 1917, another missionary, Samuel Couling (1859–1922), who helped developed the romanization system for the Cantonese language, had a much more positive entry in his *The Encyclopedia Sinica,* calling it "One of the best known, and probably the best of Chinese works of fiction…It abounds in humor and pathos, and is invaluable for anyone who would study the social life of the Chinese" (quoted in Gray, 35). Essays also began to appear more frequently praising the literary quality of the book. In 1919, yet another missionary, W. Arnold Cornaby (1861–1921), wrote in an article entitled "The Secret of the Red Chamber" that was published in *The New China Review,* that *Dream of the Red Chamber* was not just China's first genuine novel but also a work of genius. Cornaby also discussed various rumors about Cao Xueqin's life. In 1930, Harry Clemons (1879–1968), a librarian at the University of Virginia, came out with a review of Chi-chen Wang's partial translation in the *Virginia Quarterly Review.* Clemons characterized the novel as "a story that one has to assimilate slowly. I have read it bit by bit…. But each time I have lost myself in the slow movement of a chapter of the tale, there seemed to fall over these surroundings familiar to occidental life a view of oriental mystery. I have found myself moving in scenes whose meaning was only fragmentarily revealed, gazing at symbols which disappeared before I could master their significance, an untutored being reaching wistfully for knowledge that was beyond my ken" (quoted in Gray, 35).

In 1938 the American novelist Pearl S. Buck in her Nobel Prize acceptance speech called *Dream of the Red Chamber* "the document of family life and human love." In 1943, the great and still commonly used reference book *Eminent Chinese of the Ch'ing Period* appeared. It contained the first detailed biographical essay in English of Cao Xueqin as well as the first bibliography of English writings on the novel. The noted Chinese historian Fang Chaoying wrote that essay and observed that *Honglou meng* is "Such a panorama of complex human emotions and tangled relations involving tens of masters and hundreds of servants [that it] constitutes source material of supreme value for a study of the social conditions in affluent households of the Ch'ing period" (738). The eminent Swedish sinologist and philologist Bernard Kalgren (1889–1978) in 1952 entered the controversy over the authenticity of the novel's last 40 chapters. In an article for *The Bulletin of the Museum of Far Eastern Antiquities*, Kalgren using a detailed grammatical analysis of these chapters, argued that they were highly similar to the novel's original 80 chapters and that they were genuine. In 1953, for the first time, a widely used English encyclopedia, *Cassell's Encyclopedia of Literature,* had a separate entry on Cao Xueqin. And in 1959. the famous Chinese writer Lu Xun's *A Brief History of Chinese Fiction* was published in an English translation. The book contained an influential chapter on the novel.

The 1960s marked another change in English *Hongxue* because several books or significant chapters in books (albeit academic) began to appear for the first time. Moreover, all were written by eminent scholars and were published by respected academic presses. In 1961, Oxford Clarendon Press published the first book in English on *Dream of the Red Chamber.* Written by the noted scholar Wu Shih-Chang, it gave information on Cao Xueqin's life and family background, the organization of the novel, and its various manuscript versions. Wu also speculated about Cao's original plan for the story. Famed Yale University historian Jonathan Spence in 1966 published his excellent study of Cao Xueqin's grandfather Cao Yin, *Ts'ao and the K'ang-hsi Emperor,* which contained information about the reasons for the Cao family's decline. Spence also conjectured about who Cao Xueqin's father was and what served as the model for Prospect Garden. And in 1968, influential literary scholar and translator C.T. Hsia (1921–2013) published *The Classic Chinese Novel: A Critical Introduction.* Hsia's chapter on the novel, which relied upon New Criticism literary theory and takes a comparative literature approach, represents a new turn in serious Western (and Chinese) study of the novel for it moved analysis from the previous focus on matters of textual scholarship—questions about authorship, matters of editions and emendations, the dating of texts—to an approach that used literary criticism. John Minford has written that Hsia's analysis "was perhaps the first study written in English that made it possible to give (with any hope of success) to a curious friend wanting to know what the 'fuss' was about" (1999, 310).

Beginning in the 1970s, books and articles on the novel became more frequent. This was partly due to the fact that the academic field of sinology in general, and Chinese literature in particular, substantially took off with the growing interest in the West in China, which was sparked by President's Nixon's visit to the China and by the country's "opening up policy." (One well-known American book publisher went so far as to proclaim 1971 "China's year" on the cover of one of its books.) Chinese language programs expanded, and excellent translations of Chinese traditional literary works began to appear. Professional journals like *CLEAR* (Chinese Literature: Essays, Articles, and Reviews), *Renditions*, *Late Imperial China*, and the *Tamkang Review*, came into existence. At first, the topics that were discussed in these publications concerning the novel included: its allegoric, realistic, and narrative modes (in 1975's *Masks in Fiction in Dream of the Red Chamber* by Lucian Miller); literary archetypes and structural patterns (in 1976's *Archetype and Allegory in Dream of the Red Chamber* by Andrew Plaks), as well as assorted essays on the novel's lyric vision, use of allegory, and narrative point of view (in 1977's *Chinese Narrative: Critical and Theoretical Essays*, edited by Andrew Plaks). In addition, the appearance of Yangs and Hawkes/Minford translations brought much attention to the novel, making it more widely known, and providing a good reference point for discussions about it.

The 1980s saw the appearance of several illuminating essays on Cao Xueqin by Tse-tung Chow and on the novel by John Minford and Robert Hegel in the extensive 1986 work *The Indiana Companion to Traditional Chinese Literature*. Bing C. Chan's *The Authorship of the Dream of the Red Chamber: Based upon a Computerized Statistical Study of Its Vocabulary* came on the market the same year. It argued for the validity of the story's final 40 chapters. During this decade, some of the more interesting articles that were published on the novel were on maids and servants in the novel (Marsha Wagner), images of women (Kam-ming Wang), religious figures (Doughlas I-ping Ho), symbolism and the imagery of the mirror and dream (David Hawkes), and the importance of reading in the story (Haun Saussy). Since this time, even more books, articles, reviews, anthologies, and doctoral dissertations on *Honglou meng* have appeared. Established publications like the *Harvard Journal of Asiatic Studies*, *T'oung Pao*, and *The Journal of Asian Studies* began to print more essays concerning Chinese literature and the novel. Conferences on Asian studies slowly began to include individual presentations and on occasion panel discussions on *Dream of the Red Chamber*. Moreover, the range of topics discussed, and the critical approaches taken on the novel have significantly expanded. These approaches have run the gamut from cultural studies, feminist and Lacanian cultural criticism, structuralism, comparative literary analysis, historical and psychological criticism, new criticism, cognitive theory, to a combination of Western and Chinese critical theory. In the 1990s, there was analyses of stone imagery and lore in the novel (Jing Wang), a look at Communist critiques of the work and a detailed study of sexuality and gender in the novel (Louise Edwards) and a book intended to introduce the novel to general readers (Dore Levy). In addition, Anthony Yu's highly influential *Rereading the Stone: Desire and the*

Making of Fiction in Dream of the Red Chamber appeared to wide acclaim. In it, Yu strenuously argued for treating the novel as a story of fictive representation and not simply as an encyclopedia of late imperial culture. There were also during this period articles on the novel's use of doubles (Joyce C.H. Liu), a study of the adolescent world in the story, (Lucian Miller) its use of counterpoint (Angelina Yee), riddles (Irene Eber), the novel's naming system (Michael Yang), and its depictions of faces (Halvor Eifring).

Finally, for the last several decades, a plethora of new studies and topics concerning *Honglou meng* have come onto the market. The role of *qing* (love, affection, feeling, desire) in the story has received the greatest amount of scholarly attention. Maram Epstein, Halvor Eifring, Jeanne Jinsheng Yi, Xu Ma, Haiyan Lee, Wu I-Hsien, and Martin W. Huang have written on this topic. Another area of analysis is sexuality and gender, with writings about androgyny (Zhou Zuyan), incest (Andrew Plaks), and polygamy, (Keith McMahon), and the portrayal of women's sexuality in the novel (Louise Edards, Angelina Yee), being published. There have also been informative studies on the role Buddhism plays in the story by Lene Bech and Qiancheng Li. More recently, the topics of the influence of Daoism on Cao Xueqin's thinking (Zhou Zuyan, Ronald Gray, and Kam-ming Wong), and the significance of temples and clerics (Yiquin Zhou), have been discussed. Another area which has received attention by Ellen Widmer and Keith McMahon concerns the numerous sequels the Chinese have published to *Honglou meng*. In addition, Andrew Schonebaum and Chihung Yi have examined how medicine and doctors are treated in the story, and Dore Levy has helpfully written about how to read the novel's poetry. In addition, excellent character studies of Wang Xi-feng, Jia Zheng, and Jia Bao-yu have been written by Erin Brightwell, Qiancheng Li, Maram Epstein, Louise Edwards, and Mary Farquhar. Chi Xiao, Mary Scott, and Dore Levy, have analyzed the symbolism of Prospect Garden and its relationship to Chinese garden culture. And in 2012's *Approaches to Teaching the Story of the Stone*, which was edited by Andrew Schonebaum and Tina Liu appeared. This work contains short but generally informative essays on material cultural, sexual practices, medicine, servants, drama, poetry, religion, dreams, education, and other topics in the novel. Finally, in 2021, *A Companion to The Story of the Stone: A Chapter by Chapter Guide* by Hsien-Yung Pai and Susan Chan Egan was published. It provides a concise summary of the plot in each of the chapters as well as a short commentary section on these chapters.

It is also worth noting that in 2005, the international journal *The Tamkang Review* devoted a special issue to the novel, the first journal in English to do so. It contained articles by numerous noted *Hong* scholars. One area that English *Hongxue* has largely avoided but which has formed an important part of Chinese *Hongxue* is accounts of Cao Xueqin's life. Only two biographies of Cao exist in English: a 2009 English translation of a work written by the scholar Zhou Ruchang, *Between Noble and Humble: Cao Xueqin and the Dream of the Red Chamber*, and 2014's *Wandering Between Two Worlds: The Formative Years of*

Cao Xueqin 1715-1745 by Ronald R. Gray. There is clearly a need for more studies in English of Cao's life and times.

See also **Language**

Further Reading

Chan, Connie Oi Sum. "*The Story of the Stone*'s Journey to the West. A Study in Chinese-English Translation History." M.A. Thesis. Hong Kong Polytechnic University, 1999.
Dream of the Red Chamber. Translated by Wang Chi-chen. (New York: Doubleday and Company, 1958).
Fang, Chaoying. "Ts'ao Chan." In *Eminent Chinese of the Ch'ing Period*. Edited by Arthur W. Jr. Two Volumes. (Washington: Government Printing Office, 1943-1944): 737-738.
Gray, Ronald. "The Stone's Curious Voyage to the West: A Brisk Overview of *Honglou meng's* English Translation History and English *Hongxue*." *Journal of Sino-Western Communications* 3.2 (2011): 23-40.
Gutzlaff, Karl. "*Hung lau Mung*, or *Dreams in the Red Chamber*: A novel, 20 vols." *Chinese Repository* 9 (1842): 266-273.
Miller, Lucien. "The English Dream." *Tamkang Review* 36:1-2 (2005): 251-270.
Minford, John. "Foreword." *The Dream of the Red Chamber*. Translated by H. Bencraft Joly. (Tokyo: Tuttle Publishing, 2010): xi-xxii.
_____. "Pieces of Eight: Reflections on Translating *The Story of the Stone*." In *Translating Chinese Literature*. Edited by Eugene Eoyang and Lin Yao-fu. (Bloomington: Indiana University Press, 1995): 178-203.
_____. Review of Anthony Yu's *Rereading the Stone: Desire and the Making of* Dream of the Red Chamber. *China Review International*. 6.2 (1999): 307-318.
Wilkinson, William Henry. "*Where Chinese Drive*." *English Student Life By a Student Interpreter*. (London: W.H. Allen and Co., 1885).
Wong, Lawrence Kwok Pun. *Dreaming Across Languages and Culture: A Study of the Literary Translations of Honglou meng*. (Cambridge Scholar's Publishing, 2014).

Enlightenment

A Buddhist term that literally means "awakening." Enlightenment is the goal of Buddhist practice and is a state of complete or perfect wisdom or knowledge and compassion. It occurs when an individual has a jarring or shocking experience that produces contact with a deep positive reality that leads to an understanding that the concept of a self is an illusion. This transformation enables a person to meet the world in a fundamentally different way and not be restrained by the concerns generated by an egocentric and limited view of the self. The result is that one can escape from the endless cycle of rebirth and suffering and in turn possess spiritual powers. In *Dream of the Red Chamber*, Cao Xueqin expands upon this concept so that it encompasses not only a strictly Buddhist meaning. As one commentator has put it, "Cao participated in the Neo-Confucian worldview of the 18th century, which considered enlightenment in broader and more inclusive terms. Enlightenment for the educated Chinese could have a whole range of meanings: intellectual awareness, moral intuition, a new stage in a person's spiritual life, or a religious experience leading to a change of direction in life. This does not mean, however, that the basic Buddhist assumption, which considers that only by passing through the mundane world can enlightenment be achieved is neglected. To the contrary, only in this world is enlightenment possible" (Eber, 239–240).

Several characters in the novel attain enlightenment. In chapter 1, Zhen Shi-yin becomes enlightened after hearing the "Won-done Song" from the Daoist. Coldhearted Liu Xiang-lian achieves it in chapter 66 after being told by the Daoist, "I don't know where we are or who I am. I'm simply putting up here for the time being" (DRM, 3: 447). Bao-yu in chapter 22 wrongly believes for a short time that he has attained it, but because he cannot properly answer a koan posed by Da-yu, and the fact that although she and Bao-chai appear to understand Buddhist precepts they have not reached enlightenment, he concludes that it is futile for him to pursue it. He does, though, obtain it late in the story, as apparently does Jia Yu-cun.

But, as Robert Hegel has perceptively pointed out, in the novel "even detachment from world ties, in the basic Mahayana Buddhist sense, is of dubious value: it necessitates that all 'enlightened characters' abandon their families and turn away from human society altogether.... Bao-yu feels remorse and loss while Jia Yu-cun ultimately lapses into a state of lethargy and incomprehensibility.... In *Honglou meng* the emotional and spiritual release brought by Buddhist enlightenment is presented as a distinctly unattractive alternative to suffering in the 'real' world. Only Zhen Shi-yin achieves any lasting contentment. By the end of chapter 120 when the character named Cao Xueqin chides him, even Kongkong Daoren appears a gullible fool to have become so 'enlightened' by this philosophically thin tale" (Hegel, 160). Hegel contends that Xueqin, through his depiction of Buddhist figures like these, shows the limitations of "the conventional Buddhist values they represent (160)." Another scholar has noted Bao-yu's enlightenment is "qualified" because he returns to Greensickness Peak, which means "roots of desire," and the monk's remarks at the end of the tale reveal that the love karma is not yet completed. Moreover, "The Buddhist solution is qualified through an affirmation of the Confucian order. Bao-yu's final enlightenment might be a topic of irony, but the irony serves a higher sense of harmony, the prime concern being to harmonize the differences between rival conceptions of order. In the end, Bao-yu's act is legitimized by the establishment. The emperor grants him the title of Daoist Sage of the Supreme Word" (Li, 174, 240, 250).

See also **Buddhism**

Further Reading

Eber, Irene. "Riddles in the *Dream of the Red Chamber*." In *Untying the Knot: On Riddles and Other Enigmatic Modes*. Edited by Galit Hasan-Rokem and David Shulman (New York: Oxford University Press, 1996): 237–251.

Hegel, Robert. "Unpredictability and Meaning in Mid-Qing Literati Novels." In *Paradoxes of Traditional Chinese Literature*. Edited by Eva Hung (Hong Kong: The Chinese University Press, 1994. 147–166).

Li, Wai-yee. *Enchantment and Disenchantment: Love and Illusion in Chinese Literature* (Princeton: Princeton University Press, 1993).

Eunuchs

During the Ming dynasty, tens of thousands of eunuchs were employed as imperial and civil servants and often wielded considerable power. When the Manchu came to power during the Qing dynasty, they slashed this number to between 1,500 and 3,000 because they felt that eunuchs were extremely corrupt and that this had contributed to the fall of the Ming dynasty. Many of the former positions held by eunuchs were filled by bondservants. The eunuchs who remained as imperial servants were carefully monitored, but, because they were close to the emperor and the Imperial Concubines, they knew the ins and outs of the Forbidden City and continued to hold significant power. In *Dream of the Red Chamber*, most of the eunuchs the Jia family deal with are depicted as being corrupt, money hungry, and arrogant. They solicit bribes and borrow large amounts of money from Xi-feng (with no intention of paying it back), sell official titles, and are on several occasions rude to the family.

Face

The Chinese have traditionally placed much importance on the concept of face. This term refers to a person's reputation, feelings of prestige and dignity, or social standing. As a result, they are very concerned with not "losing face" in public and are careful to retain it. While most cultures understand this concept, it is more influential and nuanced in China. Whereas in Western cultures face is self-orientated and individualistic, in collectivist societies where hierarchy and social status in social groups is important, face is essentially other directed and relational and can be earned or taken away. In traditional China, the loss of one's face was considered a grievous social humiliation and was comparable to physically losing one's mouth, eyes, or nose. Consequently, in *Dream of the Red Chamber*, when a character loses face, especially if they are female, it is often devastating. When Golden, Lady Wang's principal maid, is fired from her job for flirting with Bao-yu, the result is overwhelming, so much so that she feels she has no choice but to commit suicide in chapter 32 because of the social humiliation and her loss of social standing.

Faces in the Novel

Much attention is paid in the story to the faces of characters when they are being physically described. In *Dream of the Red Chamber*, facial descriptions are based on a division of the face into three parts: the face proper (skin, chin, cheeks, forehead), organs on the face (eyes, mouth, nose, ears), and the hair on it (beard, eyebrows) (Eifring, 48–50). The passages in the novel that discuss the appearance of characters' faces usually are written as parallel couplets in semi-literary or literary Chinese. During Cao Xueqin's time, the roundness of a face was considered attractive, and facial beauty increased with how rounded it was. A white powdered face for females was prized, and dark, clear-cut eyebrows were considered beautiful because they were expressive. Bao-yu's facial features, as described in chapter 3, are a good example of what was considered beautiful: "His face was radiant as the mid-autumn moon, his complexion fresh as spring flowers at dawn. The hair above his temples was as sharply outlined as if cut with a knife. His eyebrows were black as if painted with ink, his cheeks as red as peach-blossom, his eyes bright as autumn ripples" (DRM, 1: 46). Halvor Eifring, who has studied facial features in the novel, has concluded that they are revealing because they can, on occasion, indicate a connection between a character's appearance and personality and even predict their fate. He notes, "Lin Dai-yu's frowning brows correctly anticipate her early death, while the willow-leaf brows of Xi-feng seems to indicate an early success that her early death belies. With regard to personality, Jia Bao-yu's limpid eyes and Lin Dai-yu's frowning brows and passionate eyes are expressive of their emotional and unconventional characters, and the stunning beauty of most of the young characters is expressive of a strong personality. In some cases, however, the connection between appearance and personality is explicitly denied, most notably in the case of the cruel but pretty woman Xia Jingui" (112).

FURTHER READING

Eifring, Halvor. "Chinese Faces—The Sociopsychology of Facial Features as Described in *The Story of the Stone.*" *Minds and Mentalities in Traditional Chinese Literature.* Edited by Halvor Eifring (Beijing: Culture and Art Publishing House, 1999): 46–119.

Fairy Disenchantment 警幻仙姑

Goddess of *qing* who oversees "romances and unrequited love on earth, the grief of women and the passion of man in the mundane world" (DRM, 1: 72). She resides in her spotless palace in the Land of Illusion and is first mentioned in chapter 1 where it is said that she gave the stone the title "Divine Luminescence Stone-in-waiting in the Court of Sunset Glow" (SS, 1: 53) and had collected a group of amorous spirits to send into the world to experience life's illusion. In chapter 5, Disenchantment makes her appearance when Bao-yu travels to the Land of Illusion. She is described, in classical Chinese, as being stunningly beautiful, pure, elegantly dressed, and displaying an otherworldly manner and graceful walk. Disenchantment is determined to make Bao-yu understand during his visit the illusory nature of love and human attachments (thereby fulfilling the meaning of her name). She attempts to accomplish this by employing an elaborate strategy that is intended to make Bao-yu disillusioned about his attachments. She first aims at severing his strong attachment to the girls in his life.

Disenchantment initially tries to do this by permitting him to read some poems in the Celestial Registers that foretell the fate of these females, but Bao-yu fails to understand them. So she next subjects him to a song and dance suite titled "A Dream of Golden Days," which presents Twelve Songs that foreshadow in detail the fate of the 12 beauties of Jinling. But he becomes drowsy during the performance and again fails to comprehend the meanings. An increasingly exasperated Disenchantment then gives Bao-yu a pointed lecture on love (*qing*) and desire (*yu*) and tells him that he suffers from "lust of the mind." She also says that she is attempting to change his thinking and behavior at the behest of his noble forbears, the Dukes of Ning-guo and Rong-guo, who have beseeched her to "shock the silliness out of him" (SS, 1: 137) by exposing him to the delights of the flesh so that he will become serious about his Confucian duties and concentrate on saving the Jia family from decline by ensuring that the line is maintained. Because she sizes up that Bao-yu's problem is not related specifically to sex or lust but with his excessive receptiveness to feelings of emotional affections and sympathy, Disenchantment decides as a last resort to set him up with her younger sister "Two-in-one," who combines the characteristics of Dai-yu and Bao-chai, in the hope that he will realize through the act of sexual initiation the illusory nature of human desire.

But this approach, like all the others, is to no avail, and Bao-yu continues to live an existence grounded in romantic longing and *qing*. At first glance, it might seem strange to readers that Bao-yu's ancestors would appeal to Disenchantment, the goddess of *qing*, to be part of such a thoroughly Confucian endeavor and that she would agree to it. Xu Ma has attempted to explain this apparent contradiction by postulating, "Since Dai-yu and Bao-chai represent the values of *qing* and an ideal Confucian personality respectively, Disenchantment might hope through this initiation that Bao-yu will learn to deal with desire as he negotiates between *qing* and Confucian ritualism. Only when he strikes a balance between the two can he safely rely upon his sentimental root to unfurl a new future. If not, he will fall prey to *qing*'s perversion.... Though *qing* might help the sentimental individual grow into a different social being, it gives rise to desire when used in excess, thus posing a trap for the individual of sentiment" (460). Disenchantment is mentioned again in chapter 111, where it is stated that she has chosen Faithful to take Qin-shi's place in her Tribunal of Love, and in chapter 120, when it is stated that Caltrop was going to be handed over to her after her death to have Caltrop's name entered in the celestial register.

See also **Qing**

FURTHER READING

Xu, Ma. "Can Sentimentalism Survive? Revisiting the Negotiation Between *Qing* and Confucian Ideology in *Honglou meng*." *Tsing Hua Journal of Chinese Literature* 14 (2015): 437–447.

Faithful 鸳鸯

Grandmother Jia's fiercely loyal principal maid, her name Yuan-yang means "Mandarin Duck." She is attractive, bright, extremely competent, fair in her dealing with others, and utterly devoted to and protective of Grandmother Jia, who respects her and relies upon her for advice. Jia She develops a fixation on her and aggressively attempts to make her his concubine, but she firmly rebuffs his efforts with the support of Grandmother Jia. She predicts her own suicide in chapter 46 when she says that after the matriarch dies, she will either become a nun, or if things get really bad, commit suicide, for she is happy to keep herself clean by not getting involved with a man. Faithful hangs herself in the inner room of Lady Jia's apartment in chapter 111 shortly after Grandmother Jia's death after being shown how to do it by the ghost of Qin-shi. After her death, she is given the job by Fairy Disenchantment of being responsible for settling debts of passion in the goddess's Tribunal of Love. She is also told by Qin-shi's ghost that her type of *qing* (love) is the natural state of true *qing*.

See also **Qing**

Fate

See **Foreshadowing**

"Father-in-Law Pokes in the Ashes. Auntie has it off with Nevvy"

In chapter 7, an enraged Big Jao forcefully castigates Jia Rong about the indecent behavior of certain members of the Jia family, saying, "Father-in-law pokes in the ashes. Auntie has it off with Nevvy" (SS, 1:183). This slang phrase refers to adultery between a father-in-law and his daughter-in-law, and between an aunt and her nephew. It appears to allude to the relationship between Jia Zhen and Qin-shi and a possible romantic relationship between Xi-feng and Jia Rong or possibly Bao-yu and Qin-shi. The comment is clearly used to reveal the lechery and indecency of the Jia family during this period in the novel.

See also **Big Jao**

Feng Yuan 冯渊

The poor 18- or 19-year-old ill-fated son of a country squire who falls in love with Zhen Ying-lian (Caltrop) and buys her from her kidnapper in chapter 4. He is later killed by Xue Pan's servants when he refuses to let Xue Pan have her. Yuan's relatives are bought off because the presiding magistrate,

Jia Yu-cun, is afraid of the Xue family's immense power. His name connotes "innocently encountering misfortunes."

Fireworks

Fireworks have long been an essential part of the Chinese New Year celebration, festivals, and special occasions, and the Jia family follows this tradition. They are considered a symbol of luck and happiness and are traditionally thought to drive out bad spirits. In chapter 54, the family celebrates the New Year late at night in a courtyard of the mansion with a large fireworks display with imported tribute fireworks (a further sign of the family's affluence). These fireworks have such picturesque names as "A Skyful of Stars," "Nine Dragons Soar to the Clouds," "A Bolt from the Blue," and "Ten Peals in the Air" (DRM, 2: 229). There are also several other allusions to fireworks in the novel, but they carry negative meanings. In chapter 22, lantern riddles are written during the Lantern Festival. Yuan-chun's riddle is about a firework and has been commonly interpreted as symbolically foretelling her early death. During New Year's festivities in chapter 54, Xi-feng tells a joke about a man who cannot hear the setting off of a massive rocket because he is stone-deaf. Some commentators have taken this to mean that she is oblivious to the warning the firework symbolizes about her future. Both of these allusions to fireworks might also be references to the fate of the Jia family and their spectacular rise and soon-to-be sudden and spectacular fall.

First Meeting/First Fruits

It was customary at that time in China for an older person to give a younger one a gift, when they were first formally introduced, in honor of the occasion. Thus, Xi-feng in chapter 7 gives Qin Zhong two "Top of the List" gold medallions and a length of silk, and the Prince of Beijing in chapter 15 presents Bao-yu with an aromatic rosary. The actor Bijou gives Bao-yu a crimson cummerbund in chapter 28, and Bao-yu reciprocates by presenting him with a jade pendant when they first meet, and in chapter 68, Xi-feng bestows upon Er-jie dress material, hair ornaments, and pearl and gold earrings when she first visits her. It was also customary, as Aroma points out in chapter 67, for first fruits not to be eaten before they have been offered to the ancestors.

The First Six and Other Key Chapters

The initial six chapters of *Dream of the Red Chamber* are central to understanding the rest of the story. In these chapters, Cao Xueqin impressively unfolds key features and concerns of the novel. They warrant a close reading because these chapters call attention to the novel's fictional aspect, discuss how the novel was written and transmitted, explain the origin of the plot, lay out themes, introduce key characters, and describe their respective fates. He does all of this by frequently changing perspectives and using multiple beginnings and numerous layered levels. These dimensions include the mythological, supernatural, autobiographical, narrative, allegorical, realistic, and philosophical (Daoist, Buddhist, and Confucian). From the start, the novel breaks with tradition by not having a didactic prefatory poem along with a prose commentary. It begins rather with a question concerning the origins of the story. But it then segues into the customary mythic framework and refers to a well-known legend, techniques which were customarily used to open many extended works of traditional Chinese literature. This was done to demonstrate the novel's universality and to connect it to a broad tradition (Shi, 117). The legend *Honglou meng* uses is the well-known story of the Goddess Nuwa's repairing of the sky. (While the Yang translation also has Nuwa's story, the story starts differently from the Hawkes translation because it includes an author's autobiographical note that was apparently written by Cao Xueqin's brother, and the Hawkes' translation does not.) The number of blocks she actually uses, 36,500, has special significance. It is, according to the Chinese calendar, the number of days in a century.

This use of stone imagery is not unusual in extended vernacular Chinese fiction. It is also present in two other renowned Chinese novels: the 14th-century *Outlaws of the Marsh* (which opens with an excavation of a mysterious stone tablet) and the Ming dynasty work *The Journey to the West* (which opens with the birth of a stone monkey). The place where the stone resides, Greensickness Peak, means "the root of [emotional] attachment" for the topic of love, desire, and affection will be an important theme in the novel. The fact that the stone is rejected and considered by Nuwa unfit to repair the sky and therefore feels sad and resentful because its magical powers are not recognized has been interpreted by some commentators as Cao Xueqin referring to his own status as an outcast who felt alienated from a society that did not appreciate him for his talents. The Buddhist monk (whose Chinese name means "of infinite space") and the Daoist ("of boundless time") who suddenly come upon the stone are stock religious characters who frequently populate Chinese fiction. Their strange looks and manner mimic those of the traditional Chinese sage who is usually characterized by a juxtaposition of his external ugliness and inner transcendental wisdom. These lively figures, who will appear on several occasions in the story, will carry him (the stone is identified as being male) to the human world and will accompany him back to his place of origin at the end, Greensickness Peak in the Great Fable Mountains. They perform numerous functions (as do other mysterious clerics who suddenly appear in the book), which include maintaining order, assuring moral justice, providing important background information, interceding and instructing at crucial moments when

Bao-yu is having trouble, and helping him on his spiritual journey. They are also agents of destiny. When the monk first meets the stone, which had shrunk to the size of a fan pendant, he immediately recognizes and is impressed by the stone's special magical qualities. He promises the stone that he will write an inscription on it so that people will recognize its special character (what this inscriptions says is later revealed in chapter eight of the story) and that he will take the stone to the human world so he can experience it. The two clerics then take the stone with them.

In the next scene, many eons have passed, and another monk, the Daoist Vanitas, chances upon the stone, who has completed his journey to the mundane world. Vanitas becomes intrigued by the long story that is written on the stone and proceeds to read it. Afterward, he quickly tells the stone that while the tale merits publication, it lacks several important pieces of information that are considered essential to traditional Chinese fiction writing: a verifiable reign period and an edifying subject and social message. Cao Xueqin is radically breaking with precedent here by not following these requirements and drawing attention to the fictional aspect of the story (the irony being that the reader will be taught that the illusory nature of life can be grasped by the illusion of fiction). The stone heatedly defends himself by arguing that because the story does not follow "stale old convention" (SS, 1: 49) and is based on real events and people and does not employ pompous language and stereotypical behavior, it has a freshness that other works do not have. Cao is again sharply parting here with another longstanding traditional Chinese belief—that literature was a branch of history and must be didactic and have edifying value—by insisting that literature only need provide entertainment and be truthful. Moreover, *Dream of the Red Chamber* also defies tradition by being "the first Chinese novel to utilize autobiographical experience on a large scale" (Hsia, 247). Vanitas then carefully rereads the work and concludes that it is a true record of events, not morally suspect, and that its central theme is love.

The story has a major influence on Vanitas, so much so that he undergoes a four-stage Buddhist process that results in his enlightenment. This process will mirror the novel's protagonist Jia Bao-yu's own hard-fought philosophical journey. Therefore, it is important to take a close look at its specific meaning (as applied to him): "Bao-yu comes from Void [his true nature as a Stone], contemplating a form [human body]. According to Buddhism, a form comes into being by way of desire, thus the second stage: 'from Form engendered Passion.' As to the third stage, 'transmitting Passion into Form,' it happens when the six senses come in touch with desired objects which cause attachment. In the story, this stage refers to the meeting of Bao-yu and Dai-yu, along with other 'water-like' women. The final stage, 'from Form awakening to the Void,' is when his love, Dai-yu, passes away; his earthly paradise, the Grand View Garden, lies wasted; and his family suffers a downfall. What was is no more. What remains is just a dream from which to be awakened" (Lee, 9). The fact that Vanitas changes his name from Kongkong Daoren ("empty the emptiness") to

Qing Seng ("the monk of feeling") connects two themes that will be stressed in the novel: love and emptiness.

Vanitas next goes in search of a person to publish the story after changing its title from *The Story of the Stone* to *The Tale of Brother Amor*. Each person he meets changes the title. For example, when he encounters Cao Xueqin in his study, Cao also changes the title, this time to *The Twelve Ladies of Jinling*. As Anthony Yu has observed, each of these titles (there are five) reveal a particular feature of, or theme in, the story (285). He notes that the first title, *The Story of the Stone*, "patently picks up the pervasive stone motif and imagery in the novel: the names of the many of characters, including that of Ba-yu [precious jade] and one of the females, Dai-yu [black jade], are associated with rock, stone, or nephrite" (285). The second title, *The Tale of Brother Amor*, he writes, "suggests the ironic clash of vocation and nature. A Buddhist monk is supposed to renounce all ties to world and kin, but Bao-yu is driven to enlightenment in the very experience of attachment" (287). According to Yu, the third title, *A Mirror for the Romantic*, "refers to both the reflective and fictive nature of art. Cao Xueqin often takes enormous delight in reminding his readers, subtly but repeatedly, that his engaging and apparently real depiction of life and love is paradoxically no more real than the image in the mirror" (286). The title *The Twelve Beauties of Jinling* emphasizes the novel's "sympathetic, exalted, and relentless focus on women in an aristocratic household … such depiction registers an astonishing challenge to the traditional norms of patriarchal Confucianism. Cao Xueqin's treatment of the women's beauty, their sartorial resplendence, their literary talents, their political sagacity, and their 'revolutionary or antifeudal' behavior has been frequently noted and justly praised" (287, 288). And finally, the title for which the novel is most known, *Dream of the Red Chamber*, stresses the novel's strong underlying nostalgic feel and the message of the fleeting, illusory, and dreamlike nature of life.

The reader enters the realistic frame of the novel in the next part of the first chapter and is introduced to two characters, Jia Yu-cun and Zhen Shi-yin, who will on occasion pop-up in the plot and attempt to tie up loose ends in the narrative in the final chapter. *Dream of the Red Chamber* has a sophisticated naming system regarding the names of characters and places. The novel's names for characters often carry clues to their personalities. The meaning of Yu-cun and Zhen's names are respectively "rustic fiction and false language" and "true matters concealed." Although the two are friends, Yu-cun is an extremely ambitious young man who is bent on obtaining a government position but is forced to live in a small temple due to a lack of money. Zhen is a retiring and completely unambitious individual and the father of Caltrop, who is kidnapped in the chapter and later becomes deeply involved with the Jia family. On a drowsy, hot summer afternoon, Zhen has a dream in which he overhears the previously mentioned monk and Daoist avidly discussing what had happened to the stone and their plans for his future. The monk states that when the stone was rejected by Nuwa, he aimlessly wandered around until he came to where the Fairy Disenchantment lives. She took pity on the stone and let him stay in her Sunset Glow Palace and gave him the impressive-sounding title of Divine Luminescent Stone-in-Waiting. During his time there, the stone took a liking to the beautiful Crimson Pearl Flower and began watering her every day with sweet dew, thus bringing her to life. The flower, in turn, transformed into a fairy girl, and she became obsessed with the question of how she could repay the stone for his kindness. She decided that the best way would be if they were both reborn as humans, and she would pay him back with a lifetime of tears. As a consequence, Disenchantment is about to send the Crimson Pearl down to earth, and the monk is in the process of taking the stone to her tribunal to get him cleared to also be sent to the mundane world.

Shortly after this explanation, Zhen observes the monk and Daoist disappearing through a stone archway, which is the entrance to the mythological Land of Illusion, the world of truth, where Disenchantment and her court live. A couplet is vertically written on the sides of the archway proclaiming:

> Truth becomes fiction when the fiction's true;
> Real becomes not-real where the unreal's real [SS, 1: 55].

These lines tell the reader that it is ultimately illusory to make clear and hard distinctions in both the "existing" and fictional world between truth and falsity, reality and illusion. The dialectical and complementary relationship and play of rhetoric between these categories will be a constant topic of interest in the story. Cao Xueqin is also intrigued with several paradoxes that fiction as a genre presents: the nature of truth in it and the paradoxical fact that the illusion of life is capable of being understood through the illusion of art (including fiction). The mythological relationship between the stone and the Crimson Pearl Flower will come to fruition on earth through the tragic love affair between the characters Jia Bao-yu and Lin Dai-yu. Their relationship will be doomed from the start since the Crimson Flower's fate was set when she was incarnated. The stone will be incarnated as the Jia family scion Bao-yu, and the beautiful jade that is in his mouth when he is born is a symbol of the stone's desire and his original mythological form.

Zhen Shi-yin, after undergoing a series of economic disasters, becomes enlightened at the end of the chapter. He will become an immortal being and a sage later in the novel, occasionally dispensing advice and providing important information about the plot. The event that precipitates his enlightenment is his chance meeting during the lowest point in his life with a crazed, limp Daoist who is chanting what the monk calls the "Won-done Song." Shi-yin quickly picks up on the religious message of the song and offers a riff of his own in reply. The song they sing is telling because the lyrics contain warnings about the dangers of such worldly and transient concerns as status, wealth, power, ambition, and various types of love on which, the novel will show, people often attach too much importance in their lives. It has also been asserted that both versions of the song contain clues that foretell the fate of several of the novel's characters. In chapter 2, Yu-cun makes another appearance. While he was able to obtain a government position, he was soon impeached for malfeasance. (This will be a pattern for him throughout the book; he will obtain increasingly higher positions but then be cashiered for corruption.) He is now a tutor for Lin Dai-yu, the incarnation of the Crimson Flower. While out on a walk, Yu-cun chances upon a temple that has an unusual couplet written on the sides of the gate that warns visitors about unfettered ambition and striving for achievement and the importance of stopping or drawing back in life from these matters before it is too late (a point that is similar to one of the messages of the Won-done Song). The import of the couplet ironically escapes the ambitious Yu-cun, and he meanders off to a little country inn where he runs into his old friend, the antique dealer Leng Zi-xing. They have a long conversation that provides the reader with detailed background information about the history of, and an introduction to, the current members of the Jia family. This information, which covers the foibles of specific family members and hints at the economic problems of the family that will progressively lead to the Jia's decline, neatly sets the stage for the next chapter where these characters make their appearance. During their discussion, Yu-cun also rather pompously and in great detail espouses his complex theory regarding the origins of good and evil in people, and he references a long list of famous individuals in support of it. Some critics have viewed Yu-cun's theory as a satire, while others have claimed that Cao Xueqin was being serious and advancing his own unique philosophical take on the subject.

In chapter 3, we follow Dai-yu as she makes her way to Beijing to live with the Jia family. When she arrives at the mansion, nearly all the major characters in the story are revealed, and some, like Wang Xi-feng and Bao-yu, are given a full physical description, which signifies their importance, and their strong personalities are also deftly sketched. While Jia She and Jia Zheng are not shown, their reactions to Dai-yu's presence subtly disclose aspects of their characters. We are also initiated into the architectural splendor of the Ning-guo and Rong-guo mansions. (The descriptions of the physical layout of the mansions, as well as that of Prospect Garden and its residences, are so thorough in *Dream of the Red Chamber* that Chinese editions of the book usually carry drawings of it.) Much of this chapter is visually resplendent with the beauty of the younger female members of the family and their servants, their striking clothing, and the spaciousness and luxuriousness of the mansions. In addition to being a novelist and poet, Cao Xueqin was also a painter, and his descriptive and visual skills as an artist are on full display here and throughout much of the novel. Dai-yu's intense feelings of being an outsider, which become more apparent as the story unfolds, are also expressly shown.

Chapter 4 introduces us to another branch of the Jia family, the Xues, and their powerful influence and immense wealth. Xue Pan's disreputable nature is quickly established, as well as Yu-cun's personal corruption, and the *Mandarin's Life Preserver* illustrates how common it was for powerful families to subvert the legal system during that time in China. Chapter 5 is one of the novel's most famous chapters and concerns two key topics in the novel: *qing* (love, desire, affection, and other emotional attachments) and karma or fate. The chapter describes Bao-yu's famed trip during a dream to the mythic Land of Illusion and its ruler Fairy Disenchantment's determined but ultimately unsuccessful attempt to instruct him about the illusory and destructive nature of *qing* to persuade him to study and follow the teachings of Confucius. Tellingly, Bao-yu begins the journey while sleeping in the bed of Qin-shi (whose name connotes libidinousness), whose bedroom furnishings and objects exude feelings of lustfulness and lavishness. During his time in the Land of Illusion, Disenchantment lets Bao-yu read several of the registers that foretell the fate of 15 of the story's central female characters. To drive her point home, she also has a special song and dance suite performed for him that also forecasts the fate of these characters and provides hints about the fate of the Jia family. But Bao-yu fails to grasp the meanings of these registers and songs. The novel will show that, only after fully experiencing *qing* and then the pain of disillusionment over its transitory nature coupled with a second reading of the registers, can he understand their message. A significant part of the novel's plot about him involves demonstrating how he is able in the end to accomplish this.

The supplementary registers and Disenchantment's "A Dream of Golden Days" suite are not the only foreshadowing devices used in the book to elucidate the love karma of characters. The story is full of these devices, and part of the charm of the novel for Chinese readers has long been to ferret them out. Chapter 6 warrants a brief discussion given that it helps explain an overlooked but consequential element in the story. In it, the novel's narrator complains that there are so many incidents and characters in the story to relate that it is difficult to decide where to begin and which material to include. This problem is then solved by the sudden appearance of an outsider from the countryside named Grannie Liu. This is worth noting because outsiders play a vital role in the book. They add depth to the narrative, give different and often illuminating perspectives on events and personalities (as Grannie Liu does concerning Xi-feng in this chapter), and offer useful background information. They therefore deserve special attention when reading the novel.

In conclusion, it is difficult to overestimate both the novelty and organizational brilliance of the *Dream of the Red Chamber*'s initial chapters. Cao Xueqin's painterly sensibilities are apparent in each of these chapters as shown by his slow yet adroit sketching of characters as they assume center stage and by the way he describes their physical surroundings, discusses themes, offers philosophical speculations, and effortlessly moves between numerous temporal frames, thereby setting the foundation for the rich and encyclopedic tapestry that will occur in later chapters. There are several other chapters that merit close attention and are sometimes overlooked by readers in favor of the novel's more famous scenes. These include chapters 58–64, where a protracted reversal in the Jia family's fortunes is linked to a virtual collapse of discipline and order in both houses of the clan. In these chapters, servants are pitted against servants, senior women servants misbehave, and there are instances of gambling, thievery and blowback from Xi-feng's sickness. Compounding matters are the wild antics of the family's spoiled actresses, Aunt Zhao's and Jia Jing's sudden deaths, and the lack of qualified male supervisors to control things because important members of the family have gone to ceremonies commemorating the death of the Dowager consort. Chapter 118 is also quite important because of the philosophical discussion between Bao-chai and Bao-yu, which brings to the fore a pivotal conflict that haunts and defines much of the novel and which Cao Xueqin personally must have wrestled with: the battle between the claims of family, filial piety, love, loyalty, and achievement, and the enticing pull of the great pleasures of the human world, and the opposing impulse for personal transcendence and liberation from the "quagmire of greed, hatred, folly, and passion" (SS, 5: 329) of the mortal plane, and the cleansing of the heart of illusory desires and attachments.

See also **Foreshadowing, Influences on Cao Xueqin, Land of Illusion, Naming System, Narrative Patterns and Techniques, Nostalgia Studio, Nuwa, Outsiders, *Qi*, *Qing*, Reading and Rereading, Red, Themes and Indeterminacy, The Won-done Song**

FURTHER READING

Hsia, C.T. *The Classic Chinese Novel: A Critical Introduction* (New York: Columbia University Press, 1968).

Lee, Mei-hwa. "The Interplay of Buddhism and Taoism in *The Dream of the Red Chamber* and Hermann Hesse's *Demian*." PhD Thesis, University of South Carolina, 1996.

Shi, Yaohua. "Beginnings and Departures: *The Dream of the Red Chamber*." *New Zealand Journal of Asian Studies*. 7.1 (205): 112–133.

Yu, Anthony. "Cao Xueqin's *Honglou meng*." In *Masterworks of Asian Literature in Comparative Perspective: A Guide to Teaching*. Edited by Barbara Stoler-Miller (Armonk, New York: M.E. Sharpe, 1994): 285–298.

Five Elements 五行

Ancient Chinese theory developed during the Spring and Autumn period (770–476 BC), it posits that everything in the universe is composed of five fundamental elements or material agents that are strongly interconnected. It is used to explain relationships and interactions between phenomena. The Five Elements are water, fire, wood, metal, and earth and are similar in purpose to the complementary processes of *yin* and *yang*, two central principles that were traditionally believed to control everything in the world. The theory asserts that changes in the universe occur when these elements generate or overcome their relationships with each other. The elements also represent five different colors: black/blue, red, green, white, and yellow, and the five major organs of the body: the kidney, heart, liver, lung, and spleen. The theory is heavily used in traditional Chinese medicine, martial arts, Feng Shui, astrology, music, Chinese culinary arts and is connected with the Chinese animal zodiac. It is also used in fortune telling and medical diagnoses and prescriptions as shown in the novel (see chapters 10 and 83). Some commentators have maintained that several characters in the story are directly associated with specific elements: Bao-yu is earth because he is the center of the tale, Dai-yu is wood because her name implies "forest," Bao-chai is metal because her name means "precious hairpin," Xiang-yun is water because her name means "clouds over the River Xiang," and Xi-feng is fire because of her hot temper.

Five Major Abuses

In chapter 13, Wang Xi-feng compiles a list of five long-standing major abuses in the Ning-guo mansion that need to be resolved if her management of Qin-shi's funeral is to be a success. They are the following: things are frequently lost because the household is so large and mixed; an inefficient division of labor has resulted in an acute lack of responsibility among the servants; money has been unwisely appropriated and spent because the massive allocation to the household has not been managed properly; little distinction has been made between hard and small tasks, and some people have suffered as a result; consequently, servants have become arrogant and unwilling to help out. Ironically, all of these abuses over time can also be applied to the Rong-guo house, thus reinforcing the novel's theme that inadequate supervision and a lack of understanding of the precarious economic situation of the Jia family are in part responsible for the family's fall.

Fivey 五儿

Cook Liu's only daughter and for a short time one of Bao-yu's maids. Attractive and bright, she has romantic notions about working as Bao-yu's maid, but bad luck and a sickly constitution for a long time stands in the way of her getting a position. Her friend, the former actress Parfumee, who is one of Bao-yu's maids, tries to help her. But bad luck again intervenes, and Fivey is falsely accused of stealing a bottle of Essence of Roses from Bao-yu's residence in chapter 62. She is eventually cleared but falls ill because of the bad treatment she received. When she finally does get a position, Bao-yu's personality has greatly changed, and she soon becomes disillusioned with his strange and cold behavior and eventually leaves his service.

Flowers

Honglou meng contains numerous references to, and poems about, flowers and other plants. One reason for this is because they are frequently used to show the physical appearance, character, and virtues of many of the story's main female characters. Traditionally, in Chinese literature flowers have served as a metaphor for women and as a potent image of the transience of life. Flowers also form an important part of the lives of females in the story. They hold flower viewing parties, display flowers in their residences, play flower-related drinking and card games, and their poetry club is named after a flower. Dai-yu is associated with two flowers: bamboo—her residence is surrounded by it, and it also signifies her aloofness and virtue—and the peach blossom, which symbolizes her brief life which is marked by burning desire. In contrast, Bao-chai is linked with few flowers and is primarily associated with white flowers, especially the white peony, which alludes to her austerity and reserve. Skybright's flower is the hibiscus, which traditionally symbolizes feminine beauty and is associated with common-born women who have a lofty goal. Both Xi-chun and Caltrop, are associated with the lotus, a symbol of purity and a common Buddhist metaphor for a person's true nature unsullied by the world of the Red Dust. Adamantina is linked with red plum blossom, which traditionally signifies a girl's maturing sexuality, which reveals her desire for Bao-yu. Aroma's name means "flower that attracts humans," and it represents her good-natured character. Finally, the crab flower, which forms the title of the poetry club, portrays "the feminine ideal, lyrical, aural, and pastoral dimension of the garden life. Upon its restoration in chapter 70, the club changes its name from crab flower to peach blossom, which ominously portends the pending disintegration of the botanical paradise" (Zhou, 191).

Further Reading
Zhou, Zuyan. "*The Dream of the Red Chamber*: A Shattered Dream of Androgyny." In *Androgyny in Late Ming and Early Qing Literature* (Honolulu: University of Hawaii Press, 2003): 155–198.

Food

It has been estimated that 180 different kinds of food and drink are mentioned in *Dream of the Red Chamber*. Food is eaten in all kinds of circumstance: as a snack, in meals, in special meals for sick individuals, during festival-related activities and birthday celebrations, in formal dinners and luxurious multi-dish banquets. There are also picnics and even a charming barbeque in Prospect Garden where the food eaten is described in loving detail. The novel not only shows the consumption of numerous types of mouthwatering food but also their preparation and presentation. It describes in detail how to make special delicacies like aubergine (chapter 41), discusses the price of food, and provides a realistic depiction of what is involved in running a small but busy kitchen for a large group of demanding clients (chapter 61). There are several reasons for this close attention. First, food has always been a famed hallmark of Chinese culture, arguably more so than most other cultures, and Chinese have long been extremely proud of their long culinary tradition. Consequently, Cao Xueqin, in his encyclopedic endeavor to capture essential elements of Chinese culture, had to devote space to it. Another reason for its strong presence in the story is because he knew that Chinese readers would have found the depictions of cuisine entertaining and informative. Many of these readers, who would have been literati, educated women, and members of educated merchant families, would have been gastronomes themselves and therefore would have a deep interest in and appreciation of the many types of dishes described that also formed an important part of their own lives. Cao himself was said to be an excellent cook. This strong interest by Chinese in the food culture of the novel continues even today. Books have been written on the food consumed in the story and how to prepare it. In addition, there are restaurants in China that specialize in the food described in the book.

Food plays several roles in the story's plot. First of all, its quality, variety, and cost conspicuously attest to the Jias' affluence and indulgence. Moreover, food also signals a person's status in the family. As Louise Edwards has observed, "Prior to his entrance to the garden, Bao-yu's unique and superior status in the family order was confirmed by the superior food provision through Grandmother Jia's household. Dai-yu joined this premier wing of the household upon her arrival to the mansions as well. Food stands as a marker of status even within the already privileged residences of the mansions" (166, n. 10). Food also symbolizes the Jia family's power and decline. The quality of types of food like rice and the number of references to food reflect the family's situation, and there is a noticeable drop in both when they experience a fall in their fortunes. Furthermore, as historian Jonathan Spence points out, references to food and eating are linked to subplots in the story. For example, they "add poignancy to Qin Zhong's death. In a scene of love and youthful sensuality, Qin Zhong jokes with the pretty novice, and she ripostes, 'I must have honey on my hands....' Qin Zhong's sexual initiation with the novice takes place in Wheatbread Priory ['so called because of the excellent steamed wheatbread made in the kitchens']. Qin Zhong's exhaustion after these goings-on is expressed by a 'loss of appetite' and his brief respite from death is ended with choking" (186–187).

Edwards also asserts that food and beverages significantly reinforce the novel's moral message. She writes that they "are intimately entwined with the core of the novel's engagement with the tragedy of impermanence. The consumption, preparation, transmission, and trade of food and drinks are integral to the novel's explication of the permeability of the boundaries between the pure and the profane. The extensive and exotic feasting throughout the novel creates not only a sense of luxury and privilege but also builds narrative tension as the Jia family's excessive, albeit exquisite, lifestyle is made manifestly unstable" (130–131). Finally, it has been advanced that the novel's constant depiction of the Jia family's intense desire for food and wine is intended to highlight Cao Xueqin's conviction that it is only through this extreme want, which forms an important element of the Jia family's material experience, that the illusory nature of worldly life can be shown (Edwards).

See also **Buddhism, Rice**

FURTHER READING

Edwards, Louise. "Eating and Drinking in a *Red Chambered Dream*." In *Scribes of Gastronomy: Representations of Food and Drink in Imperial Chinese Literature*. Edited by Isaac Yue and Siufu Tang (Hong Kong University Press, 2013): 113–131.

Spence, Jonathan. "Ch'ing." In *Food in Chinese Culture, Anthropological and Historical Perspective*. Edited by K.C. Chang (New Haven: Yale University Press, 1977): 259–294.

Ford of Error 迷津

During Bao-yu's visit to the Land of Illusion in chapter 5, he and Ke-qing, Fairy Disenchantment's sister, while on a walk come to the Ford of Error, an extremely deep and wide crossing. Suddenly Bao-yu is attacked by a swarm of demons and monsters who attempt to drag him down into the ford. The Ford of Error is a Buddhist term, and the beasts and demons represent passions that delude people. The only way a person can cross it is if they are fated to. Halvor Eifring has theorized that this scene is really about Bao-yu eventually understanding that his attachment to *qing* is empty. Eifring observes, "The two characters [in the novel] aboard the raft crossing the ford … [are] literally translatable as the Lay-Buddhist Wood and the Attendant Ash, and are sometimes seen as representing Bao-yu's main objects of infatuation: Dai-yu and Skybright, who both die for their love of Bao-yu. Bao-yu's awakening from his dream at the end of chapter five may be seen as an anticipation of his eventual awakening from the illusory dream of the world of desires, when he leaves home to become a monk" (302).

FURTHER READING

Eifring, Halvor. "The Psychology of Love in *The Story of the Stone*." In *Love and Emotion in Traditional Chinese Literature*. Edited by H. Eifring (Leiden: Brill Academic Publisher, 2004): 271–324.

Foreshadowing

The vast majority of Chinese during Cao Xueqin's time, whether they were Confucian, Daoist, or Buddhist, believed in some form of fate, the idea that individuals did not have any real control over much of their lives. There were several reasons for this conviction, including the Buddhist belief in karma, that the actions and intent of an individual have direct consequences for their future, and the Confucian notion that the natural process of cosmic change caused predestined outcomes. Consequently, it is an important topic in *Honglou meng*. The historian Susan Chan Egan and writer Pai Hsien-Yung have noted that Cao "uses the concept of fate to lend a sense of inevitability to the progression of events, although he makes clear that fate works itself out through a converge of people's temperament and their circumstances. Whenever it suits his artistic purposes, [he] also deploys fate as a device to create a mood of foreboding, as when the characters have presentiments of things to come" (xxiii). To do this, Cao Xueqin fashioned an elaborate and dense system of techniques in the novel that foreshadows the future of characters and the fortunes of the Jia family. They provide a dense, karmic retribution structural framework for the story, define characters, and help advance the plot. They take a wide variety of forms. These techniques include the following: (1) A character will sometimes make a causal remark that will foretell their or another individual's future. For example, Bao-yu threatens on two occasions that he is going to become a monk, which he becomes at the end of the story. Another example is You-shi's comment to Xi-feng during her birthday celebration: "Things may never be as good as this for you again" (SS, 2: 44, 366), which has an element of truth. (2) Many of the dramas performed in the novel contain hidden clues as to the future of specific characters like the Imperial Concubine or allude to the Jia family's decline. This is especially true of the dramas performed in chapters 11 and 22. (3) Drinking and other types of games often foretell the fate of the characters who participate in them. For instance, during Bao-yu's raucous birthday party in chapter 63, the game "choosing the flower" is played, and elements of Tan-chun's, Dai-yu's, Li Wan's, and Bao-chai's fates are hinted at as well as the future of Prospect Garden. (4) The biggest example of songs being used to foreshadow the fates of individuals is Fairy Disenchantment's composition "A Dream of Golden Days" song suite in chapter 5. It has also been argued that Zhen Shi-yen's song commentary on the lame Daoist's Won-done Song in chapter 1 contains hints on the fate of certain characters. (5) Riddles, like those in chapters 22 and 50, also prophesize the fates of those who write them.

(6) As for the medical diagnoses and treatment that some characters received by doctors, it has been maintained that the medical examination and diagnosis Dai-yu receives in chapter 83 "foreshadows the tragic end of the love triangle involving Dai-yu, Bao-yu, and Bao-chai ... this *fubi* [foreshadowing device] is 'reflected' on, or realized in, many of the later chapters, but most notably in one of the most important chapters of the novel, chapter 98" (Yim, 86). (7) Characters' mundane daily activities can sometimes provide clues to future events. In chapter 36, Bao-chai is shown sewing a pinafore embroidered with mandarin ducks for Bao-yu. These ducks in China symbolize

marriage, and the scene foretells their eventual marriage. In chapter 37, Bao-yu picks several sprays of cassia as a present for Grandmother Jia. This forecasts the appearance of Xue Pan's future wife Jun-gui given that she will be directly associated with this flower. (8) Various fortune-telling devices which are often accurate, but whose meanings are often misread by the fortune tellers or not understood by characters at the time. This happens in chapter 94 when word diviner Iron Mouth Liu predicts where Bao-yu's missing jade is, in chapter 95 when Adamantina uses a planchette in another attempt to find the jade, and in chapter 101 where a fortune stick foretells Xi-feng's forthcoming death. In all these cases, accurate information is divined, but no person can decipher its meaning.

(9) The names of persons and places not only describe but also periodically foreshadow future events. (10) Seemingly auspicious events are actually signs that something bad is going to happen. For example, the flowering of the crab tree in Bao-yu courtyard in chapter 94 is taken by many of the novel's characters as an auspicious sign but turns out to be inauspicious, with Bao-yu losing his jade and the Imperial Concubine suddenly after the flowering, becoming sick and dying. (11) Another technique is dreams. Bao-yu and Dai-yu have several revealing dreams that foretell aspects of their fate. (12) Explicit warnings are given by several characters about the fall of the family. Examples of this include the ghost of Qin-shi appearing to Xi-feng on several occasions, warning her that measures need to be taken to protect the Jia family from economic ruin, and in Yuan-chun's song in chapter 5, she pointedly tells her parents to "Draw back, draw back, before it is too late" (SS, 5: 141). (13) The novel's numerous literary allusions, which on occasion make subtle reference to the future of characters that either quote them or to whom they are used to refer to. (14) Buddhist and Daoist allegories foretell the consequences of certain types of actions. (15) The novel's many poems not only reflect the character of the individuals who compose or cite them but also sometimes give clues about their fate. (16) The residences, their type, and the interiors of several of the dwellings of the main characters who live in Prospect Garden can subtly forebode their owner's fate. (17) Finally, the famous registers and albums in chapter 5 contain important foreshadowing information about 14 of the novel's main female characters as well of the Jia family.

See also **Crab Tree Flowering, Drama, Fortune Sticks, Games, Medicine and The Problem of Doctors, Names, Narration, Riddles, Won-done Song**

Further Reading

Egan, Susan Chan, and Pai Hsien-Yung. *A Companion to* The Story of the Stone: *A Chapter-By-Chapter Guide* (New York: Columbia University Press, 2021).

Miller, Lucien. *Masks of Fiction in the* Dream of the Red Chamber: *Myth, Mimesis and Persona* (Tucson: University of Arizona Press, 1975).

Yim, Chi-hung. "The 'Deficiency of Yin in the Liver'—Dai-yu's Malady and Fubi in *Dream of the Red Chamber.*" *Chinese Literature: Essays, Articles, Reviews.* 22 (2000): 85–111.

Fortune Sticks

An ancient Chinese method used to tell the future. Fortune sticks are the world's oldest method of divination. Typically, individuals would enter a Buddhist or Daoist temple, kneel, and pray to a deity. Then they would take a bamboo cylinder holding 60–78 bamboo fortune sticks and shake it until a stick emerged. While this was being done, the petitioners would pray for an answer to the question or problem about which they are asking. The stick that emerges would have a number on it, and a divination book would be consulted as to its meaning, or a monk would be asked to interpret the fortune. In *Dream of the Red Chamber,* Xi-feng travels to the Convent of the Scattered Flowers to use their fortune sticks to inquire about her health. After getting her fortune, she has difficulty making sense of it, for it in part ominously refers to her returning to her home in the south. A nun from the convent tries to reassure Xi-feng by saying the fortune has an auspicious meaning, but she remains only slightly convinced. Later in a discussion with Bao-yu, Bao-chai correctly surmises that in spite of everyone believing that the divination is good, the fortune has an inauspicious meaning.

Four Books and Five Classics

See **Confucianism, Education and the Examination System**

Funerals

In Imperial China, funerals were considered one of most important rituals performed and were an expression of the central Confucian values of filial piety and ancestor worship. For Confucius, the most sacred of all ritual obligations was that of proper mourning. Consequently, "A funeral was an even more important ritual than a wedding for a family in Qing times. Because of the centrality of filial piety in this culture, the mourning of a child for a parent took ritual precedence over other demands" (Naquin and Rawski, 81). Therefore, extravagant funerals were usually not considered to be ostentatious but were actually commended because they were thought to show respect for the deceased. For the Jia family, funerals are also very important for the family's image and provide an opportunity for them to conspicuously display their affluence, high status, and elite social connections.

The two most important funerals in the novel are Qin-shi's in chapter 14 and Grandmother Jia's in chapters 110 and 111. Both of these funerals are laced with irony. To all appearances, Qin-shi's funeral is impressive. It is replete with Daoist and Buddhist monks conducting elaborate rites, and the funeral procession is long and regal and composed of colorful insignia, banners, costumes, and numerous high-ranking officials and members of the imperial family. It is capped by a wailing Jewel, Qin-shi's loyal maid, assuming the role of the unmarried daughter. But the ceremony is also rooted in a lie and a grave moral transgression that is symbolic of the underlying moral decay and prodigality of the Jia family. While Qin-shi is well liked by members of the family and even the servants, her exceedingly extravagant funeral (which includes coffin boards that were originally intended for a prince) is not proportionate to her rank as a young daughter-in-law (hence the effort to upgrade her husband Jia Rong's status by bribing the eunuch Dai Guan). Cousin Zhen is principally responsible for this excess with his highly emotional statement, "Just take everything I have—everything!" (SS,1: 259), along with his attitude toward expenses and his overwrought behavior. The commentator Red Inkstone has written that Zhen's elevation in status of his daughter-in-law "goes completely against propriety. If his parents were to die, what more could he do for them? … This is absurd [he is acting] as if his own father and mother had died. This is a detail with which the author pricks the reader into awareness" (quoted in Scott, 1989, 149). But Zhen's remark and extreme behavior run deeper than simply a father-in-law's affection for his son's wife, for the novel gives evidence that he has committed a major moral violation, incest, with her and that in fact Qin-shi committed suicide by hanging herself when their relationship was accidentally discovered by a maid. Mary Scott has clearly shown that Cao Xueqin patterned Qin-shi's death, funeral, and the preparation for it after similar scenes in chapters 60–63 of the famous Ming dynasty novel *Jin Ping Mei* (*The Plum in the Golden Vase*), noting that in both works "an inappropriately grand funeral for a woman of junior position in the household's rank order makes an open secret of an illicit sexual relationship between that woman and an elder male of the family.… [In *Dream of the Red Chamber*] this transgressive relationship is a trope for disruptions of family hierarchy and correct ritual order in general" (Scott, 2012, 265).

The funeral for Grandmother Jia is, on the surface, the polar opposite to that of Qin-shi's and is a startling public example of how far the Jia family has declined both economically and in terms of station. The Blue Jacket raid had recently occurred, and economics dominated discussions by senior family members about how much to spend on it. Because Xi-feng is ailing, and Lady Xing is extremely tightfisted about providing funds, Xi-feng's managerial skills, which were so impressive during Qin-shi's funeral, now fail. Servants ignore her orders, are completely disorganized, and provide poor service to guests. She even has to scramble to line up transportation for the procession (a sign of how low the family's fortunes have fallen); and Lady Wang, Lady Xing, and Faithful unfairly blame her for every problem that occurs. Jia Zheng complicates matters further by insisting on frugality. Only Li Wan has an understanding of the severe limitations under which Xi-feng is operating. As a result, Grandmother Jia is not properly shown the respect she deserves, and the family's status drops even further.

There are also two other funerals in the novel, and fundamental Confucian norms are also not followed during them. Cousin Zhen and his son Jia Rong in chapter 64 are depicted as not being really serious when showing their grief over the death of Jia Jing. In chapter 69, Jia Lian struggles to give Er-jie a proper funeral but is stymied by Xi-feng's refusal to provide money for it; Grandmother Jia rejects having her buried in the family's temple, and most Jia family members refuse to properly mourn or even attend the funeral itself. As a result, Lian is forced to give Er-jie a shoddy sendoff.

See also **Confucianism, Mourning Periods, Qin-shi**

Further Reading

Edwards, Louise. "New *Hongxue* and the 'Birth of the Author': Yu Pingbo's 'On Qin Keqing's Death.'" *Chinese Literature: Essays, Articles, Reviews* 23 (2001): 31–54.

Naquin, Susan and Evelyn S. Rawksi. *Chinese Society in the Eighteenth Century* (New Haven: Yale University Press, 1987).

Scott, Mary Elizabeth. "Azure to Indigo: *Honglou meng*'s Debt to *Jin Ping Mei*." PhD Thesis. Princeton University, 1989.

———. "*The Story of the Stone* and its Antecedents." *Approaches to Teaching Cao Xueqin's Dream of the Red Chamber*. Edited by Andrew Schonebaum and Tina Liu (New York: Modern Language Association of America, 2012): 259–273.

Games

The playing of games fills much of the time of the characters during birthdays, festivals, drinking parties, picnics, and other social gatherings of the Jia family and their friends. The novel is full of a wide variety of amusements that were popular among upper-class Chinese families in the 18th century. They add a further layer of realism to the story, and Chinese readers would have found accounts of them entertaining. These games include board games like Go, dominoes, backgammon, and the writing of regular and lantern riddles. There are also humorous scenes where characters participate in drinking games, which range in difficulty from "pass the plum" (where one must tell a joke), "pass the goblet," and Plumstones to complicated games requiring quotations from poems or prose, song titles and lyrics, and puns. For example, for Bao-yu's birthday in chapter 62, participants must "quote one line from a classical essay, one from an old poem, one domino's name, one name of a melody, and one line from the almanac. All these together must make up a sentence … after drinking, [one has] to name some sweetmeat or dish and link it with human affairs" (DRM, 2: 361). Gambling games like "dice grabs" and "driving the sheep" and ones involving flowers like "match my flower" and "choosing the flower" are also popular in the story, especially among females. In addition, there are simple games that maids and young members of the Jia family love to play like "guess fingers," "Racing Go," and "faithful fish." In addition to being sources of amusement, these games often reveal participants' characters and, on occasion, provide clues that foretell their future.

See also **Go, Guess Fingers**

Gatha

A verse usually mentally recited as part of Buddhist mindfulness practice in daily life or in meditation. It is intended to set a direction for practice, engage a person's mind, and make them aware of their breathing. Bao-chai quotes two famous *gathas* regarding the mind in chapter 21.

Gazette (Peking)

A Qing dynasty government publication for officials that provides official news, reports from government agencies on public policy, and information on court and legal affairs. It was also read and discussed by members of the gentry and educated individuals who lived in the cities. In *Dream of the Red Chamber*, Jia Yu-chun confirms a rumor that ex-officials like him have been reinstated by reading the *Gazette*. In chapter 99, a worried Jia Zheng reads in the *Peking Gazette* about the status of Xue Pan's murder case and the punishment of the local magistrate he had pressured to help in the case. And in chapter 101, a concerned Jia Lian comes across a report in the *Gazette* by the Board of Punishments about several corrupt officials, one of whom is connected with the Jia family.

Ginseng

This greatly valued medicine was strictly controlled by the Qing government. The Manchu banner groups held a monopoly on the production and supply of ginseng during the middle of Emperor Kangxi's rule. In 1709, a quota system was created concerning the amount of ginseng sold and its cost. Ginseng was a large and important source of revenue for the Imperial Household Department. Later, surplus ginseng was sold by the agency, and princes and high officials could purchase it, often at a cheap rate. In *Dream of the Red Chamber*, there are frequent references to this medicine. The Jia family's use of ginseng shows their affluence and connections, as well as their moral corruption, and is another symbol of their economic decline. In chapter 12, Xi-feng maliciously sends a small amount of old, broken bits of the medicine to an ailing Jia Rui. Later, in chapter 77, Lady Wang complains about the family's lack of ginseng and the poor quality of the material they do have, saying that in the past they always had large amounts of it. It is also stated that she has none and that the ginseng Xi-feng has consists of just whiskers and dry leaves and that even the high-quality ginseng Lady Jia possesses has turned bad. As a result, the Jia family is forced to turn to the Xue family's ginseng buyers to obtain the plant.

Go

Go is a very popular Chinese board game that is more than 3,000 years old. The goal of the game is to occupy territory on a square wooden board by completely enclosing vacant squares using one's stones. Go is much more complicated than chess in that a player typically has a choice of over 200 possible moves, whereas in chess there are usually 20, and in Go the board and scope of play is larger. In chapter 19, Bao-yu plays "Racing Go" with his maids. In this version of the game, Go pieces are quickly moved across the board using dice, the goal being to get to the opposing side before the other participant. Xi-chun and Adamantina like to play the game with each other.

God of Longevity 寿星

He is a symbol of longevity and noted for his large and deeply lined forehead, long eyebrows, snow-white beard, thick lips, and having three holes in each ear. It is believed that he has enjoyed a long life because of his tranquil nature, meditative skills, and ability to follow the course of nature and not be distracted by cares and worries. In chapter 38, Wang Xi-feng draws a humorous connection between Grandmother Jia's forehead, which had an indentation from when she hit her head on a wooden peg after accidentally falling into the water when she was a young girl, and the God of Longevity's forehead.

Gold Kylin

A kylin is a mythical Chinese unicorn. It is depicted as having the body and legs of a deer, the hooves of a horse, and the tail of a fox. It is a symbol of good luck and thought to be benevolent, intelligent, and lively. In chapter 29, Bao-yu is presented, by a Daoist monk at Lunar Goddess Temple, with a small red-gold kylin. Because it is like one possessed by Shi Xiang-yun, he decides to keep it for her. Unfortunately, he later loses it in Prospect Garden, but Shi accidentally finds it in chapter 31. Because of this connection and the fact that the subtitle for this chapter states, "And a lost kylin is the clue to a happy marriage" (SS, 2: 108), some have argued that Cao Xueqin had originally intended for Bao-yu and Xiang-yun to be married.

Government

Cao Xueqin spends a great deal of space, much more than the usual traditional Chinese novel, listing the numerous government agencies and positions held by characters or even listing ones with which they dealt. Among the governmental departments mentioned are these: the Board of Punishments, the Board of Civil Office, Board of Rites, Board of Justice, Council of Ministers, Imperial Board of Astronomy, Ministry of Works, College of Physicians, Department of Sacrifices of the Board of Rites, Imperial Victuallers, Censorate, Court of Censors, War Department, and Privy Purse. The novel also notes over 35 governmental positions ranging from the President of the Board of Revenue and Chief Secretary of the Empress to the Superintendent of Shipyards and Harbor Maintenance Soochow-Yangchow Area and the Mayor of the Metropolitan Prefecture.

The main reason why Cao Xueqin listed these details was to concretely show how intertwined the Jia family was with the existing power structure and to highlight their vast social network. They also contribute to the encyclopedic and realistic design of the story. During the Qing dynasty, the top echelon government agencies were the six ministries: the Ministry of Rites, Ministry of Justice, Ministry of Personnel, Ministry of Revenue, Ministry of War, and the Ministry of Works. The Ministry of Rites was concerned with ritual-related affairs, and the Jia family heavily relied upon annual emoluments from the Department of Sacrifices of the Board of Rites (chapter 53). This ministry oversaw the civil service examination that Jia Lan, Zhen and Jia Bao-yu took at the end of the story. This agency also gave Cousin Zhen and Jia Rong leave to return home in chapter 63 after the sudden death of Jia Jing. The Ministry of Justice administered the judicial and penal system and would have been involved in Xue Pan's prosecution for murder. The Ministry of Personnel oversaw government appointments, promotions, and demotions. Jia family members who held government jobs, like Jia Zheng, would have had contact with it. The Ministry of Revenue was the top fiscal agency that oversaw the assessment and collection of taxes, the population census, and distributed government money. This agency also had a special granaries section, so when Jia Zheng briefly held the post of Grain Intendant, he would have worked with this agency. The Ministry of War was responsible for advising the emperor on all military-related matters. At one stage in the novel, Jia Yu-cun holds the post of President of the Board of War. Finally, the generally efficient Ministry of Works was concerned with government construction projects, the printing of types of money, and the upkeep of roads and waterways. Jia Zheng was primarily employed by this ministry and dealt with these matters. In chapter 94, he is depicted working on a file dealing with the estimates for city wall repairs and on accounts for several provincial cities. Later in the story, after his disastrous stint as Grain Intendant, Zheng is promoted to the high position of Permanent Secretary in this agency and oversees mausoleum construction for the ministry. Finally, because the Jias were imperial bondservants and Yuan-chun was an Imperial Concubine, they would have had much interaction with the Imperial Household Department.

See also **Imperial Household Department**

Grand Canal

The oldest and longest man-made waterway in the world with a length of 1,500 miles, the Grand Canal is located in China and was first built in the 4th century BC. By Cao Xueqin's time, it passed through four provinces and extended from Hangzhou in the south to Beijing in the north. The canal was a major transportation hub with cotton, soldiers, luxury wares, textiles, grain, and people moving on it. It almost certainly would have also had a special significance for Cao Xueqin himself because it is highly likely that he and his family took the canal to Beijing in 1728 after their property was confiscated by the government and his father arrested. He was 12 or 13 at the time, and the long trip up the canal must have been a trying experience for him. This can be seen in the references in the novel to the canal for nearly all of them reflect feelings of anxiety about the future, sad partings, loneliness, and even anger. In chapter 3, Dai-yu sadly takes a boat up the canal to Beijing after bidding a tearful farewell to her father, fearful about her future with the Jia family, whom she has never met. Caltrop, in chapter 48, recalls a forlorn scene during her trip on the waterway to the capital after she is sold to Xue Pan. In chapter 12, Jia Lian and Dai-yu take it south because her father is very ill. In chapter 99, it is mentioned that a barge is being sent for Tan-chun by her future in-laws for her upcoming marriage and that she will have to take a long trip on the canal for it. Jia Zheng, in chapter 118, is delayed on it by a military convoy while taking Grandmother Jia and Dai-yu's coffins to the south. He then finds himself short of money and writes a letter to Steward Lai's son, who is employed at a nearby yamen, asking for a loan but is offended when he fails to send the amount he requested. And in the final chapter, Jia Zheng in his trip back to Beijing gets caught in a snowstorm, and in a deserted section of the waterway, he has a brief but emotional reunion with Bao-yu for the last time.

Grandmother Jia 贾母

She is the Jia family's matriarch, Jia Dai-shan's widow, Jia Zheng and Jia She's mother, and Bao-yu's grandmother. Generous, big hearted, plain spoken, and usually tolerant, she is respected, occasionally feared, and beloved. She is also a Confucian traditionalist, especially concerning the topics of marriage and love, the education of women (in chapter 92, she states that she has no problem with "women learning their letters. But needlework always comes first"

[SS, 4: 249]), and their role in life. Grandmother Jia is partial to Xi-feng, spoils Bao-yu, and has a great liking for Grannie Liu and Bao-qin. But she also has a complicated and difficult relationship with both of her sons, particularly Jia She. She thrives in small family gatherings and parties and enjoys spending time with the younger female members of the family. She is highly susceptible to gossip and first impressions and is unaware of the family's grave economic problems, Xi-feng's devious intrigues, and the odious behavior of the family's male members. Her elaborate 80th birthday (a key age in Chinese culture) party in chapter 71 is the last major celebration in the story before the Jia family's sudden fall. In chapter 106, she walks into her residence's courtyard, kneels in great sorrow over the recent Embroidered Jacket raid, makes an offering of incense, and prays to Buddha. She also, in typical Confucian fashion, assumes ultimate responsibility for what has happened and states that it occurred because she had grievously failed to properly educate the younger members about morality. She dies a peaceful death in chapter 110, at age 82, after saying goodbye to members of the family. It has been speculated that Grandmother Jia is based on Cao Xueqin's grandmother, who was Cao Yin's wife.

Grannie Liu 刘姥姥

One of the most famous characters in the novel. Plainspoken, practical, and provincial, she is also remarkably shrewd about others and a good storyteller. She is one of several outsiders in the story who provides key information and a fresh and often objective perspective on happenings. From her first appearance in chapter 6, her countrified ways are often an object of much mirth among the younger members of the Jia family, but she cheerfully accepts the ridicule. She provides much of the humor in the novel, especially in chapters 39 and 40 when she spends several days with the family and visits Prospect Garden. She quickly becomes a favorite of Grandmother Jia and develops a special relationship with Xi-feng. As the novel takes a dark turn, Liu comes up with a useful plan that protects Wang Xi-feng's daughter Jia Qiao-jie from the machinations of unscrupulous relatives and also helps arrange a marriage for her. She is also a source of comfort for the dying Xi-feng.

Guanyin 观音

In Chinese Buddhism, she is the Goddess of infinite compassion and mercy. Guanyin is a Bodhisattva, one who has earned the right to leave the world of suffering and become a Buddha but who has elected to forgo Nirvana and help others. In chapter 17, it is mentioned that Adamantina moved from Soochow to the capital, in part because she had heard that a relic of Guanyin was there and she wanted to see it. And in chapter 50, Bao-yu alludes to Guan-yin's "vase" in a poem he composes.

Guess Fingers

A popular Chinese game involving two people that is played with the hands and fingers, usually while drinking or eating. It involves each player raising their right forearm at an agreed-on signal, extending it, and sticking out zero to five fingers at the other player while shouting a number that is between one and ten. The winner of the round is the person who yells a number that is equal to the total number of fingers that are extended by both participants. Traditionally, the loser must drink a cup of wine or another alcoholic beverage. If no one guesses the correct number of extended fingers, the bout moves on to another round. The game is continued for as long as the players want. In *Honglou meng*, the maids and young members of the Jia family like to play this amusement. Because several pairs of people in the novel play the game at the same time, they are noisy events.

He San 何三

A wastrel and adopted son of the servant Zhou Rui, he worked as a servant in the Ning-guo mansion but was angrily cashiered by Jia Zhen for fighting with Bao Er. He then provided inside information about the Rong-guo mansion to a gang of thieves and joined them in a successful burglary of it in chapter 111. He was subsequently killed in a rooftop fight by Bao Yong.

Homosexuality

In *Dream of the Red Chamber*, homosexuality is common and generally accepted. This was not unusual given that China, in comparison to other countries, has been historically quite tolerant of it and writings on it. Unlike the West, Chinese religious attitudes toward homosexuality have been lenient. Even Confucianism, which placed a great deal of importance on the virtues of public reticence and a strong sense of personal propriety concerning sexual matters, seemed "to have been little concerned with sexual relationships between men. Though it promoted marriage, its insistence on the seclusion of women and their inferiority, the high value it placed on male friendship, and the closeness of the master-discipline bond it fostered, may have subtly facilitated homosexuality" (Crompton, 221). Generally speaking, Confucianism considered the practice to only be a problem when its pursuit clashed with an individual fulfilling his social and familial responsibilities and producing a son to carry on the family's name.

In the novel, many male characters engage in homosexual behavior. Jia Lian, Xi-feng's amorous husband, has sexual encounters with his handsome male servants when he has no access to women. Xue Pan is an aggressive lecher and constantly on the prowl for new (often male) sexual partners. The Jia family clan school is a den of licentious homosexual behavior and contains students willing to prostitute themselves to individuals like Xue Pan for financial gain. There are hints in the story that Bao-yu may have had dalliances with several male characters including, possibly, Qin Zhong. There are also insinuations that certain other male members of the Jia family may have had relationships with distant male family members (for example, Cousin Zhen with Jia Qiang). And finally, in chapter 75, when several of the male members of the family and their friends attend their gambling parties, young male prostitutes are brought in to entertain the guests, and characters like Lady Xing's brother De-quan drunkenly flirt and trade sexual innuendoes with them. Some of the novel's male characters are fixated on male actors (especially those specialized in playing females), or "singing boys." The inclusion of male prostitutes in men's social activities was common among upper-class Chinese in Beijing during this time. One 18th-century Chinese writer noted that homosexuality was so widespread in the capital "it is considered in bad taste not to keep elegant manservants on one's household staff, and undesirable not to have singing boys around when inviting guests for dinner" (quoted in Mackerras, 45). There is also a hint of lesbianism in the story in the relationship, in chapter 58, between the actresses' Ti-kuan and Ou-kuan, who in real life mimic the role they played as a married couple on the stage. The title couplet for this chapter calls their relationship "a strange kind of love" (SS, 3: 116).

See also **Drama**

FURTHER READING

Crompton, Louis. *Homosexuality and Civilization* (Cambridge: Harvard University Press, 2003).

Mackerras, Colin P. *The Rise of the Peking Opera: Social Aspects of the Theater in Manchu China* (Oxford: Oxford University Press, 1972).

Humor

In addition to being a highly realistic, encyclopedic, and sophisticated work of fiction, *Dream of the Red Chamber* is also humorous. It abounds with jokes (several of them scatological), puns, funny drinking contests, jocular riddles, comic characters and behavior, and social gatherings where people are often convulsed with side-splitting laughter. Examples include Grannie Liu's bumpkin behavior in chapter 41, Wang Xi-feng's witty retorts and joke-telling skills, Jia Zheng's unsuccessful attempts to humor his mother, the rollicking linked verse contest in chapter 50, Dai-yu's sardonic jabs at Bao-chai, Xue Pan's frequent clownish doings, and Bao-yu's elaborate joke in chapter 19 on Dai-yu, which involved him making a pun on her name in an attempt to cheer her up. Weihe Xue has gone so far as to argue, "Humor actually infuses or suffuses the novel's style, discourse, characterization, structure, and theme.... *Honglou meng* is simultaneously conceived in a peculiarly humorous vein which accents and deepens its pathos, i.e., in the vein of pathetic humor" (7). On a personal level, Cao Xueqin was known for his quick wit and sardonic sense of humor. A friend wrote that he was "elegant, funny, and adept in improvising stories according to the circumstances" (quoted in Xue, 136).

FURTHER READING

Xue, Weihe. "Novel Ridens in Ming-Qing Fiction: Pathetic Humor in and of *Honglou meng*." PhD Thesis. Washington University, 1991.

Immortals of the Islands 八仙

According to Chinese mythology, eight legendary Daoist immortals dwell on Penglai Mountain Island and four other islands in the Bohai Sea on the northeastern coast of China. The mountain is a base where the immortals meet. The climate is mild, and the fruit that is grown there is famous for curing any medical problem and grants longevity. In chapter 7, Bao-chai describes in detail to Zhou Rui's wife a special medicine she takes for her occasional bouts of illness caused by her tendency to overheat. She states that this exotic medicine was prescribed by a scabby monk who told her it was passed down from the Immortals of the Islands.

Imperial Household Department

The Imperial Household Department was a famous and unique Qing dynasty agency that served a wide variety of purposes. Its primary task was to take care of the emperor and imperial family's private needs. This included providing food, clothing, and managing the activities of the Inner Palace in The Forbidden City. By the end of the 18th century, it employed, not including eunuchs, clerical and menial workers, a staff of over 1,600 personnel. Staff members mainly came from the ranks of Manchu, Chinese, or other nationality imperial bondservants who were attached to banner groups. These special bondservants were all legally owned by and served at the whim of the emperor. Many performed governmental roles that previously had been undertaken by eunuchs in other dynasties. (Cao Xueqin's own family was famously employed by the department for several generations.)

The Jia family would have had a close relationship with this organization because it appears they are Chinese imperial bondservants. The department also would have been heavily involved in the life of the Imperial Concubine Jia Yuan-chun, considering she lived in the Imperial Palace. Yuan-chun, throughout the story, is constantly giving her family gifts that are described in detail. She presents them with food (cakes and pastries) from the imperial kitchens (chapter 42), many expensive items like scepters, rosaries, and tributes during her visit (18), imperial household gauze (4), and two small glass bottles of "Essence of Cassia Flowers" (34). The inventory of the family's goods discovered during the Embroidered Jacket raid reveals that she also gave them numerous pieces of furniture, properties, and other items (105). All of these gifts would have been facilitated by the Imperial Household Department. One scholar has contended that these imperial objects are intended to remind readers, "The Jia family's current favor with the emperor is an extension of his favor towards his daughter, their presence thus underlines the fragility of the family's high position ... the objects are attenuated into an overall sadness and sense of loss and foreboding, an impression that times are not only not what they used to be, but they are getting worse. The discussion of imperial gauzes in chapter 40 typifies this feeling. The gauzes themselves are quite old, and the new ones, says Grandmother Jia, cannot rival them" (Scott, 114).

See also **Bondservants**

FURTHER READING

Scott, Mary. "Azure from Indigo: *Honglou meng's* Debt to *Jin Ping Mei*." PhD Thesis. Princeton University, 1989.

Incense

Incense has been used for a variety of purposes in China for more than 2,000 years. It has been employed in ancestral rites, religious ceremonies, traditional Chinese medicine, to keep time, as an art form, and simply for everyday use. During Cao Xueqin's time, incense was often burned in beautiful, exquisitely designed copper, bronze, silver, porcelain, or metal incense burners. The Jia family burn many types of incense as part of their daily lives. Chapter 43 mentions that Bao-yu carries powdered incense for different occasions in the silk sachet he wears suspended from his neck. In chapter 22, Dai-yu's foreshadowing lantern riddle is about an incense clock. In chapter 41, Aroma hurriedly throws a handful of it into the incense burner in Bao-yu's bedroom to cover the noxious smell of Grannie Liu, who took a nap in his bed. Chapter 53 states that pine and cedar and Hundred Blend incense is burned in the main reception room of the Hall of Exalted Felicity during the Fifteenth Night celebration, and in Grandmother Jia's rear courtyard Hundred Blend incense, a gift from the palace, burns in an elegant three-piece metal incense set. Dai-yu, in chapter 70, lights a stick of Sweet Dream incense during a meeting of the poetry club, and Xi-chun is told by Faithful that she should use Tibetan incense sticks when she is making copies of the Buddhist text the *Heart Sutra* in chapter 88. In chapter 97, several sticks of heavy gum benzoin incense are lit in an attempt to make a distraught Bao-yu sleep. And in chapter 112, a burglar uses a potent narcotic incense to paralyze Adamantina so he can abduct her.

Influences on Cao Xueqin

Cao Xueqin, even for a literatus from an upper-class family, was extremely well-read. Moreover, while growing up in Nanjing, he would almost certainly have had access to his grandfather's famous and enormous library. We also have a good idea of what literary and philosophical works influenced him based upon the books and poems that are mentioned and allusions made in *Dream of the Red Chamber*, as well as comments made by close friends like the Dun brothers and Red Inkstone. Reading appears to have played an important part in his troubled life, as it does with several of the main characters in the novel. In terms of Cao's own reading, the following is a list of some of the Chinese works that clearly impacted his writing. First of all, he would have been well acquainted, as all Chinese were, with the three famous classic novels of traditional Chinese literature: the 14th-century, 100-chapter work *Outlaws of the Marsh* by Shi Naian, a story that details the exploits of 108 bandit heroes under the leadership of Song Jiang and their uprising against the corrupt government during the Song dynasty; the 14th-century, 120-chapter historical epic *The Three Kingdoms* by Luo Guanzhong, which is set in the final years of the Han dynasty and depicts the rise and fall of the Three Kingdoms of Wu, Wei, and Shu; and Wu Chengen's 16th-century, 100-chapter work *Journey to the West*, a rollicking and adventure-filled account of exploits of the Monkey King, Monk Sanzang, Greedy Pig, and Friar Sand's long search for Buddhist sutras. Like all educated Chinese, he would have read and reread all these wildly popular stories, seen plays based upon them, and heard storytellers recite famous scenes from them.

Outlaws of the Marsh appears to have had the biggest influence on *Dream of the Red Chamber*. Commentators have noted that the two novels are thematically and structurally similar and that there is a sharp contrast in both works between the temporal and the celestial worlds. It has been argued by some scholars that *Honglou meng's* beautiful and talented young women are directly patterned after the 108 brave heroes in *Outlaws of the Marsh* and that Bao-yu is loosely based on the outlaw leader Song Jiang, who is also an immortal who was sent to earth. It has also been observed that dreams play an important role in both stories. In *Outlaws of the Marsh*, dreams "create and reinforce the psychological, philosophical, religious, and aesthetic complexities of the novel. These conclusions equally apply to the *Dream of the Red Chamber*, though in a far more intense and aesthetically satisfying manner" (Wu, 17). Additional similarities have been seen between the utopia in Shi Naian's novel and Prospect

Garden. "For, like *Outlaws of the Marsh*, *Dream of the Red Chamber* overlaps dreaming and gathering to assemble certain special characters in this special garden, which is a little different from and at first, a little happier than the rest of the world. As in *Outlaws of the Marsh*, one point of distinction between the special place and the rest of the world is that it is cleaner" (Widmer, 174). Furthermore, both novels describe their authors in almost identical ways. Cao's novel shows the "author as wretched and regretful, anchors its dream outside of fantasy in the still more real world of the author's pain, just as *Outlaws of the Marsh* does" (Widmer, 130). Finally, the renowned Redologists Hu Shi and Yu Pingbo have claimed that *Honglou meng*'s missing final chapter, which was supposed to have contained the Fairy Disenchantment's *Roster of Lovers*, was based on the "stone table" list of heroes in the final chapter of Shi's book. It has also been maintained that *Journey to the West*'s elaborate Buddhist structure, trope of the monkey, and motif of life as a journey influenced Cao. In addition, Jing Wang has asserted that it and *Dream of the Red Chamber* employ "the myth of the magic stone: one assumes the shape of a stone egg; the other, that of an engraved precious stone. Both attain enlightenment at their journey's end" (97).

There is, in addition to these three classic novels, one other long, but very controversial, Chinese novel that scholars have increasingly contended had a large impact upon Cao Xueqin. *Jin Ping Mei* (also known as *The Plum in the Golden Vase*) is a 100-chapter Ming dynasty novel that details the rise and quick fall of a corrupt and ambitious merchant. It was considered pornographic and was banned during the Qing dynasty and is still technically banned in China even today (although it is easy to purchase books on it). Research has shown that its organization (chapter structure, open textuality, structuring techniques, encyclopedic nature, use of complex binary symmetry and hot and cold imagery to show the main family's fortunes), themes (sensory pleasures, desire and beauty are transient, the prevalence of social and personal corruption at that time, and the belief that the boundaries between truth and illusion are porous and often false), specific scenes (depiction of funerals and family gardens, and the story's ending), character description, importance placed on names, and philosophy (Neo-Confucian self-cultivation, and *qing*), all exerted a substantial influence upon Cao Xueqin's writing (Scott, 1989, 2012). There was also another literary genre in which he was very interested and which has a significant presence in *Dream of the Red Chamber*: drama. Cao had long had a deep fascination with the theater and originally considered writing *Honglou meng* as a play. He was particularly impressed with the very popular Yuan dynasty drama *The Romance of the Western Chamber* by Wang Shifu and the Ming dynasty masterpiece *The Peony Pavilion* by Tang Xianzu, so much so that both plays are quoted from, performed, and alluded to in the novel. They also play an important part in the relationship between Dai-yu and Bao-chai. Moreover, Cao was also much taken with Tang's notion of *qing* in his play.

Finally, the famous scholar Zhou Ruchang has written that four other celebrated Chinese works also had an impact on Cao Xueqin's thinking and writing: the *Writings of Zhuangzi,* a collection of works by the celebrated Warring States period Daoist philosopher Zhuangzi; *The Poems of Du Fu,* an anthology of poems by the Tang dynasty writer Du Fu; *The Records of the Grand Historian,* a mammoth history of ancient China by the Han dynasty historian Sima Qian; and the Warring States period poet Qu Yuan's narrative poem "Encountering Sorrow." There is one final well-known writer worth noting whom we know Cao Xueqin greatly admired and after whom he modeled himself: Ruan Ji, the eccentric Late Eastern Han dynasty and Three Kingdoms period poet and musician. Ruan Ji was noted, like Cao himself, for his unconventional behavior, outspoken opinions, strong interest in Daoism, and love of drinking. His most famous work is *Poems From my Heart,* a collection of 82 pentameter poems that describe his tormented quest to find stability and purity in an unstable and immoral world. Ruan Ji's poetry is famed for its subjective and introspective nature. Cao Xueqin thought so highly of Ruan Ji that he styled himself as Mengruan ("Dreamer or Admirer of Ruan Ji"), and his friends compared him to the poet because of their similar behavior and attitude toward life.

See also **Drama,** *The Peony Pavilion,* **Qing, Reading and Rereadings, Roster of Lovers,** *The Western Chamber,* **Zhuangzi**

FURTHER READING

Scott, Mary. "Azure from Indigo: *Honglou meng*'s Debt to *Jin Ping Mei*." PhD Thesis. Princeton University, 1989.

———. "The Story of the Stone and its Antecedents." *Approaches to Teaching Cao Xueqin's Dream of the Red Chamber.* Edited by Andrew Schonebaum and Tina Liu (New York: Modern Language Association of America, 2012): 259–273.

Wang, Jing. The Story of Stone: *Ancient Chinese Stone Lore and the Stone Symbolism of Dream of the Red Chamber, Water Margin, and* Journey to the West (Durham: Duke University Press, 1992).

Widmer, Ellen. *The Margins of Utopia: Shui-hu houchuan and the Literature of Ming Loyalism* (Cambridge: Harvard University Press, 1987).

Wu, Yenna. "Dream Encounters and Intimations of Transcendence: *Water Margin*'s Influence on *Dream of the Red Chamber*." *Selected Papers of the 1997 Southwest Conference on Asian Studies* (Fall 1998): 11–27.

Zhou, Ruchang. *Between Noble and Humble: Cao Xueqin and the* Dream of the Red Chamber. Edited by Ronald R. Gray and Mark S. Ferrara (New York: Peter Lang, 2009).

Inner Apartments

Women, especially upper class, during the Qing dynasty were commonly heavily segregated. They were prevented from having contact with nonfamilial males, and their domestic quarters included an area or areas that were set aside as secluded space for them. This clearly can be seen in *Dream of the Red Chamber.* The inner apartments for women in the novel are particularly sacrosanct and strictly reserved for their use. Men and women who were not related were expected to have no physical contact or social interaction with each other. Even men and their female in-laws were required to abstain from much contact. The reason for this segregation was not just an attempt to subordinate females; "rather it represented the sexes as fulfilling complementary roles of equal dignity [if not equal power]. Men and women controlled different domains, in which the other should not intrude. The female domain was the inner, domestic one [although we should be aware of presuming absolute coincidence between Chinese and Western meanings of 'domesticity'], and the male domain was the outer one, the two were complementary" (Bray, 1997, 128).

This segregation explains why Aunt Xue has to communicate with Zhang De-hui about his upcoming trip with Xue Pan only through a secluded window in chapter 48 and why Jia Lian in chapter 103 is enraged that Jing-gui's adopted brother Xia San is present in the women's inner apartment when her death is being investigated. Moreover, even outside female servants in the story are prevented from entering the inner apartments unless they are requested to do so. The fact that Bao-yu spends much of his time in the women's inner quarters also would have been considered very bad form and not the behavior of a well-brought-up gentleman, who normally would have spent his time in the male-dominated outer quarters. Despite these constraints placed on women, historians have recently argued, "Within the context of late imperial society and its cultural ideas, the existence of 'separate spheres' could offer some advantages and satisfactions and that it was not uncommon for life in the inner quarters to be experienced as active and gratifying" (Bray, 2005, 259). As the novel shows, these advantages included the development of emotional bonds between female relatives, poetry writing and reading, the care of their children, who lived with them until the age of ten, and feelings of having some privacy and agency in their lives because husbands usually were expected not to be present in the inner quarters during the day. Moreover, although women were expected to remain segregated when they sometimes ventured outside of their residences, it was not uncommon for them to visit temples and friends, to travel, and even attend women's poetry clubs.

FURTHER READING

Bray, Francesca. "The Inner Quarters: Oppression or Freedom?" In *House Home Family: Living and Being Chinese.* Edited by Ronald G. Knapp and Kai-Yin Lo (Honolulu: University of Hawaii Press, 2005): 259–260.
Technology and Gender: Fabrics of Power in Late Imperial China (Berkeley: University of California Press, 1997).

Jade

This valuable stone has been highly regarded by the Chinese since ancient times. Its popularity among Chinese is similar to that of diamonds or gold in the West. It was believed that jade had magical healing and spiritual properties because of its strength and translucence. The stone, which is known for its green, red, yellow, and white colors, is also associated with purity, wisdom, power, moral bravery, and immortality. Confucius, in *The Book of Rites*, stated that it exemplifies 11 key virtues: loyalty, justice, morality, compassion, propriety, truth, credibility, intelligence, earth, heaven, and music. Jade has been used in China for the making of a wide variety of objects, some of which are ceremonial. These objects include charms, amulets, rings, cups, plates, bowls, chopsticks, table screens, tools, and sacrificial vehicles. It is even used as a chime stone. Jade also formed part of many scholars' studios as they were used in rests for brushes, brush pots, wrist rests, and inkstones. In *Dream of the Red Chamber*, Bao-yu's famous jade symbolizes his spiritual nature and worldly desire.

Jade Emperor 玉皇

The supreme God in Chinese tradition and the first Chinese emperor, he rules over the universe, is the custodian of morality, and is known for his benevolence and mercy. It was said that he judges people on New Year's concerning their behavior during the previous year. In chapter 39, Grannie Liu refers to him in her story about the woman who prayed to the Jade Emperor for a grandson.

Jia and *Zhen* 贾甄, 假真

The family names of Jia and their counterpart Zheng have special significance. *Jia* is a homophone for "False" and *Zhen* for "True." This fits into the novel's emphasis on the illusory nature of the concepts of real and unreal, truth and falsity, and the ultimate impossibility of distinguishing between them.

Jia Bao-yu 贾宝玉

The protagonist of the story, he is ostensibly Jia Zheng's and Lady Wang's son, Tan-chun's and Yuan-chun's brother, and Grandmother Jia's grandson. In reality, Bao-yu is the incarnation of the celestial stone, which was not picked by the Goddess Nuwa to repair the broken sky. Bao-yu's name means "Precious Jade," and he was born with a jade talisman in his mouth. The jade is a symbol of his origin as a stone, his spiritual nature, and his worldly desire (the "yu" in his name being a pun for the word "desire"). Moreover, because the jade was located in Bao-yu's mouth, this traditionally signifies that he possesses great spiritual understanding. Bao-yu is fated to eventually return to his place of origin, Greensickness Peak, after he has learned the emptiness of passion and the necessity of detachment in the world of illusion. *Dream of the Red Chamber* is, on one level, his *bildungsroman*, the story of his hard-fought-and-won psychological, moral, and philosophical development. Bao-yu is young in the story; in chapter 3 it is noted that he is seven, in chapter 25, it is stated that it has been 13 years since he left Greensickness Peak, and at the time he obtains enlightenment in chapter 116, he is 16. He is arguably the novel's most complex character: handsome, sensitive, eccentric, headstrong (but also often weak in the face of authority), well educated, and precocious. He can be very charming and considerate of others, but he is also thoroughly spoiled, has a great fear about adulthood and its responsibilities, and doggedly refuses through most of the novel to grow up. His Prospect Garden residence, House of Green Delights, reveals additional aspects of his personality. The numerous cages of exotic birds in the courtyard's gallery signify his strange and unworldly character. The dwelling's crab trees are associated with Skybright and Dai-yu. The residence's five rooms are a maze of beautifully carved bookshelves and partitions that contain antique bronze tripods, miniature gardens, swords, vases, scrolls, and imitation curios. Its complicated and elegant interior symbolizes Bao-yu's intricate mind and tangled feelings, his propensity for self-deception and love of beautiful things. The dwelling also has a deceptive full-length mirror that is one of the tropes in the novel for him. Finally, the red in the name of the residence (in the Yang translation it is called Happy Red Court, and its prior title before the Imperial Concubine changed it was "Crimson Joys and Green Delights") refers to his fascination with rouge and red-colored things, which stands for his attachment to the mundane world, the realm of ignorance and delusion, with all of its concerns (in Buddhist terminology, the Red Dust).

Bao-yu is oppressed by the fact that he is the scion of the Jia family and therefore has the onerous responsibility of maintaining (and later restoring) the Jia family's status and "making some return for 'Heaven's favor and his ancestors' virtue'" (SS, 5: 330) by doing well on the imperial civil service examination and obtaining a prestigious government position. His failure to properly prepare for the hated exam results in a running battle with his father, Jia Zheng, who views him as a mollycoddled idler. Bao-yu's distaste for the examination system was not unusual for the time. In addition, he also has scorn for Confucian notions regarding hierarchy, the status of women, achievement, and the belief that he should serve as a moral model for young members of the family. He is infamous in the story for often ignoring social conventions and letting sentiment, rather than status and hierarchy, dictate the way he treats people. Specifically, he fails to follow Confucian rules governing gender, hierarchy, master and servant relationships (he treats maids as friends), and standards governing the behavior of older and younger friends and relatives (as seen in his interactions with Qin Zhong and Jia Huan). Bao-yu in part represents the clash that was felt by many individuals at this time in China between a Confucian self that is highly ritualized, stresses duty and self-restraint and is hierarchical in relationships with others versus an opposing self that is authentic, autonomous, and values *qing*.

Although enormous expectations are placed upon Ba-yu, he is given remarkable license largely because of Grandmother Jia, who dotes upon and constantly defends him, much to the irritation of his father. He is allowed to live in Prospect Garden among his numerous, young, unmarried female relatives, the only male to do so (which, given Confucian injunctions regarding the separation of women and men, would almost certainly not have occurred in real life). He also creates his own elaborate, aesthetic world that centers on the elevation of young, unmarried females with whom he largely identifies. This is seen in the numerous euphoric remarks he makes about them and the fact that he loves eating lipstick, has a great knowledge of makeup and powder, collects women's combs and hairpins, pens several extended poems on two females ("The Winsome Colonel" and "The Spirit of the Hibiscus"), and has mawkish reactions to sentimental stories and portraits of them. He is also a talented poet whose verse impresses even his highly critical father. (But surprisingly, the poems he writes for the Garden's poetry club are usually judged to be poor in quality.) His raucous and drunken birthday party, in chapter 62, represents the height of Bao-yu's popularity and excessive behavior. In short, he can in large part be described as being a feminized male aesthete, which was not unusual for that time. The cultural historian Wu Cuncun has written, "A survey of other romances from the first half of the Qing dynasty would reveal that the feminization of male images was widespread.... Bao-yu's appearance or feminization is in complete accord with the prevailing aesthetic of the time.... It is also interesting to note that, like many other authors of his time, when Cao Xueqin portrays a male character with a feminine appearance it is always as an indication that the author views him positively. Whenever a character is portrayed as having a more masculine appearance [it] is a signal the author does not approve of him" (27, 26).

Bao-yu's unusual personal qualities probably strike today's (especially Western) readers of the novel as extremely odd and even off-putting, but as Maram Epstein has observed, the popularity of the novel at that time (and even today) in China "demonstrates that many readers identified with or at least felt sympathetic to Bao-yu's free and poetic nature. As a literary creation, Bao-yu gave voice to a widespread frustration with the social expectations for elite men. His relationships with his maids and cousins give life to many eighteenth-century fantasies about companionate marriages between equally talented men and women. Much of his attraction for readers was precisely his wholehearted pursuit of an identity that lay outside the prescribed official and ritual order.... Many of the qualities that may strike modern readers as queer, and I mean *queer* in the broadest sense possible, are markers of his authentic nature. His ambiguous gender and sexuality are very much part of his resistance to the ritually proper social roles his father would have him assume" (322, 317). Moreover, the Qing dynasty historian Pamela Kyle Crossley has argued that Bao-yu's apprehensions about the future and upcoming responsibilities accurately mirror the fears of elites in that period. She writes, his "terror of going out into the world, beyond the comfortable studios and gardens where he plays as a boy, is so deep that he actually sees his personality as split into two: a conforming, adult, definitely male 'Bao-yu' who survives, and another Bao-yu who is a perpetual child who must remain in the garden, in company with the images and creatures of his imagination, and with his equally undefined [and therefore immortal] companions. Bao-yu's predicament reflects elite discomfort with the transition from military to civil society, from a protected environment to increasing uncertainties, from prosperity to decline" (126–127). Bao-yu also has a doppelganger, Zhen Bao-yu, whose exact role in the novel has been widely speculated on by critics. Bao-yu's romantic relationship with his cousin Lin Dai-yu is one of the most famous love stories in Chinese literature and is another major reason for *Dream of the Red Chamber*'s great popularity. Their romance is doomed from the start for she is the incarnation of the Crimson Pearl Flower whom the Stone daily watered with sweet dew. When the Stone is reborn in the world of illusion, the Flower decides to join him to repay with tears his kindness. Hence, their love is fated to have a tragic outcome.

Bao-yu takes an emotional battering on his long road to enlightenment, having to endure the deaths of Dai-yu, Ying-chun, the Imperial Concubine, Grandmother Jia, Qin-she, his close friend Qin Zhong, Er-jie, Xi-feng, Cassia, Jia Rui, Jia Jing, Concubine Wang, and Skybright; the suicides of Faithful, Golden, Er-jie, and San-jie; Adamantina's abduction, a vicious beating by his father, having witchcraft performed on him by his godmother, the purging of his maids, the loss of his jade, his father's impeachment for mismanagement, an attempt by Jia Huan to disfigure him with molten wax, a shocking attempted "rape" by Skybright's cousin's wife, a litany of heated disagreements with Dai-yu, the government's raid on the Jia family compound, several eye-opening trips to the Land of Illusion, the burglary of the Rong-guo mansion, the dissolution of the idyllic Prospect Garden community and the destruction of all it represented, as well as several mental breakdowns. And all of this occurs in a relatively short period of time. It is not difficult to see the emotional and physical toll this would collectively take on a sensitive individual like Bao-yu and why it would lead to his disillusionment and his choice to take the route of Buddhist transcendence by becoming a monk. But it also underlines the novel's point that his reading and rereading and remembrance of the registers in the Land of Illusion are not enough for his spiritual development; he must realize the truth of their messages through personal experience and with the help of the monk in chapter 117, who reminds Bao-yu of his origins. When Bao-yu finally realizes his origins, his act of offering to give the monk his jade symbolizes his renunciation of desire and that he understands he no longer needs it because the jade represents desire. At the end of the story, Bao-yu is careful to perform two very important acts of filial piety—doing well on the imperial examination and producing an heir with Bao-chai—but he also ironically leaves the Jia family forever by departing with the Daoist and the Buddhist monk and returning to his place of origin, Greensickness Peak. Some commentators have argued that Cao Xueqin based Bao-yu on himself when he was young, but it is more plausible that he is a composite of several people Cao knew.

See also **Doubles and Doubling, Education and the Examination System, Mirrors,** *Qing*

FURTHER READING

Crossley, Pamela Kyle. *The Manchus* (Oxford: Blackwell Publishers, 1997).
Edwards, Louise. *Men and Women in Qing China: Gender in the Red Chamber Dream* (Leiden: E.J. Brill, 1994): 33–49.
Epstein, Maram. "Making Sense of Bao-yu: Staging Ideology and Aesthetics." *Approaches to Teaching Cao Xueqin's Dream of the Red Chamber.* Edited by Andrew Schonebaum and Tina Liu (New York: Modern Language Association of America, 2012): 317–333.
Wu, Cuncun. "'Beautiful Boys Made Up as Beautiful Girls': Anti-Masculine Taste in Qing China." In *Asian Masculinities: The Meaning and Practice of Manhood in China and Japan.* Edited by Kam Louie and Morris Low (New York: Routledge, 2003): 19–40.

Jia Dai-ru 贾代儒

The head of the Jia family clan school and grandfather of Jia Rui, his name connotes "arrogant and conceited." He is a stereotypical conservative Confucian scholar and educator. Narrow-minded and pedantic, Dai-ru is a firm believer in zealously following rules. He is very strict with Jia Rui and severely punishes him after he comes home late after being caught in a trap set up by his love obsession Xi-feng. In chapters 81 and 82, Dai-ru attempts to instruct Bao-yu on the mechanics of writing the Octopartite Composition (Eight-Legged Essay).

See also **Education and the Examination System**

Jia Family Economics

Much time and detail are spent in the novel describing the precarious financial state of the Jia family and the economic reasons for their decline. As early as chapter 2, there is an allusion to the family's chronic inability to economize. In chapter 5, the third song, which is associated with Yuan-chun, has her warning her parents to "Draw back, draw back, before it is too late" (SS, 1: 141) and not tempt fate. When Qin-shi's ghost appears before Xi-feng in chapter 13, she ominously warns her about the necessity for the family to make certain backup plans, like investing in land and property, because their prosperity will not last. (Ironically, Xi-feng will argue for the implementation of some of Qin-shi's recommendations in chapter 92, but by that time, it is too late.) Xi-feng is the only character who fully realizes the family's economic straits. She tells Patience in chapter 55 that the family's main economic problem is, "expenses have increased while our income's dwindled; yet we still have to manage all affairs large and small according to our ancestors' old rules, in spite of less money coming in every year. If I economize too much, outsiders may jeer and their Ladyships will feel the pinch, while the rest of the household complain of my stinginess. On the other hand, if I don't devise ways to save money in good time, another few years may see us bankrupt" (DRM, 2: 244). Consequently, there are increasing signs in the story of the growing problematic nature of the family's finances. In chapter 53, a detailed list is given showing the yearly food and sales yields from the Jias' eight or nine farms in the south, and comments are made that they are much lower than in the past. Even Tan-chun's grand plan to use the fruits of Prospect Garden to save costs fails in the end.

Despite these worrying trends and clues and remarks, the family makes few adjustments, and excuses are made by Jia Lian, Cousin Zhen, Jia She, and Jia Zheng when economic realities are raised by others. In chapter 53, Cousin Zhen erroneously tells the bailiff of the Ning-guo farms that his house's finances are fine, but those of the Rong-guo mansion are problematic. In chapter 93, when Jia Zheng says in a conversation with his friend Feng Zi-ying and Jia She that the family is "living on borrowed time, and one day it will run out" (SS, 4: 26), She replies that the discussion has become depressing and quickly changes the topic. When the high-ranking domestic Lin Zhi-xiao tells Jia Lian in chapter 72 that the family's large staff needs to be cut, he readily agrees but says that Jia Zheng is the one who has to make the decision. When Zheng is confronted in chapter 106 with the facts that the family's income has long been outstripped by expenses, that rents from their estates have been halved, that there were additional expenses relating to the burial of the Imperial Concubine, and that many servants have servants of their own, he is enraged but at a loss over what needs to be done. When Grandmother Jia is told about the situation, she orders some needed changes, but it is too little too late.

Cao Xueqin spent all this time going into these financial matters not only to illustrate the moral corruption of the Jia family and the inability of senior male members of the family to decisively lead and instruct but also because he thought the details would interest readers. He also wanted to warn them about excesses, economic and ethical, and highlight the theme of the ephemeral nature of all things. The novel's realistic and detailed depiction of the economics of running a large-scale family household has so impressed three current Hong Kong business professors that in 2001 they published an informative paper on the accounting and management practices in the story. In it, they argue that *Dream of the Red Chamber* "has historical significance and is relevant to the study of accounting and management controls in 18th century China, especially as alternative documentary evidence is nonexistent" (Chan, Lew, and Tong, 314) and that it actually offers insights on how to creatively teach management accounting today and on understanding how Chinese family-owned businesses are managed. Their paper provides tables explaining how duties were divided among servants in the Ning-guo House and a chart of the family's system of cash flow as instituted by Xi-feng. Their conclusion, which is based on the novel, is that during the early Qing dynasty "Big family households clearly recognized the importance of, and made distinct achievements in, accounting and management controls. They mastered the segregation of duties, the control of cash, the use of budgets for planning, the containment of costs, and the efficiency of operations. However, social and cultural factors that were prevalent during the Qing Dynasty impeded the effectiveness of such practices. The obsession with preserving harmony in society and the family eventually led to excessive power distance and rigid rules, at the expense of flexibility and professionalism" (311).

FURTHER READING

Chan, K. Hung, Albert Y. Lew, and Marian Yew Jen Wu Tong. "Accounting and Management Controls in the Classical Chinese Novel: *A Dream of Red Mansions.*" *The International Journal of Accounting* 36 (2001): 311–327.

Jia Huan 贾环

Jia Zheng and Aunt Zhao's wayward son, he is intellectually and morally limited, lazy and develops into a libertine. His name is a homonym for "trouble or disaster." Xi-feng compares him to a singed kitten looking for a warm corner in which to curl up. He is extremely jealous of Bao-yu because of his popularity, status, and good relationship with Hua's maid Sunshine. As a consequence, he purposely spills some hot candle wax on Bao-yu's face and tells Jia Zheng the lie that Bao-yu raped and beat the maid Golden, which results in Bao-yu receiving a terrible beating by Zheng in chapter 33. Huan is constantly egged on by Aunt Zhao to stand up for himself. He has a taste for what Zheng calls "spooky poetry." Late in the novel, he concocts, with Jia Yun and Wang Ren, a dastardly but ultimately unsuccessful plot to essentially sell Xi-feng's daughter, Qiao-jie, to a Mongol prince. By the end of the story, he has receded into disgrace. It has been argued that Hua is intended to be the inverse of Bao-yu.

Jia Jing 贾敬

Ostensible head of the Ning-guo branch of the Jia family. He is Cousin Zhen's father and Grandmother Jia's nephew. His name literally means "Respect" and connotes "Quietism." Although a Palace Graduate, second class, he was a mediocre official. After his retirement, Jing moved to a Daoist monastery named Dark Truth outside Beijing. There he pursued Daoist practices like breath control, yoga and "other kinds of Taoist hocus-pocus" (SS, 3: 241). He suddenly dies after taking a special mercuric elixir in an attempt to obtain immortality. Jing's abdication of his duties as Jia family head contributes to their numerous problems. From a Confucian perspective, by isolating himself in a monastery, he grievously failed to observe his key filial obligations of serving as a moral model and properly instructing others.

Jia Lan 贾兰

Li Wan's conscientious and studious son and Bao-yu's nephew. Quiet, industrious, and a fair poet, he is a model son. But Bao-yu is shocked by the Confucian rhetoric Lan uses when discussing the importance of good character during their meeting with Zhen Bao-yu in chapter 114, considering it cliché-ridden, distasteful, and priggish. He and Bao-yu take the imperial examination together, and he does well, ranking 170th. Lan appears to be destined for high office, according to the 11th song of the song suite in chapter 5. In the final chapter, Shi-yen hints that Lan will help restore the fortunes of the Jia family.

Jia Lian 贾琏

Wang Xi-feng's husband and Jia She's and Lady Xing's son. Although Lian is not as bad as many of the male members of the Jia family, his avid lechery, with both women and men, gets him into continual trouble. His affairs with "the Mattress" and illegal and bigamous marriage to You Er-jie end with both women's deaths because of Xi-feng's extreme jealousy. He has limited managerial skills and understanding of economic matters, is gullible, and a slow learner, but he also is capable of loyalty and compassion. His marriage with Xi-feng is fraught with difficulties, and, by the end of the novel, he has become alienated from her. He eventually comes around and appreciates devoted Patience and makes her his wife.

Jia Qiao-jie 贾巧姐

Jia Lian and Wang Xi-feng's young daughter. She was born on the seventh day of the seventh month, which is considered an unlucky date. So Xi-feng asks Grannie Liu in chapter 42 to give her an auspicious name in an attempt to turn her luck. Liu recommends Qiao, which means happy coincidence, and jie, which means boy—in traditional China, it was considered flattering to call a girl a boy. Early in the novel, she contracts chicken pox (which was a common but deadly disease during this period) but survives. She develops a friendship with Grannie Liu's granddaughter Qing-er, and Liu becomes her godmother. There are hints that she is personally quite headstrong, and in chapter 117, Jia Lian warns Lady Wang that her temperament is more difficult than her mother's. Later in the story, her uncle, Wang Ren, along with Jia Huan and Jia Yun, concoct an insidious plot to essentially sell her to a Mongol prince as a concubine. The plot eventually fails, thanks in large part to Grannie Liu, who takes her away to safety in the countryside, disguised as Qing-er. In chapter 119, Qian-jie becomes engaged to a member of the rich Zhou family, who are neighbors of Grannie Liu.

Jia Rong 贾蓉

Cousin Zhen and You-shi's son and Qin-shi's husband. At the beginning of the story, he is 20 years old and an Imperial College student. His father is able to obtain a commission for him as a captain in the Imperial Guard for prestige reasons for Qin-shi's funeral by bribing the eunuch Dai Quan. Like his father, Rong is a womanizer. There are hints in chapter 6 that he may have had an affair with Xi-feng. On orders from Xi-feng, he and Jia Qiang harassed Jia Rui in chapter 12, actions which contributed to his eventual death. Rong also shamelessly and aggressively flirts with the You sisters during the mourning period for his grandfather's death and then goads Jia Lian to secretly illegally marry Er-jie.

Jia Rui 贾瑞

Grandson of the headmaster of the Jia clan school Jia Dai-ru. He is an orphan and strictly brought up by his grandfather. Rui is an inept and corrupt teacher at the clan school who shows favoritism to students like Xue Pan who supply him with gifts. In chapter 11, he develops an obsession with and pursues Xi-feng who strings him along to humiliate him. After he returns late at night to his grandfather's house after being disgraced by Jia Rong and Jia Qiang in a trap set by a vindictive Xi-feng, he is severely punished by his traditional-minded grandfather and becomes seriously ill. A Daoist monk suddenly appears with a magical mirror devised by the Fairy Disenchantment and tells Rui that he will be cured of his lovesickness in three days if he looks only at the back of the mirror and never at the front. When Rui looks at the back of the mirror, he sees the frightening image of a smiling skull. But in spite of the monk's warning, he also examines out of curiosity the front, which shows Xi-feng inviting him to join her, which he does, and they make love. Rui then constantly looks at the front of the mirror and eventually dies of sexual exhaustion and is taken away in the mirror by two figures carrying chains. Rui is generally taken to symbolize the bewitching but dangerous power of desire.

Red Inkstone and other commentators have also maintained that Cao Xueqin, in this scene, is warning readers about how to properly read the novel—that they need to read *Dream of the Red Chamber* like the mirror in the story—from the back, in order to understand the story's underlying meaning, and not just the front, which is only the novel's surface meaning.

See also **Mirrors**

Jia She 贾赦

Grandmother Jia's eldest son, Jia Zheng's brother and Jia Lian's and Ying-chun's father. He is married to Lady Xing, who toadies to his every demand. His name literally means to pardon and is similar in sound to the Chinese word for sex. She is hot tempered, arrogant with a strong sense of entitlement, a reprobate who is mainly interested in spending time with his numerous concubines and living a life of ease as an aesthete. He acutely fails in his Confucian responsibilities as the male head of the family and to serve as a moral model. He treats his children, especially Ying-chun, badly (particularly in arranging her marriage to the odious Sun Hao-zu, who behaves so badly toward her that she eventually dies) and has a major run-in with his mother over his determination to make her favorite maid Faithful his concubine. Moreover, he is entirely oblivious of the financial problems of the Jia family. She is arrested during the government raid and charged with misusing his authority to force the owner of some antique fans that he coveted to give them up and is sentenced to penal service in a Mongolian border military post and stripped of his hereditary rank. He becomes ill at this post but recovers and is pardoned by the emperor at the end of the story and returns home.

Jia Tan-chun 贾探春

The second of the Three Springs. Tan-chun is the daughter of Jia Zheng and Aunt Zhao. Her name means "Seeking Spring," and her motif is the kite. According to Bao-yu's servant Joker, her nickname among the servants is "rose" because of her prickly personality and beauty. Competent, levelheaded, and agreeable, she is considered comparable to Xi-feng in terms of managerial ability but lacks Xi-feng's malice. The interior of her residence in Prospect Garden, The Autumn Study, is revealing. It is spacious, which shows her open-mindedness and forthrightness, and her numerous books of calligraphy, and inkstones, and writing and painting ink brushes indicate her love of study. Tan-chun's toughness is clearly shown when she resolutely defends her maids and stands up to a rude servant during the raid on Prospect Garden. But she is also extremely sensitive about, and hampered by, her toxic relationship with concubine Zhao, who treats her badly. She is also hindered by the Chinese cultural prejudice against the offspring of concubines, especially in matters of marriage. She demonstrates her administrative ability and thoroughness in chapters 55 and 56 when she temporarily replaces an ill Xi-feng and is tested by a duplicitous servant and when she comes up with a plan to contract duties in Prospect Garden to help reduce the Jia household's large duplication costs. Her experience working in "The Jobs Room" with Li Wan is important because it provides her with a practical education in how to manage a large and complicated household, gives her an opportunity to put into practice what she has learned, and helps her to gain confidence in her excellent decision-making abilities. Tan-chun is also one of the few characters in the novel who realizes the import and ramifications of Lady Wang's authorized raid on Prospect Garden. She appears to have a successful marriage with the son of the commandant of the Haimen Coastal Region but has to travel far from Beijing for the nuptials. But at the end of the novel, she is able to return to the capital for a long visit.

Jia Xi-chun 贾惜春

She is the youngest of the "Three Springs" and the daughter of Jia Ling and Cousin Zhen's younger sister. Her name means "Treasuring Spring." Xi-chun is characterized as having a "perverse contrariness" (SS, 3: 480), and she develops in the novel into an intolerant and highly righteous individual. This can be seen in her behavior during the raid on Prospect Garden when she panics and stubbornly refuses to defend her innocent servant and in her nasty attack on You-shi and her family. She does have a good relationship with Adamantina. Early in the story, she is given the task by Grandmother Jia of painting a picture of Prospect Garden for Grannie Liu and spends much time struggling to complete it. In chapter 117, she announces that she will kill herself if she is not allowed to become a Buddhist nun. Xi-chun decides to make this controversial decision because she is disgusted by the bad behavior of some of the members of the Jia family and because she wants to escape from problems associated with being a female and to keep herself uncorrupted. You-shi, Lady Wang, and Lady Xing grudgingly agree to her demand, but Lady Wang insists that Xi-chun not shave her head. At the end of the novel, she moves to Prospect Garden's nunnery accompanied by Nightingale, Dai-yu's former maid.

Jia Ying-chun 贾迎春

She is the oldest of the "Three Springs" and the daughter of Jia She. Her name means "Welcoming Spring." Quiet, pretty, kind, and easygoing, Ying-chun is also extremely passive, indecisive, weak and lacks the intelligence and wit of her cousins. She is taken advantage of by her avaricious servants and ill-treated by Jia She and Lady Xing. She marries heartless Sun Shao-zu, who viciously bullies her. Her family fails to protect her, and Ying-chun is slowly worn down by Sun and his family's harsh treatment and tragically dies within a year of marriage.

Jia Yu-cun 贾雨村

A distant relative of the Jia family, Yu-cun is an ambitious and corrupt careerist and a friend of Zhen Shi-yin. His name means "false language enduring, rustic fiction, and false words," and his hometown's name is Hu-zhou, whose homonym is "gibberish." These names stress his untrustworthy nature. At the beginning of the novel, he is a poor student living in the tiny Bottle-gourd Temple, which is located next door to Zhen Shi-yin's residence. Thanks to Shi-yin's generosity, he is able to travel to Beijing to take the imperial examination, does well on it and is appointed a magistrate. While he is a competent administrator, he is soon impeached for his high-handed behavior. This will be a pattern for Yu-cun throughout the story. He will advance to increasingly higher positions, including Mayor of the Metropolitan Prefecture and President of the Board of War, but his cupidity and arrogance will continually lead to his downfall. Early in the novel he becomes a tutor for Dai-yu and accompanies her to Beijing, where he is able to ingratiate himself with the Jia family and establish a good relationship with Jia She and Jia Zheng. He is a regular visitor to the mansion and uses his connection with the family to further advance his career. He also provides services for the family, which include shielding Xue Pan from a possible murder charge and helping Jia She illegally obtain some beautiful antique fans. At the end of the story, Yu-cun is yet again in disgrace, having been convicted of embezzlement. He is released under a general amnesty and encounters Shi-yin at Wakeness Ferry where they had met years ago. (But Shi-yin had refused to recognize him). This time, Shi-yin acknowledges him, and they have a discussion about unresolved matters in the plot, including Bao-yu's spiritual nature, the Jia family's future, Calthrop's death, and the question of why so many women in the family suffer such bad fates. Yu-cun also meets Vanitas and confirms the truthfulness of the stone's tale and recommends that Vanitas meet Cao Xueqin to discuss its possible publication.

But several scholars have contended that, contrary to popular perceptions, Yu-cun is more than a stock character who regularly appears in traditional Chinese literature: the overtly ambitious and duplicitous official whose reach exceeds his ability. Zhou Zuyan, for example, has argued that the constant ups and downs of Yu-cun's life has Daoist elements and that he in fact becomes enlightened at the end of the novel. Zhou writes, "The vicissitudes that he experiences in officialdom—promotion, impeachment, deposition, reinstatement, demotion, arrest, imprisonment, and finally, release, in a general amnesty—illustrate the Daoist belief in the dangers of the useful and the value of the useless…. Yu-cun's departure from the Bottle Gourd Temple marks the start of an indispensable phase in his spiritual journey. Enlightenment in Daoist literature is often preceded by the subject's indulgence in desire in a dream-like experience; the futility of such endeavor will eventually awaken the blind pursuer. This Daoist mode of enlightenment also informs Yu-cun's cultivation … [his] shift from career pursuit to obsessive slumber marks the beginning of his enlightenment. His deep hibernation in the gourd-like cottage suggests his final return to his 'gourd' origin, his 'real home' in a Daoist sense" (164, 165, 170).

See also **Zhuangzi**

Further Reading

Zhou, Zuyan. *Daoist Philosophy and Literati Writings in Late Imperial China: A Case Study of the* Story of the Stone (Hong Kong: Hong Kong University Press, 2013).

Jia Yuan-chun 贾元春

Bao-yu's elder sister and Jia Zheng's and Lady Wang's daughter. Her name means "First Spring." Originally a palace lady-in-waiting, she is promoted to Imperial Concubine and lives in the Forbidden City. Yuan-chun is portrayed as a good-hearted and much-loved individual, especially by the emperor, who is loyal to her and helps take care of her family. She was especially close to Bao-yu when he was very young and helped teach him, their relationship being similar to that of a mother and son, and she keeps close tabs on him after she enters the palace. While her visit in chapter 18 is a happy and proud occasion for the Jia family, it is also a poignant experience for her for it brings to the surface her strong feelings of homesickness. Cao Xueqin is quite good at describing the insular and isolated world she occupies in the Forbidden City. Because the Jia family are imperial bondservants, their fortunes are very much dependent upon Yuan-chun's position and status, so they are highly sensitive about any rumors regarding her. She falls ill twice in the story, first in chapter 83, where she laments not being with her family, and eventually tragically dies in chapter 95 of a chill she contracted after a late-night banquet. Her song in the "Dream of Golden Days" song cycle has her warning her parents about tempting fate. It has been argued by some scholars that Yuan-chun is based on the daughter of Cao Xueqin's grandfather, Cao Yin, who was married to the Manchu Prince Nersu.

Jia Yun 贾芸

Impoverished Jia family relative related to the Rong-guo house. He begins the novel as a sympathetic and ambitious individual but becomes corrupt and brazenly self-serving over time. Initially, he attempts to obtain needed jobs from Xi-feng by giving her presents. Because his mother is a widow and his uncle unreliable, he is forced to turn to the Drunken Diamond for a loan to buy these presents. This approach initially works, and he is given the position of overseeing tree planting in Prospect Garden. But he finds it impossible to receive any more jobs from her. He then turns his sights on Bao-yu, whom he humorously calls his father, and presents him with a rare pure white crab flower. But this relationship collapses when he incurs Bao-yu's enmity when Yun tactlessly tries to be a matchmaker for him. Because he has lost his clout with the Jia family, he is unable to help the Drunken Diamond when he is arrested by Jia Yu-cun. At the end of the novel, Yun has run up huge gambling debts and is spending time drinking with reprobates like Jia Huan and Wang Ren and some corrupt servants and becomes involved in their unscrupulous and unsuccessful scheme to make Xi-feng's daughter a concubine to a Mongolian prince. As a result, Jia Lian banishes him and orders that he never be given another job.

Jia Zhen 贾珍

"Cousin Zhen" is You-shi's husband, Jia Jing's son, and the father of Jia Rong. He is also acting head of the Ning-guo branch of the Jia family. His name ironically means "precious" for he is a hot-tempered and disagreeable person as well as an inept administrator. Zhen, like Jia She, acutely fails to fulfill his Confucian duties as a moral example and instructor. There are also hints in the story that he committed adultery with his son's wife, Qin-she. The novel contains numerous examples of his bad behavior and vicious temper, including mistreating his son and servants, agreeing to Jia Lian's secret marriage to You Er-jie during the mourning period for his father, setting up a gambling house during another mourning period, and having several run-ins with more than a few important palace eunuchs and vice presidents.

Jia Zheng 贾政

Grandmother Jia's youngest son, father of Bao-yu, Tan-chun, Jia Huan, Jia Zhu, and Ying-chun, and grandfather of Jia Lan. He is married to Lady Wang, and his concubines are Aunt Zhou and the notorious Aunt Zhao. His name literally means "politics or administration" and connotes "righteousness." Scrupulously honest, serious, a loyal son, and basically a good person, he places great importance upon traditional values. But he is also extremely strict, inflexible in his beliefs, gullible, and an incompetent manager of people. While he has some understanding of the moral flaws and economic problems of the Jia family, he lacks the confidence and imagination to concretely do anything about them and defers too often to Jia She on key issues. Zheng has a contentious relationship with Bao-yu, considers him spoiled and not serious about his studies and frequently misunderstands him. On one occasion he becomes so infuriated with him, believing Jia Huan's lie that Bao-yu had raped and badly beaten Lady Wang's maid Golden, that he nearly beats Bao-yu to death. But at the end of the novel, he finally realizes Bao-yu's special nature. Zheng occupies several high-level government positions, including Commissioner of Education, and Grain Intendant (though he is impeached for incompetence when he holds this post) but is primarily employed by the Ministry of Works. Li Qiancheng has argued that Zheng has not been given the critical attention he merits, writing, he "is arguably the center of the family, sustaining it in various ways and shouldering the consequences of its collapse. He seems to be the most sensitive grown-up man, poignantly aware of an imminent doom. His desperate attempts to educate his son can be better understood if his side of the story is considered (3)."

FURTHER READING

Li, Qiancheng. "Jia Zheng: Self, Family, and Religion in *Honglou meng*." *Tamkang Review* 36. 1–2 (2005): 3–33.

Jia Zheng's Literary Gentlemen

One of Jia Zheng's favorite pastimes in the novel is to spend time with his "literary gentlemen." This is a reference to a traditional Chinese custom called *qingke* where affluent families invited males to live with them who were thought to have the possibility of making significant contributions in the future to the person who asked them to stay. Zheng has invited five of these gentlemen: Zhou Guan, Shan Pingren, Cheng Rixing, Hu Si-lai, and Bu Guxiu. All of them are depicted as disingenuous flatters, shameless sycophants, and avid social climbers. Moreover, their names reveal their dishonesty. Tellingly, all of them, except for Chen Rixing, vanish after the Embroidered Jacket raid. The fact that Zheng is taken in by and surrounds himself with individuals like them demonstrates his naiveté about people. It would seem that Cao Xueqin did not approve of this tradition.

See also **Naming System**

Jiang Yu-han 蔣玉函

Popular actor-manager known for his female roles, he is a close friend of Bao-yu. His stage name is Bijou, and he is patronized by the Prince of Zhong-shun. Bao-yu first meets him at a drinking party in chapter 28. At the party, Yu-han presents him with a summer crimson cummerbund as a first meeting gift, which was given to him by the Prince of Beijing. When Bao-yu's maid Aroma discovers it while going through his clothes, she is appalled and lectures him about the dangers of associating with disreputable characters like actors. Ironically, she will eventually marry Yu-han. In chapter 33, he mysteriously disappears, and Bao-yu is heatedly questioned by the Prince of Zhong-shun's chamberlain as to his whereabouts. When he reappears in chapter 93, he is giving a performance at the Earl of Linan's residence. Bao-yu attends the event and is rapturously taken with Yu-han's portrayal of Master Qin in the drama "The Queen of the Flower" and concludes that Yu-han is a "romantic, completely unique" (DRM, 3: 181).

Joker 兴儿

Bao-yu's mischievous inner-gate servant. He is impulsive, playful, and generally loyal to Bao-yu (but finds him difficult to understand). In chapter 65, Joker provides newlywed Er-jie and her sister with a humorous and somewhat inaccurate, but generally correct, overview of the personalities of key members of the Jia family. In chapter 67, he reveals under duress by a furious Xi-feng that Jian Lian has married Er-jie.

Kang

A type of traditional Chinese bed. It is an earthen or masonry platform that is primarily used in Northern Chinese houses to heat a room. It is warmed by a fire under it and covered with mats for sleeping. All of the Jia family residences have it, and Lady Wang's expensively covered large *kang* is described in chapter 3.

Kites

One of the more memorable scenes in the novel is the kite-flying episode in chapter 70. Cao Xueqin has a strong interest in kites, and there has long been a rumor that he once wrote a book on the subject. While kites frequently have been used for military purposes in Imperial China, they were also flown for recreational purposes. It was a popular belief during Cao Xueqin's time that cutting the string of a flying kite would cast off a person's bad luck or illness. In this scene, a detailed description is given of each of the kites flown by the participants, and what is on the kites often reveals the owner's character or (sometimes ironically) their fate. Dai-yu's kite has a pretty lady on it, Skybright's sports a big fish (homophonically associated with abundance), Bao-yu's flashes a pretty lady. (He originally had a crab kite, but it was given to Jia Huan the day before.) Bao-qin's kite displays an auspicious large red bat (which represents happiness and longevity), Tan-chun's presents a phoenix (a symbol of virtue and grace), Bao-chai's boasts a line of seven geese flying (a symbol of marriage), and Carmine's, Jia She's new concubine, shows a butterfly (which symbolizes long life and elegance). Moreover, during the event, another kite appears. In the Yang translation of the novel, this kite, which is the size of a door and has the Chinese character for good luck on it, gets tangled up with Tan-chun's kite, and the two kites fly away. Throughout the story, Tan-chun is associated with the image of a kite. In chapter 22, her riddle is about a kite, and in chapter 5, her register picture shows two individuals flying a kite. This leitmotiv is intended to show that she is fated to have to leave the family eventually.

Koan

A Zen Buddhist technique designed to show the limitations of logical thinking and to get people to see the world differently by loosening the hold of the self. It is employed to gauge a student's progress in Zen or to produce enlightenment through the use of a paradoxical story, dialogue, a question, or riddle. *Koans* are discussed and utilized in several episodes in the novel. In chapter 1, Zhen Shi-yin, after hearing the Won-done Song, obtains understanding and goes off with a Daoist. Liu Xiang-lian, in chapter 66, after hearing a koan from a Daoist monk, becomes enlightenment and disappears with the monk. In chapter 22, Dai-yu gives Bao-yu a koan in the form of a question about his name, but he is unable to understand it.

Kotow

A type of traditional Chinese bowing used to show deep respect or submission. The formal process of kotowing has been described thus: "You begin by standing up straight, then you kneel down and lean right forward until your forehead touches the floor. Now raise your torso and bow again so that your forehead once more brushes the carpet, and repeat once more. After that stand up again, then go through the whole business on two more occasions. So you stand, genuflect, bow down to the carpet three times—and then repeat that ritual twice more with appropriate dignity and reverence" (Patten, 245). Government officials during the Qing dynasty kotowed before the emperor, children kotowed before their parents, and family members kotowed during ceremonies before their ancestors. The novel contains numerous examples of individuals kotowing. They include Patience, Xi-feng, and Jia Lian kotowing before Grandmother Jia, Lady Xing, and Lady Wang to apologize for the fracas they caused in chapter 44, and Jia Rong in chapter 68 vigorously kotows to Xi-feng to apologize for helping Jia Lian secretly marry Er-jie.

FURTHER READING

Patten, Christopher. *East and West: China, Power, and the Future of Asia* (New York: Random House, 1998).

Lady Wang 王夫人

Bao-yu's fiftyish mother, Jia Zheng's wife and Aunt Xue's sister. Generally, she is a kind and tolerant individual, a lenient mistress, and a protective mother, but she can also be intolerant and vindictive, especially regarding maids she thinks are sexually loose in their behavior or interested in developing a romantic relationship with Bao-yu. Hence, her strong (but unfair) dislike of Golden, Skybright, and Parfumee. Moreover, she orders the disastrous raid on Prospect Garden and is capable of baldly lying, as she does about Golden to Bao-chai and about Skybright to Grandmother Jia. Because of her supposedly bad health, she has relegated the duties of overseeing the household to her eager niece Xi-feng.

Lady Xing 邢夫人

Jia She's wife and Jia Lian's mother. Her name connotes "to follow," and she is infamous for agreeing to all of Jia She's wishes, no matter how foolhardy they appear. She is extremely tightfisted, stubborn, gullible, and narrow-minded, trusts no one, and is willing to take the advice of only a few people. Lady Xing is also thoroughly disliked by most of her servants as well as members of the Jia family. She incurs Grandmother Jia's wrath when she pressures her maid Faithful to become Jia She's concubine. She treats Ying-chun, her niece Xiu-yan, and Xi-feng badly and late in the story falls for the plot to give Xi-feng's daughter to a Mongol prince. All of her servants and property are confiscated during the Embroidered Jacket raid on the Ning-guo House, but her property is restored on order of the emperor at the end of the novel.

Land of Illusion 太虛幻境

Mythical realm ruled by the Fairy Disenchantment. All of its inhabitants have fully understood the important doctrine of the illusory nature of worldly, especially *qing*-related, attachments. Bao-yu famously visits this land in chapter 5. The realm has a large stone archway that serves as a gateway between the mundane world and the Land of Illusion, with a couplet expounding the porous relationship between truth and fiction and the real and unreal and the impossibility of making distinctions between them. The Land of Illusion represents the truth, while Prospect Garden represents the mortal realm of human affairs and the illusory nature of life. The distinction (and similarities) between the two realms sets up *Dream of the Red Chamber*'s dialectical interplay between the binaries mentioned on the archway, which helps drive the story's plot. This mythical land also has a large and pristine palace with many buildings containing departments related to aspects of *qing*. The fairyland to a degree mirrors the strict social ranking of the mundane world. This can be seen in the Department of Ill-fated Fair, which contains registers that contain albums foretelling the fate of the novel's 12 main female characters. The young mistresses are kept in a main register and the maids in a supplementary register, and Aroma, because she fails to commit suicide after Bao-yu suddenly vanishes, is relegated to the secondary supplementary register. In chapter 116, Bao-yu returns to the realm, which is now called The Paradise of Truth (Shi-yin tells Yu-chun in chapter 120 that both worlds "are one and the same") (SS, 5: 371) and has an archway with two different couplets, again about fate, and the relationship between fiction and truth, the real and unreal. Bao-yu encounters female characters who include Dai-yu, Skybright, Xi-feng, and Faithful, who have recently died and ascended to the land, is able to read some of the albums again, and this time he can understand most of their hidden meanings. In a highly influential paper, Yu Ying-shih has written about the close connection between the ideal but illusory world of Prospect Garden, which is the realm of sentiments and love, and the real world of the Land of Illusion, which is the realm of the transcendence of *qing*. As one scholar has put it, "In the last analysis, in *Honglou meng* the dialectics of reality and illusion is also the dialectics of feeling and transcendence of feeling" (Li, 156).

FURTHER READING

Li, Wai-yee. *Enchantment and Disenchantment: Love and Illusion in Chinese Literature* (Princeton: Princeton University Press, 1993).

Yu, Ying-shih. "The Two Worlds of *Hung-lou Meng*." Translated by Diana Yu. *Renditions* 2 (1974): 5–22.

Language

Dream of the Red Chamber is written in the vernacular rather than classical Chinese (except in the main for passages of parallel line descriptions of characters like Xi-feng, Dai-yu, and Bao-yu in chapter 3, and most of the poetry that is composed in the story, which is written in literary Chinese). The spoken Chinese of Beijing during the Qing dynasty was influenced by the rulers of the country who were not Han, so "Elements of Manchu [who ruled China from 1644 to 1912] grammatical style, Manchu-Chinese combination of place names, Manchu words, and Manchu-style Chinese words are scattered through the novel" (Rawksi, 37). It is reported that Cao Xueqin retained the Nanjing Mandarin of his Southern hometown throughout his life and refused to adopt the Beijing vernacular. In spite of this, the dialogue in the novel is considered a first-rate example of Beijing Mandarin dialect, which formed the basis for modern spoken Chinese. In fact, during the 19th century, *Dream of the Red Chamber* was commonly studied by foreigners, especially British diplomats, when learning Chinese, because of its excellent use of the Beijing dialect. Although *Honglou meng* is over 200 years old, most educated Chinese today would generally have no major problems reading it.

FURTHER READING

Rawksi, Evelyn S. "The Prosperous Age: China in the Kangxi, Yongzheng, and Qianlong Era." In *China: The Three Emperors 1662–1795*. Edited by Evelyn S. Rawksi and Jessica Rawson (London: Royal Academy of Arts, 2005): 22–40.

The Last 40 Chapters

There has long been great controversy over the authenticity of the last 40 chapters of *Dream of the Red Chamber* ever since the novel's publication in 1792. This controversy continues to spark heated debate even today and sharply divides scholars. This is because all of the existing manuscript copies of the novel cover only the first 80 chapters and because of the circumstances in which the final 40 chapters were found and published. When the 120-chapter version of the novel first appeared, it came with prefaces and a joint foreword by Cheng Weiyuan, a painter and literatus, and Gao E, a minor official and poet. They claimed that Cheng had found an incomplete manuscript of the story written by Cao Xueqin that contained the final 40 chapters and that Gao E had simply edited and polished it, ironing out inconsistencies and continuity problems and that they only wanted to produce a complete version of the novel. The debate revolves around the question of whether Cheng and Gao E were telling the truth. Those who believe that the chapters are not genuine contend that an unfinished draft by Cao Xueqin was either heavily edited or substantially rewritten or that the chapters were completely forged by Gao E. They point out as evidence that the literary quality and character descriptions in these chapters are considerably inferior to those of the first 80, the imagery and language used are often stock, and there are more supernatural elements than in the previous chapters. These critics also maintain that these 40 chapters, unlike the earlier ones, foist a conformist moral order on the plot, which stresses the importance of orthodox Confucian values, and that Bao-yu finally buckling down and passing the imperial exam is unrealistic given his strong objections to it throughout the first 80 chapters.

Finally, proponents of this position have also asserted that these chapters frequently and significantly deviate from Cao Xueqin's original intentions as expressed in the predictions made in the registers and Fairy Disenchantment's song and dance suite in chapter 5. For example, they believe the ending gives the Jia family a much happier fate than what is prophesied about them in the epilogue to the suite, which states:

> "When food is gone the birds return to the wood;
> All that's left is emptiness and a great void" [DRM, 1: 84].

These lines have been taken by some of these critics to foretell that at the end of the story a great fire will completely destroy the Jia's mansions, thereby purifying the family of all their sins and offenses. It has also been posited that this fate is also foreshadowed by the burning down of Zhen Shi-yin's residence in chapter 1 and the fire in the Rong mansion's stable in chapter 39 (Wu, 167). Furthermore, it also noted that Red Inkstone, who knew Cao Xueqin and helped edit the novel, in his/her famous commentary has mentioned different outcomes to the story from what actually occurs. The scholar Zhou Ruchang has gone so far as to claim that the final 40 chapters are a complete forgery and that the novel really consists of only 108 chapters. He also claims that Gao E was working together with high officials in the imperial court circles to purge the novel's original conclusion because it showed the Jia family being treated badly by the government and that this had offended these officials.

Defenders of the authenticity of the 40 chapters readily admit that they were edited by Gao E but also assert that he made no significant changes and did the best he could with Cao's original but fragmentary material and that there is an essential unity between these chapters and the prior ones. They note that in the main, Cao Xueqin's original intent was retained, pointing out that the vast majority of the predictions made in chapter 5 come true. (For example, all of the major female characters have the fate that was foretold for them.) And those that did not come true (including other foreshadowing hints in the story) turned out that way simply because Cao, as authors frequently do, changed his mind about those parts of the story or committed an oversight. They also insist that the epilogue to the song suite does not necessarily forecast such a tragic fate for the Jia family. These defenders also state that some of the supernatural elements and foreshadowing techniques used (for example, the fateful fish game in chapter 81) in these chapters seem forced, and some of the novel's most superbly written and memorable scenes, like Dai-yu's death, the meeting of the two Bao-yus, the Embroidered Jacket raid, Bao-yu's second visit to the Land of Illusion, and the intriguing philosophical debate between Bao-chai and Dai-yu in chapter 118 take place in the last one-third of the book. In addition, it is observed that Bao-yu's decision to get serious about his studies and take the imperial examination is not a sign of him caving in to the system, for he undercuts his actions and violates his Confucian familial obligations by deserting his family and pregnant wife and becoming a Buddhist monk. It is also argued that the open-text nature of the story's ending, its ambiguity regarding themes and skepticism concerning the ultimate value of any one belief system, gives the novel (even in the last 40 chapters), a pluralism that overrides any singular stress on Confucian values.

Finally, several scholars have conducted statistical analyses of the grammar and vocabulary used in the early and later chapters and have concluded that there are considerable similarities between the two. (To be fair, there are also other statistical studies that have argued for the forgery position.) Furthermore, John Minford, the distinguished co-translator of the Penguin edition of *Dream of the Red Chamber*, has made an influential 298-page close study of these chapters and has concluded that Gao E basically told the truth. While the debate about the veracity of the final chapters continues, there is now a growing consensus among Western scholars, including David Hawkes, C.T. Hsia, Anthony Yu, John Minford, Dore Levy, Tina Lu, Susan Chan Egan, Pai Hsien-Yung, and others that these chapters are on the whole genuine. But the number of Chinese scholars who believe this continues to be small.

Further Reading

Chan, Bing C. *The Authorship of* The Dream of the Red Chamber: *Based on a Computerized Statistical Study of Its Vocabulary* (Hong Kong: Joint, 1986).

Minford, John. "The Last Forty Chapters of *The Story of the Stone*: A Literary Appraisal." PhD Thesis, Australian National University, 1980.

Wu, Shih-Ch'ang. *On the* Red Chamber Dream: *A Critical Study of Two Annotated Manuscripts of the XVIIIth Century* (Oxford: Clarendon Press, 1961).

Zhou, Ruchang. *Between Noble and Humble: Cao Xueqin and the* Dream of the Red Chamber. Edited by Ronald R. Gray and Mark S. Ferrara (New York: Peter Lang, 2009).

Legal System

One of the things that makes *Dream of the Red Chamber* such a fascinating novel is that Cao Xueqin realistically described so many aspects of Qing dynasty life. This includes the legal system. During his lifetime, China had institutionally a sophisticated and detailed (436 articles) legal code (called *Ta Tsing Leu Lee* or *The Great Qing Legal Code*) and judicial system. The novel realistically describes how this system operated in its account of Xue Pan's court case when he is arrested for causing the death of a waiter. Pan's case follows the usual course that capital cases like his would have taken. At first, it went to the county level where the county magistrate investigated the crime scene and called and questioned the witnesses. Magistrates at this level had no power to try the case; instead they sent a report to their superiors. The case would then advance to the prefectural level, after that to the circuit court, and then to the Provincial Supreme Court. In Pan's case, the case was then handed back to the Metropolitan Governor for further investigation and recommendation. The Board of Punishment was also involved in the process because it is a capital case, and it had to review the case and make a final ruling. In the end, he is found guilty of "homicide by blows" and sentenced to be executed by strangulation during the autumn assizes (the eighth month in the lunar calendar). The final step in the long process occurred during the autumn assizes, when a final determination was made about the death sentence he received, again because it was a capital case. This determination was made by the emperor himself in consultation with the imperial body The Three High Courts of Judicature, which was charged with reviewing all capital sentences, but the emperor made the final decision following the annual autumn assizes. In the novel, Xue Pan is extremely lucky and saved in the end when the emperor decreed a national amnesty (which would not have applied to those who were considered a serious threat to society or national security) to celebrate the return of peace on the coastal frontiers. He is then released after Xue Ke pays his commutation fine and the Board of Justice agrees to take the money for the settlement. Nearly all of these legal steps are mentioned in the novel.

Cao Xueqin is not afraid to show the dark side of the legal proceedings: the easy corruption of some of the judges and the unfair influence of rich and powerful families. The novel also explicitly depicts the important role money plays in the process for ensuring that the accused is treated well in prison, for influencing witnesses, court officials, relatives of the victims, and judges (one judge in Xue Pan's case demanded several thousand taels), and for employing proper scriveners (*songshi*), legal specialists who prepared legal documents and performed other legal roles. (In Xue Pan's case, a scrivener gives Xue Ke useful advice on how to pressure the district magistrate to remove the death penalty sentence.) It also describes the huge economic toll these demands place even on rich families like the Xues, who go bankrupt because of all the costs. (In the end, the Xue family becomes so impoverished by Pan's legal costs that Aunt Xue has to borrow money to pay for Pan's commutation fine.) But the system to a certain extent works in the novel in part because of the numerous checks placed on judicial power. Although the Jia family actively attempted to subvert justice at every level of the process, even though Xue Pan was obviously guilty of the crime, they are ultimately unsuccessful in their attempt. The real facts about the case eventually come out during court proceedings, and Pan is given a sentence that is legally appropriate for his crime. (Xiaohuan Zhao has speculated that the family was unsuccessful because they had lost much of their power and influence owing to the deaths of the Imperial Concubine and Wang Zi-teng, Xue Pan's uncle who held a high government position before his sudden death when he was on his way to Beijing.)

See also **Corruption**

FURTHER READING

Zhao, Xiaohuan. "Court Trials and Miscarriage of Justice in *Dream of the Red Chamber*." *Law and Literature* 23.129 (2011): 1–25.

Leng Zi-xing 冷子兴

Jia Yu-chun's friend who is married to Zhou Rui's daughter. He is an antique dealer and appears to be of somewhat questionable character. He became involved in a lawsuit over the sale of some objects and also got into trouble when he was drunk and picked a fight with a person who, out of revenge, said he doesn't have proper papers and should be deported to his village in the South. His wife pressures her mother to get Xi-feng to help him. But Zi-xing has an important role in the novel for he is one of several outsiders, like Grannie Liu and Bao-qin, who provide crucial background information for the reader or offer different perspectives on events that normal characters do not see or of which they are unaware. In chapter 2, during a long discussion with Jia Yu-chu, he provides key information about the Jia family, including their current economic situation as well as problems concerning the morality of the young male members of the family. He also accurately introduces and describes key male members of the family, including Bao-yu, and their respective personalities.

Li Bo 李白 701-765

Widely considered one of the greatest of Chinese poets, if not the greatest. He wrote during the Tang dynasty, the golden age of Chinese poetry. Li Bo was a romantic in his approach to life, and his highly influential poetry is celebrated for its simplicity, clear imagery, directness, and imaginary localities. His noted poem "On Phoenix Terrace" is mentioned in chapter 17 of the novel, and in chapter 115, Jia Bao-yu, obeying the polite conventions of the time, hyperbolically calls Zhen Bao-yu a reincarnation of Li Bo when they are first introduced. Bao-yu's choice of Li Bo is highly ironic because Bo was famous for his unconventionality, love of drinking, drunken behavior, and tumultuous life.

Li He 李贺 791-817

Late Tang dynasty poet famous for his allusive and ironic style, rich diction, and strange imagery. He is also known for his depiction of the emotionally fraught lives of high-class courtesans. Li He's poem "Return from Gui-ji" is alluded to when Jia Zheng's "literary gentlemen" are discussing a poem by Bao-yu in chapter 78 and also later in the same chapter in Bao-yu's "Spirit of the Hibiscus" elegy. Cao Xueqin's close friend Dun Cheng compared Cao's poetry with that of Li He's.

Li Sao and *The Summons of the Soul* 离骚与招魂

Two renowned poems from the famous ancient Chinese anthology *The Songs of the South*, after which Bao-yu models his elegy to Skybright in chapter 78. The first is by the noted Warring States period poet Qu Yuan (c. 340–278 BC). *Li Sao* means "Encountering Sorrow" and is Qu Yuan's best-known poem. It is a complex, lyrical, 379-line, first-person autobiographical monologue (which was unusual for his time because most poetic voices were anonymous) that mixes the imaginative, biographical, and mythological. In the poem, Yuan despairingly chronicles the slanderous plots against him when he served as a court official and his being forced to leave by the emperor and his shamanistic spiritual trips to several mythological realms and discussions with divine beings. In the end, he derives no comfort from these experiences and commits suicide out of despair. The second poem has also been attributed to Qu Yuan, although there is still some debate about this. This four-part poem also contains shamanistic elements and concerns the wandering soul of the narrator, who is in shock because of the tragic turns in his life. In the poem, his soul is summoned or invoked back by the temptation of a succulent feast at his home (which is symbolic of worldly delights). The purpose of this summons of the soul, which was commonly used in ancient China, was to call back the wandering soul or a troubled or sick person to their body before the soul permanently leaves it. It is said that Qu Yuan wrote this poem in order to talk himself out of committing suicide because of pressing political problems. Bao-yu was clearly attracted to these works because of their autobiographic and melancholic nature, their mixture of regret and anger, and their obsession with the past. He would also have especially liked *The Summons of the Soul* because of its stress on invocation and return, which fit the mood and tone of his elegy to Skybright.

Li Wan 李纨

Jia Lan's mother, Jia Zhen's and Lady Wang's daughter-in-law, and widow of Bao-yu's deceased older brother Jia Zhu. Her name means "Plain Silk" and connotes "Finished, Doomed." Her father was an education official who firmly believed that women need not be highly educated but should instead concentrate on sewing and spinning. He gave her the name Li Wan to stress the importance of women knowing how to sew. She is in her 20s and is quiet, well-mannered, and dedicated to her son. Her simple straw hut residence in Prospect Garden's Sweet-rice Village with its farm animals, apricot and mulberry trees, and rows of vegetables, reveals her simple lifestyle, modesty, and retiring nature. But Li Wan is not entirely a passive individual. She is capable of standing up to Xi-feng when she thinks she is wrong, as she does in chapter 45 when Xi-feng is pressuring people to contribute money for her birthday celebration. She also stays with Dai-yu when she is dying and presses Nightingale to get her burial clothes ready. She is also one of the few characters who clearly understands the severe limitations Xi-feng is operating under when she is trying to manage Grandmother Jia's funeral in chapter 110. There are hints that she feels isolated and frustrated with her status.

Her main job in the novel, besides bringing Jia Lan up, is to keep watch over her female cousins in the garden and supervise their poetry club. While Jia Lan seems destined to become a high official, according to the song about her in chapter 5, it also implies that she will die shortly afterward. The novel suggests that Cao Xueqin was very critical of how widows like Li Wan were treated in China at that time, including the tradition that they were not expected to marry again and the effect this had upon the women. This can in part be seen in the lines that are written in her register in the Land of Illusion: "Against your ice-pure nature all in vain/ The tongues of envy wagged; you felt no pain" (SS, 1: 135).

Lin Dai-yu 林黛玉

Granddaughter of Grandmother Jia, daughter of Lin Ru-hai and Jia Zheng's sister, Jia Min, and the incarnation of the Crimson Pearl Flower. Her name means "Black Jade." Dai-yu's ill-fated relationship with Bao-yu is one of the most famous in Chinese literature. The Naid's House, her residence in Prospect Garden, gives telling clues about her character. The dwelling, Xiao xiang quan, is named after the hundreds of green bamboos that surround it. Xiao means the sound of falling rain, which is a reference to Dai-yu's tendency to cry often. Xiang is "speckled bamboo," which alludes to the famous legend about the two queens of the Emperor Shun who went to the banks of the Xiang River to find him after he died. They then turned into river goddesses, and their tears of grief became spots on the bamboo that grew near the river. In Chinese culture, bamboo is a symbol of virtue, honesty, and longevity because it is strong and tall, has firm roots, and stands upright. The residence's name also implies that Dai-yu is an ethereal person. A narrow, zigzagging path, which is covered with moss, leads to her place. The path symbolizes her restricted introspective nature and hints that the course of her life will not be smooth. In traditional Chinese poetry, moss frequently grows in front of the houses of hermits. Therefore, the path's moss might signify Dai-yu's solitary nature and the sad fact that she is not visited often. The flowering pear tree that stands in her courtyard represents her lonely existence because she is an orphan, while a homophone for pear tree in Chinese is *li*, which means "to be separated." Finally, her well-stocked collection of books shows her intellectual side. She is also directly associated in the novel with the moon, which in Chinese culture is symbolic of feminine energy, while the full moon represents a family reunion and peace. Dai-yu selects the moon as a topic for a poem for Caltrop in chapter 48 and also uses it in a poem in chapter 76. In addition, on one famous occasion she dresses as, and is compared to, the Moon Goddess Chang E. All of these references are intended to indicate her otherworldly nature. Moreover, the fact that, unlike many other characters, her clothing is never described in detail reinforces her ethereal quality.

Dai-yu is by far the novel's most complicated and conflicted female character. She is highly intelligent, well educated, articulate, and possesses a great knowledge of literature and music. She is capable of great charm and thoughtfulness, honest, and is the poetry club's most talented poet. But underneath her rather aloof nature, she is also a passionate individual, a person of great sentiment (*qing*), as seen in her emotional reactions to the plays she reads, the poetry she writes, and in her feelings about Bao-yu. She is also unduly sensitive, self-centered, highly introspective, and has a strong need for constant attention and affirmation. Dai-yu ultimately sees herself as a victim, and on a certain level she sadly is one. Her deep feelings of anxiety and insecurity, which often exasperate others and become more pronounced in the story, are essentially due to several factors. First, she is haunted by the fact that she is an orphan and that she has to completely rely upon the Jia family for all of her needs. Because of her ambiguous status, Dai-yu strongly feels she is an outsider and has doubts about whether she is really accepted by the Jia family. Consequently, she is extremely sensitive to any remotely negative remarks made about her by her relatives and servants. Compounding these insecurities is the fact that throughout the story she has intense feelings of homesickness about her birthplace in the south.

Second, her health is increasingly problematic, and she suffers from what appears to be pulmonary tuberculosis, which greatly contributes to her moodiness, impatience, sharp tongue, and periods of depression. Third, the noted literary scholar Anthony Yu, who has written several sympathetic and sensitive studies of Dai-yu, has attributed much of her vexation "to her inability to resolve the conflict between duty and desire, between the need to acquire the traditional social virtues of self-restraint and deference to others and the self-assertive impulse to compete, to achieve to excel" (231). And finally, topping it all, is of course her tempestuous and emotionally draining romantic relationship with Bao-yu. It is important to emphasize that their tragic love affair was fated from the start because, when Dai-yu was the Crimson Pearl Flower, she decided to come to the real world to pay Bao-yu (when he was the stone) back with tears for watering her in her previous incarnation. Because of this, they are fated to have an unsatisfactory relationship and are prevented from even directly and completely communicating their love for each other. As chapter 64 states, although the two "had grown up side by side and were kindred spirits who longed to live and die together, this was tacitly understood by both but had never been put into words" (DRM, 2: 405). Nor would it ever be in the story. As the novel progresses, Dai-yu displays a deepening sense of mortality, transience, despair over her relationship with Bao-yu, and feelings of being trapped. The tipping point occurs when she discovers that Bao-yu will marry Bao-chai. She dies on the very day they are married, thereby completing her payment in full.

Despite her many character flaws, Dai-yu has long remained a favorite character among Chinese readers of *Dream of the Red Chamber*. As one scholar has pointed out, "By eighteenth century standards, Dai-yu is the most feminine character in the novel: she is also the most representative of the cult of sentiment. Ethereally beautiful, she evokes the stunning but ephemeral beauty of spring blossoms.... Modern United States readers might find her instability to be a flaw, but traditional Chinese readers were drawn to her emotional honesty and sincerity. Unlike the cold and reserved Bao-chai, whom some commentators dismiss as hypocritical in her shows of deference to family elders, Dai-yu embodies the authentic and aesthetic ideals heralded by the cult of sentiment" (Epstein, 326). Yu believes that she is mainly admired by readers for her great love for Bao-yu, "because she places his freedom for self-affirmation above his obligatory allegiance to family. A love that has the potential to challenge some of the most cherished values of culture must appear, for that very reason, perverse and anarchic, for it threatens to repudiate or revise the long-accepted norms of that tradition. But a love of such quality, I suspect, is also what endears her to readers traditional and modern, because it registers the eloquent intimation of tragic nobility. She never demanded her lover be anything other than what he is; all she has ever hoped from him is the unambiguous assurance of his love" (241).

See also **Bond of Gold and Jade, Chang E, Drama, *Qing***

FURTHER READING

Epstein, Maram. "Making Sense of Bao-yu: Staging Ideology and Aesthetics." *Approaches to Teaching Cao Xueqin's* Dream of the Red Chamber. Edited by Andrew Schonebaum and Tina Liu (New York: Modern Language Association of America, 2012): 317–333.

Yu, Anthony. *Rereading the Stone: Desire and the Making of Fiction in* Dream of the Red Chamber (Princeton: Princeton University Press, 1997).

Linked Verse

Two of the most memorable scenes in the novel involve Shi Xiang-yun, Lin Dai-yu, and sometimes others participating in linked verse contests where participants are expected to finish a couplet that has been started by a previous person and come up with a line to begin a new one. The scenes vividly capture the personalities of the participants, their quick wit, and impressive literary ability. The first contest, which occurs at Prospect Garden's Snowy Rushes Retreat in chapter 50, is a boisterous and uproarious affair and involves the use of what is called linked verse rhyme eyes. The contest quickly turns into an intense battle of wits between Bao-qin, Dai-yu, and Xiang-yun to imaginatively complete the couplets. For the second contest, Cao Xueqin employs his frequently used technique of replicating scenes with a twist to underline the novel's theme of decline. It occurs in chapter 76, and the versifiers are again Xiang-yun and Dai-yu, but the setting, atmosphere, and number of participants is vastly different from the first. It is now the Mid–Autumn festival, and a strong sense of foreboding and melancholy is present. Dai-yu and Xiang-yun are alone and feeling neglected because everyone else is with their families. It is late at night, and they are at the garden's deadly quiet Concave Pavilion. In an attempt to raise their spirits, they decide to compose linked pentameters. This time the imagery they use has an undercurrent of sadness and morbidity, so much so that Adamantina, who accidentally comes upon and overhears them composing, tells them that she finds their poetry slightly ghoulish and unhealthy.

Lion

The lion in Chinese culture symbolizes power, prestige, and majesty. Lions were also believed to protect people from evil spirits. A pair of stone statues of lions were commonly placed in front of the main gates to government offices and residences during the Qing dynasty. The lion on the left would be male with his right paw resting on a ball (which represents the unity of the empire). The lion on the right would be female with her left paw holding a cub (which represents flourishing offspring). The Ning-guo House is noted for the two large stone lions located in front of their triple gateway. In chapter 66, Xiang-lian contrasts the purity of these lions with the moral corruption of the Jia family, angrily telling Bao-yu, "The only clean things in that East Mansion of yours are those two stone lions at the gate. Even the cats and dogs there are unclean" (DRM, 3: 444).

Liu Xiang-lian 柳湘莲

Dedicated amateur actor who specializes in romantic roles. His name literally means "Lotus in the River Xiang," and connotes "To Love One Another" and "To Pity One Another," which is a reference to his tragic relationship with San-jie. Xiang-lian is from an excellent family but was not able to finish his education because his parents died. Young, handsome, impulsive, and a spendthrift, he is considered to have a cold disposition. He is a friend of Bao-yu and helped take care of Qin Zhong's grave. He gives an aggressive Xue Pan a thrashing when he tries to set up a homosexual rendezvous with him and then disappears. Xiang-lian later suddenly reappears and saves Pan when the group he is traveling with on a business trip is attacked by robbers. When Jia Lian by chance comes upon the two, he offers to broker a marriage between Xiang-lian and San-jie, who has loved him for five years after seeing him in a performance. Xiang-lian readily agrees to the proposal and gives Lian a family heirloom, his duck and drake swords, to symbolize his pledge to marry her. Later, he has doubts about San-jie's character and decides to retract his promise. When she hears this, San-jie kills herself in despair with one of the swords. Xiang-lian quickly realizes that he was wrong about her and soon afterward encounters a Daoist with a disabled leg in a rundown temple. The monk gives him a koan, and Xiang-lian immediately understands the vanity of human affections and goes off with him.

See also **Duck and Drake Swords, Enlightenment, Koan**

Lives of Noble Women

Anthologies of biographies of exemplary women have traditionally been popular in China ever since the Han dynasty. During Cao Xueqin's time, they were a major part of the publishing industry. These works presented "Confucian lessons on how wives, daughters, chaste women, and daughters-in-law should properly behave. The novel contains two references to these books. In chapter four, it is mentioned that while Li Wan's conservative father objected to her seriously studying books, she was allowed to read to *Lives of Noble Women* so that she could understand some Chinese characters and in order that she might be acquainted with some traditional models of female virtue. In chapter 92, Xi-feng's daughter, Qia-jie, tells Bao-yu that she has been reading the same anthology. Cao Xueqin appears to have disliked such works because they were often used to keep women in their place and not fully educated. During Qia-jie's conversation with Bao-yu, he makes fun of the genre by inventing a category of his own of special women which he calls 'Famous Beauties'" (SS, 4: 248). Tellingly, several of the celebrated women that he mentions were not considered examples of Confucian virtue.

Lord Red Beard 关羽

Guan Yu, a renowned general who served under Liu Bei during the Easter Han dynasty. He is commonly depicted as having a red face (which symbolizes his loyalty and courage) with a large beard. He was executed by enemy forces in 219 and is immortalized in the classic historical novel *The Three Kingdoms*. Guan Yu is considered a moral paragon and is a very popular personage in Chinese folk religion, Buddhism, Daoism, and Confucianism. For Buddhists, he is a Sangharama Bodhisattva, a defender of the *dharma*, and a protector of temples. Aunt Zhao, while undergoing her terrible ordeal in chapter 113, begs "Lord Red Beard" (Guan Yu) to stop killing her and promises him that she will never be bad again.

Maids and Other Servants

Many of the characters who populate the novel are maids and servants. They range in position from chief maid, junior maid, maid attendant, senior domestic, and nannies to principal page, page, chief steward, junior steward, senior servant, senior stewardesses, granary foreman, chief groom, clerk of stores, cook, farm bailiff, nurse, and wet nurse. Cao Xueqin clearly had personal knowledge of all these positions and what they entailed because he had grown up (until his family's confiscation) in a residence that accommodated 114 servants. (There has also been a long-standing rumor that he had experienced an unhappy romance with a maid early in his life, which might in part explain his sympathy for their plight.) Despite their often low status, many of them have a strong physical presence and exert an important influence in the Jia family. They are often confidants, even friends and, on occasion, lovers of members of the family. Many of them are also memorable, vividly drawn individuals, with distinct personalities, and are frequently more sympathetic characters than their masters. The novel spends much time detailing their daily lives, concerns, and hopes for the future, thus providing an "Upstairs Downstairs" element to the story. This depiction was unusual for traditional Chinese novels, where fully defined maids, in particular, were usually found only in dramas where they served as intermediaries and interlocutors for main characters. It is difficult to exaggerate how little time members of upper-class families, especially adolescents, spent alone. As *Dream of the Red Chamber* shows, they were virtually always surrounded by people, mainly maids and servants, to feed and dress them and tend to their daily needs, to accompany them inside the mansion and on outings outside it. They instructed them and monitored their behavior for others and slept near them at night. The number of servants who were assigned to characters like Bao-yu was amazingly large. In chapter 3, it is noted that he has "one wet-nurse ... four other nurses to act as chaperones, two maids as body-servants to attend to cleaning, running errands and general duties" (SS, 1: 105). When Bao-yu moves into Prospect Garden, he is assigned "two old nurses and four maids in addition to [his] existing maids and nannies, and there were other servants whose sole duty was sweeping and cleaning" (SS, 1: 459). When he leaves the mansion in chapter 52 for a party, a large entourage of male servants accompanies him. Bao-yu, at times, finds this lack of freedom and space smothering, and at one stage complains to a friend, "Every move I make is known, and there's always someone trying to stop me or dissuade me, so whatever I say, I can't do a thing" (DRM, 2: 101). Sentiments that Cao Xueqin must have also felt while growing up.

It is important to understand the special background and ranking of the Jia family's maids. They are not slaves and, as Aroma notes, are generally not ill-treated by the family, which was not necessarily the case in many upper-class Qing dynasty families at that time. (This good treatment would have reflected well on the family's image.) They were not forced to work for the family but rather were sold to the Jias by their impoverished families or were house born. Moreover, when they reached a certain age, their families could buy them out of service. Indentured servants had a higher status and were paid more than the house born. There is also, in the novel, a sharp distinction made between maids who are senior or body servants, like Aroma and Patience, and junior or little maids, like Crimson. Senior maids, who received a fixed monthly salary, spend their time taking care of their masters or mistresses. Junior maids were subject to the orders of senior maids and could have contact only with their master or mistress if they were summoned. But if the maid was lucky and had a good relationship with their master, they could be made a chamber wife or concubine, like Aunt Zhao, and if they were very fortunate, like Shi-yin's aptly named maid, Lucky, in chapter 2, they could become principal wife, as happened to her when Jia Yu-cun's first wife died.

Maids and servants play several vital roles in the novel. The personalities of some of the servants are mirror images of or complementary to main characters. This technique helps to further characterize the novel's main characters. Skybright mirrors Dai-yu in that they are both beautiful, orphans, intelligent, passionate, have a sharp tongue, are prone to jealousy, and die early deaths. Aroma mirrors Bao-chai in that both are eminently practical, modest, traditional, and rational in their thinking. In addition, the servants of the disreputable members of the Jia family, like Lady Xue, Jia Lian, Jia She, and Cousin Zhen, reflect their bad behavior, thereby reinforcing the novel's theme of the family's avid corruption and widespread moral decline. But several well-intended maids also correct or provide balance to their masters' or mistresses' behavior. Aroma provides checks on Bao-yu's misbehavior; Patience helps minimize Xi-feng's autocratic manner. Faithful is protective of Grandmother Jia, and Nightingale on occasion provides comfort to a sensitive and moody Dai-yu. Furthermore, maids and servants also function as facilitators, providing important information that helps advance the plot and as explicators explaining or commenting on what occurs and giving insight on actions or the thinking of other characters (Wagner, 265).

Finally, Marsha L. Wagner has observed that perhaps Cao Xueqin's greatest accomplishment in his depiction of these characters lies in his emphatic understanding of their precarious status. She perceptively writes, "It has often been pointed out that in the traditional Chinese view, individuality must be defined in terms of relationships to others within the social context. However, perhaps since in Cao Xueqin's own experience the social order was profoundly insecure, the individual in *Honglou meng* is often portrayed as out of place or searching for position, and this is particularly true of members of the lower ranks. The novel brilliantly depicts the poignant sufferings of characters who lack a reliable, supportive social community … it is no accident that the two maids who are best developed as individuals, Aroma and Skybright, are seen in their own family environments outside the social context of the Jia household. Indeed, most of the servants in the novel act in some way which implies a questioning of social conventions, whether through suicide, religiosity, flagrantly immoral behavior, outspoken criticism, or direct revenge" (280). Their tenuous status is also shown by the fact that they could very easily be dismissed if they run afoul of their masters or mistresses, as shown by what happened to Golden,

Skybright, and Chess. And if they had the misfortune to work for a family who ran into trouble with the government, like the Jias, they could legally be taken away and sold, as occurred with Jia She and Lady Xue's servants after the Embroidered Jacket raid.

FURTHER READING

Lupke, Christopher. "The Capillaries of Power: Hierarchy and Servitude in *The Story of the Stone*." *Approaches to Teaching Cao Xueqin's* Dream of the Red Chamber. Edited by Andrew Schonebaum and Tina Liu (New York: Modern Language Association of America, 2012): 283–295.

Wagner, Marsha L. "Maids and Servants in *Dream of the Red Chamber*: Individuality and the Social Other." In *Expressions of Self in Chinese Literature*. Edited by Robert E. Hegel and Richard C. Hessney (New York: Columbia University Press, 1985): 251–281.

Manchu Salute

A form of greeting used by the Manchus that involves dropping to one's right knee and touching a hand to the ground. Because the Jia family are imperial bondservants, the novel shows them sometimes using this salute. Jia Rong uses it to greet Xi-feng in chapter 6, and a buyer in chapter 8 greets Bao-yu using it. Moreover, the senior members of the Jia family kneel in Manchu style when they receive imperial messages.

See also **Bondservants**

Mandarin's Life Preserver

A secret list, mentioned in chapter 4, of the most powerful families in the province where Jia Yu-cun is magistrate. It is written in doggerel verse and informs the reader early in the novel of the power and affluence of the Xue and Wang families and also reveals that they are not to be trifled with legally. While Yu-cun is initially hesitant about letting it influence his decision regarding the murder charge against Xue Pan, he quickly understands the importance of the list and, in cahoots with the court usher, is able to prevent Pan from being prosecuted for the murder of Feng Yuan.

Marriage

During Cao Xueqin's time, marriage in China was primarily seen as a union between different families and not something that was determined by the couple's own wishes and affection for each other. It was considered the most important contractual agreement in Chinese society and, along with funerals, was the most significant life cycle ritual. Generally speaking, families chose brides from other families who were comparable to, but a bit lower than, their own social status. This was because it was believed that this helped ensure dutifulness in the bride, thereby creating a peaceful household. Upper-class families like the Jias would have chosen their brides from a selective pool of other well-established families. Factors like the social status and wealth of the family under consideration and the bride's character were of prime importance. Marriages enabled elite families to cement relationships, broadened their social and elite network, reinforced their image and status, and provided them with added security in times of trouble. There were specific and strict rules governing all aspects of the marriage process, including the selection of the bride, the use of fortune tellers, the behavior of the couple and their families before the marriage, the marriage itself, and the obligatory visit to the bride's family after the nuptials.

Dream of the Red Chamber provides a good overview of how this process worked in an upper-class family. In the initial phase, prospective partners would be offered and discussed by family members, friends, matchmakers, and even religious figures (as Abbott Zhang does about Bao-yu). When the couple has reached the acceptable age for marriage (most people during this period were engaged and married in their late teens), potential candidates were narrowed down, and usually the parents of the groom, in consultation with seniors in the family, would take the initiative with the help of a matchmaker. Discreet inquiries would be made about the candidate, and, if they were satisfactory, the matchmaker would negotiate the amount of bridal money and the type of gifts to be given to the bride's family, as occurs in Xing Xiu-yan's and Xue Ke's case in chapter 57. From the time of the engagement until the marriage ceremony itself, the couple would not be allowed to see each other and also, theoretically, had to shun all contact with their future in-laws and even their domestic staff. Bao-chai follows this rule much to Bao-yu's confusion because he is unaware that he is secretly engaged to her. Moreover, he is perplexed as to why Lady Xue is cold to him, for she is also appropriately obeying the rule. The next step in the process, as shown in chapter 97, was to bring in a fortune teller who would gather astrological information on the bride and groom, draw up a comparison horoscope using the Stem and Branches method to calculate birth dates, and create a bridal card. Then, based on the almanac, an auspicious day would be chosen for the bridal gifts to be delivered to the bride's family to formally complete the engagement process. Bao-chai's gifts included gold jewelry, 120 bolts of silk, and 120 garments. During these steps, ancestral sacrifices were usually made.

On the day of the marriage, the bride, who on this day would permanently move to the residence of her husband and his family, first paid deep "obeisance to her parents and ancestors, received a brief lecture on her wifely duties, and entered the gaudy red sedan chair that would take her on a noisy, ostentatious, and circuitous journey to her new husband's home. There, [she] performed various acts designed to show subservience to her husband and his family, and for the first time, perhaps—at least in most elite matches—the bride and groom actually saw each other's faces. After these ceremonies, the bridal pair reverently worshipped tablets representing Heaven and Earth, the ancestors of the groom, and the major household deities of the groom's family, especially the God of the Hearth. These activities highlighted the cosmological and familial dimensions of the match" (Smith, 357). The color red, which symbolized happiness, good luck, and prosperity, would be conspicuous in decorations, in the silk garments worn by the groom and bride, on lanterns, screens, and candles, and in the wedding chamber. The bride would wear a red veil over her face, which would be raised by her husband at the appropriate time. Fireworks would be set off, and the wedding procession would be accompanied by loud music. A large and sumptuous banquet would follow the ceremony, and longevity noodles, which symbolized martial harmony, would be eaten. The marriage of Bao-chai and Bao-yu had some special additions. Firstly, it followed court practice, which meant "a sedan chair with eight bearers and twelve pairs of lanterns" (DRM, 3: 228) were used to transport Bao-chai. Secondly, because the Jias were originally from the south, the southern custom of tossing dried fruit on the marriage bed was also observed.

In chapter 97, when it is brought to Grandmother Jia's attention that Dai-yu is ill because she is in love with Bao-yu, the matriarch heatedly exclaims, "Ours is a decent family. We do not tolerate unseemly goings-on. And that applies to foolish romantic attachments. If her illness is of a respectable nature, I do not mind how much we spend to get her better. But if she is suffering from some form of lovesickness, no amount of medicine will cure it and she can expect no further sympathy from me either" (SS, 4: 342–343); she is expressing a widely held belief of that time concerning not just love but also its place in marriage where factors like family interests usually trumped the personal feelings of the couple involved. As Anthony Yu has pointed out, Grandmother Jia, in her remarks, is reiterating "the venerated dogma that within the structure of familial authority, there is no place for 'private' or 'selfish' desire. In accord with the cultural ideas of long standing, her words maintain that the concerns of what the Chinese name as the larger, communal 'I' of family and the state must take precedence and priority over the solitary, little 'I'" (217). But it should also be noted that it was often thought during this period that in an arranged marriage a couple could, over time, develop strong affection and respect for each other, and evidence does indicate that this did occur for a sizeable number of couples.

Virtually all of the marriages that occur in *Dream of the Red Chamber* go against Confucian and social norms governing them and provide further proof of the Jia family's increasing moral corruption. Jia Lian's secret marriage to Er-jie in chapter 65, which took place with the approval of Cousin Zhen, violates important Confucian and governmental injunctions against nuptials being performed during a period of national and family mourning and without the permission of one's parents. The unsavory reason for Jia Ying-chun's ill-fated marriage to the tyrannical Mr. Sun is because Jia She owed the Sun family money. In addition, because Ying-chun comes from a prominent family, she should have received respect and consideration by the Sun family. The fact that she didn't and the Jia family failed to make any attempt to protect her other than to simply say, as Grandmother Jia does, that it was her fate and she just had to bear it because nothing could be done, is revealing. And finally, the marriage of Bao-yu and Bao-chai is based on an elaborate deception whose sole purpose is to turn his bad luck. He is cruelly led to believe that he is actually marrying Dai-yu, much to Bao-chai's embarrassment. Even Jia Zheng has deep reservations about the propriety of going through with the marriage. The ceremony itself is truncated, and there is a shabby feeling to the entire proceedings. Furthermore, in direct contrast to the event, and serving as an additional critique of it, are Dai-yu's dying as it occurs and one of her maids, who is close to Dai-yu, being pressured to leave her deathbed and attend the proceedings in an attempt to further fool Bao-yu. These three marriages effectively serve as a damning indictment of the senior members of the Jia family members' moral failings and their failure to properly follow Confucian and social norms regarding the institution.

FURTHER READING

Smith, Richard J. *The Qing Dynasty and Traditional Chinese Culture* (Lanham: Rowman & Littlefield, 2015).

Yu, Anthony. *Rereading the Stone: Desire and the Making of Fiction in* Dream of the Red Chamber (Princeton: Princeton University Press, 1997).

Medicine and the Problem of Doctors

One aspect of the novel that Western readers might find puzzling is the enormous amount of time that is spent discussing doctors and detailing the prescriptions given by them for the numerous maladies from which various characters suffer. There are several reasons for this attention. First, it contributes to the much-lauded realism of the novel. Chinese have traditionally long been interested in wellness and longevity as shown "not only in sexual practices and related therapeutic techniques (including Daoist 'inner alchemy'), but also in medical tracts, encyclopedias, almanacs, popular proverbs, religious practices, and secular symbolism" (Smith, 363). In spite of this interest, average life expectancy during the mid–Qing period China in the most prosperous region in the country, the southern lower Yangtze valley, where Cao Xueqin was born, was exceedingly low. For females at birth, it was 27.2 years, and for males at birth, 28.4 years. Childhood deaths were high. If a female was able to survive to the age of 10, her expectancy rate jumped to 41.1 years, for a male at the same age, it increased to 42.2 years (Smith, 365). Consequently, there was constant concern with the health of individuals, especially females. As the novel shows, there was a wide variety of types of doctors who used differing methods to treat patients. Some of these methods were text and theory based and mainly used herbal medicines, others employed acupressure and acupuncture, a few relied on folk remedies and massages, and there were doctors who employed the religious practices of exorcism and Shamanism. The orthodox approach, which is utilized in virtually all of the cases in *Dream of the Red Chamber*, relied upon the diagnostic technique of carefully "reading" a patient's pulses. This involved the doctor placing three of his fingers over three sections of the radial artery of the sick individual's wrist and determining the rate, depth, and quality of their pulse. A good pulse (there are 29 different ones) is regular, calm, smooth, and "soft" which indicated good *qi* and blood. In addition, as the story makes plain, because women at home were segregated from outside males, when doctors examined them, they were allowed only to see their lower arm in order to take their pulse, and the rest of the woman's body was hidden from sight. (This rule results in several serious medical misdiagnoses in the novel.)

The purpose of traditional Chinese medications was to restore the balance of the Five Elements and *yin* and *yang*, which sustain human life, in the sick person's body. While the Qing period had many famous and gifted doctors, "the vast majority of individuals who practiced the medical arts in China were low-status individuals, 'artisans' who were viewed by Chinese society as mere technicians. To the degree that they were well educated, they might enjoy considerable status, but their occupation itself was not socially esteemed. In this respect, doctors were like fortune tellers.... Doctors and fortune tellers embraced the same cosmological principles and used several of the same evaluative techniques with their clients" (Smith, 364). Consequently, it was difficult at times for people to find competent medical practitioners. The fact that, on several occasions, an elite and prosperous family like the Jias had problems locating capable doctors (while they had a family physician, Dr. Wang, who was also a court physician, he was not always available because he also served in the imperial army) and that several of the ones they did find were criminally incompetent, is telling. For example, the physician who treats Skybright thinks she is male and, as a result, prescribes dangerously strong medicine for her cold. Qin-shi's early doctors do not properly diagnose her illness, and, when a competent doctor is finally found, it is too late. Er-jie's physician does not realize that she is pregnant and gives her medicine that results in a miscarriage. Another glaring case of medical incompetence occurs when Lady Xue's brother Wang Zi-teng dies traveling to Beijing after a doctor gives him the wrong medicine.

The story's detailed descriptions of the specific types of illnesses of certain female characters also have symbolic meaning and divulge aspects of their personalities. For example, Xi-feng's protracted illness, which resulted in a constant loss of blood, represents the Jia family's increasingly hemorrhaging economic situation and lack of morality. Traditional Chinese medicine holds that there is a strong causal relationship between an individual's bodily and emotional states. This belief can be seen in the way the illnesses of females are portrayed in *Dream of the Red Chamber*. In it, the reason for most of their sickness is "emotion-desire (*qing*), and absence and loss enhance the affective power of *qing*.... Dai-yu, Caltrop, Qin-shi, Skybright, and Xi-feng all suffer from a wasting disease brought on by unrestrained *qing*, desire. Each manifests the symptom set of a consumptive who suffers from passion, grief, worry, or ambition.... They die of fatigue and taxation, according to their debts to *karma* or their debts to each other. Their earthly retribution is still *karmic*, since being put on earth to suffer is part of the grand design to teach the lesson of detachment from human emotion and the suffering it causes" (Schonebaum, 2012, 173, 184). It has been argued that several of the medical treatment and diagnosis sections of the story (especially those relating to Dai-yu in chapter 83) serve as foreshadowing devices that predict a tragic ending to the Dai-yu, Bao-chai, and Bao-yu love triangle because they "correlate references to the *yin-yang* and the Five Elements in Dai-yu's diagnosis and treatment with the archetypal relations between [her and them]" (Yim, 93). Finally, there is no doubt that Cao Xueqin had a considerable and impressive knowledge of medicine for modern physicians have attested to the accuracy of the medical prescriptions in the novel. In fact, Andrew Schonebaum has persuasively demonstrated that *Honglou meng* can be viewed as a medical casebook, albeit one in which most of the patients are female. He writes, the "novel acts as an encyclopedia and can be used to diagnose character types based on symptom sets and illness based on character traits ... [it] presents selected cases as examples of illnesses that can be avoided by the reader and explicitly posited itself as literati medicine and implicitly as warning of the dangers of repressed desire. In doing so, it reproduced fabricated medical realities found in doctor's casebooks" (2005, 229, 241).

See also **Five Elements, Melancholy and Sleep, Qing, Yin and Yang**

FURTHER READING

Schoenbaum, Andrew. "The Medical Casebook of *Hong Lou Meng*." *Tamkang Review* 36:1–2 (2005): 229–250.

———. "Medicine in *The Story of the Stone*: Four Cases." *Approaches to Teaching Cao Xueqin's* Dream of the Red Chamber. Edited by Andrew Schonebaum and Tina Liu (New York: Modern Language Association of America, 2012): 164–185.

Smith, Richard J. *The Qing Dynasty and Traditional Chinese Culture* (Lanham: Rowman & Littlefield, 2015).

Yim, Chi-hung. "The 'Deficiency of Yin in the Liver'—Dai-yu's Malady and Fubi in *Dream of the Red Chamber*." *Chinese Literature: Essays, Articles, Reviews* 22 (2000): 85–111.

Melancholy and Sleep

The topics of melancholy and sleep are not commonly associated with nor discussed concerning *Dream of the Red Chamber*. But both are linked with a subject that does figure prominently in the novel and that Cao Xueqin personally suffered from: depression. When taken as a whole, in spite of the memorable scenes of excited poetry club meetings, happy family gatherings, delectable meals, lazy, carefree summer days in Prospect Garden and the novel's luxurious settings, the story is full of blasted hopes, fits of despair, debilitating and recurring illnesses (often depression related), tragic love affairs, troubling visits to another world, sexual improprieties, a case of insanity (Bao-yu is described as mad on two occasions), suicides, sudden deaths, murder, and deep and widespread anxieties about the future. Moreover, its main plot concerns the protagonist's long and anguished quest for meaning, and coloring everything is the economic and moral decline of a once illustrious family. So it comes as no surprise that melancholy and depression are widespread among the story's characters. Victor Mair has found 736 sleep-related references attesting, "some word for resting in bed or sleeping occurs, on the average, on more than half of the pages of the book" (1). This number is unprecedented in Chinese narrative fiction and indicates that Cao Xueqin must have had some special reasons for this large number of references to sleep.

Mair claims the main purpose was to illustrate Cao's belief that sleep was the best remedy for the widespread depression in the novel: "The bed is seen as the best location to avoid others and 'sleep' is thought of as the most efficacious and readily available ointment for salving one's spiritual wounds" (19). Andrew Schoenbaum, expanding upon Cao Xueqin's focus on depression, has contended that *Honglou meng* was intended to be "both preventive medicine and palliative. It serves as a guidebook for identifying dangerous behaviors and extremes of emotion, also removes the reader from his melancholy by engrossing him in a finely wrought work of fiction. It warns against the sort of excessive longing that can result in the loss of *yang* essence if matters are taken into the reader's own hands and describes the dangers of excessive female emotion and desire that results in depression" (187). In addition, Schoenbaum argues that Cao also wanted to cure the reader of depression and illnesses related to it through the use of what he calls "emotional counter-therapy," which he defines as "The treatment of the ills brought on by excess of one emotion by bringing on its opposite emotion" (187). In short, Schoenbaum believes that by presenting examples of excessive melancholy and desire, the novel warns the reader about the effect of these emotions on the body while at the same time making them forget their own troubles.

See also **Medicine and the Problem of Doctors**

FURTHER READING

Mair, Victor H. "Sleep in Dream: Soporific Responses to Depression in *Story of the Stone*." *Sino-Platonic Papers* 143 (July 2004): 99 pages.
Schonebaum, Andrew. "For the Relief of Melancholy: The Early Chinese Novel as Antidepressant." In *Depression and Narratives Telling the Dark*. Edited by Hilary Clark (Albany: Suny Press, 2008): 179–194.

Mencius 孟子 (c. 372–289 bc)

The most important Confucian philosopher after Confucius. The influential book *Mencius* is his teachings as collected by his followers. It is one of the classic Four Books of Confucian thought. Mencius famously believed that human nature is essentially good. He maintained that benevolence and wisdom did not originate from the outside but in man initially and that evil would vanish if people reclaimed their authentic internal goodness and followed their original child heart. Mencius also contended that governments needed to model their policies on the compassionate leadership of the Zhou dynasty. Like Confucius, his philosophy was highly ethical, focused more on the individual than the state, and stressed the centrality of filial piety. Jia Zheng and Bao-yu, in chapter 84, discuss a quotation from *Mencius* regarding the power of good breeding and culture. In chapter 118, Bao-yu and Bao-chai debate the meaning of Mencius's phrase "the heart of a newborn babe," with Bao-chai defending Mencius and Bao-yu countering with a Daoist critique.

See also **Confucianism**

Mirrors

Mirrors have traditionally symbolized the mind in China. In Chinese literature, mirrors have been used for a number of purposes. They have served "as means for the investigation of the self and of others, and for the representation of love and death. [Mirrors] can also symbolize self-knowledge and self-deception, the world that appears to us or the world beyond" (Motsch, 117). In *Dream of the Red Chamber*, mirrors are employed for several reasons. Chapter 1 mentions that an alternative title for the novel was *A Mirror for the Romantic*, which is the name of the Daoist mirror given to Jia Rui by the monk in chapter 12 in an unsuccessful attempt to cure him of his lovesickness. This mirror was created by the Fairy Disenchantment to counter the effects of lust. Various theories have been offered to explain the meaning of this famous episode. Monika Motsch has argued, it "assumes the role of a prologue which symbolically foreshadows developments in the plot: Thus, Bao-yu enters the Mirror of Sensuousness, so that later, through the death of Lin Dai-yu and ruin of his family, he should learn to know the reverse side of the mirror and become a monk" (120). The Qing dynasty commentator Red Inkstone has claimed that it is intended to warn the reader about reading only the surface appearance of the novel and ignoring its underlying meaning. Bao-yu is also strongly linked in the story with mirrors. He collects them (chapter 57), writes a poem that references them (23), composes a riddle whose subject is a mirror (22), has a dream about his double Zhen Bao-yu that Aroma claims was caused by a mirror (56), and alludes to a mirror while singing a song during a drinking party (28). Moreover, his residence famously has a mirror door that opens to his bedroom (26, 41). When he has his celebrated dream in Qin-shi's bedroom, an antique mirror that once belonged to Empress Wu Ze-tian is on a table in the room (5), and a monk shines a mirror in his face during his second visit to the Land of Illusion (116). It has also been maintained that mirrors represent Bao-yu's divided self, contradictory nature, or his quest for self-knowledge. Some critics have taken this association to have Buddhist and Daoist import since mirrors have a special symbolic importance in both philosophies. In Buddhism, a mirror is a metaphor for the mind whose purity must be kept "wiped, clean, and polished" through meditation and Buddhist practices so as not to be darkened by desire, passions, or attachments. In Daoism, mirrors also stand for the mind. According to the philosopher Zhuangzi, the perfect man uses his mind like a mirror: he goes after nothing, welcomes nothing, and responds to things but does retain them.

See also **Monkey**

FURTHER READING

Motsch, Monika. "The Mirror, and Chinese Aesthetics: A Study of *Honglou meng*." *Ming Qing yanjiu* (1996): 117–136.

Missing Bracelet

In chapter 52, Patience's shrimp whisker bracelet is stolen. The bracelet was given to her by Xi-feng. It is quickly discovered that the culprit was Bao-yu's junior maid Trinket, who is summarily dismissed. Mary Scott has observed that this seemingly small incident is designed to highlight the numerous thefts and disappearances that have appeared prior to this one. She argues that they are emblematic of "the breakdown of authority in the household. It all started innocently enough with the loss of a pearl from Bao-yu's hair-clasp in chapter 21, which Xiang-yun notices as she helps him braid his hair, and the maid Crimson's lost handkerchief in chapter 24, which is finally returned to her, in chapter 37 a misplaced agate dish is eventually located and returned. But the series continues with the theft of Patience's shrimp whiskered bracelet, in the course of which it is mentioned that some jade has been stolen several years earlier. At this point the thefts begin to turn ominous. The thief turns out to be Trinket, the little maid who returned Crimson's handkerchief as a token of Jia Yun's love" (107). And this will not be the end of the thievery, for even graver acts of theft will occur later in the story. Ying-chun will have items stolen by her nannie to cover her gambling debts; controversy will erupt over the missing bottle of Essence of Roses; many of Grandmother Jia's possessions will be stolen by a group of thieves; Bao-yu's jade will be taken by a monk; and Adamantina will be kidnapped.

Further Reading

Scott, Mary Elizabeth. "Azure to Indigo: *Honglou meng's* Debt to *Jing P'ing mei*." PhD Thesis. Princeton University, 1989.

Money and Measurements

It has been estimated that the word money, *qian*, is mentioned in *Honglou meng* 544 times. Cao Xueqin was obviously concerned with illustrating the cost and value of things in order to show the affluence and corruption as well as rampant spending habits of the Jia family and their resulting economic decline. In terms of raw currency numbers, one tael at that time was roughly equal to one Chinese ounce, or 1.208 English ounces, of pure silver. It was also equivalent to 1,000 copper cash. To put these numbers in practical terms in relation to the novel, the following examples are informative. Xi-feng earned a profit of 1,000 taels a year loaning money out (chapter 39). The Jia family's four senior maids receive one tael a month; junior maids earn 500 in copper cash; and Aroma gets one tael and a string of cash, which is later increased to two taels (36). Lady Wang is allotted a personal allowance of 20 taels a month. Aunt Zhao and Aunt Xue are paid one tael a month, and Aunt Zhou is given an additional tael because of Jia Huan (36). In chapter 65, 15 taels are given for Er-jie's expenses. The cost of holding social events, parties, and ceremonies is quite high. In chapter 43, more than 150 taels are collected for Xi-feng's birthday, and the cassia viewing party in chapter 39 costs 20 taels. In chapter 50, 50 taels are collected for a future snow party, and nine to ten taels are outlaid for the snow-viewing party in chapter 49. Several thousand taels are spent on Grandmother Jia's birthday celebration (72). And Jia Jing's funeral costs 1,110 taels; Lady Jia's funeral puts the family in debt for four to 5,000 taels; and 50 taels is given to Aroma for her mother's funeral expenses (54). There are also some revealing additional costs. These include Jia She's purchase of a concubine for 500 taels (47), Jia Lian paying the family of Bao Er's wife 200 taels after her suicide so they don't create problems (44), and Lady Wang giving Golden's family 50 taels after her suicide (32). The novel also mentions the costs associated with bribing officials and others. In chapter 68, 200 taels are allocated to bribe the censor (notwithstanding the vast sums of money the Xue family paid judges so that they will make a favorable ruling about Xue Pan's case). Twenty taels are paid to Er-jie's fiancé to break off her engagement. Xi-feng charges a family 3,000 taels for her to break a marriage contract (15), and in chapter 13, Jia Zhen happily pays 1,000 taels to a eunuch for Jia Rong to be appointed a captain in the Imperial Guards. In addition, Aunt Zhou agrees to pay Mother Ma 500 taels to place a curse on Bao-yu and Xi-feng. Concerning food prices, the hen eggs Grannie Liu is given as a joke in chapter 40 cost one tael each, while Cook Liu complains in chapter 61 about the scarcity of chicken eggs, saying that hen eggs cost ten cash.

When it comes to large incomes and expenses, Zhou Rui, the bailiff in charge of the Jia family's farms in chapter 53, notifies Cousin Zhen that 400,000 taels passes through his hands every year. Because of the confiscation, Xi-feng loses 30,000 taels of her savings, and she and Jia Lian also have an additional 60,000 taels confiscated (106). The biggest expense for the family is the construction of Prospect Garden, which totaled 50,000 taels. To put all these numbers in perspective, Grannie Liu states in chapter 39 that just 20 taels would sustain a farmer's family for one year. (In 1700, the yearly income of a farmer was around five taels). Gerald Brown has argued that Cao Xueqin purposely inflated many of these prices and values, particularly in the last 40 chapters, in order to underscore the sharp fall of the Jia family and to provide a warning about the failure to understand the real value of money (805, 806).

There is also a special form of money, spirit money (also known as joss paper), mentioned in chapter 58. This money was burned as offerings during ancestral worship ceremonies during holidays or special occasions. In this chapter, the actress Nenuphar burns some gold paper spirit money in memory of her dear friend Pivoine, who had died. This gets her in trouble because she does it in Prospect Garden, which is considered an improper place to do this. Bao-yu castigates her and tells her that she should never use this paper again, that it was a foolish superstition and that if she wanted to honor her friend, she should instead reverently light some incense in a burner, put out some water or tea and flowers or fruit. In terms of measurements that are used in the novel: for weight: one tael equals one and a third ounces which equals 37.783 grams, and for distance: one *li* equals a third of a mile.

FURTHER READING

Brown, Gerald Tristan. "The Metaphorical Dimensions of Symbolic Prices and Real World Values in *Honglou meng*." *Tsing Hua Journal of Chinese Studies, New Series*, 41.4 (2011): 795–812.

Monkey

The monkey is viewed by Chinese as a smart, powerful, flexible, brave, and mischievous animal and a protective God. It is also the ninth sign in the Chinese horoscope. Buddhism, which regards the monkey as both a wise and rash animal, uses a host of monkey metaphors to describe people's "monkey mind"—the flighty, psychologically unnerving, false, and restless nature of human consciousness. Bao-yu is directly associated with this animal. In chapter 22, his behavior during a lantern riddle party is compared to that of a captive monkey that has been let loose. In chapter 73, he compares himself to Monkey, a famous character in the celebrated Chinese novel *Journey to the West*. And in chapter 50, Bao-yu correctly guesses the answer to a riddle about a performing monkey. These references were clearly employed by Cao Xueqin to show the unsettled and agitated nature of Bao-yu's "monkey mind." The image of a monkey is also used to foretell the fall of the Jia family. Qin-shi's ghost visits Xi-feng in her bedroom one night to warn her: "Our house has prospered for nearly a hundred years. If one day it happens that at the height of good fortune the 'tree falls and the monkeys scatter,' as the old saying has it, then what becomes of our cultured old family?" (DRM, 1: 174).

Monks, Nuns, and Temples

There are 15 clerics in the novel, and they are one of two types: archetypal immortals and regular members of monasteries. The former traditionally represent and impose order, righteousness, and moral justice. Customarily, they are depicted as being ugly in appearance and eccentric in manner, and a contrast is drawn between these qualities and their sagacity and transcendental wisdom. In *Dream of the Red Chamber*, they are described as being deformed, lame, scabby-headed, dirty, quirky, loud, and even mad. They offer cures (for lovesickness and the effects of witchcraft), instruct, and embody or are vehicles for enlightenment. But they also differ from traditional immortals. As Robert Hegel has observed, although the Daoist and the monk who frame the story in the first chapter "maintain a kind of order: they punish Bao-yu for his attachment by 'sentencing' him to a life in the Red Dust of mortal existence. Yet once his initial attachment is conceived in innocence and is essentially selfless, this result seems unjust, as inappropriate for its sorrowful consequences.... That the Buddhist and Taoist figures of *Honglou meng*'s celestial realm are only agents of inscrutable destiny and not acting in their own right further problematizes the moral uprightness of that higher order" (159).

On the other hand, virtually all of the regular clerics associated with temples, both monks and nuns, are depicted in a highly negative fashion and are shown to be corrupt, sexually promiscuous, unspiritual, snobbish, and rapacious. Examples of these types of misbehavior include: One Plaster Wang conning people with his medications, the prioress Jingxu of the Water-moon Priory bribing Xi-feng to break up an engagement, the nun Sapientia carrying on a secret affair with Qin Zhong, and the young nuns of the Priory flirting and drinking with Jia Qin. There are 13 temples mentioned in the novel. Yiqun Zhou has argued that there is a significant difference between those that were founded by the Jia family and those that were not, noting, "Three of the private temples—Temple of the Iron Threshold, Water-moon Priory, and Convent of the Savior King—and the other temples patronized by the Jias have much in common. They readily become stages where the author displays a variety of monastic vices. In fact, because the private temples play a more important role in the Jia's social and ritual activities than do those temples not founded by the family, they provide the setting not only for the fullest revelations of conventional clerical vices but for various family members to engage in morally and ritually questionable behavior" (269).

It was a widely held belief at that time, which is reflected in traditional Chinese literary works, that clerics were in general greedy, lascivious, parasitic, and untrustworthy individuals. Therefore, it was considered shocking if persons became monks or nuns, especially if they came from an upper-class family. Moreover, if the person were male, like Bao-yu, it was thought to be highly objectionable because he would then be unable to perform his Confucian and familial responsibilities. (This view can be seen in Aroma's anguished remark to Bao-yu in chapter 120: "I suppose you think this is enlightenment. But what sort of enlightenment is it for you to abandon your own wife?" [SS, 5: 358].) Critics have often argued that Cao Xueqin's anti-clerical attitude in the story is directed at the crooked, self-serving, and profane way in which religion was practiced by clerics, and the institutions that supported them, and not against Buddhist or Daoist doctrine or philosophical tradition. Zhou finds this point too simple, contending that Cao was also critiquing the foolish nature of some popularly held religious concepts. She writes that the novel "as a whole hangs in the balance between anti-clericalism and the pursuit of enlightenment, but Cao Xueqin does so while grappling with the role of *qing* in human lives…. By casting the Land of Illusion and its earthy projection in the image of a splendid temple [the main reception hall in Prospect Garden], the author intimates that, after all, religion provides the ultimate framework with which to conceptualize the relationship between illusion and truth, and between passion and enlightenment, and that a religious edifice furnishes the most appropriate site for the planning and enactment of a human drama centered on the entanglement of *qing*" (309, 308).

It should be mentioned, as the novel shows, that temples in China during this time were not only places of worship but also served a wide variety of social functions. They were places to exchange gossip, enjoy entertainments like dramas, and were venues for popular fairs where books and crafts and other items were sold. Temples were also used to display art and provided locations for poetry and discussion clubs, and some even operated libraries. Finally, as shown on several occasions in the story, they also were used as lodging.

See also **Adamantina, Qing**

FURTHER READING

Hegel, Robert. "Unpredictability and Meaning in Mid-Qing Literati Novels." In *Paradoxes of Traditional Chinese Literature*. Edited by Eva Hung (Hong Kong: The Chinese University Press, 1994): 147–166.
Zhou, Yiqun. "Temples and Clerics in *Honglou meng*." *Harvard Journal of Asiatic Studies* 71.2 (2011): 263–309.

Moon Cake

A delicious small cake that is eaten during the Chinese Mid–Autumn festival, an occasion for moon watching and family gatherings. It is traditionally made in a round shape to represent a full moon and is composed of wheat flour, fat or oil, maltose, and sugar. Numerous ingredients are used for the stuffing, including lotus seed paste, fruits, pine nuts, almond, and sweet bean paste. Chapter 75 has a scene that gives the novel a nice bit of conversational realism. In it, Grandmother Jia discusses with Jia Zhen the quality of that year's moon cakes, which were made by a new pastry chef. They both agree that they are good.

Mother Ma 马道婆

Bao-yu's duplicitous and greedy godmother. She is a Buddhist priestess (according to the Yang translation) and ostensibly has used her spiritual powers to protect him since infancy. She is also a secret practitioner of black magic and is not afraid to use her powers, even for monetary gain. Ma makes her appearance in chapter 25, where she persuades Grandmother Jia to purchase five pounds of sesame oil a day to be burned as an offering to the Bodhisattva (a being who is worshipped as a God but has not yet reached Nirvana, so they can help others) of Universal Light so that Bao-yu will be shielded from devils and other evil spirits. During her spiel to the matriarch, she gives a detailed description of invisible imps that make trouble for the children of rich families. The noted commentator Red Inkstone has remarked that Cao Xueqin had personally experienced this type of illogical and unethical babble himself and that Ma's story is not entirely fictional. After visiting with Grandmother Jia, Ma meets other members of the family, including Aunt Zhao, who tells her that she wants Ma to use her black magic to kill her sworn enemies Xi-feng and Bao-yu. Ma eventually agrees and gives her 12 paper cutouts of figures to be placed under each of the two's beds after Zhao gives her a promissory note for 500 taels. Zhao places the figures, and Xi-feng and Bao-yu are soon struck with life-threatening illnesses caused by demons, but a monk suddenly appears and uses Bao-yu's jade to save them. The next year, Ma is arrested by the secret police for practicing her dark arts and is sentenced to death. It is discovered that she has been employing her witchcraft for several noted families. Grandmother Jia and others then realize that Ma had caused Bao-yu and Xi-feng to be possessed. They also conclude that Zhao was probably also involved in the plot, but, fearing a public scandal and lacking hard evidence against her, they decide to be patient and wait for Zhao to show her true colors. Red Inkstone has written that Cao Xueqin's purpose in depicting Mother Ma was to warn readers about the dangers associated with allowing religious professionals into a person's house, to stress the importance of being on one's guard against them and to describe how hard it is to keep them away once they have entered.

Mourning Periods

Filial piety and ancestor worship were traditionally considered central Chinese values, and there were precise and involved Confucian rituals and practices governing how they should be expressed. This was especially true when a family member died, because Confucius believed that proper mourning was the most sacred of all ritual obligations. In Imperial China, there were specific Confucian ritual responsibilities called the Five Degrees of Mourning that members of the deceased's family, regardless of their status in society, were expected to observe. These determined the duration and degree of their mourning depending upon their relationship to the deceased. Among these obligations were that a man was required to mourn the death of his parents for three years (the length of time it took to wean a child) and for his grandparent a year or less. This meant he could not marry or attend weddings during this time, take examinations, or participate in communal festivals. Government officials were given extensive leaves during this period, offerings were regularly offered at the grave, and anniversaries of the deceased's death were also observed. In addition, there were national mourning periods when members of the imperial family died, as shown in the novel. The failure to follow these rules was considered a serious transgression. The sordidness and moral decline of the Jia family can be seen in the chronic failure by male members of the family to follow these responsibilities concerning mourning periods. Cousin's Zhen's and Jia Rong's support of Jia Lian's secret marriage to Er-jie and the marriage itself were formally illegal because the two were supposed to be observing the mourning periods for their father and grandfather Jia Jing, respectively. Moreover, their inability to display proper emotions while publicly mourning and behave appropriately in a public setting in chapter 64 is particularly revealing, as is Jia Rong's crude behavior soon after with the You sisters and their maid in chapter 63. Later, in chapter 71, Cousin Zhen, finding the ban on amusements during the mourning period bothersome, comes up with a plan to use archery (which was not banned) as an excuse to set up a gambling establishment at the residence. Finally, all of these violations occur during a period of state mourning because of the death of the Imperial Concubine Zhou, which makes Jia Lian's marriage to Er-jie even more problematic.

Naming System

The names of characters, places, and objects have special importance in *Honglou meng*. The commentator Red Inkstone was the first person to point out this significance. Michael Yang, who has extensively studied the novel's elaborate naming system, has written, "The various names, which often assume allegorical or symbolic significance, shed light on the theme, plot, setting, objects, and characters greatly reinforcing the meaning inherent in the work.... Because of the special nature of the Chinese language, which abounds in homonyms, many names are polysemous through the association of homonyms or near-homonyms, and utilized in a great variety of ways to illuminate various aspects of the novel" (69, 70). Names are frequently used ironically or to show their opposite meaning in an effort to get readers to read critically and between the lines and to reinforce the novel's theme of the difficulty of making distinctions between appearance and illusion and reality and truth. They also explicitly disclose the true nature of certain characters. For example, the names of Jia Zheng's literary gentlemen connote their parasitic natures: Zhan Guan ("Taking Advantage Of"), San Pingren ("Good at Deceiving People"), Cheng Rixing ("Having Fun Everyday"), Hu Si-lai ("Doing Crazy Things"), and Bu Guxiu ("Having No Sense of Shame") (Yang, 95). Names can also show individuals' jobs. In chapter 90 women are picked to take care of Prospect Garden, and their names suggest their duties: Zhu Ma ("The Caring of a Bamboo Grove"), Tian Ma ("The Caring of a Rice Field"), and Ye Ma ("The Caring of a Flower Garden") (Yang, 90). Yang also notes that the novel's names are used to criticize or comment on aspects of Chinese society, like the custom that widows (like Li Wan) should not remarry. Attempts have been made in this guide, when possible, to explain the meaning or connotation of character's names and some place names.

FURTHER READING

Yang, Michael. "Naming in *Honglou-meng*." *Chinese Literature: Essays, Articles, Reviews* 18 (1996): 69–101.

Narration

The way *Honglou meng* is narrated differs from other works of traditional Chinese vernacular fiction. In them, the narrator often intrudes in the story and gives the reader tips, summaries, predictions, or detailed remarks on plot developments, characters, and themes. In Cao Xueqin's novel, this role has been expanded to include various individuals in the story. Among these are supernatural beings who possess information about the future, like the Fairy Disenchantment, the scabby monk, the lame Daoist, and enlightened persons like Zhen Shi-yin. They also include outsiders, like Leng Zi-xing and Grannie Liu, and even minor characters like Xue Ke and Bao-qin, who tell the reader what to think about specific characters or stumble upon meanings that others have not seen (Rolston, 344). When the narrator does make comments in the novel, it is about practical matters, the writing and transmission of the text, and narrative details. When central characters are discussed, for example, in chapters 3 and 17 about Bao-yu, the narrator's remarks are frequently ironic or not clear (Rolston, 347). In addition, Cao Xueqin also requires readers to be active and critical readers and to discern meaning through a sophisticated system of foreshadowing devices that includes dramas, songs, dreams, drinking games, poems, Buddhist and Daoist allegories, riddles, names, literary allusions, and casual remarks made by characters, and to read between the lines.

See also **Foreshadowing**

FURTHER READING

Rolston, David L. "Everything at Once: The '*Honglou meng*.'" In *Traditional Chinese Fiction and Fiction Commentary: Reading and Writing Between the Lines* (Stanford: Stanford University Press, 1997): 329–348.

Narrative Patterns and Techniques

Cao Xueqin uses a diverse array of narrative patterns and techniques to organize and communicate the novel's plot. Many of them have long been employed in traditional Chinese literature, but he also uses some of them in new ways. The following are 12 of the most important of these patterns and techniques. (1) Formulaic narrative patterns, some of which "represent general cultural or social patterns of Chinese society. The author uses them to reflect and embody the mythic mode" (Miller, 278). These patterns include "male children spoiled through maternal love.... Inherited patrimony versus success in the Civil Service Examinations.... The ill-fated orphan.... Male inferiority, female superiority, and female decline.... The figure of enlightenment" (278, 289, 280, 281). (2) Red Inkstone, in his famous commentary on the novel, noted that the story uses more than 35 narrative techniques, many of which were influenced by the methods of painting. Three of the most commonly employed techniques that Red Inkstone mentions are these: (a) "laying down the thread," in which an outwardly innocent comment is made which is later expanded on and becomes a major scene. For example, in chapter 2, Jia Yu-cun states that he once tutored Zhen Bao-yu, and Leng Zi-xing makes the prediction that Yuan-chun would be made Imperial Concubine. Both of these remarks are more fully developed later in the novel. (b) The second method is what Red Inkstone calls "beating the grass to startle the snake," where "the author sometimes pretends to write about A when he really wants to describe B, as though trying to fool the reader." (c) The third is referred to as "The gray line of the grass snake," where a key image or symbol is repeated throughout the story for a special purpose or to create unity. For example, certain flowers are associated with female characters. Tan-chun is linked with a kite, Dai-yu with the moon, and Bao-yu with mirrors (Wang, 1978, 209–210). Another example of this technique occurs in chapter 3 when Dai-yu, after arriving at the Jia family mansion and meeting the female members of the family, goes to pay a visit to

Jia She. Red Inkstone comments that it is important for the reader to understand that this scene is really about Jia She and not Dai-yu (Wang, 1978, 210).

(3) The repetition, or repetition with variants, of certain major scenes or situations. Obvious examples of this are the two major funerals in the story, those of Qin-shi and Grandmother Jia, and the novel's numerous social occasions, such as birthday celebrations, drinking parties, and dramatic performances, especially the way they are portrayed early in the novel when they are used to show the power and affluence of the Jia family and later when they are utilized to illustrate the family's moral and economic decline. In these incidents, an ironic contrast is drawn between the initial and later replicated scenes and situations to stress the family's steep fall. In addition, there are also subtle repetitions of locations that are revealing. For instance, near Xi-feng's residence is a small enclosure surrounded by walls and buildings. Early in the novel, Jia Rui is forced to endure a cold and wet night when Xi-feng lays a trap for him for his unwanted advances. Later, in chapter 44, during her birthday celebration, Xi-feng receives her own comeuppance when she encounters a maid in this same place who informs her that Jia Lian is carrying on with another woman. Dai-yu comes across the maid Simple, who tells her that Bao-yu will marry Bao-chai in the same place where they had their famous flower burial scene and first read the play *The Western Chamber*. Red Inkstone and other commentators have written that repetition in *Dream of the Red Chamber* can also mean "either the exact repetition of a word or symbol, or repetition of similar situations or ideas" (Wang, 2005, 2). John Wang has argued that this type of repetition "is a conscious artistic device by which the author achieves a certain purpose: to make for unity, for example, to drive home a point; or to bring a person or a situation into sharper focus" (2). Wang also contends that repetition also greatly contributes to the overall artistic unity of the story: "Reading *Dream of the Red Chamber* is not unlike listening to a great symphony. The notes may sound disconnected, even discordant, in the beginning; but through the artful repetition with variations of some key notes gradually a discernable movement begins to appear. All the individual sounds in the piece begin to fall into place much like the many tributaries, at once different and similar, slowly but surely flowing to form a great full-bodied river that twists and turns on its way to an open sea" (14).

(4) Angelina Yee has maintained in a famous paper that the novel frequently uses the narrative procedure of counterpoise. "Many characters in *Honglou meng* are conceived in pairs, whether as opposites, doubles, or mutual complements. This is immediately obvious even to the most casual reader: the Buddhist monk and the Daoist priest.... Zhen Shi-yin and Jia Yu-cun, Dai-yu and Bao-chai.... Such coupling is not confined to the presentation of characters within particular scenes, but extends to the grouping of similar episodes such as parties, birthdays, and love affairs, in which various characters are juxtaposed, and events echo each other" (613). Yee contends that the technique of counterpoise enables characters to be illuminated by implication or refraction,

adds an underlying tension to, integrates, and livens up the plot and that the novel's many contrasts and comparisons "subtly shape an implicit system of values, wherein the individual characters find their place" (613). (5) The fundamental, cosmic, complementary, opposing, and interdependent principles of *yin* and *yang*, which Chinese at that time believed controlled all things in the world, are utilized in the story to illustrate the themes of the interconnection and the dialectical nature of the concepts of truth and falsity, illusion and reality, dreams and daily life, fortune and calamity, masculinity and femininity, and life and death. (6) Another narrative pattern that is employed is the contrasting levels of meaning in the story (especially in the initial chapters): allegorical, realistic, mythological, and philosophical. (7) The employment of puns in names of characters and places provides clues as to their real nature. (8) Outsiders, like Xue Bao-chai, Grannie Liu, and Dai-yu are often brought in to provide vital background information and to offer objective perspectives on Jia family members and events in the story.

(9) Cao Xueqin also places in the narrative a wide variety of foreshadowing devices like poems, dramas, riddles, and drinking games to foretell future events and the fate of individual characters. (10) Lucian Miller has claimed that the concept of "meaningful chance" also plays an important narrative role in the novel. He writes, "The concept of time in the novel involves the union of chance and predestination and the aesthetic pattern of the work may be understood in part in terms of synchronicity" (287). Instances of this include the love affair between Qin Zhong and the Buddhist nun, the violent conflict between Xue Pan and Feng Yuan, and Jia Bao-yu's meeting with Zhen Bao-yu. (11) The story's detailed descriptions of the appearance and layouts of the Jia family's mansions and Prospect Garden "set a procession of architectural images, a sort of movie presentation, before the reader. Through images, one understands. But such total immersion in architectural images also determines in part the reader's sense of narrative development. Thus, space not only forms the platform of the story, but it influences its very workings" (Li and Yeo, 52). (12) Finally, *Dream of the Red Chamber*, through its skillful use of irony, satire, the clash between surface meanings and real meanings, and emphasis on the importance of reading critically and between the lines, weaves a level of ambiguity into the text that encourages multiple interpretations. These narrative patterns and techniques contribute to the unification and comprehensive scope of the story, tightens its interconnected elements, and contributes to the novel's realism and open-text nature.

See also **Drenched Blossoms Bridge and Pavilion, Doubles, Foreshadowing, Naming System, Outsiders, Reading and Rereading, Themes and Indeterminacy, *Yin* and *Yang***

FURTHER READING

Li, Xiaodong, and Yeo Kang-shua. "The Propensity of Chinese Space: Architecture in the Novel *Dream of the Red Chamber.*" *Traditional Dwellings and Settlements Review* 13.2 (2002): 49–62.

Miller, Lucien. *Masks of Fiction in the* Dream of the Red Chamber: *Myth, Mimesis and Persona* (Tucson: University of Arizona Press, 1975).

Wang, John. C.Y. "The Chih-yen-chai Commentary and the *Dream of the Red Chamber*: A Literary Study." In *Chinese Approaches to Literature*. Edited by Adele Rickett (Princeton: Princeton University Press, 1978): 189–220.

———. "Redundancy as an Artistic Device in the *Dream of the Red Chamber*: A Preliminary Investigation." *Journal of Oriental Studies* 38: 1&2 (2005): 1–15.

Yee, Angelina. "Counterpoise in *Honglou meng*." *Harvard Journal of Asiatic Studies*. 50.2 (1990): 613–650.

Nightingale 紫鹃

Dai-yu's principal maid. She was previously a second-grade body servant for Grandmother Jia who gave her to Dai-yu when she first arrived. She becomes over time extremely loyal to Dai-yu. Fearful that Dai-yu would return to the south and she would have to leave her family, she foolishly tests Bao-yu in chapter 57, much to the ire of Grandmother Jia, by telling him that Dai-yu is going back to Soochow to be with her family, temporally plunging him into a form of dementia. Nightingale is one of the few people who is with Dai-yu when she dies. In chapter 113, while thinking over a conversation she has just had with Bao-yu, whom she initially blames for Dai-yu's death, she unknowingly stumbles on the origins of Dai-yu and Bao-yu when she ironically concludes that it is better to have "the destiny of plant or stone, bereft of knowledge and consciousness, but blessed at least with purity and peace of mind" (SS, 5: 255). As one critic has noted of this scene, "Unconscious as she is of her mistress's original nature, Nightingale has seen through the illusion of romantic attachment more clearly than any other member of Bao-yu's household, including his own wife, with the possible exception of his cousin Xi-chun" (Levy, 56–57). It is therefore not surprising that at the end of the novel Nightingale decides to become a nun and serve Xi-chun.

FURTHER READING

Levy, Dore. *Ideal and Actual in The Story of the Stone* (New York: Columbia University Press, 1999).

Nostalgia Studio

The name of the studio in chapter 1 where Cao Xueqin worked on the Stone's tale for ten years. He rewrote the story five times, divided it into chapters, came up with chapter titles, and added an introductory quatrain. He also changed the title of the story to *The Twelve Beauties of Jinling*. The Chinese name for this studio is Dao Hong Xuan, which means "mourning over the world of the Red Dust," which is one of the themes of the novel. Red Dust is a Buddhist word referring to the mortal, busy, and deluded human world, which is focused on worldly concerns and success.

Nuwa 女娲

Chinese goddess and creator of human beings, she is the younger sister and wife of the first of three legendary emperors, Emperor Fuxi. She is usually depicted as having the body of a serpent and a human head. Nuwa is famous for restoring order by mending the sky after it had been damaged by Gong Gong, the Water God, in a fit of anger after losing a fight with Zhurong, the Chinese God of Fire, over who could assume the throne of heaven. Gong Gong had struck his head against one of the pillars located at Mount Buzhou, which held up the sky, thereby causing the earth to tilt and creating a black hole from which intense rain and wind poured down to the earth. This resulted in great flooding, chaos, and hardships. Nuwa, feeling sorry for humans because of all the suffering this had caused, gathered stones of five colors, melted them down, and used the material to fill the open holes in the sky. She also sliced off a celestial turtle's feet and placed them as pillars to reset the out-of-balance earth. Cao Xueqin incorporated this myth into the story in chapter 1 to explain how the Stone came into existence and gained its spiritual powers. He adds new details to the myth by stating that Nuwa used 36,500 blocks of stone to mend the sky and that these huge blocks were 72 by 144 feet square and by inventing a stone that was not picked by Nuwa and having it reside at the foot of Greensickness Peak. By beginning his story with a myth that does not mimic history, Cao went against the Chinese literary tradition in which the narrative is presented as a historical narrative and a form of history.

See also **The First Six Chapters**

One Plaster Wang 王一贴

Daoist priest in charge of Tian Qi Temple which is located outside the West Gate of Beijing. In chapter 80, Bao-yu visits the temple to burn incense to repay a vow Grandmother Jia had made for his recovery. Father Wang, who has traveled widely and has a worldly attitude, is noted for his plasters, pills, and powders, which purport to cure individuals of a wide host of aliments. As with many of the monks in the novel, he is a rogue, albeit a very humorous and self-deprecating one. During Bao-yu's stay at the temple, Wang freely admits that his plasters are "tomfoolery" and that if they really worked, he would have taken them himself "so as to become an immortal instead of coming here to fool around" (DRM, 2: 699).

Outsiders

Outsiders play a prominent and highly significant role in *Dream of the Red Chamber*. Characters like Grannie Liu and the antique dealer Leng Zi-xing, who are not related to the Jia family; distant relatives like Jia Yu-cun and Jia Yun (both appear during the early part of the story); Xue Ke, Xue Bao-qin, and Jia Yun, and orphans like Lin Dai-yu; because of their status as outsiders, all provide important background information to the reader and perspectives that insiders do not have. A short verse (which is in the Yang translation but not the Hawkes), which occurs at the beginning of chapter 2 underlies the important viewpoint outsiders offer:

> Who can guess the outcome of a game of chess?
> Incense burned out, tea drunk—it's still in doubt.
> To interpret the signs of prosperity or decline
> An impartial outsider must be sought out [DRM, 1: 19].

Proving this point, Leng, in this same chapter, furnishes Jia Yu-cun (and the reader) with crucial information about the Jia family and introduces the novel's main characters. In the next chapter, these characters make their appearance, and we are able to see them and the palatial Jia family mansions, like Dai-yu, for the first time, and through her eyes. Several chapters later, we are further introduced via the perspective of Grannie Liu to one of the novel's main characters Xi-feng and her luxurious residence. Later in the novel, Bao-qin helps the reader visualize the magnificence and formality of the Jia family's New Year's ancestral sacrifice in chapter 53. Lucian Miller has observed that Cao Xueqin's use of "The 'outsider' approach also represents a variation upon the theme of 'true' and 'false' Jia.... Cao repeatedly indicates that that which is intuitive, indirect, and removed, is more viable than that which is objective, direct, and declared" (284).

Cao Xueqin's interest in outsiders and marginalized individuals almost certainly derived in large part because of his own status in Chinese society. As Martin W. Huang has insightfully noted, "Perhaps no other literati novelist suffered more from marginality than Cao Xueqin. Cao's ancestors were Han Chinese who had lived as Manchu after being captured by the Manchus.... Thus, strictly speaking, Cao Xueqin was both a Han Chinese and a creature of the Manchus, or neither. His family, because of their close relationship with the Kangxi emperor, once enjoyed tremendous wealth and power, but at the same time, they were Manchu banner 'bondservants.' In a sense they were both masters and servants, or neither. Cao's family had long lived in Nanjing, but after they lost favor with the imperial court, they moved to Beijing. Consequently, he was both a southerner and a northerner, or neither. In a word, he belonged to no clearly identifiable social category, and is almost a perfect case of borderline marginality" (84–85). But it was also Cao's position as a marginalized outsider that provided him with a unique viewpoint that enabled him to write such a critical, encyclopedic, and seemingly modernistic novel as *Dream of the Red Chamber*.

FURTHER READING

Huang, Martin W. *Literati and Self-Re/Presentation: Autobiographical Sensibility in the Eighteenth-Century Chinese Novel* (Stanford: Stanford University Press, 1995).

Miller, Lucien. *Masks of Fiction in the* Dream of the Red Chamber: *Myth, Mimesis and Persona* (Tucson: University of Arizona Press, 1975).

Painting

One of the most impressive features of *Dream of the Red Chamber* is its visually resplendent nature. Much of this is due to the fact that in addition to being a novelist and poet, Cao Xueqin was also a painter. He was a good enough one that it provided some of his livelihood during the poverty-stricken last years of his life. This influence can also be seen in the fact that the novel's principal commentator and editor, Red Inkstone, often used terms used in painting when discussing Cao's writing techniques. The scholar Zhou Ruchang has aptly compared *Dream of the Red Chamber* to a long, traditional Chinese scroll painting woven from the threads of the lives of numerous men and women in the story. Zhou has also likened the way Cao has depicted characters to the realistic portrait paintings of the celebrated Jin dynasty artist Gu Kaizhi. Moreover, Emanuel Pastreich has gone so far as to assert, "In *Honglou meng* certain chapters are filled with details, or packed with action, whereas others are less eventful. It is the larger aesthetic pattern that Cao strives to construct. The alternation between scenes involving large numbers of characters and descriptions of characters alone also serves to weave a larger fabric, a narrative whose gentle washes are best represented by analogy to landscape painting" (255). There are numerous examples of Cao's visual flair and painterly details in descriptions in the book. Among these are the way he carefully and colorfully describes and situates Prospect Garden and the Jia family mansions, the way he slowly introduces the mansions to Dai-yu (and to the reader) in chapter 3, the way he picturesquely describes rituals like the New Year's Eve ceremonies in chapter 53, the well-drawn way in which he individualizes characters through their character and clothing, and the aesthetic and visual delight he takes in discussing furnishings and objects. Finally, *Dream of the Red Chamber* also provides an excellent primer on the practicalities of painting via Xi-chun's struggling and ultimately unsuccessful attempt to paint a picture of Prospect Garden for Grannie Liu. In chapter 42, Xi-chun has a discussion with Bao-yu, Bao-chai, Dai-yu, and Xiang-yun about the painting, and Bao-chai gives her an extensive list of material she will need. The list details numerous types of brushes and the type of material needed for paint. The scene also offers advice about the steps involved in painting, the type of paper to be used, as well as information on perspective and how to place figures in the drawing and the amount of time she will need to complete the work. Clearly, Cao intended this part of the story to provide information to readers on how they can create, if they are interested, their own painting, and to provide added realism to the novel.

FURTHER READING

Pastreich, Emanuel. "The Novel in the Painting: An Allegory of Literature in Cao Xueqin's *Hongloumeng*." *Sungkyunkuan Journal of East Asian Studies* 3.1 (2003): 238–258.
Wang, John. C.Y. "The Chih-yen chai Commentary and the *Dream of the Red Chamber*: A Literary Study." In *Chinese Approaches to Literature*. Edited by Adele Richard (Princeton: Princeton University Press, 1978): 189–200.

The Palace

See **Beijing**

Palanquins or Sedan Chairs

A covered and self-enclosed litter used to convey a person. It was usually carried on the shoulders of four persons through the use of poles. They could be elaborate and ornate depending upon the status of the individual. In *Dream of the Red Chamber*, the palanquins used by the prince of Beijing in chapter 14, and the Imperial Concubine in chapter 18, are large and well decorated. The Imperial Concubine's palanquin is gold topped and has yellow curtains brilliantly embroidered with phoenixes and is carried by eight eunuchs. The type of sedan chair used by ministers and lower officials depended on their ranking. But all of them, when officials were traveling on a street, were surrounded by attendants and were preceded by gongs heralding their approach. People were required to get out of the way and be quiet, or they were punished. This is shown in chapter 104, when the Drunken Diamond gets into trouble with Jia Yu-cun when he refuses to get out of the way of his procession. The number of attendants and sedan bearers used in the procession was determined by the official's rank. Private sedans were usually simply made and constructed out of wood or bamboo. Dai-yu takes one to the Rong mansion when she first arrives in the capital. In chapter 114, Wang Xi-feng, on her deathbed, calls for a sedan chair to take her back to Jinling "to be entered on the Registers" (SS, 5: 216). Special sedans were used for hire on wedding days for the bride and were covered by red-covered silks.

Parfumee 芳官

Actress attached to the Jia family's troupe, later Bao-yu's maid and then a Water-moon Priory nun. Beautiful, intelligent, willful, and a bit spoiled, she has a tumultuous life. She is at first a child actress who is purchased by the Jia family in the south to perform during the Imperial Concubine's visit. When this troupe is disbanded, Bao-yu, who is quite taken with her, makes Parfumee one of his maids. Zhou Zuyan has written that the two have a close spiritual connection that is "symbolically presented in chapter 63, when they are first mistaken for 'a pair of twin brothers' while engaged in an exciting game of guess-fingers at Bao-yu's birthday party. Later they lie side by side on a bed in inebriated negligence of the cultural imperative of division of the sexes. The maid wins unusual favor from Bao-yu thanks to their shared nonchalance vis-à-vis social conventions: her tender age has kept her a sort of 'uncarved block' [a Daoist concept which is a metaphor for the original primordial state of the mind before being shaped by experience], impervious to the cultural dictates that define human gender and social status. Her ambiguous gender identity at the birthday party, along with her defiance of household seniority, reveals a spiritual affinity to the chaotic *hundun* [in Daoism, the mythic primordial disorder] state that strikes a ready chord with Bao-yu" (151–152). Bao-yu changes her name (which is Feng-guan) to Yelu Hunni, after dressing her up as a foreign servant. He then changes it to the French word Aventurin. She is swept up in Lady Wang's purge of Bao-yu's maids and decides to become a nun at Water-moon Priory. Although she is serious about her vows, another scandal erupts concerning some of the former actresses at the nunnery, and she and they are summarily sent back to the south.

See also **Zhuangzi**

FURTHER READING

Zhou, Zuyan. *Daoist Philosophy and Literati Writings in Late Imperial China: A Case Study of the Story of the Stone* (Hong Kong: Hong Kong University Press, 2013).

Parrot

According to traditional Chinese culture, parrots are a symbol of a loose woman and also serve as a warning for people to stay faithful because the bird is considered talkative. Dai-yu has a parrot named Polly as a pet and teaches it her favorite poems. In chapter 35, Polly recites a line from the famous Yuan dynasty play *Romance of the Western Chamber* and sighs like Dai-yu, much to the amusement of Nightingale. By associating Dai-yu with a parrot, Cao Xueqin is obviously not suggesting that Dai-yu is a loose woman, but he rather wrote the scene for humorous effect. Moreover, the association emphasizes her sense of isolation, as well as her sensitive and passionate nature.

Patience 平儿

Wang Xi-feng's principal maid. As her name implies, she is an even-tempered person. She is also loyal, empathetic, and competent. She is very protective of Xi-feng and is her closest confidant. Xi-feng heavily relies upon Patience for advice and frequently follows it. Patience is also capable at times of standing up to Xi-feng's husband, Jia Lian. She is also quite aware of Xi-feng's flaws, her avarice, jealousy, and malice, and, on occasion, goes behind her back and tries to alleviate the trouble she has caused, as she does, for example, in Er-jie's case. She attempts to curb Xi-feng's faults by keeping her grounded and attuned to what is really going on in the mansion, but she also acutely knows that Xi-feng is intractable about certain subjects like money and Jia Lian's infidelities and can be pushed, even by her, only so far. Patience is well liked and respected by both servants and members of the Jia family. At the end of the novel, Jia Lian comes around and finally appreciates her good qualities and makes her his proper wife.

Pear Tree Court

Originally the Duke of Rong-guo's retreat during the final years of his life. The pear is a symbol in China of longevity and compassionate administration. The wood of this tree was traditionally used to make printing blocks for books. The court is small but elegant and has a door that opens onto the street. The Duke and his brother the Duke of Ning-guo established the Jia family's name and status, so it is highly ironic and suggestive, and a subtle mark of the family's decline, that the Xue family and, in particular, Xue Pan, live there and that Pan uses the court's door to the outside to embark on his scandalous behavior.

The Peony Pavilion 牡丹亭

Romantic tragicomedy Southern-style *Kunqu* drama written by the well-known Ming dynasty playwright Tang Xianzhu. It is considered the greatest work of traditional Chinese drama and was first performed in 1598. The 55-act play tells the story of a shy 16-year-old cloistered maiden named Du Liniang, the daughter of an important government official, who yearns for love. She has an erotic dream in her bedroom following a stroll in her family's peony-filled garden. In the dream, she meets a young handsome scholar, and they have a passionate love affair that culminates in them making love in the garden's Peony Pavilion. Du awakens from the dream when a flower petal falls upon her during the height of the couple's passion. From that point on, she incessantly thinks about the dream and becomes overwhelmed by longing. She soon falls ill from a wasting disease, which continues for several months, and eventually dies after painting her self-portrait. But her desire is so intense that she returns to the real world as a ghost after three years. In the garden near the shrine her parents have erected in her honor, Du encounters the handsome scholar who was in her dream who is named Liu Mengmei (Willow Dream of the Plum). He is staying in Du's former residence while recovering from a sudden illness. After his recovery, Liu came across Du's self-portrait and quickly fell in love with her. They meet and promise to love each other forever. She then informs him that she is really a ghost and begs him to exhume her remains so that she can be brought back to life. He does, and they elope. Liu then passes the highest level of the imperial examination, and their secret marriage is recognized by the emperor. The drama is lyrical with patches of earthy humor, rich in symbolism and philosophical insight, and has well-developed characters. When it first appeared, it was wildly popular, especially with the females who read it. But it was also considered shocking because of Du's independent and passionate nature, the fact that she chose her husband and the story's commemoration of love over social convention. The work had a major influence upon Cao Xueqin because of its concept of *qing*. In the play, Tang Xianzu attempted to show "*qing* in its highest development, as true love between man and woman, embraces sexual attraction, physical passion, but also sentiment, empathy, devotion—the virtues of that broader love that exists outside of the sexual relationship" (Birch in Tang, x).

In *Dream of the Red Chamber*, *The Peony Pavilion* is closely associated with Bao-yu and especially with Dai-yu. In chapter 23, she overhears the Jia family's 12 young actresses rehearsing several scenes from it in Prospect Garden and is emotionally overcome by the beauty and imagery of the drama's poetry. The scenes also bring to her mind several lines from the play *The Romance of the Western Chamber*, which she had just read. Anthony Yu has contended that this scene contains several important themes. "It is no random detail that Dai-yu is moved to ardent longing by two dramatic texts of Chinese literary history not only most forceful in their glorification of heterosexual love, but also most daring in their portraits of young women living through their sexual awakening.... Through the eyes of yearning she shares with the dramatic heroine [Du Liniang], Dai-yu is already viewing her own environment from the perspective of its incapacity to endure as any dwelling of lasting happiness. The new for her already takes on the ominous potential of the old and the dying, and in this manner her reception of the dramatic verse anticipates the eventual, fated decline of the garden.... Dai-yu's hearing of fiction suddenly thrusts her into the terror of impermanence" (207, 208).

See also **Drama, Qing, *The Romance of the Western Chamber***

FURTHER READING

Tang, Xianzhu. *The Peony Pavilion*. Second Edition. Translated by Cyril Birch (Bloomington: Indiana University Press, 2002).

Yu, Anthony. *Rereading the Stone: Desire and the Making of Fiction in* Dream of the Red Chamber (Princeton: Princeton University Press, 1997).

Plague God

In Chinese folk religion, there are deities who are answerable for diseases and the plague and are thought to release them as punishment when people commit transgressions. These calamities are also believed to be caused by evil spirits. Consequently, offerings and prayers were given to appease these deities and to disperse the bad spirits, and many temples were built to honor these gods. Grannie Liu, in chapter 39, concocts a tale about a badly maintained shrine in the countryside that honors a mysterious snow maiden. The story spellbinds a gullible Bao-yu, who immediately sends Tealeaf out to find the shrine and quickly report back. When Tealeaf returns, he states that all he could find was a rundown temple that contained a large statue of an ugly Plague God.

Poetry

There are more than 200 poems in *Dream of the Red Chamber*. This is not unusual for poetry was commonly used in traditional Chinese prose narrative. The poems in the novel are chiefly written in classical Chinese and almost all the central verse forms in traditional Chinese poetry are used: regulated verse (chapter 38), linked verse (50, 76), the ballad (27), and *ci* song lyric (7). In addition, over 50 poets, many of them famous, are alluded to, and some of their poems quoted. Cao Xueqin was greatly admired for his skill at writing verse, and was called "the poet" in several poems written by his close friend Dun Min. Unfortunately, none of his poetry exists other than what he wrote for the novel. Unlike the West, the writing of poetry in traditional China was considered "a companionable art, for private and social use ... the Chinese lyric at its best was conceived as the highest form of speaking to someone else, an activity appropriate to all human beings on certain occasions and in certain states of mind.... The Chinese understood the lyric as speaking not to humanity as a whole but to *someone* else, some person or group the poet knew or would like to know. This someone would be a person the poet hoped that would know *him* through the poem" (Owen, 295). The composition of poetry formed a routine part of the lives of scholars and officials, and educated Chinese were expected to have both a good knowledge of poetry and the ability to compose passable verse. *Honglou meng* gives one the best and most detailed depictions of how poetry was socially practiced by educated gentry in traditional China. It shows how poems were commonly written during occasions like banquets, parties, celebrations, and the special poems that were exchanged when friends went on a long trip or moved to another place.

What makes *Dream of the Red Chamber* different from other traditional works of Chinese fiction is that virtually all of the poems penned in it are by women. This probably will come as a surprise to readers, given the overall status of women at that time in China. By the 18th century, it was not uncommon for upper-class Chinese women to be educated in such subjects as calligraphy, painting, music, and poetry (especially in the southern regions) mainly because it was believed it would increase their marriage prospects. While these upper-class women remained largely confined to the inner quarters of their family's compounds, they were able to pursue activities like the writing of poetry, and in certain circumstances to even publish it. One noted historian has written that "During the High Qing era, published work by women came into its own. The first anthologies of women's writing, edited by women, appeared in print. Elite families reveled in the achievements of erudite mothers and daughters and published their writings in separate editions.... In the context of the High Qing period, women's poetic voices had new meaning. It was more audible, it was more controversial, and it engaged directly with men in discussion about women as writers" (Mann, 3, 9). It has been estimated that over 3,000 women poets had their works published during the Ming and Qing dynasties.

This, of course, is not to say that this development was widely accepted by these families. Many of them did not wholeheartedly approve of or frowned upon women seriously writing verse. This ambivalence is shown in *Honglou meng* by several remarks Bao-chai makes in chapters 37 and 42, when she says that writing poetry is not as important for women as embroidery nor their proper duty. It can also be seen in the reaction Bao-yu receives from his cousins when he mentions that some of their poetry has been seen by outsiders. Nonetheless, as the novel shows, the formation of poetry clubs by upper-class women was not unusual during Cao Xueqin's time. Although Qing dynasty women often lived very sheltered lives, they were allowed, like female members of the Jia family, to venture out and visit temples, attend funerals and festivals. They could also sometimes visit nearby women friends, and poetry clubs became a popular pastime among some of them. One such notable club was the Banana Garden Poetry Club in the Southern city of Hangzhou which met from 1665 to 1675 and had around seven members. A member of this club later wrote that "Each month we would meet a number of times, and at each meeting we would randomly choose a rhyme and assign a topic, and [and then we would] chant our verses until the end of the day. Moreover, each of us would recommend [for membership] female relatives. We became as friendly as 'gold and orchid' and each of us was rich in 'snow and floss'" (quoted in Itema, 472).

Dream of the Red Chamber contains three types of integrated verse: descriptive (which assumes the narrator's point of view, that is, verse that describes characters when they are first introduced to the reader, as occurs in chapter 3); allusive (literary quotations, aphorisms); and new poems that are written by the novel's characters (Levy, 197–198). Most of the poems that are composed are in regulated verse, which was commonly used in poetry in China beginning with the Tang dynasty until modern times. Regulated verse makes use of the tonal nature of the Chinese language (classical Chinese had more than four) tones, has eight lines, and is written using either heptasyllabic (seven syllables) or pentasyllabic (five syllables) meter. (David Hawkes has an informative three-page essay on regulated verse in the appendix of volume two of his translation of the novel.) Poetry serves several purposes in the novel. First, it reveals the inner lives of characters who write it and illustrates their talents. For several of the female characters the genre allows them to communicate their deep-seated and private emotions in a socially acceptable way. Dai-yu is the best and most productive poet (followed by Xiang-yun and Bao-chai). Her talent is evident in the verse she writes for the Crab Flower Club meetings and in private. Dai-yu's poetry lets her give full expression to her feelings of loneliness and acute sense of being an outsider, her grief over the passage of time, and fears about her future. This can be seen in compositions like her elegant five-quatrain "Autumn Window: A Night of Wind and Rain" in chapter 45 and her "Flower Elegy" in chapter 27. Poetry also gives the normally reserved Bao-chai the means to articulate her private feelings of despair and grief to Dai-yu in chapter 87. Linked verse contests further display Xiang-yun's witty and vivacious side as well as Bao-qin's native intelligence. Calthrop's independence and long-denied desire for aesthetic cultivation is demonstrated in her successful struggle to learn how to compose verse. Although Bao-yu is surprisingly a mediocre poet during meetings of the poetry club, he has a considerable knowledge of the genre, and the poetry he writes in private is generally impressive. His elegy for Skybright in chapter 78 poignantly foreshadows the sense of loss he will feel after Dai-yu's death. Secondly, poetry enables the narrator in several instances to describe characters and places and make remarks about aspects of the story.

The novel's poetry also foretells the future of many of the female characters, particularly in chapter 5. Furthermore, because "poetry in the Chinese tradition extends beyond the textual sphere of the highbrow. Poetic expression often becomes part of the everyday vocabulary and of both the educated and the underprivileged. This aspect of poetry is vividly captured in [the novel]" (Wu, 304). It has also been argued that all the verse in the story has "a unified purpose—to lead the reader into integration with the experience of the text, with the ultimate goal of freeing that reader from attachment to that experience. According to Cao Xueqin's note to his brother, he explicitly created a 'real' world to further transcendent ideals" (Levy, 222). Finally, the poetry contributes to Cao Xueqin's attempt to make the novel a cultural compendium and enabled him to display his knowledge of the genre. It also allowed him to play the role of poetry teacher and critic. Because poetry meant a great deal to him and he had strong opinions regarding it, the story is also a first-rate primer on how to write it. We see this in chapter 48, which describes in detail how an earnest novice Calthrop is instructed by Dai-yu (with some input from Bao-chai) on the basic mechanics and aesthetics of writing poetry. Dai-yu's choice of poets for Caltrop to study is significant because it also reflects Cao's own opinion of these poets since Dai-yu is the most gifted writer of verse.

Moreover, Dai-yu's statement that the language used in a poem is not of primary importance, rather it is "the ideas behind it. If the ideas behind it are genuine, there's no need to embellish the language for the poem to be a good one" (SS, 2: 457), and Bao-chai's earlier remark that as "long as our ideas are fresh, the language can't be vulgar" (DRM, 1: 549) undoubtedly also reflected Cao's own view.

See also **Linked Verse, Women**

FURTHER READING

Idema, Walt, and Beata Grant. *The Red Brush: Writing Women of Imperial China* (Cambridge: Harvard University Press, 2004).
Levy, Dore J. "Embedded Texts: How to Read Poetry in *The Story of the Stone.*" *Tamkang Review* 36:1–2 (2005): 195–227.
Mann, Susan. *Precious Records: Women in China's Long Eighteenth Century* (Stanford: Stanford University Press, 1997).
Owen, Stephen. "Poetry in the Chinese Tradition." In *Heritage of China: Contemporary Perspectives on Chinese Civilization*. Edited by Paul S. Ropp (Berkeley: University of California Press, 1990): 294–308.
Wu, I-Hsien. "'Enlightenment Through Feelings': Poetry, Music, and Drama in *The Story of the Stone.*" *Approaches to Teaching Cao Xueqin's* Dream of the Red Chamber. Edited by Andrew Schonebaum and Tina Liu (New York: Modern Language Association of America, 2012): 296–316.

The Power and the *Guanxi* of the Jia Family

The Jia family, in addition to being rich, wield a great deal of power and have numerous important social and political connections. This easily can be seen in several of the novel's important social occasions, for example, in the status of those who attend Qin-shi's funeral in chapter 14 and who are invited to Grandmother Jia's 80th birthday celebrations in chapter 71 and in the large number of imperial gifts the matriarch receives. They include imperial kinsmen, dukes, princes, marquis, barons, princesses, high-ranking members of government ministries, the commissioner of police, and military and civil governors. The family's power rests upon the *guanxi* they have amassed and retained over several generations. *Guanxi* is a very important concept in China; it is the complex system of social relations, personal and influential connections, and feelings of reciprocity that enable favors to be granted among participants. This system is based on trust and mutual obligation and operates on personal, familial, work-related, and political levels. During traditional times, the extended family formed the basis of this network. The Jia family's *guanxi* derives from the titles they hold, their familial link with the Imperial Concubine, the high government positions family members like Jia Zheng hold, elite marriages the family has made, and the old boy connections that male members of a family have because of their participation in the imperial examination system. *Guanxi* is very much dependent upon one's status (which is connected with the concept of face), and if there is a steep drop in it, it quickly can be lost, as happens with the Jia family toward the end of the novel when the Embroidered Jacket raid occurs. But it can also be restored, which is what occurs at the end of the novel when the emperor reinstates the family's titles, returns confiscated items, and pardons Jia She and others in part because of Bao-yu's stellar examination performance.

See also **Face**

Prince of Beijing 北静王

Young, strikingly handsome, intelligent, and unassuming member of the royal family who befriends Bao-yu and the Cao family. Shui Rong (his actual name) first appears at Qin-shi's funeral procession where he offers a libation to her coffin as it passes by out of respect for the past strong friendship between one of his forebears and the Duke of Ning-guo. When he is introduced to Bao-yu, the prince is impressed with him, gives him a rosary, and invites Bao-yu to visit his palace in Beijing. Bao-yu eventually takes him up on the offer and periodically has discussions with him. Rong later presents him with a jade that is a copy of Bao-yu's. During the Embroidered Jacket raid, the prince suddenly appears bearing a second edict from the emperor that states only Jia She is to be arrested and the Prince of Xi-Ping is to supervise the investigation. He also consoles Jia Zheng about what has happened.

Prospect Garden 大观园

China has long been famous for its elegant and sophisticated gardens. For many Chinese, the country's most famous garden is a fictional one: *Daguan yuan* (Prospect Garden), the palatial and other worldly garden in *Dream of the Red Chamber*. This garden has generated a massive amount of interest among devotees of the novel, not just in regard to what it looked like and its meaning but also the question of what garden it is modeled after. Reams of books and articles have been published on the subject, and most books on the novel contain, as a matter of course, detailed drawings of what the garden looked like as well as of the dwellings that comprise it. Prospect Garden was constructed after one year of labor for a visit by the Imperial Concubine Jia Yuan-chun. It is a combination of two older Jia family gardens, the Ning-guo's All Scents Garden and the original Rong-guo garden. Chinese garden design is considerably different from Western design. In the West, buildings dominate the surroundings, and their interiors and exteriors occupy distinct space. In traditional Chinese gardens, spaces are created to reflect and reproduce elements in the natural world like mountains, lakes, and rivers; the aim is to provide a unity between natural and man-made beauty. They also contain flowers and plants that are believed to be auspicious, animals like storks, rabbits, deer, chicken, and geese that are considered ornamental, and goldfish and carp in ponds. Pavilions, decorative ceremonial halls, lodges, zigzag bridges, winding paved pathways, tunnel passageways, twisting galleries, and other structures are integrated with the natural properties of trees, rocks, and water. Chinese gardens, which ranged in size from massive, like the Summer Palace (Yuanmingyuan) in Beijing, to tiny city gardens, display an ornamental gate and are usually surrounded by a white plastered wall whose color is intended to provide a pleasing contrast to the garden's plants and flowers. These gardens also displayed *yin/yang* duality. Buildings were purposely set amidst natural features, rock foundations resembling mountains were set near water, empty places with filled ones, and areas which were light in color interspersed with dark. Prospect Garden has all of these elements (as well as a small village and Buddhist nunnery) and is an excellent example of Southern Jiangnan ("South of the Yangtze") garden style that was popular in Suzhou and Songjiang provinces. This style was noted for its elegance, irregular and meandering nature, and use of space, which was designed to induce feelings of infinitude. Literati frequently made their gardens into a three-dimensional landscape painting with uniquely shaped rocks, artificial hills, and trees that were carefully placed so they could be enjoyed from pavilions, balconies, and the latticed windows of buildings. Gardens were considered to be places for self-cultivation and were frequently locations for Daoist retreat, where an individual could find peace, reflect, and escape from society and responsibilities even if they were living in a bustling city. In addition, they were also viewed as a microcosm that symbolized the variety and fertility of the universe.

Because much of the story's action occurs in Prospect Garden, and it occupies such a central role (the important commentator Red Inkstone called it the arteries and veins of the novel), much attention has been focused on its meaning. First of all, its presence fits in with the encyclopedic nature of the novel, for the garden "is a summing up, a composite picture of the entire range of Chinese garden art" (Plaks, 187). It also would have been of great interest to Qing dynasty readers, many of whom would have had gardens of their own. On one level, Prospect Garden is a symbol of the Jia family's affluence and status. When Yuan-chun visits, the family is at the pinnacle of their power, and the garden is used not just to honor her but also to conspicuously display this fact. But its massive size and opulence (which she strongly criticizes) also symbolizes the family's extravagance for they have economically strained themselves constructing it, and the lavishness will contribute to the family's eventual fall. The garden has importance because the style and interior decorations of the dwellings, as well as the trees, flowers, and plants that surround them, reveal personality traits of the individuals who inhabit them. Prospect Garden is clearly depicted as an oasis, with Bao-yu at the center, for those who live in it because it is physically set apart from the "real" world of the Jia family mansions and the demanding outside public world. It is an insular and aesthetically pleasing realm where normal social rules and responsibilities concerning such matters as hierarchy and gender relations do not apply. The garden's world is governed by love and sentiments; relationships in it between the cousins and even their maids are forthright and natural, and conventional manners are frequently ignored. It is an idyllic place of freedom, charm, youth, and beauty. This juxtaposition of the garden's enclosed and ideal world alongside the debased world outside it is one of the novel's major structures.

As is true of many areas in *Dream of the Red Chamber*, there is still considerable debate over the main purpose of the garden and the precise reasons for its breakdown. Yu-shih Yu, in a seminal article, has contended that there is a close connection between the garden and the mythic-fantastic Land of Illusion and that the two realms are opposed but also intertwined. Yu also astutely points out that the utopian world of the garden with its stress on beauty and cleanliness was doomed to eventually collapse because it was erected on a location in the real world that is infested with unclean acts and behavior, namely All Scents Garden. This is the place where Qin-shi hanged herself (a scene which was depicted in the original version of the story but was subsequently cut, although there are still subtle allusions to it in the novel), where Jia Rui first met and lusted after Xi-feng, and where Ning-guo's original garden stood, which was used by Jia She, one of the dirtiest characters in the story. Moreover, the garden's water supply system, which is greatly admired by Jia Zheng and his literary friends, flows "contaminated" water into the garden from the original gardens. In short, in an ironic twist, the greatest purity, Prospect Garden, is founded on the worst vice. Yu concludes that these unpleasant realities about the garden illustrate the novel's theme: "As cleanliness originally came from squalor, so in the end to squalor it must ineluctably return. I believe that this is the central significance of the tragedy of *Dream of the Red Chamber*, and to Cao Xueqin, it must have been the greatest tragedy known to man" (21). One scholar who has studied the literary and allegorical tropes relating to the garden has taken a different tack, contending that they provide support for the novel's "perhaps most fundamental and pervasive theme: the absolute necessity of egress from the self-contained world of the garden" (Plaks, 201). For the inevitable decline of the garden world "is not a question of guilt, either personal or cosmic, but simply a part of existence ... the configurations of change that take effect within [Prospect Garden] partake of the same processes of creation, growth, decay, and dissolution that characterize the entire phenomenological world outside its walls. The analogy to the stages of human life—pre-natal, self-containment, unselfconscious childhood, maturity, marriage, regeneration, aging, and death—needs no further elaboration" (205, 201).

Critics have also linked the garden's meaning with *qing*, with one maintaining, "Once within its walls, people act on the basis of their desires [*qing*] and are only minimally constrained by the ordained social hierarchies. Because *qing* is necessarily personal, it can easily degenerate into self-centeredness which is unlikely to be checked by a sense of one's place in the larger structure of Confucian human relations.... If it is not to destroy the structure of society, *qing* must be channeled into socially structured relationships. If it exceeds those bounds, it is destructive to the human community.... The garden-dwellers futile attempt to always live in the springtime of the present leads finally to the garden's ruin" (Scott, 94). It has also been claimed that *Daguan yuan* is "a miniature world that exists simultaneously on several levels: physical, metaphoric, allusive and allegorical. Each level of the garden is interreferential in the world of the novel and metareferential in encompassing the world of the reader ... the growth of awareness of the outside world plants the seeds of the garden's destruction, spoiling its sanctity as a refuge from responsibility, adulthood, and time" (Levy, 115, 118). There has also been much speculation by Chinese scholars as to what real-life garden served as the model for Prospect Garden. Some have argued that it is based on the luxurious Xitang ("West Court") Garden in Nanjing, which was part of the official residence of the Textile Commissioner and where Cao Xueqin spent his early years. Others have asserted that it is patterned on the small but elegant garden in the palace of Heshen, a close associate of the Qianlong emperor, in Beijing; it has also been asserted that the massive imperial garden of Emperor Yongzheng, the Garden of Perfect Brightness, also in Beijing, was the model, and some have posited that it is based in part on an infamous fictional garden in the Ming dynasty novel *Jin Ping Mei*. The most plausible answer is that it is an imaginative amalgamation of several gardens with which Cao was familiar.

See also **Qing**

FURTHER READING

Keswick, Mary. *The Chinese Garden: History, Art, and Architecture* (Cambridge: Harvard University Press, 2003).
Levy, Dore. "The Garden and Garden Culture in *The Story of the Stone*." *Approaches to Teaching Cao Xueqin's* Dream of the Red Chamber. Edited by Andrew Schonebaum and Tina Liu (New York: Modern Language Association of America, 2012): 115–132.
Plaks, Andrew. *Archetype and Allegory in the* Dream of the Red Chamber (Princeton: Princeton University Press, 1976).
Scott, Mary. "The Image of the Garden in *Jin Ping Mei* and *Honglou meng*." *Chinese Literature: Essays, Articles, Reviews* 8 (1986): 83–94.
Yu, Ying-shih. "The Two Worlds of *Hung-lou Meng*." Translated by Diana Yu. *Renditions* 2 (1974): 5–22.

Proverbs

Chinese are famous for their coining and frequent use of proverbs in conversation and writing, and they have long formed an important part of Chinese cultural life. This can easily be seen in *Dream of the Red Chamber* where the citing of proverbs is ubiquitous. The novel contains nearly 150 proverbs, and most are used during conversations between characters and are drawn from the fields of literature, history, poetry, and other writings. They have ethical or philosophical import and concern aspects of everyday life. At that time, and even today, a good command of proverbs and the ability to aptly use them was considered a sign of an individual's knowledge of history, literature, philosophy, level of education, and wisdom. Furthermore, it has also been believed that they provide a link between the past and the present and help solidify a sense of cultural continuity and stability. The proverbs cited in the novel cover a wide variety of subjects, from stressing the virtues of proper behavior, self-reliance, honesty, and acceptance, offering advice on dealing with adversity, difficult people, and life's unpredictability to remarks about personality traits and the role of fate in human affairs. Sometimes, the proverbs come fast and furious in the story. In chapter 16, Xi-feng, during a discussion with Jia Lian in which she describes her supervision of Qin-shi's funeral, fires off four proverbs in short order in support of her (disingenuous) depreciation of her managerial ability. *Honglou meng*'s numerous proverbs add to the realism in the story, help to further define the characters who use them, and reinforce several of the novel's themes.

Qi 气

In chapter 2, Jia Yu-cun has a long conversation with his friend the antique dealer Leng Zi-xing. Among the topics they discuss is Yu-cun's elaborate theory that explains why people turn into good or bad individuals. Yu-cun's speculations are based on the notion of *qi*, an important concept in Chinese philosophy and traditional medicine. The term is rather difficult to adequately render into English, but it can broadly be defined as meaning vital force, energy, or life force that animates living things and constitutes inanimate objects. "In popular parlance, *qi* is applied to the air that we breathe, steam, smoke, and all gaseous substances. The philosophical use of the term underlies the movement of *qi*. *Qi* is both that which really exists and what has the ability to become. To stress one at the expense of the other would be to misunderstand *qi*" (Zhou, 45). Yu-cun posits, "The generative processes operating in the universe provide the great majority of mankind with natures in which good and evil are commingled in more or less equal proportions" (SS, 1: 76). He further asserts that cases of unusual goodness or badness are respectively the result of being born during prosperous and peaceful times or dangerous and unstable periods. As a result, "The good bring order to the world, the bad plunge it into confusion. The good embody pure intelligence, the true essence of heaven and earth; the bad, cruelty, and perversity, the evil essence" (DRM, 1: 27). During good times, "the over-abundance of good essence, having nowhere to go is transformed into sweet dew and gentle breezes throughout the Four Seas. But because there is no place under the clear sky and bright sun for the essence of cruelty, and perversity, it congeals in deep caverns … should it meet the pure essence, good refuses to yield to evil while evil envies good—neither can prevail over the other" (DRM, 1: 27–28). The result is that humans who are infected by these mingling forces are not capable of being wholly good or bad. But if we put them "in the company of ten thousand others, you will find that they are superior to all the rest in sharpness and intelligence and inferior to the rest in perversity, wrongheadedness, and eccentricity" (SS, 2: 78). Yu-cun then provides a long list of these types of people and later adds Bao-yu to it.

Critics have generally not taken Yu-cun's theory seriously. It has been called an "oddball queer-beer thesis in which Yu-cun endeavors to account for Bao-yu's character type" (Miller, 133) and "a spoof on the part of Cao Xueqin, surely" (Minford, 318). It has also been argued that the theory "provides a cosmological explanation to set the stage for an epic father/son struggle [between Bao-yu and Jia Zheng]" (Levy, 34). But some Chinese scholars have taken it seriously. Zhou Ruchang has maintained that in addition to being a great novelist, Cao Xueqin was also a great philosopher and that he was advancing with this theory under the influence of the Neo-Confucian philosopher Li Zhuowu, a radically new philosophy of *qi*. Zhou contends that Cao was attacking the traditional Chinese belief that *qi* determined one's social station and that good people were born with positive *qi* and bad people with negative *qi*. Zhou also states "to write about a group of people born with *jian qi* [impure energy] who were not immortal [as traditional commentaries suggested] but rather talented individuals. This idea that people born with a combination of both pure and impure *qi* incessantly in conflict with each other challenged traditional notions of the harmony of *yin* and *yang*.... Cao thought that [the traditional] theory revealed little about human nature, which he believed was not so easily measured in terms of broad concepts like good and evil. In Cao Xueqin's view, some people were simply beyond relative moral categories" (133, 132).

FURTHER READING

Levy, Dore. *Ideal and Actual in* The Story of the Stone (New York: Columbia University Press, 1999).
Miller, Lucien. *Masks of Fiction in the* Dream of the Red Chamber: *Myth, Mimesis and Persona* (Tucson: University of Arizona Press, 1975).
Minford, John. Review of *Rereading the Stone: Desire and the Making of Fiction in* Dream of the Red Chamber. *China Review International.* 6.2 (1999): 307–318.
Zhou, Ruchang. *Between Noble and Humble: Cao Xueqin and the* Dream of the Red Chamber. Edited by Ronald R. Gray and Mark S. Ferrara (New York: Peter Lang, 2009).

Qin 琴

A seven-string traditional Chinese musical instrument similar to the zither. It has been in use for over 3,000 years and dates back to the Han dynasty. The *qin* is considered the most elegant of all the Chinese musical instruments and is associated with Confucius, who was a master of the instrument. In

Confucianism, it was thought to typify learning and morality. Well-educated individuals were traditionally expected to know how to play it, and the instrument was a symbol of the literati and Chinese high culture. The *qin* was used in both civic and religious ceremonies, and at banquets for entertaining guests. The instrument is constructed from a long box of lacquered wood and has an oblong resonator body inlaid with 13 small disks that show pitch possibilities. Players place the *qin* horizontally on a table, sit, and face the side of the instrument. They pluck the string using their right hand while pressing down the strings with their left hand and move their fingers along the strings to change the pitch. There are more than 200 finger positions. In chapter 86 (and part of 89) of the novel, Dai-yu provides Bao-yu with an extensive introduction to the *qin*. She discusses how to play it, what clothing to wear while playing it, where to play it, and the philosophy behind it. She also explains to a fascinated Bao-yu that playing it is conducive to meditation and that its purpose is "to induce self-restraint, curb passion, and suppress license and extravagance" (DRM, 3: 93–94). Dai-yu's considerable knowledge of the instrument has greatly impressed Chinese commentators on the novel. The *qin* is also used by Cao Xueqin to reveal Dai-yu's passionate and troubled character, as shown in chapter 87 when Adamantina is shocked while listening to her play the instrument when Dai-yu strikes such a high note that it loudly snaps a string while she is singing a mournful and autumnal song she has composed. Finally, this focus on the *qin* is another example of a subject that would have interested Cao Xueqin's readers because the instrument played an important role in Chinese culture, and he attempted to incorporate key elements of Chinese culture into the story.

FURTHER READING

van Gulik, R.H. *The Lore of the Chinese Lute: An Essay in Ch'in Ideology*. A Monumenta Nipponica Monograph (Tokyo: Sophia University, 1940).

Wu, I-Hsien. "'Enlightenment Through Feelings': Poetry, Music, and Drama in *The Story of the Stone*." *Approaches to Teaching Cao Xueqin's Dream of the Red Chamber*. Edited by Andrew Schonebaum and Tina Liu (New York: Modern Language Association of America, 2012): 296–316.

Qin-shi 秦氏

One of the most controversial characters in the novel, she is Jia Rong's wife and Jia Zhen's daughter-in-law. Her name connotes "Feeling, Emotion, and Love," but it also suggests libidinousness. Tellingly, her father's name, Qin Bangye, connotes "Love Abets Karma," which refers to the Buddhist belief that love and emotions are attachments to the self that keep the cycle of karma going. Qin-shi is beautiful, charming, and well liked and is especially close to Xi-feng. But she is also depicted as a very passionate woman, as shown by the numerous voluptuous objects she displays in her bedroom that originally belonged to famous historical and mythological women noted for their sensuality. It is also revealing that when Bao-yu makes his first visit to the Land of Illusion, he has a sexual encounter with Fairy Disenchantment's sister Two-in-one, who is also called Ke-qing, which is Qin-shi's childhood name. Cao Xueqin had originally planned to include a scene in the novel that would have indicated that Qin-shi had an incestuous relationship with Jia Zhen and that she hanged herself when the affair was accidentally discovered by a maid. But supposedly a relative strongly objected to it on moral grounds, so Cao cut it. Nevertheless, what remains still appears to indirectly indicate that Qin-shi did have an affair with her father-in-law. Moreover, the song about her in chapter 5 seems to imply that she did hang herself. (For a detailed discussion of this controversy see Edwards [2001].) Qin-shi's ghost appears to Xi-feng on two occasions, warning her about the decline of the Jia family and ironically (given her major moral transgression) offering Confucian advice on how to prepare for it. She also appears again late in the novel to show Faithful how to kill herself by hanging and makes a final appearance in chapter 116 when Bao-yu briefly sees her in The Paradise of Truth. Qin-shi's extravagant and costly funeral (along with the Imperial Concubine's visit) exhibits the Jia family at the height of their power and affluence.

FURTHER READING

Edwards, Louise. "New *Hongxue* and the 'Birth of the Author': Yu Pingbo's 'On Qin Keqing's Death.'" *Chinese Literature: Essays, Articles, Reviews* 23 (2001): 31–54.

Qin Zhong 秦钟

Bao-yu's close friend and Qin-shi's young brother, his name connotes "The Affectionate One" but also suggests, like his sister Qin-shi's, "Libidinousness." Shy, bright, and mischievous, he attended the Jia family clan school with Bao-yu and has a romantic relationship with the Water-moon Priory novice Sapientia. When his father, a low-ranked government official, discovers this relationship, he severely beats Zhong and dies several days after from the exertion. Zhong then suddenly dies from a combination of a cold he had contracted in the country while sporting with Sapientia, the effects of the beating, guilt over his father's death, and worries about Sapientia's future.

Qing 情

One of the most important concepts in *Dream of the Red Chamber* is *qing*. This word is difficult to translate into English because of its very wide-ranging and complex meaning in Chinese. (One scholar has come up with 13 definitions for the term.) It has been broadly construed as meaning love, affection, compassion, kindness, and empathy. Halvor Eifring has come up with probably the best definition for how this term is used in the novel. He defines it as a "positive emotion between human beings ... free flowing, spontaneous, and often incontrollable feelings towards and desire for others...[there is also] a strongly eroticized *qing,* like the *qing* Jia Rui nourishes for Wang Xi-feng in chapter 12, often translatable as 'desire' ... [and] a less strong erotized *qing* like the *qing* Jia Bao-yu nourishes for the young girls of the family, explained by the Red Inkstone commentary as *titie* 'sensitivity, empathy, and caring'" (276). During the Ming dynasty and Cao Xueqin's time, Chinese scholars and writers were fascinated with the subjects of romantic sentiment and desire or physical lust (*yu*). This widespread interest commonly has been referred to as the "cult of *qing*." This label is a bit of a misnomer because the movement was not as unified as popularly supposed. It should be more accurately viewed as a general trend that had many interconnected and often opposing elements and covered the areas of philosophy, literature, and the theater (Lee, 86). The philosophical underpinnings for this trend were established by the Ming dynasty Neo-Confucian thinker Wang Yangming, who famously argued for an egalitarian conception of Confucian selfhood and the idea that man's moral nature and original goodness were grounded on an all-encompassing *qing* that naturally flowed from the first principle of things. Wang also believed that if individuals based their actions in accordance with this feeling and used their will to actualize it, they could become perfected. This theory had a strong influence on many Ming and Qing dynasty intellectuals.

These intellectuals included writers like the Ming dynasty author Feng Menglong, whose book *Qingshi* was a massive collection of 850 stories on aspects of *qing*. In it, Feng maintains that *qing* is a cosmic principal and that his aim was to prophesize about its power. Wang's philosophy made a strong impact upon the Ming dynasty dramatist Tang Xianzu, author of one of China's most renowned plays *The Peony Pavilion,* which depicted the emotion-ridden love affair between the young love-obsessed Bridal Du and her suitor Liu Mengmei, who exemplifies true feeling. The drama became one of the most influential promoters of *qing* and contributed to discussions of the subject at the time because of Tang's "attempt to idealize *qing* by endowing volition, imagination, and longing with transformative power, and the interplay of high and low diction to bring about the fulfillment of *qing* in the mundane world" (Li, 255). This discourse on *qing* was also very much part of the popular aesthetic vogue for male actors among the literati during this period. These philosophical and dramatic writings about *qing*, while differing in emphasis, did share several beliefs. The most important of these was the notion, "Sentiment rather than the manifestation of intellectual desire, was the original nature from which desire was only a deviation toward excess.... Sentiment, therefore was made the first principal and took on an ontological property. And it was in this capacity that sentiment was celebrated in drama and fiction, as a spontaneous energy, a medium of self-expression, and the basis of a radical subjectivity" (Lee, 87).

This attention on *qing* also had an enormous influence upon Cao Xueqin. This can be seen in the fact that *Dream of the Red Chamber* is rich in references to it. In chapter 1, Vanitas notes that the main theme of the novel "was love" (DRM, 1: 5). In the same chapter, Zhen Shi-yin overhears a conversation between the Daoist priest and Buddhist monk in which it is mentioned, "A love drama is about to be enacted, but not all its actors have been incarnated" (DRM, 1: 7). The Goddess Disenchantment who is in charge of *qing* famously gives Bao-yu a lecture in chapter 5 on love and desire, telling him that he suffers from "lust of the mind," a malady that is characterized by "a blind, defenseless love with which nature has filled [his] being" (SS, 1: 146) and unsuccessfully tries to get him to understand the ultimate vanity of human attachments. In addition, the prelude to her famous song and dance suite asks the perennial question, "How did love begin?" (SS, 1: 139). Jia Rui, in his obsession with Xi-feng, demonstrates the destructive nature of excessive *yu*, as do the You sisters and Qin-shi and her brother Qin Zhong (both of whose names suggest libidinous). Furthermore, one of the names of the monk Vanitas is *Qing seng* (Brother Amor, the Passionate Monk) because he believes that truth could be apprehended through passion. In chapter 111, Disenchantment's younger sister Ke-qing informs Faithful about the true meaning of love: "Before the emotions of anger, grief, and joy stir within the human breast, there exists the 'nature state' of love; the stirring of these emotions causes passion. *Our* kind of love, yours and mine, is the former natural state. It is like a bud. Once opened, it ceases to be true love" (SS, 5: 210). Moreover, the novel includes scenes where *The Peony Pavilion* is performed during family gatherings and in which Bao-yu and Dai-yu quote from it. Feng Menglong's classification of the types of love in *Qingshi* possibly served in part as a model for the mysterious missing *Roster of Lovers* table that was supposed to be in the novel's final chapter. This table was said to have classified 60 of the novel's female characters according to the type of *qing* they exemplified.

Because of the novel's focus on *qing*, the topic has recently received increasing attention by scholars. The following are some of the more interesting interpretations of the role of *qing* in the story. Martin Huang, in his extensive study of desire in late imperial Chinese fiction, has contended that, when compared to other works of literature that discuss *qing*, this concept in *Dream of the Red Chamber* is a great deal more sophisticated and subtle. Huang specifically examines the form of *qing* that Bao-yu represents, which he calls the "lust of intent … spiritual love" (272). He points out that the commentator Red Inkstone, who was a personal friend of Cao Xueqin, in an attempt to further clarify this special type of *qing*, wrote that it could be called *qing buqing*, that is, to have feeling for the unfeeling, to love someone or something that is not definitely able to return this love, and that Bao-yu feels it throughout the novel. When Bao-yu experiences these feelings of intense empathy, there is a breakdown between his self and the subject of the emotion. These subjects not only include people but also plants and even a lady in a painting. Huang argues, "Bao-yu's reluctance to grow up is obviously related to his desperate attempt to cling to his idea of *qing* and his freedom to pursue his 'lust of intent.' However, since growing up is an unavoidable part of life, the logical conclusion is that Bao-yu must outgrow his lust of intent. Throughout the novel, *qing* or the lust of intent is often associated with attempts to resist or defy the passage of time" (293). Huang concludes, "One important achievement of *Honglou meng* is its pervasive demonstration of how difficult it is to invent a *qing* that can transcend *yu* without excluding the latter" (314). The distinguished literary critic C.T. Hsia has argued, "The schematic presentation of love and lust in the novel runs to this formula: those sunk in the mire of gross passions make no attempt to extricate themselves, while those whose love, given the chance to blossom, could have seriously challenged the ideal of renunciation and represented another kind of fulfillment [and the author's sympathy fully entitles us to this expectation] are systematically destroyed so as to leave room for the Buddhist-Daoist moral" (265–266). Maram Epstein believes that Bao-yu's propensity for *qing* is the "connecting thread of the novel" (155) and that paradoxically the story shows, "*Qing* treated as the basis for the authentic self, eventually leads to a collapse of identity unless it is contained and regulated by ritual practices" (173). It has also been maintained, "Every act of the Jia clan to preserve familial stability and prosperity—by dogged espousal of threadbare orthodoxies, by reliance on royal connections and sycophancy, by blatant greed and corruption, by desperate gestures of altruism—is also an act of unenlightened desire" (Yu, 218).

Another scholar has contended that the conventional view that there is a conflict between the *qing* and orthodox Confucianism in the novel is wrong and that Cao Xueqin was actually trying "to use *qing* as an alternative scheme of self-identification to achieve the authentic Confucian ideal and thus redeem the collapsing Confucian order" (Xu, 443). Halvor Eifring has taken an entirely different interpretation by offering a psychological interpretation of the role *qing* plays in the story, claiming that *Dream of the Red Chamber* "is a psychological novel built around a core of conflicting inner impulses" (23). As a result, he writes, its obsession with *qing* is rooted "in a psychological resistance against boundaries and responsibilities, an unwillingness to let go of the sense of wellbeing and unity associated with the child's early state of primary narcissism and with its privileged relation with a number of girls" (274). Eifring also observes that the passages in the novel that directly describe "*qing* and the fear and shame surrounding it have little of the irony that is so typical of the passages expressing self-reproach on the one hand and non-attachment on the other. The lack of irony reflects a lack of psychological distance…. The conflicts relating to *qing* dominate the mental universe of the novel to such extent that there is little room for the smiling afterthought that is typical of irony…. But it may be seen as a strength, making the novel more directly psychologically expressive than any previous work of Chinese fiction, and giving us an intimate view of the emotional battlefield underlying the narrative" (323). Finally, the noted scholar Zhou Ruchang has put forward an expansive and philosophic take on how Cao Xueqin views *qing*. He maintains that Cao was a great philosopher who gave new meaning to the concept of *qing* and that the central theme of the novel (as exemplified in Bao-yu) was *gong qing* (love and compassion for all). Zhou asserts, "In *Honglou meng*, *qing* refers to a noble relationship between persons and is manifested as caring, sympathy, pity, humanity, and compassion. As such, *qing* not only occurs between a man and a woman, but extends to all creatures, indeed to all those upon whom misfortune has visited" (93). Zhou also thinks that the *qing* in the novel is not simply "a doctrine but a living conception inextricably tied to context and the manner of using and giving *qing*" (94).

See also **Confucianism, Drama, Fairy Disenchantment, *The Peony Pavilion*, Prospect Garden, Red Inkstone, The Roster of Lovers**

FURTHER READING

Eifring, Halvor. "The Psychology of Love in *The Story of the Stone*." In *Love and Emotion in Traditional Chinese Literature*. Edited by Halvor Eifring (Leiden: Brill Academic Publisher, 2004): 271–324.

Epstein, Maram. "Reflections of Desire in *Honglou meng*." In *Competing Discourses: Orthodoxy, Authenticity, and Engendered Meanings in Late Imperial Chinese Fiction* (Cambridge: Harvard University Press, 2001): 150–197.

Hsia, C.T. "*Dream of the Red Chamber*." In *The Classic Chinese Novel: A Critical Introduction* (New York: Columbia University Press, 1968): 245–297.

Huang, Martin W. "Qing and the Reluctance to Grow Up in *Honglou meng*." In *Desire and Fictional Narrative in Late Imperial China* (Cambridge: Harvard University Press, 2001): 271–316.

Lee, Haiyan. "Love or Lust? The Sentimental Self in *Honglou meng*." *Chinese Literature: Essays, Articles, Reviews* 19 (1997): 85–111.

Li, Wai-yee. "Languages of Love and Parameters of Culture in *Peony Pavilion* and *The Story of the Stone*." In *Love and Emotions in Traditional Chinese Literature*. Edited by Halvor Eifring (Leiden: Brill, 2004): 233–270.

Xu, Ma. "Can Sentimentalism Survive? Revisiting the Negotiation Between Qing and Confucian Ideology in *Honglou meng*." *Tsing Hua Journal of Chinese Literature*, 14 (2015): 437–447.

Yu, Anthony. *Rereading the Stone: Desire and the Making of Fiction in* Dream of the Red Chamber (Princeton: Princeton University Press, 1997).

Zhou, Ruchang. "None the *Red Chamber* Message Hears: Art as Living Philosophy." *Tamkang Review* 36.1–2 (2005): 89–103.

Reading and Rereading

Dream of the Red Chamber places as much importance on the ability to read carefully as it does on the benefits of actively and critically reading and rereading. Books form a considerable amount of the material that is read in the novel (along with registers, songs, and poems). They are read out loud (chapter 23), imitated and parodied (22), quoted from (22), secretly purchased (23), carefully hidden

(23), burned (36), and spilled on (9). Scenes from books are performed both publicly and privately. The reading of works of poetry, drama, philosophy, history, and fiction in the story is significant in large part because they frequently disclose elements of characters' personalities. In chapter 25, Cao Xueqin nicely captures the excitement and sheer joy of reading when Bao-yu and Dai-yu pore over, for the first time, the famous drama *The Romance of the Western Chamber*. The experience also provides a way by which they can express their feelings for each other. The novel also contains detailed descriptions of numerous poetry club meetings where the proper reading (and writing) of poetry is discussed and debated, as well as quiet scenes where characters like Dai-yu do their own private but revealing reading from works from their personal library. It was common during this time for the printed version of most of these books to publish a commentary in them written by a critic or critics who offered insights and opinions on the text. David Rolston, who has made a detailed study of Chinese fiction commentary, states, "Fully developed commentaries included as many as fifteen prefatory essays and charts, chapter comments before and after each chapter [sometimes both], marginal comments about the texts, interlineal comments between the lines, and a variety of emphatic punctuation" (4). Consequently, the act of reading was bounded by levels of commentary, which had an important effect upon the way readers understood the text. Moreover, as Rolston points out, this form of close reading "involves the apprehension of a hidden message. Commentators can lay claim to our attention only by promising to show us something that would otherwise elude us. They are thus in the business of reading between lines as well as of writing between them" (1).

Similarly, one of Cao Xueqin's purposes is to instruct the reader on how to read his novel and, by implication, how to read or understand life itself. Cao's approach to reading was undoubtedly influenced by the commentary editions of many of the works of literature he had read himself and the emphasis they placed upon the ability to read between the lines. This can be seen in *Honglou meng*'s marked stress on the significance of engaged, but also evaluative, reading and rereading. From the first chapter, when Vanitas has to read the stone's story twice to comprehend it, to Bao-yu's misreading of the registers and albums in chapter 5, to his largely successful rereading of the registers in chapter 116, the whole novel, on a fundamental level, can be viewed as an extended lesson on how the reader should properly read the text: namely, critically and skeptically. The novel constantly tells readers that they need to read between the story's lines through the subtle use of a wide variety of techniques: paradox, myths, allegories, parody, irony, subversion, sophisticated and widespread foreshadowing devices, indeterminacy and contingency, and frequent changes in form and perspective. This message is also underscored in the story's frequent disconnect between surface appearances and reality, public ideology and private practices, and its self-reflexive nature. All of these elements raise the self-consciousness of readers and force them to be active readers, to read critically and reread and to think about the text in order for them to grasp the full import of the novel's meaning. As Robert Hegel has perceptively observed, "By generally destabilizing the predictive potential of certain major elements of his narrative, [Cao Xueqin] signals the implied reader about the appropriate way to read and how to regard *reality* at the same time: in this text the usual 'rules' simply do not apply with any exactness; similar 'rules' may mean no more in the reader's own life" (158). A point that Zhen Shi-yin underlines at the end of the novel when he discusses Bao-yu's finally reaching understanding: "Could two readings of the registers and the whole lifetime of experience fail to bring enlightenment?" (SS, 5: 371).

See also **Drama, Foreshadowing, Narrator, Registers**

FURTHER READING

Hegel, Robert E. "Unpredictability and Meaning in Mid-Qing Literati Novels." In *Paradoxes of Traditional Chinese Literature*. Edited by Eva Hung (Hong Kong: The Chinese University Press, 1994): 147–166.

Rolston, David L. *Traditional Chinese Fiction and Fiction Commentary: Reading and Writing Between the Lines* (Stanford: Stanford University Press, 1997).

Red

The color red has a special importance in Chinese culture. It can mean, depending upon the occasion, luck, youth, vitality, happiness, the summer season, success, and celebration. Red is also an auspicious color that is thought to ward off evil; hence brides during that time wore red and their heads were covered with a red cloth, the groom wore a red belt, and the wedding chamber would be decked out in red decorations. During festivals like Chinese New Year, traditionally lanterns are red colored and money is given out in red envelopes. In *Dream of the Red Chamber*, the color has several important meanings. First, it forms part of the novel's title (*hong*). As Anthony Yu has written, "There is little doubt that coupled with the towered buildings [in the novel's title] it describes, red chamber or red mansion conjures up an image of power, wealth, and baronial opulence for most readers. After all, gates, and pillars of the rich were painted bright red in traditional China, and vermillion steps fronted royal palaces. Varying shades of red are employed in countless ways throughout the narrative to evoke the baroque splendor of the Jia mansion and the plutocratic existence of its inhabitants" (288). David Hawkes has pointed out, "The pervading *redness* of this Chinese novel … red as symbol—sometimes of spring, sometimes of youth, sometimes of good fortune or prosperity, recurs again and again throughout it" (SS, 1: 43). Red in the story is also a reference to the Buddhist concept of the "Red Dust," the temporal, ever-changing human world. Moreover, the red flowers in the story, red peony, red plum, and so on, signify human desire. Thus, much of the redness in the novel also signifies the many and varied charms of the sensual world.

FURTHER READING

Yu, Anthony. "Cao Xueqin's *Honglou meng* (*Story of the Stone* or *Dream of the Red Chamber*)." *Masterworks of Asian Literature in Comparative Perspective: A Guide for Teaching.* Edited by Barbara Stoler Miller (Armonk, New York: Sharpe, 1994): 285–298.

Red Inkstone 脂砚斋

Mysterious commentator on and editor of *Dream of the Red Chamber*. When Cao Xueqin was writing his novel, he was aided by several persons who gave him valuable feedback. The most important of these commentators was Zhiyanzhai, commonly known as Red Inkstone. (Odd Tablet was the other significant commentator.) This pseudonym comes from the fact that the comments were written in red on handwritten manuscript copies of the novel. Red Inkstone was a close friend of Cao Xueqin, knew his family well, and was present during some of the events that are chronicled in the story that occurred in real life. The identity of Red Inkstone remains unclear. It has been speculated that the commentator was Cao's uncle, his first cousin and adopted brother Cao Yufeng, or the collective voice of several individuals. Zhou Ruchang has offered the controversial theory that Zhiyanzhai was actually a woman who was Cao's cousin and second wife and that the novel's character Shi Xiang-yun is based upon her. Red Inkstone helped Cao Xueqin in several ways. He (or she) carefully edited the novel, offered key suggestions on how to improve it, and monitored the progress he made. They also collated the various manuscripts, many of which were circulated among friends and relatives and loaned out for money. This was a difficult task because some of the manuscripts were lost or damaged. Finally, Red Inkstone provided needed support during the years it took Cao to write it. Zhiyanzhai's extensive commentary is extremely valuable because it gives detailed, illuminating, and helpful information on literary techniques used in the novel, important scenes, themes, characters, and names in the story as well as details on aspects of Cao Xueqin's life. Unfortunately, Red Inkstone's entire commentary has not been translated into English, but the article and book listed below contain useful excerpts from it.

See also **Narrative Patterns and Techniques**

FURTHER READING

Wang, John C.Y. "The Chih-yen chai Commentary and the *Dream of the Red Chamber*: A Literary Study." In Adele Rickett, ed., *Chinese Approaches to Literature* (Princeton: Princeton University Press, 1978): 189–200.

Zhou, Ruchang. *Between Noble and Humble: Cao Xueqin and the* Dream of the Red Chamber. Edited by Ronald R. Gray and Mark Ferrara (New York: Peter Lang, 2009).

Red Plum

The plum, peony, lotus, and chrysanthemum are symbols of the four seasons, with plums representing winter. Plums also have a host of other meanings. According to R.H. van Gulik, "The Plum tree is closely associated with creative power and fertility. Because of the fact that black and seemingly lifeless branches of an old plum tree still produce tender blossoms, the Chinese ascribe to this tree an unusual amount of *Yang* power, of vital energy, and have made it a symbol of longevity. Blossoming when winter has barely ended, it is a symbol of the New Year, and the revival of nature. Because of this and other associations, the plum tree and plum blossoms are often used in metaphors relating to woman and female beauty. A slender waist is compared to the twig of the plum tree, a beautiful woman is called a plum blossom, a rose-and-white face is called a plum blossom complexion. In Chinese literature one often reads stories of plum blossoms that took the shape of beautiful girls" (143). In *Dream of the Red Chamber,* blooming plums are also used as a metaphor for the beauty of several of the young women in the story. In a celebrated scene in chapter 49, Bao-yu, as a penalty for not participating in a linked verse contest, is required to obtain from Adamantina a branch from a red plum tree which is located in Green Bower Hermitage. He is successful and brings back a beautiful flowering plum branch that is placed into a vase. Poems were then written on the flower by Xing Xiu-yan, Li Wen, and Bao-qin. The red plum is clearly meant to refer to the beauty of these young women (including that of Adamantina). Because it is an early blooming flower, it also symbolizes, in the Chinese poetic tradition, the temporal nature of feminine unfettered happiness, youth, and innocence and conjures up images of loss and solitude, thus foretelling the sad fate of many of the girls in the story. In addition, Bao-qin's future is explicitly linked with that of a late-blooming plum flower because she is fated to have a late marriage. There is one other allusion to a plum flower in the novel in chapter 110. Here, Bao-yu compares the flower, because of its "incomparable purity of whiteness, the unsurpassable freshness of and delicacy of its scent" (SS, 5: 206), with the recently deceased Dai-yu.

FURTHER READING
van Gulik, R.H. *The Lore of the Chinese Lute: An Essay in Ch'in Ideology.* A Monumenta Nipponica Monograph (Tokyo: Sophia University, 1940).

Registers

Records of the past, present, and future of girls in the world kept in cupboards in the Department of the Ill-Fated Fair by the Fairy Disenchantment in her palace in the Land of Illusion. In chapter 5, Bao-yu travels in a dream to the Land of Illusion, and Disenchantment lets him read them as part of her determined effort to disabuse him of his feelings of desire, from supplementary records number two, concerning the "12 Beauties of Jinling," the most exceptional girls in his home province. He reads poems and examines the accompanying pictures in the records that depict the fates of Skybright, Aroma, Caltrop, Dai-yu, Bao-chai, Yuan-chun, Tan-chun, Xiang-yun, Adamantina, Ying-chun, Xi-chun, Xi-feng, Qiao-jie, Li Wan, and Qin-shi. Unfortunately, Bao-yu fails to understand the meaning of any of them. But, in chapter 114, he thinks back to this experience and promises himself that if he ever has another dream like this one, he will be much more observant so that he can understand things better and be able to foretell the future. His remark highlights *Dream of the Red Chamber*'s emphasis on the importance of reading and rereading. Finally, in chapter 116, he has a dream in which he travels to The Paradise of Truth, where he learns "more about the operation of fate" (SS, 5: 285) and rereads the album. This time, because of Bao-yu's hard-learned personal experiences, the recovery of his jade, and his new attitude, he is better positioned to comprehend the meaning of the registers and is now able to understand some of the predictions, while others require that he reflect upon them. But there are still several that remain incomprehensible to him.

See also **Fairy Disenchantment, Reading and Rereading**

Rice

Rice has been a staple food for most Chinese for thousands of years and has been cultivated in the hot and humid climate of the southern and central part of the country. It also has a cultural importance and is a symbol of luck, wealth, and fertility and the link between earth and heaven. Rice was an important component in traditional Chinese events like New Year's celebration, festivals, and sacrificial rites. In *Dream of the Red Chamber*, there are several references to the type of rice the Jia family consumes, and the food is also used as another sign of the economic decline of the clan. Among the kinds of rice mentioned are red emperor (which shows the Jia family's high status in that this type of rice was specifically grown for the imperial family), green glutinous, powder, rose, white glutinous, and general purpose. The servants in the novel eat plain white rice. But in chapter 75, Grandmother Jia complains that You-shi has to eat the same type of rice that the servants consume. Faithful responds by stating that meals have been downsized for economic reasons. Lady Wang then adds that because of floods, droughts, and the fact that the Jia farms no longer produce what they did in the past, rationing has occurred. Rice is also used for religious purposes in the story. In chapter 88, Faithful informs Xi-chun that she has been counting for years her "Buddha Rice," that is, collecting grains of rice to honor Buddha, which she does to express her loyalty to Grandmother Jia.

Riddles

The numerous riddles in the novel have several important functions. (In fact, it might be argued that, on one level, *Dream of the Red Chamber* is a massive and elegant literary riddle.) They reinforce several themes, like the ephemeral nature of existence and the limitations of ties of affection, and they also describe character's personalities and frequently foretell the fate of the individuals who compose them. Cao Xueqin also uses riddles to draw the reader more deeply into the story and to stress that it needs to be read carefully and critically, and not just on a surface level. Finally, these riddles would have intrigued readers since sophisticated riddle games have long been popular in China, especially among the literati, which would have been the main audience for *Dream of the Red Chamber*. There are two types of Chinese riddles. The first is based on the spoken language and uses puns and regional pronunciation. The second is more complicated and is based on written Chinese and uses complex wordplay and puns, with answers dependent on literary allusions and Chinese characters (Eber, 238). There are five instances in the story where riddles are composed or given. The most famous riddles occur in chapter 5, are rebuses, and form part of the Fairy Disenchantment's song and dance suite. They foretell the fate of 14 of the novel's major female characters and discuss aspects of their personalities, the fate of the Jia family and Dai-yu and Bao-yu's relationship and themes like the mutability of life and the dangers of *qing*.

In chapter 22, lantern riddles are written as part of the celebrations for the New Year. These stylish riddles consist of seven-character poems that foretell the tragic futures of Grandmother Jia's granddaughters. Yuan-chun's riddle is about fireworks, which represents her quick rise to the position of Imperial Concubine and her sudden death. This association is reinforced by the fact that she was born on the first day of the first month, New Year's Day, when fireworks are traditionally set off. Ying-chun's riddle is about an abacus because she will have a calculating and vicious husband who will continually remind her that she was given to him because Jia She owed him 5,000 taels of silver. Tan-chun's concerns a kite, which is her motif in the novel, because she is fated to live far from her family when she marries. Dai-yu's riddle describes an incense clock because she will, in the end, burn herself out due to illness and anger over Bao-yu's marriage to Bao-chai. Bao-chai's is associated with a bamboo wife who is doomed to live a lonely life after Bao-yu disappears. And Bao-yu's is associated with a mirror, which is one of his motifs. Mirrors traditionally have special Buddhist and Daoist meaning, and Bao-yu's connection to them, in part, symbolizes his inability to understand who he really is. Ironically, only Jia Zheng recognizes the troubling nature of these riddles, but he fails to realize that the riddles also point to the imminent fall of the Jia family.

In the next chapter, riddles are created based upon quotations from the Confucian *Four Books*. There are also, in this chapter, simpler riddles about everyday things, one of which is about a performing monkey, which Bao-yu correctly guesses. (He is linked with this animal on several occasions mainly because, in Buddhist terms, he possesses a "monkey mind.") The chapter ends with Bao-chai, Bao-yu, and Dai-yu reciting riddles they have composed, but the novel fails to provide the answers to them, probably because Cao Xueqin wanted readers to try to figure them out by themselves. In chapter 51, precocious Bao-qin offers ten concealed riddles about famous places and people, with each riddle containing hidden references to everyday objects. Her rapt audience tries to guess the solutions, but no one is successful, and the novel again fails to give the correct answers. There is still debate over what the solutions to her riddles are. (David Hawkes, in the appendix of the second volume of his translation, offers his solutions.) Some Chinese scholars, like Cai Yijiang, have maintained that Bao-qin's riddles contain hints about the future of several characters. Finally, in chapter 62, a complicated drinking game involving dice and the stringing together of quotations from prose and verse and the names of food is played during Bao-yu's birthday celebrations. One riddle during the game foretells the unhappy ending of Bao-yu and Bao-chai's marriage. Many of these riddles also gave Cao Xueqin the opportunity to raise several philosophical issues in which he and other intellectuals at that time were interested. Among these was "the problem of fate: whether a life is destined to be what it is, or whether a person has the means of changing destiny. Moreover, how can one know and act, when 'ignorance' [in the Buddhist sense] prevents one from knowing" (Eber, 247).

See also **Golden Kylin, Mirrors**

FURTHER READING

Eber, Irene. "Riddles in the *Dream of the Red Chamber*." In *Untying the Knot: On Riddles and Other Enigmatic Modes*. Edited by Galit Hasan-Rokem and David Shulman (New York: Oxford University Press, 1996): 237–251.

The Romance of the Western Chamber 西厢记

Two celebrated Chinese dramas have a strong presence in *Honglou meng*: The Yuan dynasty *zaju* (northern drama) *The Romance of the Western Chamber* (also known as *The Story of the Western Wing*) by Wang Shifu and *The Peony Pavilion*. *The Romance of the Western Chamber* is a 21-act play that has been called China's "Lover's Bible." It dramatizes the intense secret love affair between the talented and lovely maiden Cui Yingying (Oriole), the daughter of a high Tang dynasty official, and a young handsome scholar named Student Zhang. They meet in the garden of a temple where Cui and her mother are staying and fall passionately in love at first sight. After enduring, with the help of Cui's loyal maid Crimson, a series of misunderstandings, adventures (including dealing with a local bandit leader named Sun the Flying Tiger who lays siege to the monastery because he wants to marry Cui), tests (Cui's mother agrees to Zhang marrying her only if he travels to Beijing and passes the imperial examination, which he does), and a long separation, they are happily reunited in the end and marry. The play is China's most popular love comedy, and numerous sequels to, and parodies of, it have appeared. The story is told with psychological realism and was admired for Wang's criticisms of aspects of traditional Chinese society. It was hated by moralists who considered the work immoral because it showed a couple pursuing a love relationship outside the boundaries of marriage and because of its theme that young people should have the freedom to choose their marriage partners, which went against the norms of Chinese traditional morality that held that marriages were arranged by families and not to be based on love.

The play had a strong influence on the development of Chinese drama, short stories, and novels. It also had a big impact on Cao Xueqin. Stephen West and Wilt Idema, who have translated the drama into English, have gone so far as to argue, "*Dream of the Red Chamber* itself might never have been written if *The Story of the Western Wing* had not already established in vernacular literature the images of the talented student, the beautiful maiden, the stern parent, and the witty girl servant" (in Wang, 4). *Honglou meng* contains several references to the play. In one of the best-known scenes, Dai-yu discovers Bao-yu in chapter 28 secretly reading the drama in Prospect Garden, and he hands it over for her to read. Both are completely taken with the beauty of its language and the passion of the main characters. And as one commentator has neatly put it, when Bao-yu lends the book to Dai-yu, "the spreading contagion of desire at once seals the fate of their reading" (Yu, 204). Like many young devotees of the play, they also see themselves as the protagonists in the story. On several occasions, Bao-yu teases Dai-yu by quoting from the play, and although she is offended when he does this, and on one occasion warns him that she will report him to his parents for reading it, her objection is not because she is so "resistant to the idea conveyed by these citations as she is to the nuance and circumstance of its conveyance" (Yu, 205). For she is haunted by the drama and quotes from it when she is alone (chapter 35) and even publicly during a party (35), much to the chagrin of Bao-chai, who later rebukes her for doing so (42). These scenes show that she identifies with the heroine Yingying, and like her (and the heroine in *The Peony Pavilion*), Dai-yu becomes filled with romantic longing. In short, the text of *The Romance of the Western Chamber* gives Dai-yu and Bao-yu a way to view their relationship and a language to communicate their feelings for each other.

See also **Drama, Marriage, *The Peony Pavilion***

FURTHER READING

Wang, Shifu. *The Story of the Western Wing*. Edited and Translated by Stephen H. West and Wilt L. Idema (Berkeley: University of California Press, 1995).

Yu, Anthony. *Rereading the Stone: Desire and the Making of Fiction in* Dream of the Red Chamber (Princeton: Princeton University Press, 1997).

Roster of Lovers

According to the commentary of Red Inkstone, the final chapter of *Dream of the Red Chamber* was supposed to have contained a *Roster of Lovers* compiled by the Fairy Disenchantment. This roster was intended to be a supplement to the Twelve Songs written by the Fairy Disenchantment in chapter 5 and a structural device that would have completed the mythic sequence of the story. This list would have the names of 60 female characters in the story divided into five groups of 12, with each name ranked. Each female would have represented a different kind of love, based in part on their position in the primary and supplementary registers in chapter 5. For example, the first group would have been called "pure love," the second "conscientious love," and so on. The purpose of this roster was to "disenchant" or warn readers about certain types of love. Unfortunately, this missing chapter has never been found, but there has been much speculation concerning what it would have contained. CCSR International in Ontario has come up with their own version of the Roster: see http://www3.sympatico.ca/ccsr/truelove.html. There have also been numerous conjectures about where Cao Xueqin got the idea for the Roster of Lovers. The famous scholar Hu Shih has written that it is similar to the "posthumous Honors List" in the 18th-century novel *The Scholars* as well as the "stone tablet" in *The Outlaws of the Marsh*. Zhou Ruchang has interestingly argued that it originates in the late Ming dynasty collection of love stories, *Ching-shih*, by Feng Menglung. The 24 stories in this anthology are organized around a specific kind of love.

See also **Qing**

Samadhi

A Hindu and Buddhist term that literally means "to direct together." In the Buddhist Noble Eightfold Path, it is the last of the eight elements and is a form of enlightenment. In chapter 48, an impressed Bao-yu humorously tells Caltrop that she has attained *samadhi* after hearing her explicate a poem by Wang Wei.

Scholar and Beauty Romances

A very popular type of vernacular fiction (*caizi jiaren*) that first appeared in the 17th century and was widely read during Cao Xueqin's time. There are two types of these romances: the erotic and the chaste. "The chaste beauty-scholar romance can be defined as a [short] novel about a young man and woman who represent the best in intelligence, looks, and moral character that civilization has to offer. They meet by chance and get to know each other, often through the exchange of literary messages, especially love poetry…. Mean people try to steal the woman away … but fail because the youths are more clever and virtuous. Their love exists just outside—but too far from—the traditional system of marriage according to 'ritual.' ... The match of the beauty and scholar is for their own benefit rather than their parents, although they ultimately obtain their parents [sic] blessing ... the classic romances are devoid of descriptions of sex ... the language is correspondingly polite and elegant, rarely obscene or colorfully colloquial as in other fictions of the period" (McMahon, 103–104). Erotic scholar-beauty romances emphasize sexuality, and the characters in them are sexually active. In erotic romances the males are favored and are polygamists, unlike chaste romances where females are elevated.

Dream of the Red Chamber has several negative references to these romances. In chapter 1, the stone, in a conversation with Vanitas, sharply distinguishes his tale from that of *caizi jiaren* romances, labeling them stereotypical, pedantic, and highly unrealistic. Chapter 54, which has the title "Lady Jia Ridicules the Clichés of Romantic Fiction" (SS, 3: 21), has Grandmother Jia complaining that these romances do not accurately portray the real lives of well-brought-up girls from scholar-official families. She also states that their authors either envy the wealth of such families or want to discredit them and that no well-brought-up woman from these families would behave the way women do in these stories. But as is true of many incidents and conversations in *Honglou meng*, there is an underlying irony to Lady Jia's comments. For she also readily admits that she likes, on occasion, to listen to storytellers relating these romances. Moreover, on a certain level, the relationship between Bao-yu and Dai-yu roughly follows the pattern of these romances (except for how their relationship ends). Nevertheless, there are major differences between Dream *of the Red Chamber* and these romances. The women in it are considerably more complex, conflicted, and individualized than those in *caizi jiaren*, and there is much more realism about their lives. Moreover, although Cao's female characters are talented, unlike the women in the romances, they are unable to display this characteristic outside of the confines of the garden. And although Bao-yu is the only male who is aware of their special qualities, he clearly does not behave as a scholar because of his hatred of the examination system and the path to officialdom and his dogged refusal to fully participate in the masculine world.

FURTHER READING

McMahon, Keith. *Misers, Shrews, and Polygamists: Sexuality and Male-Female Relations in Eighteenth Century Chinese Fiction* (Durham: Duke University Press, 1993).

Screen Wall

Traditional Chinese houses usually had a special wall commonly made of brick, tile, or stone either inside or outside their gates. These walls were intended to hide rooms from the views of outsiders and to prevent evil spirits from entering. The Jia family mansions would have had numerous screen walls. Moreover, as chapter 33 notes, there were also screen walls that covered gateways that led from the inner to outer areas of the mansions.

Seating Arrangements and Sitting Style

Observant readers of *Honglou meng* notice that much time is spent on minutely describing the seating arrangements of characters during social gatherings like dinners, parties, and dramatic performances. This can be seen, for example, in the descriptions of Dai-yu's first dinner with the Jia family in chapter 3, the informal lunch party in Grandmother Jia's apartment in chapter 35, and the cassia viewing party in chapter 38. The reason for this focus on seating arrangements is that they reveal the shifting social relations between characters as well as a character's current status. Although hierarchy (age, sex, family relationship, and status) formally dictated where a person sat and who they sat next to, these rules are sometimes ignored, when an individual has gained favor with a person of higher status, or lowered when they are out of favor. The noted Redologist Yu Pingbo once famously drew a detailed chart that documented where each of the characters sat who attended Bao-yu's birthday party, in chapter 62, because he thought it revealed important information about the status and relationships among these characters. There were also specific rules governing how to sit in certain social situations. For example, in chapter 4, Jia Yu-cun asks the court usher, given that they were acquainted in the past, to be seated instead of standing before him. The usher then carefully and deferentially "perched [himself] sideways on the edge of a chair" (DRM, 1: 55), as was required when an individual of lower status sits near a superior. On another occasion, when Wang Xi-feng asks her maid Patience to join her on the *kang* for dinner, Patience makes sure that she is not fully sitting on it because she is Xi-feng's servant.

Sequels

When *Dream of the Red Chamber* was finally published in 1792, nearly 30 years after Cao Xueqin's death, it was so popular that sequels to it soon appeared. The first, *The Later Dream of the Red Chamber,* was published in 1796, just five years after the novel was published. By 1805, five sequels had appeared, and by 1824, there were four more. In 1877, the first extant novel written by a woman, Gu Chun, was published, and it was a sequel titled *Honglou meng ying.* By the end of the Qing dynasty in 1911, 15 had been written, including a science fiction sequel that was published in 1905 in which Bao-yu traveled to 20th-century Shanghai. (Beijing University Press, Beijing Normal University Press, and Yue Lu publishers have reprinted many of them.) Since then, a large number of sequels have continued to appear to today. These sequels were penned for a variety of reasons. Some were attempts to give the novel a much happier ending; other were composed to clear up inconsistencies in the story or to further develop characters who were liked. Recently, these sequels have received a great deal of critical attention by scholars who are interested in what they reveal about attitudes toward the original novel and the status of women, who were the primary readers of these sequels. One of these scholars, Keith McMahon, has observed, "We can see in the dozens of sequels to *Honglou meng* the irresistible urge that authors felt to resurrect the mesmerizing world of Cao Xueqin's original novel. Readers and sequel writers debated the opposing virtues of Bao-chai and Dai-yu. They loved to resent Bao-chai, Wang Xi-feng, and Xiren for 'stealing' Dai-yu from Bao-yu. The unrelenting flow toward dissolution in the latter half of the novel left writers and readers craving a resolution in which the dead come back to life, wronged victims were vindicated, and villains were punished. Sequel writers also longed for stability and thus added chapters about the easygoing daily life of a highly placed family in which people ate well, played games, arranged marriages, and raised children. A number of them also took the opportunity to desublimate the 'mind-lust' of the original Jia Bao-yu by giving him or his reincarnation multiple sexual partners" (98). A sequel and a retelling of *Dream of the Red Chamber* have even appeared in English. In 2012, Pauline Chen came out with the best-selling novel *The Red Chamber*, a vivid reimagining of the novel's main story, which attempted to iron out some inconsistencies and further develop several of the main characters. And more recently, in 2019, an English translation of a Japanese novel *Murder in the Red Chamber* by Ashibe Taku was published. It is a mystery about a series of murders that take place in Prospect Garden. In it, a murder is committed in Prospect Garden and Bao-yu assists the local magistrate who conducts the investigation.

Further Reading
Chen, Pauline A. *The Red Chamber* (New York: Alfred A. Knopf, 2012).
McMahon, Keith. "Eliminating Traumatic Antinomies: Sequels to *Honglou meng*." In *Snake's Legs: Sequels, Continuations, Rewritings, and Chinese Fiction*. Edited by Martin W. Huang (Honolulu: University of Hawaii Press, 2004): 98–115.
Taku, Ashibe. *Murder in the Red Chamber*. Translated by Tyran C. Grill (Kuma-gun, Japan: Kurodahan Press, 2019).

Shi Xiang-yun 史湘云

One of the novel's most popular and endearing characters. Vivacious, intelligent, warmhearted, outspoken, and outgoing, she is an orphan and the beloved great niece of Grandmother Jia and Bao-yu's younger second cousin. Xiang-yun lives with her wealthy uncle, Shi Ding, the Marquis of Zhongjing, whose household does not treat her well. Her name implies "Clouds over the River Xiang," so she is given the pen name of Cloud Maiden for the poetry club, which captures her lofty and charming manner. She is also highly imaginative and a talented poet, as demonstrated in the boisterous linked verse contest in chapter 50. One of the most famous scenes in the story occurs in chapter 62, where she is found tipsy and asleep on a stone bench, completely covered with crimson petals, her fan on the ground half covered with petals, her head neatly resting on a petal peony pillow, and butterflies and bees hovering above her in Prospect Garden during a party in which drinking games were played. She is a great friend of Aroma and Bao-chai, is tomboyish, and loves to dress up in male clothing. In chapter 49, she draws much attention because she is clad in a large fur coat with a red hood and deerskin boots and a colorful green tunic and red satin riding skirt underneath, thereby projecting "the somewhat masculine appearance of her figure with its graceful, athletic bearing" (SS, 2: 479). Some commentators have maintained that Cao Xueqin had originally intended for her to marry Bao-yu. Like most female characters in *Dream of the Red Chamber*, she experiences tragedy. While she has a successful marriage, her husband, soon after they are married, contracts tuberculosis and does not have long to live.

See also **Golden Kylin**

Simple 傻大姐

Foolish, hefty, 14-year-old maid of Grandmother Jia's who helped with heavy work, she is extremely naïve but kind. Her nickname, Sha Daijie, means "Big Sister Ignorance," which is representative of a central Buddhist ideal. Simple's nickname belies her importance considering she is inadvertently the cause of two important events in the novel: she discovers the purse in Prospect Garden and informs Lady Xing about it, thereby precipitating the raid on the garden, and she also tells Dai-yu about the secret marriage plans for Bao-yu, information which directly leads to Dai-yu's death.

Skybright 晴雯

One of Bao-yu's senior maids, Skybright is intelligent, beautiful, industrious when it is needed and extremely loyal to Bao-yu. But she is also hot tempered, outspoken, impatient, and has a sense of entitlement because she is his maid (as shown in her treatment of Crimson). She has no memory of her parents and was raised by her cousin and bought when she was ten years old by Chief Steward Lai Da to serve his wife. But Grandmother Jia was so taken with her that she was given to her as a present. The matriarch had such a high opinion of Skybright's ability that she eventually gave her to Bao-yu. She is his maid for five and a half years. During that time, she has several frequently testy arguments with him but is there for him when he has troubles. She famously shows her great loyalty to him in chapter 52 when she, though ill, is able to repair a burned hole in his Russian, gold, peacock snow cape. In one of the novel's many ironic turns, while she is still recovering from this illness and is in a weakened condition, she is brought before a scornful Lady Wang, accused of wanton behavior, and eventually dismissed. After her dismissal, she moves to her cousin's house where she is mistreated by him and his promiscuous wife. She dies a sad and lonely death there at age 16. Shortly before her demise, Bao-yu pays a tearful visit, and her conflicted feelings of despair, happiness, surprise, and love for him are revealed. After her death, he writes a heartfelt eulogy in honor of her and becomes convinced that she has turned into a hibiscus flower fairy.

Smallpox Goddess 逗神娘娘

A Daoist goddess who controls smallpox and is attached to the celestial Ministry of Education, her Chinese name is T'ou-Shen Niang Niang, and she is sometimes depicted as wearing a large shawl to keep the cold off her infected skin. She is infamous for her capricious ways and is said to especially enjoy causing smallpox in young children, particularly those who are attractive. As a result, parents had their children wear ugly masks during festival times to fool her. People prayed to her, asking her to show mercy. During the Ming and early Qing dynasty, smallpox was a major problem and killed many children. The Manchus were especially afraid of the disease because it rarely occurred in the region from which they came, and most of them were not immune to it. Several prominent members of the imperial family died from it, including the Shunzhi emperor. In 1687, the Kangxi emperor decreed that all lineage children had to be inculcated against the disease after their first birthday. In chapter 21 of the novel, Xi-feng's baby daughter Qiao-jie contracts smallpox, and a strict protocol is immediately followed by the family. Patience and Xi-feng worship the goddess every day, fried and sautéed food is avoided, a ritually purified room is set aside for the doctors, and a special dark red dress is made for Qia-jie. Moreover, Jia Lian is required to move out because the parents of the patient were traditionally required to practice sexual abstinence during the period of the illness. But Jia Lian fails to follow this rule and starts an affair with the notorious Mattress, which eventually leads to a major public dustup between him, Xi-feng, and Patience, when Xi-feng finds out about it in chapter 44, and to Mattress's suicide.

"Song of Everlasting Grief" 长恨歌

Famous melancholic, long narrative poem by the popular Tang dynasty poet Bai Ju-yi (772–846). It narrates the tragic love affair between Tang Emperor Xuanzhong and his favorite consort Yang Guifei. The poem describes Yang Guifei's rise to power, the emperor's obsession with her, and her subsequent death by soldiers. It also describes an emotional conversation from the world of the shadows, after her death, between her and a grief-stricken Xuanzhong. One of the themes of the poem is the conflict between love and duty. Ju-yi was noted for the verbal simplicity of his verse and for his belief that literature should have a didactic role and serve a social function. Bao-yu quotes two well-known lines from this poem to himself while thinking of Dai-yu in chapter 109. Bao-chai overhears him and immediately chides him for comparing Dai-yu to Yang Guifei.

See also **Yang Guifei**

The South

Cao Xueqin was born and lived in the southern region of Jiangsu in China until the government confiscated his family's property in 1727, and they were sent to live in Beijing. This prosperous region was an important trade and cultural center during the Qing dynasty and famous for its beautiful scenery and historic sites. There is a definite and nostalgic southern presence in the novel. The story, on the realistic level, begins in a southern city. There are allusions to southern food (like lyceum tips) and customs: Prospect Garden contains flora from the southern Yangtze valley; members of the Jia family make periodic visits to the south; the family has farms and holdings upon which they are dependent in the south; and the family graveyard is also there. (Jia Zheng takes Grandmother Jia's and Dai-yu's bodies to it for burial at the end of the novel.) The family's counterpart, the Zhen family, live in the south. Xi-feng, the Xues, Caltrop, Dai-yu, and others are also from the region. In chapter 87, Tan-chun, Dai-yu, the Li sisters, and Xiang-yun have a conversation about the south, with Xiang-yun tellingly stating that some members of the Jia family "are northerners, others were born in the south, still others were brought up in the south and then came north. Our coming together now in one place shows that everyone's fate is fixed. Each individual is destined for different places" (DRM, 3: 99). Later, in the same chapter, Dai-yu longingly recalls the South's "spring flowers and autumn moonlight, limpid streams and lucent hills, Yangchow's twenty-four bridges and Six Dynasties' relics" (DRM, 3: 100).

Spirit Money

See **Money and Measurements**

Spirit Writing

"Passive" or "automatic" writing in which spirits, gods, other worldly beings, and immortals were believed to communicate with this world through a divining instrument that was operated by a spirit medium who transmitted spirit messages. This practice was known as "wielding the planchette" and was especially popular with the educated elite during the Qing dynasty who used it to foretell whether a candidate would successfully pass the imperial civil service examination and even to get advance notice about upcoming key exam questions. Spirit writing was also sometimes employed in the legal field and in party games. It was also believed by some that famous poets and writers could communicate through the planchette and author poems, letters, and even dramas. Cao Xueqin appears to have taken a rather jaundiced view of this practice. There are several instances in *Dream of the Red Chamber* when spirit writing is used. In chapter 4, it is falsely employed by Jia Yu-cun to protect Xue Pan from a murder charge. And in chapter 95, a reluctant Adamantina uses the planchette wand to summon the spirit Iron Crutch Li to find the location of Bao-yu's missing jade. While the answer the spirit sends in reply is seemingly correct, Li Wan, Bao-yu, and others fail to completely understand it.

Spiritual Tablets

The most important symbol of Chinese ancestor worship, it signifies filial piety, and written on it is the name of a past ancestor. In *Dream of the Red Chamber*, the tablets are kept in the family's ancestral hall, as mentioned in chapters 13 and 53. The tablet is considered an effigy of the dead ancestor. When rites are observed, incense is burned in front of the tablet, food is placed before it for the spirit, and participants bow. By Cao Xueqin's time, "domestic ancestor worship had become a cultural universal in China.... Enriched by Confucian, Buddhist, and Religious Daoist ideas, ancestor worship buttressed the Chinese family system not only by cementing social relationships and reinforcing status obligations, but also by fostering a profoundly conservative precedent mindedness at all levels of society. Important decisions within the family, whether made by peasants or by the emperor himself, required the 'consent' of the ancestors, and all major social events were symbolically 'shared' with them" (Smith, 154).

See also **Confucianism, Funerals, Mourning Periods**

Further Reading

Smith, Richard J. *The Qing Dynasty and Traditional Chinese Culture* (Lanham: Rowman & Littlefield, 2015).

Spitting At/On

There are at least 11 occasions in the novel in which characters in a fit of anger spit at another person (frequently on their face). It is done by both male and female members of the Jia family and even servants. Among these incidents are when Jia Zhen orders a page to spit on Jia Rong for laziness; Xi-feng spits on servants in several chapters for misbehavior, and at the ghost of Qin-shi out of fright; You-shi spits at Jia Rong for hiding Er-jie's secret marriage to Jia Lian; Bao-yu spits on Jia Yun for aggressively trying to get him to agree to a marriage he has cooked up for him; Jia Lian does it to Jia Yun for not properly supervising the mansion's night watch; and Faithful vigorously spits on the face of her ambitious sister-in-law who pressures her to become Jia She's concubine. The Chinese character for spitting is 啐 (which also has the meaning of contempt or despise); in most cases it does not mean that saliva was actually expelled but rather that the sound of spitting was made. For example, Chinese commentators have pointed out that when women in the novel feel deep resentment, they will expel saliva, as Xi-feng does; when they are simply angry, they will just make the sound. Spitting was, in certain situations, an acceptable practice among superiors who could do it to subordinates. It was very rarely done by individuals of a lower status to a person of higher status. While it was thought to be very offensive, it was acceptable when it was done as a joke or even as a sign of closeness between friends and acquaintances (using only the sound).

Su Dong-po 苏东坡 (1037–1101)

The pen name of the great multitalented Song dynasty poet, critic, statesman, hydrological engineer, painter, philosopher, and calligrapher Su Shi. Su is famous for his mastery of nearly all the Chinese literary forms: prose essays, poetry, calligraphy and painting. He is primarily celebrated for his poetry, which is noted for its emotionally unrestrained character, optimistic transcendental perspective, and stylistic novelties. Sun is mentioned in a poem by Dai-yu in chapter 38 and on a drinking cup owned by Adamantina in chapter 41. And in chapter 8, it is stated (ironically, given his limited ability) that Jia Zheng is having an afternoon nap in a small study located in the mansion's Su Dong-po rooms.

Suicide

Traditional Chinese literature abounds with characters, the vast majority being women, who commit suicide, and *Dream of the Red Chamber* is no different. There are ten suicides in it, and eight of them are committed by women. While the taking of one's life was thought during Cao Xueqin's time to be a shocking event because it involved an act that went against the important Confucian precept of filial piety, which held that his/her body was a gift from their parents and could not be harmed without their consent, it was also frequently viewed as evidence of virtue when women did it, which was common in the 18th century. The novel captures this ambivalent attitude well. Female characters in the story take their lives for a variety of reasons. Golden kills herself out of loss of face after being unfairly cashiered by Lady Wang for flirting with Bao-yu. Qin-shi probably does herself in out of shame when her adultery with her father-in-law is discovered. Her maid Gem kills herself out of loyalty to her, or, it has been argued, because she is the person who comes across Qin-shi *in flagrante delicto* with Jia Zhen. Jia Lian's mistress, the notorious "Mattress," hangs herself out of shame after her very public spat with Xi-feng. You San-jie destroys herself out of disappointment and anger when Liu Xiang-lian suddenly cancels their engagement because of doubts about her character. Her sister Er-jie commits suicide because of ill treatment by Xi-feng and fears that she is losing the love of Jia Lian. (The tragic deaths of the sisters can also be explained it part by the fact that it was common in Qing dynasty vernacular literature for "women from tainted backgrounds to [resort to] suicide to save face and restore their reputation" [Zamperini, 82].) Ying-chun's tempestuous principal maid Chess commits suicide (an act that earns the praise of Xi-feng) when her mother refuses to let her marry her cousin. Grandmother Jia's loyal maid Faithful hangs herself soon after the matriarch's death, in part out of fear of Jia She, who has designs on her. And Lin Dai-yu, while suffering from tuberculosis, wills her own death out of her love for Bao-yu when she learns he will marry Bao-chai. (In terms of the male suicides: Chess's cousin kills himself out of despair over her suicide, and it is stated that the government determines that Stony's, the owner of the set of antique fans that Jia She stole, death was due "to his own eccentricity" [SS, 5: 141].)

Honglou meng is also accurate in its description of the methods used in committing this act. Upper-class women frequently swallowed gold, as Er-jie does, or starved themselves to death, which Dai-yu attempted to do. Servants and maids often hanged themselves, like Faithful, or drowned themselves, as does Golden (Zamperini, 88). (Chess and Gem die by ramming their heads against a wall, and San-jie uses a sword.) In addition, the novel also touches on a common belief at the time concerning individuals who committed suicide: that they could come back as a ghost, especially if they were a wronged woman. In the story, Qin-shi returns as a ghost on three occasions, twice to give Xi-feng Confucian advice on how to shore up the family's fortunes and once manifestly to Faithful to show her how to hang herself. San-jie appears to Er-jie to warn her about Xi-feng. In these incidents, the apparitions "become disturbing harbingers of the Jia family's decline" (Theiss, 204). The topic of female suicide in Imperial China has recently received much attention by scholars as part of a general trend in Western women's studies, which attempts to ascribe some agency and power to Chinese women during this period and not view them only as passive victims of ruling standards regarding gender or virtuous martyrs. Specifically, it has been argued that female suicides during China's late imperial period can also be seen as an "almost instinctual assertion of personal integrity and interests, which was thus neither an act of resistance against dominant gender norms nor an expression of accommodation to them.

In suicide and in myriad other ways, women struggled to define chastity for themselves and to defend their own sense of morality against the standards of propriety asserted by family authorities and the state" (Theiss, 207). Moreover, Paula Zamperini, who has studied late imperial literary representations of women's suicide, has argued that they are usually depicted as "acts of passion and self-assertion, rather than as being construed as defeat in the face of adversaries, a response to abuse suffered, or as a last resort to preserve chastity.... [They are] presented as a path of independence" (77). This is generally true of the motivations for many of the female suicides in *Dream of the Red Chamber*. Cao Xueqin also uses several of the suicides in the novel to warn readers about the destructive power of unbridled *qing*.

See also **Qing, Qin-shi**

FURTHER READING

Theiss, Janet. *Disgraceful Matters: The Politics of Chastity in Eighteenth-Century China* (Berkeley: University of California Press, 2004).
Zamperini, Paula. "Untamed Hearts: Eros and Suicide in Late Imperial China." *Nan Nu* 3.1 (2001): 77–104.

Sun Shao-zu 孙绍祖

The reprehensible husband of Ying-chun, he is one of the most despicable characters in the novel and is compared to the infamous wolf of Zhong-shan in the seventh song of Fairy Disenchantment's libretto "A Dream of Golden Days." This famous Chinese fairy story describes an ungrateful wolf who viciously turns on a kind but naïve scholar who saved him from a hunting party and tries to eat him. In the end, the wolf is punished. The story's moral concerns the dangers of not having a realistic understanding of the world and the virtues of doing good. Sun is nearly 30, holds the position of military provost in the city garrison and is thought to have a good future. Although he is an impressive-looking individual, tall, strong, has a military bearing, and can be charming when necessary, he is also vindictive, a spendthrift, has a deep animus against the Jia family (supposedly because they owe Sun's family money), and treats Ying-chun abominably. Jia Zheng did not approve of the marriage because he believed that the Sun family were uneducated and lacking in class. But Jie She ignored his objections. Sun and his family's continual and vicious bullying of delicate Ying-chun eventually results in her lonely death.

Supernatural

It was not uncommon for works of traditional Chinese literature to contain supernatural and mythological elements, and *Dream of the Red Chamber* is no different. Modern Chinese scholars of the novel have often been rather embarrassed by its presence in the story and have usually either ignored it or instead stressed the realistic elements of the story. When they have discussed the topic of the supernatural in *Hunglou meng*, they have frequently attempted to explain it by saying it is "the dregs of a 'feudal belief system'" (Shi, 113) or that it was just formulaic narrative scaffolding that was commonly used in extended Chinese fiction. They have also differentiated between the supernatural happenings in the book's first 80 chapters and the last 40 chapters, saying that the latter are pertinent to key themes in the story, and the former were fabricated by another author, namely, Gao E., the editor of the first printed version of the novel, and are superfluous to the plot. Among these supernatural incidents in the initial two-thirds of the novel are: chapter 1's mythological framing of the story; Zhen Shi-yin's dream about the monk and Daoist; Bao-yu's visit to the Land of Illusion; the Daoist priest's unsuccessful attempt, with his magic mirror, to cure Jia Rui of his lovesickness for Xi-feng; Qin-shi appearing as a ghost to Xi-feng; Mother Ma's hex on Bao-yu and Xi-feng and the monk who suddenly appears and uses Bao-yu's jade to dispel the evil spirits attacking them; the argument between the minions of the underworld while Qin Zhong is dying; and the sounds of melancholy sighing from the Jia family's Ancestral Temple which disrupts Jia Zhen's Mid–Autumn Festival's outing with his family.

Two of the most prominent advocates of this interpretation are Wu Shih-Chang and Yu Pingbo. Wu has argued that these events are "relevant to the theme of the novel or to other significant stories. The first mythological, pre-natal account of the hero and heroine is really an introduction to the novel, it is not part of the mundane drama, as is Zhen Shi-yin's dream in the first chapter. Bao-yu's dream in chapter five is a revelation of stories in the whole book.... The Daoist priest with his 'Precious Mirror for Romantic Life' illustrates the moral of the novel.... The 'ghost story' at the death of Qin Zhong is an obvious parody in which the author lampoons the snobbery of the 'ghosts' and their 'squad leader.' The story about the priestess Ma's black magic is less defensible from our point of view, but at least it shows the antagonism between the high handed Xi-feng, the much doted on Bao-yu, and the embittered concubine Zhao.... The strange sounds coming from the Ancestral Temple in the Mid-Autumn night was interpreted as 'sighs' by those who were suffering from psychoneurosis caused by their fear of the clan's decline, and is meant to be a sign of depression rather than a superstitious ghost story. We can see that in Cao Xueqin's work each of these stories has its significant point besides being a story" (309–310). Wu also maintains that in contrast to the novel's first 80 chapters, the supernatural elements in the last 40 chapters "are obviously too superstitious to be convincing. They are hardly relevant to the central theme or to other stories ... so many of them must be boring to any reader; and the great space they occupy does little justice to the novel" (309). The influential scholar Yu Pingbo has drawn a distinction between what he believes is Cao Xueqin's skillful use of supernatural allegories and parables and what he considers Gao E's patently superstitious beliefs, as exemplified in the last third of the novel.

Although both scholars raise some interesting points about the functions of the story's supernatural elements in the first 80 chapters, they seem oblivious to the literary quality and importance of some of the "superstitious" incidents in the last 40. (Even if we assume, as they do, the controversial theory that these chapters are forgeries.) For example, Cao's depiction of the meeting of the two Bao-yus is imaginative and raises issues that are germane to several of *Dream of the Red Chamber*'s themes as well as to the consequential philosophical debate that occurs between Bao-yu and Dai-yu shortly after the Bao-yus meeting. The scene where the Daoist monks "capture" the evil spirits that infest Prospect Garden in the end reads as a clever parody rather than as an expression of the author's superstitious beliefs. The return of Bao-yu's jade by the monk and his attempt to give it back to him is a logical development of Bao-yu's quest for philosophical understanding and reinforces the novel's stress on the concepts of origins and return. In the end, as Yaohua Shi has concluded, "neither Wu Shichang nor Yu Pingbo makes a convincing case for the interpolation theory" [114].)

See also **Doubles and Doubling, The Last 40 Chapters**

FURTHER READING

Shi, Yaohua. "Beginnings and Departures: *The Dream of the Red Chamber.*" *New Zealand Journal of Asian Studies*. 7.1 (2005): 112–133.

Wu, Shih-Ch'ang. *On the Red Chamber Dream* (Oxford: Oxford University Press, 1961).

Sutras (Diamond and Heart)

The canonical scriptures of the Buddha, they are records of discussions of the Buddha and/or his enlightened disciples. Two seminal sutras, the Diamond and Heart, are mentioned in chapter 88 of *Dream of the Red Chamber*. In this chapter, the young women of the Jia family are ordered to make copies of both sutras to help celebrate Grandmother Jia's upcoming 81st birthday. The *Diamond Sutra* is the world's oldest printed book and the most studied of all the sutras. It consists of 6,000 words and 32 sections, and its major themes are the illusory and empty nature of all phenomena, impermanence, the importance of nonattachment, and the idea that spiritual understanding is contingent on transcending rational categories. The word diamond in its title means that the text is designed to sharply cut through everything so that the reader can obtain enlightenment. The sutra's final chapter famously states:

> As a lamp, a cataract, a star in space
> an illusion, a dewdrop, a bubble
> a dream, a cloud, a flash of lightening
> view all created things like this [Red Pine, 429].

In chapter 110 of the novel, a dying Grandmother Jia requests that copies of the *Diamond Sutra* be made and distributed. The *Heart Sutra*, in contrast, is very short and discusses the emptiness of phenomenal reality. It attempts to show that an awareness of this emptiness results in a release from the cycle of death and rebirth and leads to wisdom. Karl-Heinz Pohl has argued that the concept of non-duality in the *Heart Sutra* is central to understanding *Dream of the Red Chamber*.

See also **Buddhism**

FURTHER READING

The Diamond Sutra: The Perfection of Wisdom. Text and commentaries translated from the Sanskrit and Chinese by Red Pine (New York: Counterpoint, 2001).
Pohl, Karl-Heinz. "The Role of the *Heart Sutra* in *Dream of the Red Chamber*." *European Journal of Sinology* 5 (2014): 9–20.

Swastika

In traditional Chinese culture, the swastika was a Buddhist symbol signifying spirituality, eternity, and plurality centuries before the Nazis appropriated it. The word comes from the Sanskrit and means auspicious. In chapter 19, Bao-yu's servant Tealeaf attempts to seduce a girl who is named Swastika because her mother dreamed of a piece of brocade that had a pattern of lucky swastikas on it before she was born. She is given this name in the hope that she will have a lucky future.

Themes and Indeterminacy

There is still not a firm consensus among scholars over what the central or core theme is of *Dream of the Red Chamber*. New theories continue to appear, and sometimes old ones reappear with new packaging. The main problem is that the novel itself is so inclusive and indeterminate, and the text at times so contradictory between surface and underlying meaning, that it is difficult to clearly discern an all-embracing vision and message. As a result, it is possible to marshal arguments for a wide variety of interpretations. It has been argued by two prominent scholars that the work's "contrasting levels of 'reality,' whether the mythical world of goddesses, sylphs, and divine stones, or any of the social levels that appear in quotidian detail throughout its length, deliberately leave the reader confused over the author's or authors' vision and purpose" (Minford and Hegel, 454). David Rolston has observed, "Many readers have found a home in *Honglou meng* because there is so much room to inhabit, if for no other reason than its obviously unfinished state tempts readers to move in and start making repairs" (347). Li Qiancheng has written, "The 'incompleteness' of *Honglou meng* again testifies to this: too many contradictions remain unresolved; perhaps they are not resolvable, or perhaps they are not meant to be resolved" (17–18). Anthony Yu has noted, "The several names of the narrative and their allusive resonance relative to its content, may not indicate indecisiveness of authorial intent, but they surely help explain why scholars find it difficult to arrive at a consensus on the novel's main theme or meaning" (289). Lucian Miller has picturesquely likened the novel "to a great ball of silken yarn we weavers weave into endless patterns and colors" (263). In addition, it has also been contended that it, in the end, even undercuts major Chinese conventional religious belief systems at the time: "The Buddhist Confucian messages vibrating so strongly throughout the book are both denied a functioning purpose in human life at the end of the novel. Bao-yu's final choice to exit from the mundane world and return to his primal form of a rock not permeable to human attachment denounces both Confucianism and Buddhism as a way of a happy life: they appear equally inadequate and illusory and therefore abandoned" (Jinsheng, 171). And Robert Hegel has gone so far as to surmise that Cao Xueqin "strived throughout the last years of his life to *de*stabilize his text—to create *more* logical inconsistencies, *more* moral paradoxes, as his way of revealing his fundamental skepticism about the moral validity of didactic elements in popular fiction and even in conventional worldviews of his time" (Hegel, 162).

Some of this confusion also lies in the fact that Cao Xueqin gives contradictory statements about what the purpose of the novel is in the text itself. In chapter 1, Vanitas concludes, after reading the stone's tale, that the main theme is *qing* (love). In the same chapter, the Stone says that he hopes that readers of the tale would "heed its lesson and abandon their vain and frivolous pursuits, and by doing so obtain some small arrest in the deterioration of their vital forces" (SS, 1: 50), and there is also a short poem that laments, "All men call the author fool; None his secret message hears" (SS, 1: 51). In chapter 120, Vanitas, after carefully reading the story, surmises that its main message is, "Things are not as they seem, that the extraordinary and the ordinary, truth and fiction, are all relative to each other" (SS, 5: 374). Later, Cao Xueqin himself laughingly undercuts the veracity of the story, telling Vanitas that it is "a fictitious rustic tale … that serves to while away the time with a couple of friends after wine and food, or to dispel loneliness some rainy evening under the lamp by the window. It doesn't have to be vouched for or launched by men of consequence" (DRM, 3: 586). As a result, an amazed Vanitas says to himself, "So, it's all hot air-fantastic! Neither author, transcriber, nor readers can tell what it is about. It is nothing but a literary diversion to entertain readers" (DRM, 3: 586). Then to further complicate matters, the book ends with a four-line *gatha* that declares:

> A tale of grief is told,
> Fantasy most melancholy,
> Since all live in a dream.
> Why laugh at other's folly? [DRM, 3: 586]

Consequently, scholars have advanced a wide range of possible central themes for the novel. Since it was first published, it has been contended that Cao Xueqin intended for it to be a veiled depiction of the Qing court; the sad tale of a Manchu prince's illicit and failed love affair; a revealing roman à clef; an anti–Manchu and pro–Han Chinese tract arguing for the restoration of the Ming dynasty; a hidden autobiography; a strong Confucian critique of Qing era society; a sharp attack on China's feudal society; a story about the fictive nature of art; an epic vision of life; a Buddhist parable concerning disenchantment and enlightenment; a Daoist-inspired fictional text; a Chinese *bildungsroman*; an arresting account of a tragic love triangle; a brilliant novel of manners or sentiment; a graphic depiction of the unreliable nature of the real world (the world of the Red Dust) and the categories of truth/falsity and the real/unreal and the importance of seeing through and transcending it; a homage to and discussion of female talent; a narrative of the vanity of desire; a tale illustrating the idea, "Everything produces its opposite; the human condition is mutability; life is but a dream" (Miller, 57); and a vast tribute to women. But that is not all. It has also been maintained that Cao was a great philosopher who was attempting to show the importance of *qing* and the various forms it takes. Moreover, it has been claimed that *qing* is the central thread in the novel that connects and drives the story. The famed Redologist Yu Pingbo famously felt that Cao simply wanted "to say nothing else but that he began with a life of happiness but ended in a rather miserable state; and he painfully recollects his life and is nostalgic about his previous joys" (cited in Bonner, 557). And still others have taken the main theme to be that nothing in this world can be relied upon, and even true and innocent love will be destroyed in the end. The important commentator and friend of Cao, Red Inkstone, stated that the major theme is "Life is a dream.... This grand book narrates a dream, Bao-yu's affections are a dream, Jia Rui's lust is a dream.... What's more these criticisms are written in a dream" (quoted in Edwards, 13). Expanding on this idea that life is a dream, it has also been advanced that the novel's central message is Buddhist and cautionary in nature and that we can be awakened from our illusions about life only by seeing through our net of desire and learning to distinguish the differences between the real and the fictional, truth and falsity.

But sometimes in the discussion the important point gets lost that *Dream of the Red Chamber* also has a strong underlying skepticism as shown in its frequent use of irony, satire, ambiguity, subversion, critical self-reflexivity, and ambivalence, characteristics that make it, in several ways, a strikingly modernistic novel. As Wai-yee Li has correctly observed, "In its encyclopedic inclusiveness, *Honglou meng* in a sense sums up Chinese culture, but the greatness of the book lies more in the way it asks difficult questions of that culture. It poses as problems the way systems of order [whether sociopolitical, moral, philosophical, religious]" (655). It also seems plausible to argue that the reason why a consensus has not been reached regarding the novel's main theme is because Cao Xueqin decided *not* to present an all-embracing and all-sustaining theme, creed, or vision and that the power, distinction, and artistry of the book ultimately lie in the probing questions it asks and not in the solution it offers. In this way (and others), it is quite similar to the famous novel *Jin Ping Mei*, which had a major influence on Cao. As Gu Mingdong has noted about this Ming dynasty work, "The underlying principle that holds all the ... differing and different elements [of *Jin Ping Mei*] together is not to be found in any overarching vision, but [is] to be found in an artistic vision which is deconstructive in nature.... The author sees life as a continuum of paradoxes and makes full use of them in his creative act. He plays different ideological visions and modes of presentations one against each other and refuses to allow any vision or mode to have the last word, thereby creating a vortex of artistic tension that endows the novel with multivalence and polysemy" (199). Mingdong goes on to explain that *Jin Ping Mei's* "narrative form conveys an artistic vision which sees the structure and texture of the novel grounded on a language which transforms, parodies, contradicts and undermines surface meanings. This may explain why different readers may find different layers of meaning which clash and conflict with one another" (199). This might also be true of *Dream of the Red Chamber*.

This, of course, is not to say that *Dream of the Red Chamber* does not have themes, recurring perspectives and concerns, for it obviously does. A novel of this size and scope would naturally have a host of them. Bao-yu's arch of philosophical development clearly shows that it is a tale in part about the quest for identity, the search for understanding of life's meaning. Cao Xueqin is also greatly interested in the concept of *qing* and delineating its various types, as seen in his Roster of Lovers as well as in the dialectical relationship between truth and falsity, the real and unreal. The subject of corruption—governmental, legal, social, and personal—is another area of great concern in the novel. Another constant and underlying theme that runs throughout the story, as observed in characters like Bao-yu and which comes to the fore in his philosophical debate with Bao-chai in chapter 118, is, as C.T. Hsia has concisely put it, a "nostalgia for, and tormented determination to seek liberation from, the world of Red Dust" (297). This tension is brilliantly captured in the story by the stark contrast between the worldly material and cultural splendor of the Jia family's lifestyle and the impulse expressed by some of its characters for transcendence and personal salvation. While the story contains definite Buddhist and Daoist elements and narrative structures, it remains an open question as to whether they are, as Zhou Ruchang and some other scholars have contended, in the end, simply structural paradigms that are borrowed for organizational, formal, and traditional purposes to help propel the narrative and to retain the reader's interest and do not reflect a presiding ideology.

In short, it might be more plausible to view *Honglou meng* as a work that is primarily diagnostic and not prescriptive in nature. In other words, that

Cao Xueqin was more concerned about identifying problems with and posing fundamental questions about the human condition and society and not so much with providing solutions or systems of beliefs to rectify them. (At the risk of being accused of committing the biographical fallacy, there is no clear evidence that Cao personally believed in any comprehensive and systematic religious or philosophical ideology or that he was able to successfully resolve in his life the central tension shown in the novel between worldly attachments and transcendence. We do know that his death was greatly hastened by the sudden demise of his young son. These biographical facts might very well be reflected in his work.) Furthermore, it does seem clear that he is also attempting, as philosophical novelists do, to provoke self-reflection and examination, critical thinking, and skepticism in the reader. The novel's repeated emphasis on reading (and rereading) between the lines and looking beyond surface meanings impels readers to view their own life critically. Its indeterminacy also ultimately forces them to turn their attention to, and to question, themselves and even life itself. Cao Xueqin does not spoon-feed his readers, he does expect them to involve themselves imaginatively and actively in the story and then think and consider. At the same time, the open-text nature and lack of a specific dominating ideological vision in the novel gives readers the freedom to discover within the work themes and concerns they can pursue on their *own* and reach their *own* conclusions. (It has long been held by the Chinese that the way one views this novel is dependent on the stages a person is going through in life.) In short, *Dream of the Red Chamber* provides the basis for readers to create and craft their own philosophy of life.

See also **Critical Reception—Chinese**; **Critical Reception—Western**; **Influences on Cao Xueqin**; *Qing*; **Reading and Rereading**

FURTHER READING

Bonner, Joey. "Yu P'ing-po and the Literary Dimensions of the Controversy Over *Hung lou Meng*." *The China Quarterly* 67 (1976): 546–581.

Edwards, Louise. *Men and Women in Qing China: Gender in the* Red Chamber Dream (Leiden: E.J. Brill, 1994).

Hegel, Robert. "Unpredictability and Meaning in Mid-Qing Literati Novels." In *Paradoxes of Traditional Chinese Literature*. Edited by Eva Hung (Hong Kong: The Chinese University Press, 1994): 147–166.

Hsia, C.T. "*Dream of the Red Chamber*." In *The Classic Chinese Novel: A Critical Introduction* (New York: Columbia University Press, 1968): 245–297.

Jinsheng, Jeannie. *The* Dream of the Red Chamber: *An Allegory of Love* (Paramus, New Jersey: Homa & Sekey Books, 2004).

Li, Qiancheng. *Fictions of Enlightenment*: Journey to the West, Tower of the Myriad Mirrors, *and* Dream of the Red Chamber (Honolulu: University of Hawaii Press, 2003).

Li, Wai-yee. "Full-Length Vernacular Fiction." In *The Columbia History of Chinese Literature*. Edited by Victor H. Mair (New York: Columbia University Press, 2001).

Miller, Lucien. *Masks of Fiction in the* Dream of the Red Chamber: *Myth, Mimesis and Persona* (Tucson: University of Arizona Press, 1975).

Minford, John, and Robert Hegel. "*Hung-lou Meng*." In William Nienhauser, ed. *The Indiana Companion to Traditional Chinese Literature* (Bloomington: Indiana University Press, 1986): 452–456.

Mingdong, Gu. "Paradox of Vision and Poetics of Paradox: Ideology and Form in the *Jin Ping Mei*." *Journal of Oriental Studies* 37.2 (1999): 175–203.

Rolston, John. "Everything at Once: The '*Honglou meng*.'" In *Traditional Chinese Fiction and Fiction Commentary: Reading and Writing Between the Lines* (Stanford: Stanford University Press, 1997): 329–348.

Yu, Anthony. "Cao Xueqin's *Hongloumeng* (*Story of the Stone* or *Dream of the Red Chamber*)." In *Masterworks of Asian Literature*. Edited by Barbara Miller. *Comparative Perspective: A Guide for Teaching* (Armonk, New York: Sharpe, 1994): 285–298.

Zhou, Ruchang. "None the *Red Chamber* Message Hears: Art as Living Philosophy." *Tamkang Review* 36.1–2 (2005): 89–103.

Three Springs

Nickname for Jia Ying-chun, Jia Tan-chun, and Jia Xi-chun. It comes from the word "chun," which means spring.

Top of the List Gold Medallions

Medallions that are given to imperial examination candidates in the hope that they will score first in the examination results. Patience, in chapter 7, selects two of these medallions for Xi-feng to give to Qin Zhong in honor of their first meeting.

Tortoise

The turtle is greatly admired by the Chinese for its endurance and long life. It is considered noble, sacred, auspicious, and a symbol of power and tenacity. Turtles also symbolize the shape of the universe; their dome-shaped back represents the vault or sky, and their belly, the earth. The turtle motif was also common in traditional Chinese tomb construction. In chapter 23, during a heated argument with Dai-yu, Bao-yu says that if he had wished to insult her, "I'll fall into the pond tomorrow and let the scabby headed tortoise swallow me, so that I change into a big turtle myself. Then when you become a lady of the first rank and go at last to your paradise in the west, I shall bear the stone table at your grave on my back forever" (DRM, 23: 336–337).

Tripitaka

A Sanskrit term that means "Three baskets," it refers to the three early authoritative texts of the Buddhist canon. Li Wan jokingly compared Patience in chapter 39 to the famous Tang dynasty monk who is named after the Tripitaka who traveled to India in search of these three Buddhist texts.

The Twelve Songs of the Suite of "A Dream of Golden Days"

This song and dance suite was composed by Fairy Disenchantment for Bao-yu and was performed by 12 dancers in chapter 5 in the Land of Illusion. It is part of her determined attempt to instruct him in the illusionary nature of attachments of love and sentiment (*qing*). The suite is important because it, along with the previous supplementary registers, provides hidden clues that prefigure the fates of 12 of the novel's main female characters, who are referred to as "the 12 beauties of Jingling." The prelude to the suite poses the question of "how did love begin?" (SS, 1: 139). The songs forecast the tragic fates of the beauties in the following order: Lin Dai-yu and Xue Bao-chai, Jia Yuan-chun, Jia Tan-chun, Shi Xiang-yun, Adamantina, Jia Ying-chun, Jia Xi-chun, Wang Xi-feng, Jia Qiao-jie, Li Wan, and Qin-shi. The suite also, in the epilogue, offers a summing up of what has happened in the story and makes a prediction of what will happen to the Jia family. There also have been some questions over the exact meaning of some of these predictions, especially in terms of the ninth song, which refers to Xi-feng's fate. Moreover, some critics have long argued that some of these prognostications do not occur in the manner in which they are described and that the epilogue refers to the Jia family suffering a far-more-terrible fate than is shown in the finale of the story. These critics also maintain that these discrepancies are evidence that the last 40 chapters of the novel were not written by Cao Xueqin and were in fact fabricated by Gao E. Nevertheless, a close reading of the songs seems to indicate that virtually all of the predictions about the beauties are fulfilled in the story, but there remains some uncertainty about what the epilogue means about the fate of the Jia family.

See also **The Last Forty Chapters**

Tyrant King 桀

A possible reference to King Jie of Xia (1728–1675 BC). He was infamous for his tyrannical behavior and reckless and massive appetite for luxury, food, alcohol, and sex. In chapter 39, Li Wan compares Xi-feng's overbearing behavior to his.

Vanitas

Daoist monk in search of immortality who chances upon the stone at Greensickness Peak. His importance is shown by the fact that he appears at both the beginning and the end of the novel. Vanitas (*kongkong daorem*, which means "empty the emptiness") reads the long inscription on the stone and then criticizes the stone for not providing the elements that were considered necessary in writing prose fiction. The stone replies by offering a spirited defense, saying that he is simply describing things the way they occurred, and Vanitas gives the story a close second reading and concludes that it is a truthful account based on real events, and its main theme was love. This second reading has such a strong impact upon him that he undergoes the process of enlightenment: beginning in the Void (truth); then proceeding to the understanding of Form (illusion); which gives rise to Passion; through the communication of Passion, again entering into form; and then finally arriving at the understanding of the Void (truth). The message, which is stressed throughout *Dream of the Red Chamber,* is that enlightenment is obtained through experience and passion, that the two are means to realizing their illusory nature (Levy, 12). This Buddhist process foreshadows Bao-yu's later conversion in the novel. Vanitas's transformation results in him changing his name to Brother Amor, or the Monk of Feeling, and the novel's title from *The Story of the Stone* to *The Tale of Brother Amor.* As one commentator has put it, when Vanitas initially reads the story, his "delusion lay in his attachment to the characters and the world of the stone's experiences. In Cao Xueqin's scheme of things, this is just as empty, just as illusory, as sexual desire, maternal love, or pity. By capturing not only the essence but details of real life, it functions as a substitute for real life. And not just any life, but one in which the tides of desire and experience have been shown to lead to spiritual liberation. A second reading persuades Vanitas that he has actually fallen into the trap of attachment by reading the novel, until the narrative rescued him. His conversion to Buddhism is therefore a sign that he understands his previous 'enlightenment' was illusory, as it was not grounded in experience of form and passion" (Levy, 12). Vanitas is so impressed by the stone's story that he goes in search of a publisher for it.

At the end of the story, Vanitas returns to Greensickness Peak and carefully rereads the inscription on the stone again as well as a new section that has been added by the stone to tidy up some loose ends in the story. After finishing his reading, Vanitas concludes that the stone's experiences in life have given him special spiritual understanding and that the tale should be copied down and published so that its message "that things are not as they seem, that the extraordinary and the ordinary, truth and fiction, are all relative to each other" (SS, 5: 375) is better known. He then sets off to find a publisher again, this time with the new version in hand, but the individuals he meets have no interest in publishing it. He does encounter Jia Yu-cun, who verifies the truthfulness of the story, and Cao Xueqin himself, who warns him of the dangers of searching for facts in the tale and insists on the fictionality of the text. A nonplussed Vanitas laughs at Cao's remarks, tosses the manuscript on the ground, and concludes that the story was simply fantastic nonsense and a clever literary diversion that was written for fun and to entertain the reader.

See also **The First Six and Other Key Chapters**

FURTHER READING

Levy, Dore. *Ideal and Actual in The Story of the Stone* (New York: Columbia University Press, 1999).

Wang Ren 王仁

Wang Xi-feng's duplicitous brother. His name connotes "forgetting benevolence." He is an unscrupulous individual who is always on the lookout for ways to get money. We first hear about him when Jia Lian complains to Xi-feng about Ren erroneously celebrating her other brother's birthday so he could make money. Ren behaves abominably after her death and immediately tries to find out from Xi-feng's daughter Qiao-jie how much money Xi-feng had left because he is convinced that his sister had hid a large amount of silver in her apartment. Qiao-jie quickly sizes him up and plays ignorant. In chapter 118, he becomes involved in a dastardly scheme to make Qiao-jie a concubine for a Mongolian prince. The plot fails, and, at the end of the novel, Jia Lian is set on punishing him for his actions.

Wang Shanbao 王善保

Lady Xing's servant and grandmother of the maid Chess, her husband's name is a near homonym for "to tell on someone to one's superior," which also describes her well. She has a strong sense of entitlement because she has been a trusted servant for Lady Xing since childhood and is an ambitious and notorious busybody. Moreover, she has long-standing resentments against the maids in Prospect Garden. Therefore, she jumps at the chance to lead the inspection of the garden in chapters 74 and conducts it in a high-handed manner. But it leads to unexpected and humiliating results for her when she is put in her place by an angry Tan-chun when Shanbao jokingly pretends to search her, and it is discovered that the only servant who broke the rules governing the garden is her granddaughter Chess. Because she works for Lady Xing, she, like all of Xing's servants, is taken away during the government's raid on Ning-guo House.

Wang Wei 王维 (701–761)

One of the great poets of the Tang dynasty, the golden age of Chinese poetry, Wang was also a talented landscape painter, statesman, and musician. He was employed as a scholar-official and obtained high office but was later demoted and then eventually recalled. Later, after the death of his wife and mother, he became discouraged by life and withdrew to his country house and pursued Buddhism. His poetry is noted for its simple imagery, subtlety, his appreciation of nature and contemplative attitude toward the world. *Dream of the Red Chamber* contains several allusions to his writings. When Dai-yu is instructing Caltrop on how to write poetry in chapter 48, the first poet she tells her to study is Wang Wei. When Caltrop returns after studying a collection of Wei's poetry, Dai-yu queries her about the poems, and Caltrop talks about the beauty of the imagery in Wang's poem "On the Frontier."

Wang Xi-feng 王熙凤

One of the novel's most famous, controversial, and complex characters, she is the wife of Jia Lian, niece of Lady Wang and Aunt Xue and mother of Jia Qiao-jie. Her name means "Splendid Phoenix," and her nickname is "Peppercorn Feng" because of her hot temper. Beautiful, highly intelligent and complicated, she is known for her quick wit, great storytelling ability, and is capable of acts of kindness to those who are in trouble or poor. But she is also highly vindictive, insecure, cruel, shrewish, greedy, and willing to kill if she believes she is threatened. Her duality is neatly shown when she makes her first appearance in chapter 3 when she is introduced to Dai-yu. The short scene brilliantly and tellingly illustrates Xi-feng's charm, striking presence, and authority in the family, as well as her mercurial, opportunistic, and disingenuous side. It also indicates her importance in the novel because she is one of the few characters who is given a full physical description. It is easy to forget that she is young, only in her 20s. Xi-feng has the onerous task of managing the Rong-guo household, a job which she generally does with ruthless efficiency. Because she is insecure, she is strongly driven to prove her worth by conspicuously demonstrating her competency. The height of her power and influence occurs in her flawless management of Qin-she's elaborate funeral, and ironically, her lowest period occurs during her attempt to supervise Grandmother Jia's problem-filled funeral when she is sick. One of her major flaws that eventually undermines her and contributes to the decline of the Jia family's fortunes is her extreme avarice and obsession with making money. (The famous Chinese scholar Zhou Ruchang has humorously called her China's first capitalist.) Xi-feng is able to amass a large amount of money by illegal usury, taking bribes, theft, extorting individuals, and abusing her power, all of which she subsequently loses after the Embroidered Jacket raid. She is highly jealous of her husband Jia Lian's numerous dalliances and views them as a threat; she becomes especially outraged with his taking Er-jie as a wife and treats her so badly that Er-jie kills herself. (There are also some hints early in the story that Xi-feng indulged in some sexual transgressions of her own, specifically in regard to her nephew Jia Rong, Qin-she's husband. Moreover, her overt flirtations with the goatish Jia Rui does not reflect the behavior of a proper young wife.)

Much of Xi-feng's deep-rooted lack of confidence derives from her status as a daughter-in-law. She must perform a delicate balancing act, always deferring to her mother-in-law Lady Xing, as well as Lady Wang, and consulting with them about important decisions while at the same time performing her duties without being too independent or demanding because of her age and status. Her responsibilities are onerous, and she must constantly be on her guard against criticisms; she has few people she can depend upon for help. (She is also hampered by the fact that she is basically illiterate.) Xi-feng's dilemma is neatly captured by an understanding Faithful: "A daughter-in-law's life must be pretty impossible. If she is too meek and mild her in-laws will complain she is stupid and the servants won't respect her, yet if she shows any initiative, there is always another set of problems rising up behind her back for everyone that she deals with. In our household, where there are a number of mistresses who used once themselves to be maids, it's particularly difficult. Such people are so full of their own importance that they are always taking offense, and if they are the slightest bit crossed in anything they begin spreading stories about you or finding other ways of stirring up trouble" (SS, 3: 412). Xi-feng is lucky in that she is a favorite of Grandmother Jia and protected by her. She is also close to her always practical and loyal principal maid Patience, who provides useful advice on several occasions. Moreover, she surprisingly strikes up a friendship with Grannie Liu (who ends up protecting Xi-feng's daughter Qiao-jie) and was close to Qin-she (who appears twice to her after her death to warn Xi-feng about the necessity of making backup preparations in the event of the Jia family's decline). She does have the virtue of some self-awareness of her flaws, which she acknowledges to Patience in chapter 55, and can be quite perceptive about the strengths and weaknesses of others, like Tan-chun. She is also one of the few characters in the novel who is acutely aware of the Jia family's precarious financial situation. While Xi-feng has a strong constitution and intense need to never admit failure, the severe toll her managerial duties inflict upon her, along with the effects of the government raid, eventually results in the collapse of her health and her death.

Several critics have viewed Xi-feng's gender identity by comparing her with Bao-yu, with some arguing that her more masculine characteristics complement Bao-yu's feminine ones and that she serves as an intermediary between the feminine and the masculine. She has mainly been viewed as a classic shrew, a stock character type who often appears in traditional Chinese literature. In an illuminating essay, Erin Brightwell has taken issue with this interpretation. She contends that viewing "Xi-feng's story as that of a shrew disguises central thematic issues by isolating her negative traits and ignoring her commonalities with other characters. She is certainly a character with many faults, but they are not unique to her, and her appeal lies precisely in her refusal to conform to patterns" (820). Brightwell also argues that blaming Xi-feng for the deaths of Jia Rui, which was caused by unbounded sexual desire, and San-jie, which was in part set in motion by Jia Lian improperly marrying during a mourning period as well as the evils of sexual desire, and for the fall of the Jia family, which was also caused by improper behavior by male members of the Jia family, is unfair and fails to take into account the circumstances in which these acts occurred. Another scholar has asserted, "The success of Xi-feng as a character lies precisely in her ability to amplify the social contradictions manifested in her transgression of rigid prescriptions of power, gender, and social order" (Edwards, 86). And the noted literary historian C.T. Hsia has written that Xi-feng's evil acts are the result of her being an oppressed woman who is forced to defend and advance her interests through underhanded methods. "This defenseless struggle in the form of the outwardly polite cunning of Xi-feng constitutes the tragedy of the Chinese woman. It is her tragedy that she has become mean and cunning in order to cope with male domination, a condition of injustice to which she is nevertheless resigned" (26).

See also **Funerals**

FURTHER READING

Brightwell, Erin L. "Analyzing Gender: Wang Xi-Feng as the Shrew." *Tamkang Review* 36. 1–2 (2005): 67–87.

Edwards, Louise. *Men and Women in Qing China: Gender in the* Red Chamber Dream (Leiden: E.J. Brill, 1994): 68–86.

Hsia, C.T. *The Classic Chinese Novel: A Critical Introduction* (New York: Columbia University Press, 1968).

Western Objects

Western readers of *Dream of the Red Chamber* are often surprised by the large number and wide variety of Western objects members of the Jia family own. They include 18 clocks and watches, a glass screen, European wine, costly wooden furniture and imported glass bowls, spectacles, and a Western-style painting. Also mentioned are a large variety of textiles and a small pair of silver scissors from the Western Ocean (Europe). Jia Bao-yu, who is most associated with Western things in the novel, owns an imported large dressing mirror, which famously confuses Granny Liu, and a European toy boat. He also displays a knowledge of snuff and gives his maid Skybright the product to help clear up a nasty cold. The snuff is kept in a golden, starred glass case that shows a picture of a naked Western woman with angel wings inside its lid, which fascinates Skybright. Bao-yu also prescribes a Western plaster called "yi-fu na" for her headache. (He also interestingly appears to have a very limited knowledge of the French language, as shown in chapter 63 when he gives Parfumee the French name Aventurin.)

The Qing dynasty was not, as is frequently portrayed in Western popular culture, a monolithic or static state. China at that time was a complicated and a multivalent country that was ethically and religiously diverse. Furthermore, it had long participated in international trade, especially in East and Southeast Asia, and also had conducted extensive commerce with Europe in porcelain and other commodities since the 16th century. Moreover, Western Jesuit missionaries were employed at the imperial court during much of the 18th century, working as artisans, court painters, astronomers, musicians, and mathematicians. They also operated medical dispensaries and designed a new Summer Palace for the emperor near Beijing. Consequently, it was not uncommon at that time for Chinese upper-class families, and even members of the Qing court, to display Western objects like these in their homes to show their affluence and sophistication. In the 18th century, Qing imperial palaces were replete with numerous types of European ornaments as well as many watches, clocks, and European toys. Foreign goods at that time were greatly prized, and early Qing dynasty fiction regularly referred to clocks and textiles and other objects. (But *Dream of the Red Chamber* contains the greatest variety of Western objects.) The novel mentions that the Wang family was in charge of foreign trade, and considering that it was common for clans, because they were closely connected, to share in the advantages associated with positions like the Wangs held, it is easy to see how the Jias got to know about and obtain foreign items. However, it should be noted that Westerners rarely appeared in early Qing literature, and, when they did, they were typically depicted as being arrogant, dishonest, crafty, and physically ugly. The novel does refer to one Westerner, a young woman whom Bao-qin and her father meet while traveling. She is presented in a positive light, though, and Bao-qin recites a poem that the woman had written in Chinese, which greatly impresses her relatives.

Cao Xueqin would have had extensive knowledge of these Western items because his grandfather Cao Yin and father, Cao Fu, were involved with foreign trade owing to their official positions as Imperial Textile Commissioners. In fact, Cao Yin, in addition to his many duties as commissioner, was a purchasing agent of exotica for the Emperor Kangxi, and there is evidence that he had widespread contact with European traders. As a result, the Cao family's mansion in Nanjing would have contained many of these Western items. One Chinese scholar has suggested that Cao Xueqin's interest in Western things may have been motivated by his feelings of alienation from Chinese conventional society, his strong sense of being an outsider, and his wish to experience new things (Han).

FURTHER READING

Han, Jiaming. "The Image of the West in *A Dream of Red Mansions*." In *Images of Westerners in Chinese and Western Literature*. Edited by Sukehiro Hirakawa (Amsterdam: Rodopi, 2000): 39–52.

Wet Nurses

A special nurse who breastfeeds and looks after another person's child. According to Charlotte Furth, one reason why Chinese mothers often used one was because "breast milk has the potential to pollute babies through foetal poisoning since it was thought to be a postpartum transformation of the mother's highly polluting *yin* blood. Hiring wet nurses was one method mothers avoided blame for foetal poisoning—the burden for any infant illness passed instead to the wet nurse" (noted in Edwards, 122). In traditional China, wet nurses often had an important relationship with the family for whom they worked. This is true of the Jia family, where they enjoy special status and are treated well even after their breastfeeding duties have long ended. Nannie Li gets away with her annoying and prying behavior and her bad treatment of Aroma because she was Bao-yu's wet nurse. Nannie Liu is treated with much respect by Xi-feng and Jia Lian and is able to ask Jia Lian to employ her two sons because she was his wet nurse. But the novel also shows that some of these former wet nurses have a strong sense of entitlement and feel that they should be granted special concessions from their former wards. But there are limits even for them. People are shocked when Ying-chun's wet nurse is sternly punished after it was discovered she had stolen jewelry from her and pawned it to feed her gambling habit. Louise Edwards has argued that the marking of boundaries between the pure and the profane is an important theme in *Honglou meng*. She has gone so far as to argue, "Breast milk features frequently in the foodscape of the novel prior to the entrance of the young people into the garden. The garden walls act as a protective barrier against the threat of pollution from breast milk and its bearers, the wet nurses.... Wet nurses and breast milk are symbols of pollution into the garden and the forbidden transport of objects out of it" (122, 124). It is interesting to note that Cao Xueqin's own great-grandmother was a wet nurse to the Kangxi emperor and the family received great benefit from this connection for their relationship was close, so much so that he once visited her on one of his famous southern trips.

Further Reading

Edwards, Louise. "Eating and Drinking in a *Red Chambered Dream*." In *Scribes of Gastronomy: Representations of Food and Drink in Imperial Chinese Literature*. Edited by Isaac Yue and Siufu Tang (Hong Kong University Press, 2013): 113–131.

Furth, Charlotte. "Concepts of Pregnancy, Childbirth and Infancy in the Ch'ing Dynasty China." *Journal of Asian Studies*, 46 (1987): 7–33.

Wolf of Zhong-shan

See **Sun Shao-zu**

Women

Dream of the Red Chamber is famous and praised for its sensitive and sympathetic and seemingly progressive depictions of women of all classes and their many difficulties in Qing dynasty China. But recently, several Western scholars have questioned this long-held perception and argued that Cao Xueqin was not really that interested in the treatment and status of women during his time but in using them, as many Chinese literati did, to project his frustrated feelings as a socially borderline male writer with few options and that he, in actuality, reflected prevailing sexual beliefs regarding women. Martin W. Huang has pointed out that it had long been popular in Chinese traditional literature for male writers and dissatisfied literati to use females in their writings to symbolize their anxieties and feelings of insignificance because of women's marginalized status. Huang surmises, "Perhaps Cao's own marginalized status made him feel empathetic with women and even sometimes impelled him to identify with them. He needed to identify with those talented but doomed female characters in order to alleviate his own sense of frustration and to enhance his own visibility.... What fascinates Cao is not femininity *per se* but the feminine appearance a man assumes when he is marginalized and the question of how he can regain his masculinity" (95). Louise Edwards, employing feminist literary theory, has examined notions of female purity, pollution, and virginity, motherhood, and power in the story and concluded that the novel actually underpins traditional views of women by insisting on the customary duality that viewed women as either sacred or profane. She does, though, concede, "In the intermingling of the real and the unreal around a mythological realm free from the patriarchal dominance so striking in the mimetic realm, Cao questioned the necessity of sexual and moral distinctions. It is through posing this unspoken philosophical problem and not simply through the reversal of gender orders or the veneration of women that the novel is able to undermine comfortable assumptions about sexual ideologies" (67).

Recent scholarship on late imperial Chinese women has also "begun to move away from 'victimization' studies and to emphasize instead that Chinese women's lives have been shaped by many factors, including their own active choices and participation in social, economic, and family life. Finally, many scholars have begun to question the assumption ... that the suffering of women in Chinese society was primarily a function of conservative patriarchal Neo-Confucianism" (Paul Ropp quoted in Smith, 343). This scholarly trend has shown that many late imperial Chinese women had more agency than commonly assumed and that they were able to carve out areas in which they could exert some freedom in their lives. Several important studies have focused on elite women in the southern region of China. One noted historian, Dorothy Ko, has demonstrated how China's increasing commercialization, urbanization, rising print culture, and privatization of family life (including the belief among many upper-class families that having an educated daughter increased marriage possibilities) during the Ming dynasty led to women becoming more visible. She points out, "In the face of women's growing visibility in Chinese cultural life—as readers, audiences, authors—within and without the family, the pressing question was no longer 'What if women were literate?' but how do we conform old values to those of reality?" (159). Ko concludes that, although during the 17th century in the Southern Jiangnan region of the country educated women were allowed freedom for creative expression, it was not allowed for all because "old gender stereotypes died hard, often co-existing with more sympathetic thoughts on women in the same person" (67). This social trend largely continued into the Qing dynasty.

During Cao Xueqin's time, it was not uncommon for upper-class women to be educated, as most of the young female members of the Jia family are, in painting, poetry, calligraphy, and music. In addition, elite women were at times given greater freedom (although still limited) to write. Moreover, they carved out their own personal and safe area in the inner quarters in which they lived to pursue things in which they were interested, as characters like Dai-yu and other females in Prospect Garden do. It should also be noted that, as *Dream of the Red Chamber* shows, there was a sharp distinction drawn between how males and females were expected to behave in public and in private. In the public realm, women were expected to be submissive and passive and had few rights, but in private, they were usually allowed some space to express opinions and to exert some authority. Furthermore, mothers-in-law wielded a great deal of power and often dominated their son's wives, but over time these wives became mothers-in-law themselves and were in some cases able to exert power of their own. Moreover, elderly women frequently had considerable power within the family, as Grandmother Jia demonstrates.

But as the novel shows, traditional attitudes remained. The ideal upper-class type of woman at that time is described in the novel (with a bit of tongue in cheek) as being "sweet-tempered, beautiful, well-mannered, softly spoken, a perfect needlewoman, deft with her writing brush, nimble with her abacus, a paragon of daughterly obedience, kind and ladylike towards the servants" (SS, 4: 284). Despite being in general a tolerant person, Grandmother Jia has a very conventional attitude toward the duties of females, insisting that their primary responsibility is embroidery. This is shown in chapter 92 when she says that she has "no objection to girls learning their letters but needlework must come first" (SS, 4: 249). Because it was widely held at the time that industrious, productive manual labor (for upper-class women it was embroidery) was a sign of virtue (idleness in a woman was considered a mark of immorality) and a central responsibility of females, there are numerous scenes of females sewing in the novel. These include Skybright skillfully repairing Bao-yu's burned Russian coat, Dai-yu making a fan case and purse for him, Bao-chai helping Aroma sew a summer cover for him, and Xiang-yun being forced by her family to do embroidery until late at night. Even Bao-chai, on several occasions, echoes this traditional view. In chapter 37, she states that "spinning and sewing is the proper occupation for girls like us" (SS, 2: 235). In chapter 64, she tells Bao-yu, "A girl's first concern is to be virtuous, her second to be industrious" (SS, 3: 470). Despite these changes, it should be underscored that the situation for women in 18th-century China was terrible. The number of highly literate women in the country at the time was extremely small and limited geographically. It has been roughly estimated that they composed around "0.1% of the population and 70% of these women came from the southern Lower Yangzi region" (Mann, 4, 33). As one noted historian has observed, "It is clear that gender issues in traditional China cannot, or at least should not, be reduced to simple themes of subordination, oppression, and victimization … [but it does] appear that imperial policy and social pressures combined to create a situation that placed inordinate burdens on women for most of the Qing period…. Women in Qing China generally had few property rights. Chinese men could divorce their wives for seven reasons, including loquaciousness; Chinese women could not divorce their husbands for any reason except severe physical mutilation or the husband's attempt to sell his wife into prostitution. Chasity was expected of women, not of men. Infanticide overwhelmingly involved girls, not baby boys. Traditional Chinese rituals underscored at every turn the subordination of women to men. Moreover, demeaning expressions about women could be found everywhere, from the Confucian classics and ritual handbooks to popular proverbs…. [There was also] the pervasive notion of the 'three types of womanly obedience'—first to the father, then to the husband, and eventually to the son" (Smith, 342, 343, 365).

Cao Xueqin, on a certain level, remained the product of his times and, as is true of many great artists, was unable to completely transcend prevailing gender norms, especially regarding women. And there is little doubt that he conveyed some of the deep personal dissatisfaction he felt about his status and lack of opportunity in several of the female characters he created. But it is very difficult not to form the impression based upon the novel that he also did express a genuine interest in the treatment of women and a strong sense of empathy for *and* a good understanding of them during this period. He shows them in the novel not as the pliant, passive, and obsequious characters of Western stereotypes of Chinese women but often as active, engaged, opinionated individuals with complex interior lives. Their dreams, motivations, and daily concerns are described with remarkable realism, along with the social barriers and pressures they constantly faced. It is especially telling that most of the story's characters are female, and they are largely treated in a much more positive light than the male characters. Furthermore, the novel's protagonist and hero is an admirer of, and friendly to, all girls. Finally, according to an introduction to the first chapter of the novel, written by Cao Xueqin's younger brother, which is not in Hawkes's translation but is included in the text of the Yangs, the book is the result of Cao's wish to give a record of "all the lovely girls I have known" (DRM, 1: 1). The scholar Zhou Ruchang has also posited that Cao Xueqin's interest in the plight of women was based upon the deep disgust he felt when he learned about the terrible ways slave girls in rich families were treated by their owners (101–102).

See also **Concubines, Inner Quarters, Marriage, Poetry, Suicide**

FURTHER READING

Edwards, Louise. *Men and Women in Qing China: Gender in the* Red Chamber Dream (Leiden: E.J. Brill, 1994).

Huang, Martin W. "The Self Displaced: Women and Growing Up in the *Dream of the Red Chamber.*" In *Literati and Self-Re/Presentation: Autobiographical Sensibility in the Eighteenth-Century Chinese Novel* (Stanford: Stanford University Press, 1997): 75–108.

Idema, Walt, and Beata Grant. *The Red Brush: Writing Women of Imperial China* (Cambridge: Harvard University Press, 2004).

Ko, Dorthey. *Teachers of the Inner Chambers: Women in Seventeenth Century China* (Stanford: Stanford University Press, 1994).

Mann, Susan. *Precious Records: Women in China's Long Eighteenth Century* (Stanford: Stanford University Press, 1997).

McMahon, Keith. "Polygamy, Crossing of the Gender and the Superiority of Women in *Honglou meng.*" In *Misers, Shrews and Polygamists: Sexuality and Male-Female Relations in Eighteenth Century Chinese Literature* (Durham: Duke University Press, 1995): 176–204.

Smith, Richard J. *The Qing Dynasty and Traditional Chinese Culture* (Lanham: Rowman & Littlefield, 2015).

Zhou, Ruchang. *Between Noble and Humble: Cao Xueqin and the* Dream of the Red Chamber. Edited by Ronald R. Gray and Mark Ferrara (New York: Peter Lang, 2009).

The Won-done Song 好了歌

The "Won-done Song" by the lame Daoist and Zhen Shi-yin's commentary on it in the song in chapter 1 form an important part of the novel. Unfortunately, they are often overlooked by first-time readers. Both songs appear in a form that was popular at the time. The monk's "Won-done Song" contains a simple and thoroughly Daoist message that in order for a person to "win" in life, they must give up on the idea of trying to "attain or gain." Shi-yin cleverly elaborates on this sentiment by focusing his responding song on the unreal and mutable nature of power and wealth, romantic, marital, and familial love, fame and worldly ambition. The important commentator Red Inkstone has given a clear and edifying analysis of the meaning and themes of Shi-yin's song, writing, "On stanza one: First is described the stage: now fresh, now withered, now lovely, now decayed—an ebb and flow continuous without ever getting 'over.' On stanza two: A section on wives and concubines: the new are welcomed, the old are bid farewell: sudden affection, sudden love, sudden pain, sudden tragedy—all inextricable and impossible to get 'over.' On stanza three: A section on the shortness of life and the fluctuation of extremes: dew in the wind, frost on the grass, wealth, desire, avarice—impossible to get 'over.' On stanza four: A section on the unreliability of sons and daughters after one's death: during one's lifetime—vain figuring, endless planning, foolish doting—impossible to get 'over.' On stanza five: A section on the fortuitousness of tenure and dismissal: struggle for wealth, bitter competition, joy, and foreboding—impossible to get 'over.' On stanza six: A summary of the innumerable perennial fools who go through a stage of illusion: illusory events, jostle and jumble, day after day—impossible to get 'over'" (translated by Miller, 105–107).

It has also been maintained that Shi-yin's commentary is "an explicit exposition of the conflict between the ideal and actual in the 'real' world. Evoking the rhythm of waxing and waning characteristic of traditional interpretations of the patterns of Chinese imperial history, Zhen Shi-yin outlines the former glory of the Jias and foreshadows their decline, while others may then come into their own.... The pageant of mundane existence depends on no single individual: The flow is not stayed for anyone. The will to seek fulfillment deludes us, and salvation lies only in recognizing its emptiness and futility" (Levy, 152). And finally, some commentators have maintained that his song commentary contains allusions to specific characters in the story and their fate. For example, Red Inkstone contends there are references to Dai-yu, Bao-chai, Xi-feng, Liu Xiang-lian, Jia She, Jia Yu-chun, Jia Lan, and Jia Yuan-chun (Miller 293–297), while Wu Shih-Ch'ang believes that Shi-yin alludes to Bao-yu, Bao-chai, Shi Xiang-yun, Qin-shi, and Qiao-jie (184, 186–187).

See also **Red Inkstone, Zhen Shi-yin**

FURTHER READING

Levy, Dore. *Ideal and Actual in* The Story of the Stone (New York: Columbia University Press, 1999): 149–154.

Miller, Lucien. *Masks of Fiction in the "Dream of the Red Chamber": Myth, Mimesis and Persona* (Tucson: University of Arizona Press, 1975).

Wu, Shih-Ch'ang. *On the Red Chamber Dream: A Critical Study of Two Annotated Manuscripts of the XVIIIth Century* (Oxford: Clarendon Press, 1961).

Xi Shi 西施

The leading beauty of the four great beauties of ancient China, she was the daughter of a tea trader and lived during the Spring and Autumn period. The famous poet Su Shi compared her beauty to that of Hangzhou's renowned West Lake. There are several famous stories attesting to her natural beauty. It was said that it was so striking that when she once looked down on a pond, the fish were so dazzled by her beauty that they forgot to swim and promptly sank. Another story says that an ugly woman named Dong Shi once saw Xi Shi frowning because she was ill but thought she looked even more beautiful than usual. So the woman decided to imitate this frown to receive praise from others. But when people saw her, they turned away and avoided her because she looked even worse than before. The moral of the story is that one should not try to copy another person because you will make a fool of yourself. *Honglou meng* contains several references to Xi Shi. In chapter 3, Dai-yu is compared with Xi Shi, and later Dai-yu cites her in a poem. Lady Wang mockingly compares

Skybright to Xi Shi in chapter 74. And in chapter 30, when Bao-yu comes across a girl writing on the ground in Prospect Garden, he recalls the story about Dong Shi as told in the philosopher Zhuangzi's famous story "The Movements of Heaven." He then compares the girl to Dong Shi.

Xia Jin-gui 夏金桂

Xue Pan's shrewish and conniving wife, her name means "cassia in the summer" and has several negative connotations. This is intended to show her two-faced nature because cassias do not bloom in northern China in the summer. It also indicates that she and Xue Pan (and his family) are not compatible because her name refers to summer and his family name, Xue, connotes the winter. Her name also connotes "crowing about one's dignity." Because she was thoroughly spoiled by her widowed mother, Jin-gui is a willful and selfish 17-year-old girl who is bent on controlling every aspect of the Xue family household. Her behavior becomes increasingly worse and more outlandish over time. After exerting complete control over Xue Pan, who runs away from her, she turns her attention to Lady Xue, Bao-chai (who provides some check on her behavior) and then to gentle Caltrop (whom she forces to change her name to Lilly). She also turns on her licentious maid Moonbeam (Bao Chan, whose name connotes "satisfying one's hunger") and even attempts to seduce Xue Ke. Jin-gui is eventually undone by her constant vicious plotting when she tries to poison Caltrop but ends up, in an ironic twist of fate, poisoning herself by accident.

Xing Xiu-yan 邢岫烟

Lady Xing's niece, she is quiet, serious, and well-mannered and is engaged to Xue Ke, whom she meets on her journey to Beijing with her family. She has a difficult time living with the Jias. Her family is poor and totally reliant upon the Jia family for support. Her drunkard father doesn't care about her, and she is essentially ignored by Lady Xing. Moreover, she lives with Ying-chun, whose servants take advantage of and force Xiu-yan to spend her small allowance on them. As a result, she must pawn her winter clothes to make money. She is close to Bao-chai, who periodically helps her and gives her useful advice, as does Xi-feng, who is impressed by Xiu-yan's personality and sympathetic about her situation. She spends her time waiting for Bao-qin to marry Academician Mei's son so that she can then marry Xue Ke. She finally marries Ke at the end of the story.

Xue Bao-chai 薛宝钗

Lady Xue's daughter, Xue Pan's sister, and Bao-yu's wife, her name means "Precious Hair Pin," which is a symbol of restraint. She is considered an ideal of feminine beauty for the time and is described in this manner: "Her face seemed a silver disc, her eyes were lustrous and almond-shaped, her lips red and without rouge, her eyebrows dark without being penciled" (DRM, 1: 430). She is also a bit plump, which was then considered a mark of beauty, but she is a bit sensitive about her weight, which is shown in her reaction when Bao-yu jokingly compares her to the famous full-figured Tang dynasty beauty Yang Guifei in chapter 30. She has also been considered by many to be a model of what a traditional Chinese woman was supposed to be like: modest, filial, thoughtful, sensible, reserved, and bound by the norms of Confucian propriety, and she was thought by many readers to represent an ideal personality type. Her strong sense of austerity and even coldness is implied by her residence All Spice Court in Prospect Garden (and by her surname Xue which is a homonym for "snow"). The dwelling's five rooms are extremely bare and have few decorations (which shocks Grandmother Jia when she visits). The snow cave-like whitewashed rooms of the residence and the tall miniature mountain of rock (which may allude to her future husband Bao-yu) that hides it foretell of Bao-chai's lonely fate. The plants and herbs in her courtyard symbolize her pliant nature, and their cool fragrance represents her purity of character. She is well educated and has an impressive knowledge of many subjects, including painting, poetry, and drama. She also has been viewed by Chinese readers as a perfect complement to Dai-yu and that together they make the ideal woman with Dai-yu representing sensibility and Bao-chai sense.

But this is an oversimplification given that she is depicted in the novel as being a considerably more complicated and conflicted character than commonly assumed. This can be seen, for example, in her attitude toward poetry. On the one hand, she is the Crab Flower Club's second-most-talented poet (after Dai-yu), but several times she also expresses the conventional belief that poetry is not the correct subject for women to dabble in, that their primary concern should be on traditional duties like sewing. (She also criticizes Dai-yu for reading plays but admits that she avidly read them when she was young.) These seeming contradictions are telling and have been explained in this way by one expert on the novel: "On the one hand, Bao-chai has a great talent for composition and tremendous knowledge of poetry and poetic theory. On the other hand, she is painfully aware that the transcendence of poetry is virtually unavailable in her country. Poetry is not a woman's 'proper business' and women's poetry is not for public display.... It is not so much that she feels that poetry and plays undermine authority—she is well aware that the authority patterns in the household are already far from ideal. But she understands, with regret, that the wish fulfillment so gratifying in literature is not to be found in everyday life, even in such privileged household as this. Her critiques of poetry as an enterprise, therefore, are both ironic and self-ironizing" (Levy, 115, 119).

Bao-chai also has long suffered from the malady of "internal heat," a congenital tendency to overheat, and sometimes must take cold fragrance pills. Her disease has been taken to signify that underneath her general appearance of studied nonchalance she has intense but suppressed feelings and love for Bao-yu. (One Qing dynasty commentator has described her as being "hot within, cold without.") Moreover, Bao-chai's much-praised sense of Confucian self-control is not always apparent. She is capable of feelings of jealousy (about Dai-yu), envy, and revenge, and sometimes gloats and has a sharp tongue. She also, at times, comes across as being hypocritical and duplicitous when she easily acquiesces to elders, especially when she knows they are wrong (for example, to Lady Wang regarding Golden's suicide). Nor is she wholly innocent. She has a calculating side as seen, for example, in chapter 100, when she uses sex to deal with Bao-yu's deep depression following Dai-yu's death. (Bao-chai herself also suffers from bouts of depression in the later part of the novel over her family's situation and once reaches out to Dai-yu because of it.) Because of these negative characteristics, some Chinese readers have long been suspicious of her. But she also continues to have many strong defenders. Recently, one critic has offered an interpretation that splits the difference regarding her character and probably best explains Bao-chai in the end, writing that Cao Xueqin's purpose was not to portray Bao-chai as either a Confucian paragon or a calculating hypocrite but rather "as a fledging maiden who is striving to become a perfect Confucian gentlewoman … the novel portrays her not just as a young *lady* but as a young *girl*, who succumbs to her nature.… Although in the public eye she may appear to have succeeded in her goal—as a flesh and blood young woman—she is caught in a perennial tug-of-war between her instincts, desires, emotional impulses and subconscious thoughts, and her keen sense of Confucian propriety resulting from her education.… If her image as an ascetic paragon dehumanizes her, then [her] passionate slippages, naturalize and normalize her, making her more like the rest of us who are flawed and often unable to bridle our improper feelings, thoughts, or actions. What is particularly significant is that such outbreaks of her nature against nurture often occur under cover of her humor" (Xue, 142, 148). Bao-chai's fate is to have a lonely existence as an abandoned wife, but this will be partly offset by the solace of being pregnant with a son (Jia Gui) who will be the heir to the Jia family.

FURTHER READING

Levy, Dore. *Ideal and Actual in* The Story of the Stone (New York: Columbia University Press, 1999).
Xue, Weihe. "How Humor Humanizes a Confucian Paragon: The Case of Xue Bao-chai in *Honglou meng*." *Humor in Chinese Life and Letters: Classical and Traditional Approaches*. Edited by Jocelyn Chen and Jessica Milner Davis (Hong Kong University Press, 2011): 139–168.

Xue Bao-qin 薛宝琴

Xue Bao-qin is an often-overlooked but nevertheless consequential character in *Dream of the Red Chamber*. She is clearly the most intelligent and talented woman in the story. Moreover, it is commonly agreed by members of the Jia and Xue family that she is the most beautiful woman in the family. Bao-qin also has an engaging and warmhearted personality and quickly becomes a favorite of the matriarch Grandma Jia and even forms a close friendship with the prickly Lin Dai-yu. Although young, she is precocious, very well read, a first-rate poet, and quick on her feet, as shown by her impressive performance in the uproarious linking verse contest in chapter 50. In chapter 51, she composes ten clever riddles during an animated gathering in the Winter Room of Prospect Garden based upon famous places she visited. Each riddle contains a clue that refers to an everyday object and also foreshadows what will happen to several of the story's characters. (The noted scholar Halvor Saussy has gone so far as to argue that Bao-qin is *Dream of the Red Chamber*'s most original character because of the insight she displays in her ten riddles regarding the story's plot.) Bao-qin is Bao-chai's cousin and a niece of Aunt Xue and came to Beijing with her brother Xue Ke to complete the formalities of her engagement to the son of the Hanlin Academy scholar Mei. Unlike the other female characters in the novel, she is widely traveled, having visited more than half of the provinces in China with her father. During a trip to a southern seaport, they met a beautiful, blond foreign girl who charms them by her ability to write a poem in Chinese (which is quoted). Bao-qin is symbolically linked with the flower plum blossom because, like her, it blooms early. This association seems to imply that she will be fated to have a late or possibly difficult marriage. She is a significant character because she represents a feminine ideal that embodies many of the qualities Cao Xueqin admired and because she is one of the novel's crucial outsiders who perform the vital task of communicating important information to the reader about events and behavior that the main characters in the story take for granted or to which they are oblivious. For example, in chapter 53, we view the New Year's Eve ancestral sacrifice in the Jia family's Hall of the Ancestors from her perspective, which greatly adds depth to the formality and splendor of the Confucian ritual.

FURTHER READING

Saussy, Haun. "Women's Writings Before and Within the '*Hong lou Meng.*'" In *Writing Women in Late Imperial China*. Edited by Ellen Widmer and Kang-i-Song Chang (Stanford: Stanford University Press, 1997): 285–305.

Xue Ke 薛蝌

One of the novel's few decent male characters, he is Bao-qin's elder brother, Aunt Xue's nephew, and is engaged to Lady Xing's niece Xing Xiu-yan, whom he met on a journey to the capital. He had not been living with the Xues for long when he was given the demanding task of trying to overturn Xue Pan's murder charge. As a result, he makes numerous exhausting trips to the prison Pan is in to bring him money and to judges to offer bribes, sometimes to no effect. In the midst of all this, Ke is besieged by Pan's friends looking to take advantage of the situation and by Pan's monstrous wife Xia Jin-gui and her maid Moonbeam, who are aggressively attempting to seduce him. (But he quietly rebuffs their attempts.) Through it all, he remains loyal to the Xue family, humble, well-intended, and concerned over Xing Xiu-yan's unfortunate circumstances, although he cannot marry her until Bao-qin marries her fiancé. At the end of the novel, he is finally able to marry her.

Xue Pan 薛蟠

The wayward son of Lady Xue and Bao-chai's brother, he is known in the novel as the "Oaf King," and his name is a homonym for "to covet." Ignorant, impulsive, hot tempered, badly educated, a bisexual libertine, and spoiled, Pan is in constant trouble throughout the story because of his licentious and crude behavior and strong sense of entitlement. He kidnaps Calthrop and treats her badly, is responsible for her fiancé's death, and bribes his classmates in the clan school to have relations with him. Later, he is charged with the murder of a waiter in a dispute, and the cost of his defense bankrupts the Xue family. He is later pardoned by the emperor and has a child with Caltrop.

Yama 阎罗大王

The king of the underworld. This realm is closely structured along the lines of the Chinese government and has a complicated hierarchy of officials and bureaucratic procedures that need be followed. Yama is usually depicted as wearing a Chinese judge's cap and rules over the Buddhist *Narakas* or hells, questioning and passing judgment on the deceased and determining the course of their rebirth. When people are dying, he sends his minions to get their souls, as happens to the dying Qin Zhong in chapter 16. Those who performed good deeds are rewarded by him with good fortune, and those who did bad things are punished with torture and/or are condemned to have unhappy future lives. In chapter 90, Xue Ke wonders why Yama assigned a terrible person like Xia Jin-gui such a pampered life, but to his fiancée Xiu-yan, who is a good person, he assigned numerous hardships. Finally, a hideously tortured Aunt Zhao, in chapter 112, states that she has been called by Yama to answer questions about Mother Ma and her use of black magic and pleads with Xi-feng to put in a good word for her with him.

Yamen 衙门

The official residence or office of a Chinese official. Jia Yu-cun's yamen at Ying-tian-fu is mentioned in chapter 4, as well as Jia Zheng's in a later chapter when he is serving as Grain Intendant.

Yang Guifei 杨贵妃 (719–756)

One of the four beauties of ancient China, she was the notorious concubine of the Tang dynasty Emperor Xuanzong. Originally, she was a concubine of one of Xuanzong's sons, but he forced his son to give her to him. Xuanzong became so besotted with her that he neglected his official duties, and Yang started to amass much political power. A rebellion eventually occurred, led by her adopted son and possible lover An Lushan. She is eventually killed, while fleeing the capital, by imperial troops who were furious over her unseemly behavior. Xuanzong never got over her and died several years later a broken man. Yang is one of the few women in Chinese history who was considered beautiful even though she was obese. Her favorite fruit was lychee, and the emperor had it specially transported from the south by very fast imperial couriers for her. Her story has been immortalized in numerous Chinese plays and works of fiction. In chapter 30, Bao-yu, in a lapse of tact, jokingly compares Bao-chai to Yang (for she is a bit overweight), much to Bao-chai's embarrassment and anger given that Yang is associated with lechery and treason. And in chapter 5, it is noted that a table in Qin-shi's bedroom contains the quince that An Lushan threw at her, which bruised her breast.

Yao and Shun 尧 and 舜

Renowned sage kings of ancient China who respectively ruled in the 24th and 23rd centuries BC. Both were respected for their humility, honesty, and were revered by Confucius, who considered them models of integrity and virtue. In chapter 118, Bao-chai twice uses them as examples of individuals who were compassionate and cared for others, in support of her Confucian-based argument against Bao-yu's Buddhist/Daoist opposing notions of virtue and personal transcendence.

Yin and *Yang* 阴阳

Two fundamental principles that were traditionally believed by Chinese to exert control over everything in the world. *Yin* represents the female, water, earth, the moon, and is passive, soft, low, weak, dark, old, cold, and negative. *Yang* is considered male, active, strong, high, hard, hot, light, young, and positive and represents heaven, the sun, fire, and the south. Neither principle is superior to the other, and an increase in one leads to a corresponding decrease in the other. These dual cosmic principles are not only opposing but also interdependent and complementary. They constantly succeed each other in an unceasing cycle, and their interchange and interplay cause all things and creatures to change and grow. *Yin* reaches the height of its power during the winter solstice and *yang* with the summer solstice. A balance between the two principles is considered key. These principles work in conjunction with The Five Elements. The concepts of *yin* and *yang* have had a strong influence upon Daoism and Confucianism, the famous divination book *I Ching*, and martial arts, and are heavily used in traditional Chinese medicine. By Cao Xueqin's time, the belief in correlative cosmology and the principles of *yin/yang* were being questioned, particularly by intellectuals. This skepticism can be seen in chapter 31 in the novel where Shi Xiang-yun has a humorous discussion about the notion of correlative cosmology with her maid, who mocks these principles.

See also **The Five Elements, Narrative Patterns and Techniques**

You-shi 尤氏

Cousin Zhen's wife, Jia Rong's mother, and Er-jie's and San-jie's stepsister. She is depicted as a quiet and unobtrusive individual and one of the few members of the Jia family to gain the respect of the domestic staff. She generally enjoys a good relationship with Xi-feng and is liked by Grandmother Jia, but she also has a running feud with Xi-chun, who is extremely rude to her. Her marriage to Cousin Zhen is characterized as happy.

You Sisters
(You Er-jie, You San-jie) 尤二姐, 尤三姐

These beautiful sisters are the daughters of Mrs. You and are You-shi's stepsisters. Er-jie is the eldest, and they both have a checkered past regarding men. Er-jie once was involved in an affair with Cousin Zhen, as was San-jie. In one of the most shocking scenes in the novel, an aggressive San-jie is shown in chapter 65 turning the tables on licentious Zhen and Jia Lian by brazenly flirting with and then suddenly loudly, verbally abusing them. Both sisters eventually change their attitudes when love comes their way and become model women. Jia Lian becomes smitten with Er-jie, and she formally is made his secondary wife, although the ceremony occurs during a mourning period, and he fails to ask for the permission of his parents. Er-jie is a loyal and loving wife, and her gentle good nature charms even the denizens of Prospect Garden. But when a very jealous Xi-feng finds out about the relationship, she plots her revenge and devises an elaborate plan exploiting the fact that when Er-jie was young, she was betrothed to the son of a friend of her father (though it was never followed through) in order to besmirch Er-jie's reputation and turn Grandmother Jia against her. It works, and Er-jie eventually, after losing a child she is carrying because of an inept doctor, kills herself by swallowing gold. Meanwhile, a determined San-jie announces that she will also marry and sets her sights on Bao-yu's friend, the former actor Liu Xiang-lain. She declares that if this marriage is not possible, she will join a convent. The two become engaged, but Liu changes his mind at the last minute because he has suspicions about San-jie's reputation. She then dramatically kills herself with one of his swords, exclaiming she squandered her life for love.

Critics have offered differing interpretations of the sisters' tragic fates. C.T. Hsia has observed that in reading their love stories, "one feels not so much that Cao Xueqin fails to respect true love as that he regards true love as inherently fragile, easily shattered under the impact of the slings of a far from outrageous fortune. You San-jie, who shows sustained moral outrage in defying the voluptuaries around her, characteristically cannot bear for a minute the understandable mistrust of a person who has only heard of her reputation and knows nothing of the selfless love she is ready to offer him. [So] she impulsively kills herself" (Hsia, 265). The commentator Red Inkstone wrote, "San-jie's slashing a sword across her throat is breaking off passion and also proper passion" (quoted in Xiao, 216). Another scholar has surmised that San-jie's death "reveals the ardor of her love. Thus, she takes death as the purifying ordeal for the transformation of her own image" (Xiao, 244). And more recently, Halvor Eifring has argued that *Honglou meng* "is by no means unequivocal in assigning love as the cause of death ... the direct reason for You Er-jie's suicide is not her love for Jia Lian, but her maltreatment at the hands of Wang Xi-feng ... in its treatment of genuine love, the novel makes a distinction between love that occurs within a prescribed relation and love that violates each relation ... all the love relations that end in death somehow violate a taboo.... You San-jie pays with her life for her former sin of a sexual relation with her elder sister's husband. You Er-jie moves in with Jia Lian when he is still in mourning and not supposed to marry" (299, 300, 301).

FURTHER READING

Eifring, Halvor. "The Psychology of Love in *The Story of the Stone*." *Love and Emotion in Traditional Chinese Literature*. Edited by Halvor Eifring (Leiden: Brill Academic Publisher, 2004): 271–324.

Hsia, C.T. "*Dream of the Red Chamber*." In *The Classic Chinese Novel: A Critical Introduction* (New York: Columbia University Press, 1968): 245–297.

Xiao, Chi. *The Garden as Lyric Enclave: A Generic Study of the* Story of the Stone (Ann Arbor, Center for Chinese Studies: University of Michigan Press, 2001).

Zhen Bao-yu 甄宝玉

Scion of the Zhen family, Zhen Ying-jia's son and Jia Bao-yu's manifest double. His personality and attitude regarding girls, Confucianism, study, and the imperial examination system are strikingly similar to Bao-yu's throughout much of the novel. But this drastically changes when he becomes seriously sick and visits the Land of Illusion, where he reads and understands the registers. As a result, he completely changes his perspective and devotes himself to studying and learning the family business. Jia Bao-yu meets him twice: first in a dream and then in chapter 115 where they engage, together with Jia Lan, in a conversation. Their discussion reveals, much to Jia Bao-yu's intense disappointment and disgust, that Zhen now holds conventional convictions and that his talk is peppered with Confucian platitudes about filial piety, loyalty, and virtue. Jia Bao-yu later dismisses Zhen Bao-yu as another example of a person who is a "career worm" while talking with Bao-chai. But members of the Jia family, including Jia Zheng, are quite taken with Zhen, and Lady Wang, with the approval of Lady Zhen, makes a match for him to marry a cousin of Li Wan. At the end of the novel, he does well on the imperial examination. Numerous theories have been offered to explain Zhen Bao-yu's purpose in the story. It does seem plausible that Cao Xueqin, on one level, was exploring through Zhen a route his own life might have taken if the tragic events in his family had not occurred or if he had acted differently during it.

See also **Doubles and Doubling, Jia Bao-yu**

Zhen Family

Affluent Southern family that has long-standing and close connections with the Jia family. The head of the family is Zhen Ying-jia. Their family name means "true." They are, on a certain level, mirror images and even harbingers of events that will overtake the Jia family. Their relationship to the Jia family is so close that the Jias have received many expensive gifts from them, including imperial-use satins, gauzes, taffetas, and damasks, and for Grandmother Jia's 80th birthday, they sent an expensive 12-panel folding screen. Members of the family also visit the Jias, including Zhen Ying-jia. Their Beijing townhouse is like the Ning and Rong mansions but even more opulent. The Zhens also have their mansion raided by the government, their hereditary ranks taken away, and family members detained for questioning. (Tellingly, the Jia family receive news of this happening on the same day Prospect Garden is raided. Moreover, the Zhens also carried out a search of their compound shortly before the government raid.) In addition, their family's scion is also named Bao-yu, and he bears a striking physical similarity to Jia Bao-yu and is his manifest double. The commentator Red Inkstone, who knew Cao Xueqin, has written that it is important for readers of the novel to understand that when Cao mentions the Zhen family, he is secretly referring to his own family.

See also **Doubles and Doubling, Zhen Bao-yu**

Zhen Shi-yin 甄士隐

Caltrop's father, Feng-shi's husband, and Jia Yu-cun's friend, his name is a homonym for "true matters concealed." His significance can be seen in the fact that he (like Vanitas, Jia Yu-cun, and the monk and Daoist) appears at the beginning of the novel and at the end. At the beginning of the story, Shi-yin is in his 50s, a modest and unambitious gentleman of private means with a retiring nature. He is devoted to his only child, Ying-lian (Caltrop) and enjoys poetry and wine. Jia Yu-cun is a friend who lives in a nearby temple, and Shi-yin generously provides him with money so that he can travel to Beijing to take the imperial examination. Soon after, a series of disasters and bad luck plague Shi-yin and his wife. Ying-lian is kidnapped, their residence burns down, and he is forced to rely upon his mean-spirited and tightfisted father-in-law to survive. One day, during a walk, he encounters a mad and lame Daoist monk and becomes enlightened. Later, he meets Yu-cun again but purposely fails to recognize him. At the end of the novel, Shi-yin is an immortal, and he and Yu-cun meet a third time and have a long discussion over what has occurred in the story. Shi-yin's main role is to provide critical information to the reader: background information about the relationship between Bao-yu and Dai-yu, information about the novel's themes, and information on future developments of the Jia family. For example, in chapter 1, he chances on the monk and Daoist and overhears them discussing how the stone and Crimson Pearl Flower met and developed their special relationship. In the same chapter, he composes a song that reinforces the messages in the lame Daoist monk's Won-done Song, which contains hints as to the future of several characters and touches on some of the novel's themes. And in chapter 120, Shi-yin ties up some loose ends in the plot, as he expounds on "the nature of passion and illusion" (SS, 5: 357). He informs the reader on what is going to happen to Caltrop, Jia Lan, Bao-yu's son Jia Gui, and what the fortunes of the Ning and Rong houses will be and elaborates on the workings of karma and the dangers of human attachments. While many of his comments clarify issues, others are confusing or ambiguous, which is keeping with the open-text nature of the novel. One critic has called Shi-yin the epitome of a Quanzhen Daoist master, noting, "The echoing of Quanzhen attitudes towards the impermanence of life in Zhen Shi-yin's verses [in chapter 1]—his only elaboration on a philosophy of life in the narrative—supports the belief that this allegorical figure is conceived as a personification of Quanzhen Daoism" (Zhou, 48).

See also **Zhuangzi**

FURTHER READING

Zhou, Zuyan. *Daoist Philosophy and Literati Writings in Late Imperial China: A Case Study of the Story of the Stone* (Hong Kong: Hong Kong University Press, 2013).

Zhuangzi 庄子 (369–286 BC)

Pivotal Chinese late 4th-century BC Daoist philosopher. Daoism is a native Chinese philosophical and religious tradition. The Buddhist elements in *Dream of the Red Chamber* have tended to overshadow its Daoist aspects. But there is no doubt that Daoism, as exemplified by the thoughts of Zhuangzi, also forms a significant part of the story. One useful way to illustrate the basic tenets of Daoism is to contrast them with the other native Chinese philosophical tradition, Confucianism. Whereas Confucianism is concerned with human society and making the world a better place, Daoism is focused on nature and living in harmony with it. While Confucianism reads the human social order into nature, Daoism holds that individuals needed to model themselves on nature. While Confucianism emphasizes others, self-discipline, ritual, decorum, the regulation of behavior, and wisdom, Daoism prizes the self, personal freedom, independence, spontaneity, naturalness, and seeks the happy ignorance represented by the mind of a child. While Confucianism is noted for its stress on a strict social hierarchy, merit, privilege, and the belief that there is a natural basis for social distinctions and human ethical norms, Daoists believe in natural equality and question evaluative, ethical distinctions made between right and wrong, noble and base. For Daoists, the goal in life is tranquility and passivity, which can be obtained by comprehending and abiding with the *dao*, the "way, path, road" on which one travels in life. The *dao* is the permanent and eternal entity amid the constantly changing universe, the ultimate reality *and* method, and the truth of all things. It is also the origin of the world, and, while it is real and objective, it is without form or shape. Harmony with the *dao* can be obtained through the cultivation of *wu wei*, "actionless acting or taking no action," where an individual develops a state of being in which what they do is seamlessly associated with the natural movement of the universe. That is, doing what comes naturally through a lively, unforced, and unconscious state of mind and not through overexertion, vigorous endeavor, or willful intention. Despite these differences between the two philosophies, it should be said that Daoism, on one level, was seen in China as a natural complement to Confucianism. There is a traditional Chinese saying stating that people are Confucians in public but Daoists in private.

The defining figures in Chinese Daoism were Laozi (6th century BC), the author of the world-famous work the *Daode jing*, and Zhuangzi, whose writings are simply referred to as *Zhuangzi* (*The Words of Master Zhuangzi*). In contrast to Confucian writings, which are commonsensical and straightforward, these canonical Daoist works are highly suggestive, poetic, playful, and ironic. Of the two philosophers, Zhuangzi has the more important presence in *Honglou meng*. By Cao Xueqin's time, a certain amount of syncretism, which began during the Ming dynasty, occurred between the boundaries of the "three teachings" and affected the way that Confucianism, Buddhism, and Daoism were popularly practiced. Buddhism and Daoism, in particular, significantly borrowed from each other in terms of deities and certain key concepts. It should also be noted that, very broadly speaking, Daoism has traditionally been divided into two types (although some continuity exists between them): "philosophical" Daoism and "religious" Daoism. The first consists of the main ideas of Laozi and Zhuangzi. During the Qing period, religious Daoism was concerned with alchemy, the search for elixirs that would give immortality or longevity, with female alchemy, which was intended for women's physiology and practice, and with meditation and sexual self-cultivation. The novel strongly indicates that Cao Xueqin had a dislike for certain popular aspects of religious Daoism. Jia Jing is depicted as being derelict in the performance of his duties as head of the family because of his foolish quest for an elixir for immortality, a quest that eventually costs him his life when he ingests a poisonous mercury-based elixir. The seemingly impressive ceremony performed by the Daoist priests to exorcise the evil spirits in Prospect Garden is, in the end, undercut by an onlooker's skeptical comments. In addition, many of the novel's Daoist monks are depicted as corrupt and greedy.

It is also clear that Zhuangzi and his teachings play a significant role in *Honglou meng*. The famous Qing dynasty commentator Red Inkstone remarked that the novel is worthy of comparison to Zhuangzi's writings and that it employs terminology and concepts from them. Although the story tends to show Confucianism and Buddhism to be conservative, rigid, and oppressive, Daoism, for the most part, is portrayed in a positive light. Zhou Zuyan, in a book on Daoism in the novel, has concluded, "The *Stone* critiques the Neo-Confucian notion of purity that suppresses the natural, celebrates the Daoist ideal of purity that affirms it, and mocks the Buddhist ideal of purity that purges it" (276). Zhou also contends that Cao Xueqin's strong interest in Daoism was not unusual considering, "historically, Daoist philosophy often appealed to scholars at times of rampant hypocrisy, political degeneration, and ritual corruption. While the Kangxi-Yongzheng-Qianlong period Cao Xueqin lived in is usually taken as the golden age of the Qing dynasty due to its territorial expansion and social stability, the conflicts within the royal family and the widespread political corruption had a devastating impact on Cao's life, along with the decadent institutions held as state orthodoxy. All of these must have stimulated his critical sensibility leading to his Daoist inclinations.... The combined political, ethnic, and ideological oppression that he experienced must have induced a sense of confinement and engendered a longing for freedom, which may have led him to seek inspiration from Daoist philosophy, traditionally an ideological rival to a corrupt orthodoxy" (280, 283). Moreover, Cao was noted for his self-identification with the Neo-Daoist poet Ruan Ji, who was one of the famous Seven Sages of the Bamboo Grove, many of whom had links to the Qingtan school of Daoism. Finally, Cao Xueqin must have been specifically attracted to Zhuangzi's writings because of the philosopher's famous nonconformist and skeptical attitude, emphasis on freedom from conventional beliefs, and his imaginative use of irony, fantasy, satire, humor, and the literary quality of his prose.

Dream of the Red Chamber has ten explicit references to Zhuangzi. Nearly all of them are directly associated with Bao-yu, and he is his favorite writer (as well as Adamantina's). It has been argued that these carefully placed references can be viewed as operating like a sensitive gauge that measures and monitors Bao-yu's arduous philosophical development and that they also offer a critique of his subject dominating, analysis and emotion driven, limited point of view (Gray). The first allusion occurs in chapter 21 where Bao-yu is smarting from criticisms made by Dai-yu, Xiang-yun, and Aroma. Sulking in his room and tipsy from the wine he has drunk, he picks up and reads chapter 10, "Rifling Trunks," from the *Zhuangzi*. He then misinterprets a famous passage from this chapter and angrily pens his own version of it using the names of the girls who have recently offended him. Dai-yu later stumbles upon Bao-yu's comments and writes a short verse satirizing his complete misreading of Zhuangzi's original point. Cao Xueqin is not showing by this incident simply a case of a drunk and spoiled youngster not understanding an important philosophical idea, for the chapter Bao-yu read gives a clue to an epistemological malady that will plague him through most of the story, namely what Zhuangzi calls the "lust for knowledge." Zhuangzi states, "Everyone in the world has enough sense to inquire into what he does not know, yet we do not have the sense to inquire into what we already do know. Everyone knows how to condemn what he judges to be bad, yet we do not know how to condemn what we have already judged good. That is why we are in utter disorder.... How utterly the lust for knowledge has disordered the world" (210).

Zhuangzi contended that many of the problems people encounter in the world are the result of their failure to recognize the relativity of human perception. His skeptical perspectivism was based on the idea that everything is in a continual state of change and transformation caused by the endless dynamic interactions of opposites and that because of this situation, all of our distinctions, judgments, and perspectives are, in the end, relative. Therefore, all conscious human endeavors and acts involving the lust of knowledge, which attempt to formulate, generalize, and impose order, restrict and reduce the natural order and flow of things. It can be argued that Bao-yu's constant disputes and heated misunderstanding with others, which bracket nearly all of the novel's references to Zhuangzi, illustrate, in large part, his addiction to knowing, the harmful effects of his attachment to excessive human feeling, and his unwarranted purposeful striving. His repeated and excessive attempts at evaluating, clarifying, arguing, empathizing, and intellectualizing and emoting his way to truth throughout much of the novel all ultimately fall flat because he refuses to grasp the partiality and self-interested nature of his perspective and the deceitful character of language (Gray 181, 182). This is revealed in chapters like 22 when he tells Dai-yu during one of their frequent arguments, "There's always a reason for everything. If you tell people what it is, they don't feel so bad about it" (SS, 1: 438), and in an earlier argument with her, he exclaims, "It's the way I feel that makes me the way I am" (SS, 1: 412). According to Zhuangzi's thinking, the cognitive process that Bao-yu uses during his arguments with others is the product of his "prejudiced mind," which makes hard and fast judgments grounded on only partial knowledge, treats differences as absolute, and makes wide generalizations from language that are inherently deceptive. In short, instead of analyzing and choosing, Bao-yu needs to understand that the Way "is an unverbalizable 'knowing how' rather than 'knowing that.' The sage adapts to the course of things instead of trying to impose his will upon it, like the swimmer who stays afloat under a huge waterfall" (Graham, 186–187).

Later chapters containing references to Zhuangzi appear to continue to critique Bao-yu's lack of proper perspective and attachment to language. In the end, he is finally able to prevail over his self-centered orientation by discovering his original natural self and to live (albeit with some difficulty) with his natural dispositions. By doing so, he ontologically and epistemologically returns to his original state—that of a stone. As a result, he is ultimately able to break (albeit with some lingering resistance) with the circular cause and effect chain of discursive reasoning that provided in large part the basis for his finite perspective (Gray, 184). In the words of Zhuangzi, Bao-yu has finally learned "when to stop." Revealingly, after this change occurs, he, in true Daoist fashion, orders his maids to store his books on Daoism because he now understands and therefore no longer needs them. There is one other important motif from Zhuangzi that is explicitly associated with Bao-yu and warrants a brief discussion, namely the usefulness or efficacy of the useless. (For a detailed analysis of other Daoist motifs in the novel, like bird-fish, skull, bone, heart, beauty, imagery, notions of purity, and the rhetoric of chaos, as well as why Jia Yu-cun is a Daoist figure, see Zhou.) Zhuangzi's writings contain several parables designed to shake up commonly believed notions regarding usefulness and uselessness, success, and utility. His belief was that everything is useful in some way or another depending on the situation, and there are occasions when something that is extremely useful is useless, or, conversely, useful because it is useless. In a short verse in chapter 3 of *Honglou meng*, Bao-yu is described as, "First in this world for uselessness is he" (DRM, 1: 47).

If he is viewed through the Neo-Confucianism lens of his class and society, this would seem to be the case. Moreover, he was also a useless stone in his prior life because he had been rejected by the Goddess Nuwa. But, ironically, at the end of the story, Bao-yu, a seemingly worthless individual, suddenly becomes very useful when he does well on the imperial examination, bringing honor to and helping to restore the status of his earthly family, thereby neatly affirming Zhuangzi's position. It should also be noted that in addition to Bao-yu being associated with Zhuangzi and his ideas, he is directly linked throughout the novel with several traditional Daoist symbols. For example, in several chapters (5, 22, 56, 57), he is explicitly associated with mirrors. These mirror images can be viewed as providing a subtle reminder of Bao-yu's limited perspective and the importance of him changing it. In Daoist thought, the female is also an important symbol, and Bao-yu is strongly linked with femininity, with his passionate reverence for and identification with girls, and his effeminate appearance. His infamous remark, "Girls are made of water and boys are made of mud" (SS, 1: 76), contains two traditional symbols of Daoism:

water and the female. In Laozi's *Dao de Ching*, they are both used to explain the *dao*. Moreover, Daoism prizes natural virtue, lack of conscious will and intellectualism, and the spontaneity of children, arguing that a child's attitude provides a useful model on how to attain spiritual understanding. Bao-yu is often described in the novel as being simple and childlike and is considered by some to be silly or even stupid.

While it is clear that Cao Xueqin was deeply interested in and had a great knowledge of Daoism (especially elements of the Quanzhen school, which flourished in the Jiangsu-Zhejiang region of China where he spent his early years), it still remains an open question as to whether he seriously believed in the philosophical tradition or whether in the end it just had formal importance and was primarily used by him, as frequently occurred in traditional Chinese literature, to help structure the novel, move the plot, keep the reader's interest, and to augment the novel's realism and encyclopedic scope. Zhou Zuyan also believes that this "remains a question," observing, "Despite the pervasive inscriptions of Quanzhen values, the novel is not written essentially as a religious sermon, and the religious framework constitutes only a small portion of the narrative" (62, 63).

See also **Chinese Philosophy: Characteristics and Syncretism, Jia Yu-cun, Mirrors**

FURTHER READING

Chuang-Tzu: *The Inner Chapters*. Translated by A.C. Graham (London: Mandala, 1991).
Graham, A.C. *Disputers of the Tao: Philosophical Arguments in Ancient China* (Las Salle, Illinois: Open Court, 1989).
Gray, Ronald. "Returning to the Unpolished: Jia Bao-yu and Zhuang-zi in *Honglou meng*." *Tamkang Review* 36.1–2 (2005): 177–193.
Zhou, Zuyan. *Daoist Philosophy and Literati Writings in Late Imperial China: A Case Study of the* Story of the Stone (Hong Kong: Hong Kong University Press, 2013).

Recommended Reading

Books

Chan, Bing C. *The Authorship of The Dream of the Red Chamber: Based on a Computerized Statistical Study of Its Vocabulary* (Hong Kong: Joint, 1986).

Chen, Xunwu. *Another Phenomenology of Humanity: A Reading of Dream of Red Mansions* (Lanham: Lexington Books, 2015).

Edwards, Louise. *Men and Women in Qing China: Gender in the Red Chamber Dream* (Leiden: E.J. Brill, 1994).

———. *Recreating the Literary Canon: Communist Critiques of The Red Chamber Dream* (Bochum: Ruhr University, Chinathemen, 1995).

Gray, Ronald R. *Wandering Between Two Worlds: The Formative Years of Cao Xueqin* (New York: Peter Lang, 2014).

Hawkes, David. *The Story of the Stone: A Translator's Notebooks*. Edited by Liu Ching-chih (Hong Kong Centre for Literature and Translation: Lingnan University, 2000).

Hsien-Yung Pai, Kenneth and Susan Chan Egan. *A Companion to The Story of the Stone: A Chapter-By-Chapter Guide* (Columbia University Press, 2021).

Levy, Dore. *Ideal and Actual in The Story of the Stone* (New York: Columbia University Press, 1999).

Li, Qiancheng. *Fictions of Enlightenment: Journey to the West, Tower of the Myriad Mirrors, and Dream of the Red Chamber* (Honolulu: University of Hawaii Press, 2003).

Liu, Zaifu. *Reflections on Dream of the Red Chamber*. Translated by Shu Yungzhong (Amherst, New York: Cambria Press, 2008).

Miao, Huaming. *Cao Xueqin*. Translated by Guosheng Yang Chen, Trevor Hay, and Bo Ai (Nanjing: Nanjing University Press, 2010).

Miller, Lucien. *Masks of Fiction in the Dream of the Red Chamber: Myth, Mimesis and Persona* (Tucson: University of Arizona Press, 1975).

Plaks, Andrew. *Archetype and Allegory in the Dream of the Red Chamber* (Princeton: Princeton University Press, 1976).

Schonebaum, Andrew and Tina Liu, Eds. *Approaches to Teaching Cao Xueqin's Dream of the Red Chamber* (New York: Modern Languages Association of America, 2012).

Wang, Jing. *The Story of Stone: Ancient Chinese Stone Lore and the Stone Symbolism of Dream of the Red Chamber, Water Margin, and Journey to the West* (Durham: Duke University Press, 1992).

Wong, Lawrence, Kwok Pun. *Dreaming Across Languages and Culture: A Study of the Literary Translations of Honglou meng* (Cambridge Scholar's Publishing, 2014).

Wu, I-Hsien. *Eroticism and Other Literary Conventions in Chinese Literature: Intertextuality in the Story of the Stone* (Amherst: Cambria Press, 2017).

Wu, Shih-Ch'ang. *On the Red Chamber Dream: A Critical Study of Two Annotated Manuscripts of the XVIIIth Century* (Oxford: Clarendon Press, 1961).

Xiao, Chi. *The Garden as Lyric Enclave: A Generic Study of the Story of the Stone* (Ann Arbor, Center for Chinese Studies: University of Michigan Press, 2001).

Yan, Fang Gui (editor). *A Chinese English Dictionary of Idioms from A Dream of*

Red Mansions (Hangzhou: Hangzhou Publishing House, 2003).
Yi, Jeannie Jinsheng. *The Dream of the Red Chamber: An Allegory of Love* (Paramus, New Jersey: Homa & Sekey Books, 2004).
Yu, Anthony. *Rereading the Stone: Desire and the Making of Fiction in* Dream of the Red Chamber (Princeton: Princeton University Press, 1997).
Zhou, Kexi. A Dream of Red Mansions as Portrayed Through the Brush of Sun Wen. Translated by Qian Ren and Dorothy Zhang (New York: Better Link Press, 2010).
Zhou, Ruchang. *Between Noble and Humble: Cao Xueqin and the* Dream of the Red Chamber. Edited by Ronald R. Gray and Mark S. Ferrara (New York: Peter Lang, 2009).
Zhou, Zuyan. *Daoist Philosophy and Literati Writings in Late Imperial China: A Case Study of the* Story of the Stone (Hong Kong: Hong Kong University Press, 2013).

Articles

Alexander, Edwin. "China's Three Ways as Reflected in *Dream of the Red Chamber*." *Chinese Culture* 17 (1976): 145–157.
Bech, Lene. "Fiction That Leads to Truth: *The Story of the Stone* as Skillful Means." *Chinese Literature: Essays, Articles, Reviews* 26 (2004): 1–21.
———. "Flowers in the Mirror, Moonlight on the Water: Images of a Deluded Mind." *Chinese Literature: Essays, Articles, Reviews* 24 (2002): 99–128.
Besio, Kimberly. "Bao-chai Chasing Butterflies: Visual Culture in *Honglou meng*." *European Journal of Sinology*, 6 (2015): 84–105.
Bonner, Joey. "Yu P'ing-po and the Literary Dimensions of the Controversy Over *Hung lou Meng*." *The China Quarterly* 67 (1976): 546–581.
Brightwell, Erin L. "Analyzing Gender: Wang Xi-Feng as the Shrew." *Tamkang Review* 36.1–2 (2005): 67–87.
Brown, Tristan Gerald. "The Metaphorical Dimension of Symbolic Prices and Real-World Symbolic Values in *Honglou meng*." *Tsing Hua Journal of Chinese Studies*, 41.4 (2011): 795–812.

Chan, K. Hung, Albert Y. Lew, and Marian Yew Jen Wu Tong. "Accounting and Management Controls in the Classical Chinese Novel: *A Dream of Red Mansions*." *The International Journal of Accounting* 36 (2001): 311–327.
Chiang, Hwei-eng. "The Mirror Image in the *Dream of the Red Chamber*." *Asian Culture Quarterly* 8.2 (1980): 75–79.
Chu, Chung-Yi. "Pao-yu and the Other: Recognition of the Other as Difference." *Tamkang Review* 22.1–4 (1991): 315–328.
Cooper, Eugene, and Meng Zhang. "Patterns of Cousin Marriage in Rural Zhenjiang and in the *Dream of the Red Chamber*." *Journal of Asian Studies* 52.1 (1993): 90–106.
Edwards, Louise. "Gender Imperatives in *Honglou meng*: Bao-yu's Bisexuality." *Chinese Literature: Essays, Articles, Reviews* 12 (1990): 69–81.
———. "Jia Bao-yu and Essential Feminine Purity." *The Journal of the Oriental Society of Australia* 20–21 (1988–1989): 36–47.
———. "New *Hongxue* and the 'Birth of the Author': Yu Pingbo's 'On Qin Keqing's Death.'" *Chinese Literature: Essays, Articles, Reviews* 23 (2001): 31–54.
———. "Representations of Women and Social Policy in Eighteenth Century China: The Case of Wang Xifeng." *Late Imperial China* 14.1 (1993): 34–59.
———. "Women in *Honglou meng*: Prescriptions of Purity in the Femininity of Qing Dynasty China." *Modern China* 16.4 (1990): 407–429.
———. "Women Warriors and Amazons of the Mid-Qing Texts *Jinghua yuan* and *Honglou meng*." *Modern Asian Studies* 29.2 (1995): 225–255.
Egan, Ronald. "Red on Gold: Teaching *Honglou meng* in California." *Center for Cross-cultural Studies, City University of Hong Kong, Newsletter* 2 (n.d.).
Epstein, Maram. "Reflections of Desire: The Poetics of Gender in *Dream of the Red Chamber*." *Nan Nu* 1.1 (1999): 64–106.
Farquhar, Mary, and Louise Edwards. "Jia Baoyu in *Honglou meng*: Boyhood, Adolescence, and Adulthood in Pre-Modern China." *Tamkang Review* 36. 1–2 (2005): 35–66.
Ferrara, Mark S. "Emptying Emptiness: Kongkong daoren in *Honglou meng*." *Tamkang Review* 26:1–2 (2005): 105–116.

Fu, James S. "Liu Lao-Lao and the Garden of Takuanyuan." *Literature East and West* 17: 2.3.4 (1973): 305–314.

———. "The Mirror and the Incense in *The Tale of the Genji* and the *Dream of the Red Chamber*." *Tamkang Review* 10 (1979): 199–209.

Ge, Liangyan. "Albums in the Land of Illusion: Visualizing Baoyu's Visualization." *Southwest Review of Asian Studies* 34 (2012): 43–59.

Gray, Ronald. "Returning to the Unpolished: Jia Baoyu and Zhuang-zi in *Honglou meng*." *Tamkang Review* 36.1–2 (2005): 177–193.

———. "The Stone's Curious Voyage to the West: A Brisk Overview of *Honglou meng*'s English Translation History and English *Hongxue*." *Journal of Sino-Western Communications* 3.2 (2011): 23–40.

Greider, Jerome B. "The Communist Critique of *Hong-lou Meng*." *Papers on China* 10 (1956): 142–168.

Hawkes, David. "The *Story of the Stone*: A Symbolist Novel." *Renditions* 25 (1986): 6–17.

———. "The Translator, the Mirror and the Dream: Some Observations on New Theory." *Renditions* 13 (1980): 5–20.

Ho, Douglas I-ping. "Religious Figures in the *Dream of the Red Chamber*." *Fu Jen Studies: Literature and Linguistics* 16 (1983): 1–32.

Hsia, C.T. "Love and Compassion in the Dream of the Red Chamber." *Criticism* 5 (1963): 261–271.

Huang, Martin W. "Notes Towards a Poetics of Characterization in the Traditional Chinese Novel: *Honglou meng* as Paradigm." *Tamkang Review* 21.1 (1990): 1–27.

Hwang, Mei-shu. "Chia Pao-yu: The Reluctant Quester." *Tamkang Review* 1.1 (1970): 211–222.

Kaminski, Johannes. "Myths We Cannot Believe in: The Function of Mythological Metanarratives in Wilhelm Meisters Lehrjahre and Hong Lou Meng." *Arcadia* 48.1 (2013): 75–97.

———. "Toward a Maoist *Dream of the Red Chamber*: Or, How Bao-yu and Dai-yu Became Rebels Against Feudalism." *Journal of Chinese Humanities* 3 (2017): 177–202.

Lai, Whalen. "The Family as the Axis of Religion: Notes on the *Dream of the Red Chamber*." *Ching Feng* 35.1 (1992): 44–56.

Lam, Ling Hon. "The Matriarch's Private Ear: Performance, Reading, Censorship, and the Fabrication of Interiority in *The Story of the Stone*." *Harvard Journal of Asiatic Studies* 65.2 (2005): 357–415.

Lee, Haiyan. "Love or Lust? The Sentimental Self in *Honglou meng*." *Chinese Literature: Essays, Articles, Reviews* 19 (1997): 85–111.

Levy, Dore. "The Chiming of the Void: Poetry and Liberation in the *Story of the Stone*." *Common Knowledge* 6.3 (1997): 99–114.

———. "Embedded Texts: How to Read Poetry in *The Story of the Stone*." *Tamkang Review* 36:1–2 (2005): 195–227.

Li, Qiancheng. "Jia Zheng: Self, Family, and Religion in *Honglou meng*." *Tamkang Review* 36. 1–2 (2005): 3–33.

Li, Xiaodong and Yeo Kang-shua. "The Propensity of Chinese Space: Architecture in the Novel *Dream of the Red Chamber*." *Traditional Dwellings and Settlements Review* 13.2 (2002): 49–62.

Lianghan, Ge. "The Mythic Stone in *Honglou meng* and an Intertext of Ming-Qing Fiction Criticism." *Journal of Asian Studies* 61.1 (2002): 57–83.

Liao, Hsien-hao. "Tai-yu or Po-ch'ai: The Paradox of Existence as Manifested in Pao-yu's Existential Struggle." *Tamkang Review* 15.1–4 (Autumn 1984-Summer 1985): 485–493.

Lin, Shueh-fu. "Chia Pao-yu's First Visit to the Land of Illusion: An Analysis of a Literary Dream in an Interdisciplinary Perspective." *Chinese Literature: Essays, Articles, and Reviews* 14 (1992): 77–106.

Liu, David Jason. "The Chih-yen Commentary: An Analysis in the Perspective of Western Theories of Literature." *Tamkang Review* 10 (1979): 471–494.

Mair, Victor H. "Sleep in Dream: Soporific Responses to Depression in *Story of the Stone*." *Sino-Platonic Papers* 143 (July 2004): 99 pages.

Mao Dun. "What We Know of Tsao Hseuh-chin." *Chinese Literature* 5 (1964): 85–104.

Messmann, Stefan. "A Dream of Equality—Has it Been Achieved? Some Legal Aspects of the Facts in *A Dream of Red*

Mansions." *European Journal of Sinology*, 5 (2014): 61–75.

Miller, Lucien. "The English Dream." *Tamkang Review* 36:1–2 (2005): 251–270.

———. "Naming the Whirlwind: Cao Xueqin and Heidegger." *Tamkang Review* 12.2 (1981): 143–163.

———. "Sequels to the *Red Chamber Dream*: Observations on Plagiarism, Imitations and Originality in Chinese Vernacular Literature." *Tamkang Review* 5.2 (1974): 187–215.

Ming, Dong Gu, "The *Hongloumeng* as an Open Novel: Towards a New Paradigm of *Redology*." *Monumenta Serica* 51 (2003): 253–282.

———. "Psychological Subversion of the Patriarchal Order in the *Tao Te Ching* and the *Dream of the Red Chamber*." *Comparative Literature: East and West* 4 (2002): 105–136.

Motsch, Monika. "The Mirror, and Chinese Aesthetics: A Study of *Honglou meng*." *Ming Qing yanjiu* (1996): 117–136.

Nai, Cheng Gek. "*Hong lou meng*: An Introduction." *Asian and Pacific Quarterly of Cultural and Social Affairs* 24.1 (1992): 65–73.

Palandri, Angela Jung. "Women in *Dream of the Red Chamber*." *Literature East and West* 12.2–4 (1968): 226–38.

Pastreich, Emanuel. "The Novel in the Painting: An Allegory of Literature in Cao Xueqin's *Hongloumeng*." *Sungkyunkuan Journal of East Asian Studies* 3.1 (2003): 238–258.

Plaks, Andrew. "Completeness and Partiality in Traditional Commentaries on *Honglou meng*." *Tamkang Review* 36:1–2 (2005): 117–135.

———. "Leaving the Garden: Reflections on China's Literary Masterpiece." *New Left Review* 47 (2007): 109–129.

Pohl, Karl-Heinz. "The Role of the *Heart Sutra* in *Dream of the Red Chamber*." *European Journal of Sinology* 5 (2014): 9–20.

Roberts, Moss. "Neo-Confucianism in the *Dream of the Red Chamber*: A Critical Note." *Bulletin of Concerned Asian Scholars* 10.1 (1978): 63–66.

Saussy, Haun. "The Age of Attribution or How *Honglou meng* Finally Acquired an Author." *Chinese Literature: Essays, Articles, Reviews* 25 (2003): 119–132.

———. "Reading and Folly in *Dream of the Red Chamber*." *Chinese Literature: Essays, Articles, Reviews* 9 (1987): 23–47.

———. "The Return of the *Pingdian Pai*." *Tamkang Review* 36.1–2 (2005): 137–147.

Schoenbaum, Andrew. "The Medical Casebook of *Hong Lou Meng*." *Tamkang Review* 36.1–2 (2005): 229–250.

Scott, Mary. "The Image of the Garden in *Jin Ping Mei* and *Honglou meng*." *Chinese Literature: Essays, Articles, Reviews* 8 (1986): 83–94.

Shan, Te-hsing. "A Study of Chin-yen-chai's Commentary on the *Honglou meng*." *Studies in Language and Literature* Oct. 2, 1986: 134–156.

Shi, Yaohua. "Beginnings and Departures: The *Dream of the Red Chamber*." *New Zealand Journal of Asian Studies* 7.1 (2005): 112–133.

Steelman, David L. "An Introduction to Editions of the *Dream of the Red Chamber*." *The Scholar* June (1981): n.p. Also at: https://cti.lib.virginia.edu/HLM/hlmitre2.htm

Sychou, L. and V. "The Role of Costume in Ts'ao Hseu-chin's Novel the *Dream of the Red Chamber*." Translated by Cecelia Shickman. *Tamkang Review* 11.3 (1981): 287–305.

Tambling, Jeremy. "Inside and Outside the *Dream of Red Mansions*." *Tamkang Review* 35.2 (2003): 63–93.

Walter, Ann. "On Not Becoming a Heroine: Lin Dai-yu and Cui Ying-ying." *Signs* 15.1 (1989): 61–78.

Wang, C.Y. "Redundancy as an Artistic Device in the *Dream of the Red Chamber*: A Preliminary Investigation." *Journal of Oriental Studies* 38: 1&2 (2005): 1–15.

Wang, Ying. "The Disappearance of the Simulated Oral Context and the Use of the Supernatural Realm in *Honglou meng*." *Chinese Literature: Essays, Articles, and Reviews* 27 (2005): 137–150.

———. "The Supernatural as the Author's Sphere: Jinghua Yuan's Reprise of the Rhetorical Strategies of *Honglou meng*." *T'oung Pao* 92: 1–3 (2006): 129–161.

Wei, Shang. "Truth Becomes Fiction When Fiction is True: *The Story of the Stone* and the Visual Culture of the Manchu Court." *Journal of Chinese Literature and Culture* 2.1 (2015): 207–248.

Widmer, Ellen. "Extreme Makeover: Dai-yu and Bao-chai in Two Early

Sequels to *Honglou meng*." *Nan Nu* 8.2 (2006): 290–315.

Wong, Kam-ming. "Anatomy of *The Stone*: Dotting the 'I' of the Lychee and the Monkey." *Tamkang Review* 36:1-2 (2005): 147–176.

———. "The Butterfly in the Garden: Utopia and the Feminine in *The Story of the Stone*." *Diogenes* 209 (2006): 122–134.

Wu, Wei. "Color Symbolism of Redness in *The Dream of the Red Chamber*." *European Journal of Sinology*, 5 (2014): 76–110.

Wu, Yenna. "Dream Encounters and Intimations of Transcendence: *Water Margin*'s Influence on *Dream of the Red Chamber*." *Selected Papers of the 1997 Southwest Conference on Asian Studies* (Fall 1998): 11–27.

Yang, Jiang. "Art and the Overcoming of Difficulty—the *Dream of the Red Chamber*." *Chinese Journal of Comparative Literature* 1.1 (1983): 31–47.

Yang, Michael. "Naming in *Honglou-meng*." *Chinese Literature: Essays, Articles, Reviews* 18 (1996): 69–101.

Yang, Vincent. "The Symbolism of Naming in *Dream of the Red Chamber*." *Tamkang Review* 22.1–4 (Fall 1991-Summer 1992): 305–313.

Yau, Ka-Fai. "Realist Paradoxes: The Story of the *Story of the Stone*." *Comparative Literature* 57.2 (2005): 117–133.

Yee, Angelina. "Counterpoise in *Honglou meng*." *Harvard Journal of Asiatic Studies* 50.2 (1990): 613–650.

———. "Self, Sexuality, and Writing in *Honglou meng*." *Harvard Journal of Asiatic Studies* 55.2 (1995): 373–407.

Yim, Chi-hung. "The 'Deficiency of Yin in the Liver'—Dai-yu's Malady and Fubi in *Dream of the Red Chamber*." *Chinese Literature: Essays, Articles, Reviews* 22 (2000): 85–111.

Yu, Anthony. "The Quest of Brother Amor: Buddhist Intimations in the *Story of the Stone*." *Harvard Journal of Asiatic Studies* 49.1 (1989): 55–92.

———. "Religious Symbolism in *Hung-lou Meng*." *Studies in Language and Literature*, Oct. 4 (1990): 1–30.

———. "Self and Family in the *Hung-lou Meng*: A New Look at Lin Tai-yu as Tragic Heroine." *Chinese Literature: Essays, Articles, Reviews* 2.2 (1980): 199–223.

———. "The Stone of Fiction and the Fiction of Stone: Reflexivity and Religious Symbolism in *Hung-lou Meng*." *Studies in Language and Literature* 4 (1990): 1–30.

Yu, Ying-shih. "The Two Worlds of *Hung-lou Meng*." Translated by Diana Yu. *Renditions* 2 (1974): 5–22.

Zhan, Haiyan. "Tea in *The Story of the Stone*: Meaning and Function." *ICU Comparative Literature* 39 (2007): 83–118.

Zhao, Xiaohuan. "Court Trials and Miscarriage of Justice in *Dream of the Red Chamber*." *Law and Literature* 23.129 (2011): 1–25.

Zhou, Ruchang. "None the *Red Chamber* Message Hears: Art as Living Philosophy." *Tamkang Review* 36.1-2 (2005): 89–103.

Zhou, Yiquin. "Temples and Clerics in *Honglou meng*." *Harvard Journal of Asiatic Studies* 7.2 (2011): 263–309.

Zhou, Zuyan. "Chaos and the Gourd in the *Dream of the Red Chamber*." *T'oung Pao* 97.4-5 (2001): 251–288.

———. "A Crane Standing Amidst Chickens: Cao Xueqin's Art of Bird Symbolism Viewed Against His Kin's and Friend's Writings." *European Journal of Sinology*, 6 (2015): 62–70.

Book Chapters, Introductions and Prefaces

Bonner, Joey. "Analysis of *Dream of the Red Chamber*." In *Wang Kuo-Wei: An Intellectual Biography*. (Cambridge: Harvard University Press, 1986): 81–88.

Chang, H.C. "A Burial Mound for Flowers." In *Chinese Literature: Popular Fiction and Drama*. (Edinburgh: Edinburgh University Press, 1973): 383–403.

"Chang Hsin-chih on How to Read the *Hung-lou Meng* (*Dream of the Red Chamber*)." Translated and annotated by Andrew Plaks. In *How to Read the Chinese Novel*. Edited by David Ralston. (Princeton: Princeton University Press, 1990): 316–322.

Chou, Ju-ch'ang. "Preface." *A Dream of Red Mansions: An Abridged Chinese Reader*. Edited by Lu Wen-hua. (Beijing: Sinolingua, 1994): 3–8.

Chow, Tse-tsung. "The Origin of the Title

of *The Red Chamber Dream.*" *A Birthday Book for Brother Stone: David Hawkes at 80.* Edited by Rachael May and John Minford. (Hong Kong: Chinese University of Hong Kong, 2003): 115–118.

———. "Ts'ao Hsueh-ch'in." In *The Indiana Companion to Traditional Chinese Literature.* Edited by William Nienhauser. (Bloomington: Indiana University Press, 1986): 791–794.

Eber, Irene. "Riddles in the *Dream of the Red Chamber.*" In *Untying the Knot: On Riddles and Other Enigmatic Modes.* Edited by Galit Hasan-Rokem and David Shulman. (New York: Oxford University Press, 1996): 237–251.

Edwards, Louise. "Aestheticizing Chinese Masculinity in *Honglou meng*: Clothing, Dress, and Decoration." In *Changing Male Masculinities: Imperial Pillars of State to Global Real Men.* (Hong Kong: Hong Kong University Press, 2016): 90–112.

———. "Eating and Drinking in a *Red Chambered Dream.*" In *Scribes of Gastronomy: Representations of Food and Drink in Imperial Chinese Literature.* Edited by Isaac Yue and Siufu Tang. (Hong Kong University Press, 2013): 113–131.

———. "Painting Boundaries of Sex Segregation in Qing China: Representing the Family in the *Red Chamber Dream.*" In *The Family Model in Chinese Art and Culture.* Edited by J. Silbergeld and Dora C.Y. Ching. (Princeton University Press, 2013): 339–372.

Eifring, Halvor. "Chinese Faces—The Sociopsychology of Facial Features as Described in *The Story of the Stone.*" In *Minds and Mentalities in Traditional Chinese Literature.* Edited by Halvor Eifring. (Beijing: Culture and Art Publishing House, 199): 46–119.

———. "The Psychology of Love in *The Story of the Stone.*" In *Love and Emotion in Traditional Chinese Literature.* Edited by Halvor Eifring. (Leiden: Brill Academic Publisher, 2004): 271–324.

———. "The Ritual Death of Baoyu and Xifeng–A Close Reading of Chapter 25 of *The Story of the Stone.*" In *Studies in Chinese Language and Culture: Festschrift in Honor of Christopher Harbsmeir on the Occasion of his 60th Birthday.* Edited by Christopher Anderl and Havlor Eifring. (Oslo: Hermes Academic Publishing, 2005): 435–448.

Epstein, Maram. "Making Sense of Bao-yu: Staging Ideology and Aesthetics." *Approaches to Teaching Cao Xueqin's* Dream of the Red Chamber. Edited by Andrew Schonebaum and Tina Liu. (New York: Modern Language Association of America, 2012): 317–333.

———. "Rereading the Sentimental World of *Story of the Stone.*" *Orthodox Passions: Narrating Filial Love During the High Qing* (Cambridge: Harvard University Press, 2019).

———. "Reflections of Desire in *Honglou meng.*" In *Competing Discourses: Orthodoxy, Authenticity, and Engendered Meanings in Late Imperial Chinese Fiction* (Cambridge: Harvard University Press, 2001): 150–197.

Fan, Shengyu, and John Minford. "The Story of the Stone's Journey to the West: The History of the English Translations of *Honglou meng.*" In *The Routledge Book of the Chinese Translation.* Edited by Chris Shei and Zhao-Ming Gao (New York: Routledge, 2017): 374–387.

Fang, Chao-ying. "Ts'ao Chan." In A.W. Hummel, ed., *Eminent Chinese of the Ch'ing Period.* Volume Two (Washington: United States Government Printing Office, 1944): 737–739.

Friends, Mary Ellen. "Bao-yu Goes to High School." *Approaches to Teaching Cao Xueqin's* Dream of the Red Chamber. Edited by Andrew Schonebaum and Tina Liu (New York: Modern Language Association of America, 2012): 442–453.

Furth, Charlotte. "Five Questions for a New Reader of *The Story of the Stone*: A Historian's Primer for Volume 1." *Approaches to Teaching Cao Xueqin's Dream of the Red Chamber.* Edited by Andrew Schonebaum and Tina Liu (New York: Modern Language Association of America, 2012): 78–94.

Ge, Liangyan. "The Stone in *Dream of the Red Chamber*: Unfit to Repair the Azure Sky." In *The Scholar and the State: Fiction as Political Discourse in Late Imperial China* (Seattle: University of Washington Press, 2017): 138–169.

Han, Jiaming. "The Image of the West in a *Dream of Red Mansions.*" In Sukehiro Hirakawa, ed., *Images of Westerners in Chinese and Japanese Literature*

(Amsterdam, Netherlands: Rodopi, 2000): 39–52.

Hawkes, David. "The Disillusionment of Precious Jade." In John Minford and Siu-Kit Wong, eds. *Classical, Modern and Humane: Essays on Chinese Literature* (Hong Kong: Chinese University Press, 1989): 267–271.

Hegel, Robert. "Unpredictability and Meaning in Mid-Qing Literati Novels." In *Paradoxes of Traditional Chinese Literature*. Edited by Eva Hung (Hong Kong: The Chinese University Press, 1994): 147–166.

Hsia, C.T. "*Dream of the Red Chamber*." In *The Classic Chinese Novel: A Critical Introduction* (New York: Columbia University Press, 1968): 245–297.

Huang, Martin W. "Qing and the Reluctance to Grow Up in *Honglou meng*." In *Desire and Fictional Narrative in Late Imperial China* (Cambridge: Harvard University Press, 2001): 271–316.

———. "Readership and Reading Practices: *The Story of the Stone* in Premodern China." *Approaches to Teaching Cao Xueqin's* Dream of the Red Chamber. Edited by Andrew Schonebaum and Tina Liu (New York: Modern Language Association of America, 2012): 95–102.

———. "The Self Displaced: Women and Growing Up in the *Dream of the Red Chamber*." In *Literati and Self-Re/Presentation: Autobiographical Sensibility in the Eighteenth-Century Chinese Novel* (Stanford: Stanford University Press, 1997): 75–108.

Hung, Wu. "Beyond Stereotypes: The Twelve Beauties in Qing Court Art and the *Dream of the Red Chamber*." In *Writing Women in Late Imperial China*. Edited by Ellen Widmer and Kang-i Yun Chang (Stanford: Stanford UP, 1997): 306–365.

Kao, Yu-kung. "Lyric vision in the Chinese Narrative Tradition: A Reading of *Hung-lou-Meng* and *Ju-lin Wai-shih*." In *Chinese Narrative: Critical and Theoretical Essays*. Edited by Andrew Plaks (Princeton: Princeton University Press, 1977): 227–243.

Levy, Dore. "The Garden and Garden Culture in *The Story of the Stone*." *Approaches to Teaching Cao Xueqin's* Dream of the Red Chamber. Edited by Andrew Schonebaum and Tina Liu (New York: Modern Language Association of America, 2012): 115–132.

———. "The Retributory Power of Gossip in *The Story of the Stone*." In *Idle Talk: Gossip and Anecdote in Traditional China*. Edited by Jack Chen and David Schaberg (Berkeley: University of California Press, 2013): 194–215.

Li, Wai-yee. "Beginnings: Enchantment and Irony in *Hung-lou Meng*, Self-reflexivity and the Lyrical Ideal in *Hung-lou Meng*, Disenchantment and Order in *Hun-lou Meng*." In *Enchantment and Disenchantment: Love and Illusion in Chinese Literature* (Princeton: Princeton University Press, 1993): 152–256.

———. "Languages of Love and Parameters of Culture in *Peony Pavilion* and *The Story of the Stone*." In *Love and Emotions in Traditional Chinese Literature*. Edited by Halvor Eifring (Leiden: Brill, 2004): 233–270.

Liu, Joyce C.H. "The Doubling of the Stone: The Double Motif and the True Self in *Xiyou Ji* and *Honglou meng*." In *East-West Comparative Literature: Cross-Cultural Discourse*. Edited by Tak-wai Wong (Hong Kong: Department of Comparative Literature, University of Hong Kong, 1993): 121–150.

Liu, Tao Tao. "Hu Shih and the Story of the Stone." In *A Birthday Book for Brother Stone: For David Hawkes at 80*. Edited by Rachael May and John Minford (Hong Kong: Chinese University of Hong Kong, 2003): 185–193.

Lu, Hsun. "Novels of Manners in the Ching Dynasty." In *A Brief History of Chinese Fiction*. Translated by Yang Hsien-yi and Gladys Yang (Peking: Foreign Languages Press, 1959): 298–316.

Lu, Tina. "Dreams, Subjectivity, and Identity in *Stone*." *Approaches to Teaching Cao Xueqin's* Dream of the Red Chamber. Edited by Andrew Schonebaum and Tina Liu (New York: Modern Language Association of America, 2012): 274–282.

———. "The End of *Stone*." *Approaches to Teaching Cao Xueqin's* Dream of the Red Chamber. Edited by Andrew Schonebaum and Tina Liu (New York: Modern Language Association of America, 2012): 103–114.

———. "*Honglou meng* and the Borders of the Family." *Accidental Incest,*

Filial Cannibalism, and Other Peculiar Encounters in Late Imperial Chinese Literature (Cambridge: Harvard University Press, 2009): 201–238.

Lupke, Christopher. "The Capillaries of Power: Hierarchy and Servitude in *The Story of the Stone*." *Approaches to Teaching Cao Xueqin's Dream of the Red Chamber*. Edited by Andrew Schonebaum and Tina Liu (New York: Modern Language Association of America, 2012): 283–295.

McMahon, Keith. "Eliminating Traumatic Antinomies: Sequels to *Honglou meng*." In *Snake's Legs: Sequels, Continuations, Rewritings, and Chinese Fiction*. Edited by Martin W. Huang (Honolulu: University of Hawaii Press, 2004): 98–115.

———. "Polygamy, Crossing of the Gender and the Superiority of Women in *Honglou meng*." In *Misers, Shrews and Polygamists: Sexuality and Male-Female Relations in Eighteenth Century Chinese Literature* (Durham: Duke University Press, 1995): 176–204.

———. "Qing Can Be in One and Only One." In *Polygamy and Sublime Passion; Sexuality in China on the Verge of Modernity* (University of Hawaii Press, 2010): 31–47.

———. "Sequels to *Stone*: Polygamous Harmony and the Theme of Female Talent." *Approaches to Teaching Cao Xueqin's Dream of the Red Chamber*. Edited by Andrew Schonebaum and Tina Liu (New York: Modern Language Association of America, 2012): 381–389.

Meyer-Fong, Tobie. "A Question of Taste: Material Culture, Connoisseurship, and Character in *The Story of the Stone*." *Approaches to Teaching Cao Xueqin's Dream of the Red Chamber*. Edited by Andrew Schonebaum and Tina Liu (New York: Modern Language Association of America, 2012): 208–217.

Miller, Lucien. "Children of the Dreams: The Adolescent World in Cao Xueqin's *Honglou meng*." In *Chinese Views of Childhood*. Edited by Anne Kinney (Honolulu: University of Hawaii Press, 1995): 219–247.

Millward, James. "Bao-yu's Education." *Approaches to Teaching Cao Xueqin's Dream of the Red Chamber*. Edited by Andrew Schonebaum and Tina Liu (New York: Modern Language Association of America, 2012): 159–163.

Minford, John. "Foreword." *The Dream of the Red Chamber*. Translated by H. Bencraft Joly (Tokyo: Tuttle Publishing, 2010): xi–xxii.

———. "Pieces of Eight: Reflections on Translating *The Story of the Stone*." In *Translating Chinese Literature*. Edited by Eugene Eoyang and Lin Yao-fu (Bloomington: Indiana University Press, 1995): 178–203.

———. "The Slow Boat from China: The *Stone's* Journey to the West." *Komparative Philosophie: Begegnungen Zwischen Ostlichen und Westlichen Denkwegen*. Edited by Rolf Elberfeld, Johann Kreuzer, John Minford, and Gunter Wohlfart (Wilhelm Fink Verlag, 1998): 171–180.

———. "Truth and Fiction in the Translating of *The Story of the Stone*." *Approaches to Teaching Cao Xueqin's Dream of the Red Chamber*. Edited by Andrew Schonebaum and Tina Liu (New York: Modern Language Association of America, 2012): 334–345.

———, and Robert Hegel. "Hung-lou Meng." In William Nienhauser, ed. *The Indiana Companion to Traditional Chinese Literature* (Bloomington: Indiana University Press, 1986): 452–456.

Ming Dong, Gu. "The Art of *Honglou meng*." In *Chinese Theory of Fiction: A Non-Western Narrative System* (Albany: State University of New York Press, 200): 153–180.

Naquin, Susan. "Three Questions about *Stone*: Men, Riches, and Religion." *Approaches to Teaching Cao Xueqin's Dream of the Red Chamber*. Edited by Andrew Schonebaum and Tina Liu (New York: Modern Language Association of America, 2012): 2018–225.

Plaks, Andrew. "Allegory in *Hsi-yu Chi* and *Hung-lou Meng*." In *Chinese Narrative: Critical and Theoretical Essays*. Edited by Andrew Plaks (Princeton: Princeton University Press, 1977): 163–202.

———. "The Problem of Incest in *Jing Ping Mei* and *Honglou meng*." In *Paradoxes of Traditional Chinese Literature*. Edited by Eva Hung (Hong Kong: Chinese University Press, 1994): 123–146.

———. "Self-enclosure and Self-absorption in the Classic Chinese Novel." In *Minds and Mentalities in*

Traditional Chinese Literature. Edited by Halvor Eifring (Beijing: Culture and Art Publishing House, 1999): 30–45.

Rawksi, Evelyn S. "The Banner *Story of the Stone.*" *Approaches to Teaching Cao Xueqin's* Dream of the Red Chamber. Edited by Andrew Schonebaum and Tina Liu (New York: Modern Language Association of America, 2012): 144–158.

Rolston, David. "Everything at Once: The *Honglou meng.*" In *Traditional Chinese Fiction and Fiction Commentary: Reading and Writing Between the Lines* (Stanford: Stanford University Press, 1997): 329–348.

Saussy, Haun. "Authorship and *The Story of the Stone*: Open Questions." *Approaches to Teaching Cao Xueqin's* Dream of the Red Chamber. Edited by Andrew Schonebaum and Tina Liu (New York: Modern Language Association of America, 2012): 70–77.

———. "*The Story of the Stone* and World Literature." *Approaches to Teaching Cao Xueqin's* Dream of the Red Chamber. Edited by Andrew Schonebaum and Tina Liu (New York: Modern Language Association of America, 2012): 475–478.

———. "Unspoken Sentences: A Thought-Sequence from *Honglou meng.*" In *Studies in Chinese Language and Culture: Festschrift in Honor of Christopher Harbsmeier on the Occasion of His 60th Birthday.* Edited by Christoph Anderl and Halvor Eifring (Oslo: Hermes Academic Publishing, 2006): 427–433.

———. "Women's Writing Before and Within the *Honglou meng.*" In *Writing Women in Late Imperial China.* Edited by Ellen Widemer and Kang-i-Sun Chang (Stanford: Stanford University Press, 1997): 285–305.

Schonebaum, Andrew. "For the Relief of Melancholy: The Early Chinese Novel as Antidepressant." In *Depression and Narrative: Telling the Dark.* Edited by Hilary Clark (Albany: SUNY Press, 2008): 179–194.

———. "Medicine in *The Story of the Stone*: Four Cases." *Approaches to Teaching Cao Xueqin's* Dream of the Red Chamber. Edited by Andrew Schonebaum and Tina Liu (New York: Modern Language Association of America, 2012): 164–185.

Scott, Mary. "*The Story of the Stone* and its Antecedents." *Approaches to Teaching Cao Xueqin's* Dream of the Red Chamber. Edited by Andrew Schonebaum and Tina Liu (New York: Modern Language Association of America, 2012): 259–273.

Silber, Cathy. "Privacy in *Dream of the Red Chamber.*" In *Chinese Concepts of Privacy.* Edited by Bonnie S. McDougall and Anders Hansson (Leiden: Brill, 2002): 55–78.

Sommer, Matthew H. "Scandal in the Garden: *The Story of the Stone* as a Licentious Novel." *Approaches to Teaching Cao Xueqin's* Dream of the Red Chamber. Edited by Andrew Schonebaum and Tina Liu (New York: Modern Language Association of America, 2012): 186–207.

Spence, Jonathan. "Author's Hypotheses on *Dream of the Red Chamber.*" In *Ts'ao Yin and the Kang-hsi Emperor: Bondservant and Master* (New Haven: Yale University Press, 1966): 301–307.

Wagner, Marsha L. "Maids and Servants in *Dream of the Red Chamber*: Individuality and the Social Other." In *Expressions of Self in Chinese Literature.* Edited by Robert E. Hegel and Richard C. Hessney (New York: Columbia University Press, 1985): 251–281.

Wang, John C.Y. "The Chih-yen chai Commentary and the *Dream of the Red Chamber*: A Literary Study." In *Chinese Approaches to Literature.* Edited by Adele Rickett (Princeton: Princeton University Press, 1978): 189–220.

Wang, Xiaojue. "*Stone* in Modern China: Literature, Politics, and Culture." *Approaches to Teaching Cao Xueqin's* Dream of the Red Chamber. Edited by Andrew Schonebaum and Tina Liu (New York: Modern Language Association of America, 2012): 413–426.

Wei, Shang. "The *Stone* Phenomenon and Its Transformation from 1791 to 1919." *Approaches to Teaching Cao Xueqin's* Dream of the Red Chamber. Edited by Andrew Schonebaum and Tina Liu (New York: Modern Languages Association of America, 2012): 390–412.

———. "*The Story of the Stone* and Its Virtual Representations, 1791-1919." *Approaches to Teaching Cao Xueqin's* Dream of the Red Chamber. Edited by Andrew Schonebaum and Tina Liu

(New York: Modern Languages Association of America, 2012): 346–380.

Widmer, Ellen. "*Honglou meng* Sequels and their Female Readers in Nineteenth Century China." In *Snake's Legs: Sequels, Continuations, Rewritings, and Chinese Fiction*. Edited by Martin W. Huang (Honolulu: University of Hawaii Press, 2004): 116–142.

———. "*Honglou meng* Sequels and their Female Readers." In *The Beauty and the Book: Women and Fiction in Nineteenth Century China*. Edited by Ellen Widmer (Cambridge: Harvard University Press, 2006): 217–248.

Witke, Roxane. "Redreaming the *Red Chamber*." In *Comrade Chiang Ch'ing* (Boston: Little, Brown and Company, 1977): 276–292.

Wong, Kam-ming. "The Allure of Melancholy: The Anxiety of Illusion in *Honglou meng*." In *Symbols of Anguish: In Search of Melancholy in China*. Edited by Wolfgang Kubin (Bern, Switzerland: Peter Lang, 2001): 213–261.

———. "Point of View and Feminism: Images of Women in *Honglou meng*." In *Women and Literature in China*. Edited by Anna Gerstlacher (Bochum: Brockmeyer, 1985): 29–97.

———. "Points of View, Norms, and Structure: *Hung-lou Meng* and Lyrical Fiction." In *Chinese Narrative: Critical and Theoretical Essays*. Edited by Andrew Plaks (Princeton: Princeton University Press. 1977): 203–226.

Wong, Yoon wah. "The Impact of *Dream of the Red Mansions* on Modern Chinese Literature." In *Essays on Chinese Literature: A Comparative Approach* (Singapore: Singapore University Press, 1988): 96–108.

Wu, I-Hsien. "'Enlightenment Through Feelings': Poetry, Music, and Drama in *The Story of the Stone*." *Approaches to Teaching Cao Xueqin's Dream of the Red Chamber*. Edited by Andrew Schonebaum and Tina Liu (New York: Modern Languages Association of America, 2012): 296–316.

Xue, Weihe. "How Humor Humanizes a Confucian Paragon: The Case of Xue Baochai in *Honglou meng*." *Humor in Chinese Life and Letters: Classical and Traditional Approaches*. Edited by Jocelyn Chen and Jessica Milner Davis (Hong Kong University Press, 2011): 139–168.

Yibin, Ni. "Material Culture Matters in *The Story of the Stone*." *Approaches to Teaching Cao Xueqin's Dream of the Red Chamber*. Edited by Andrew Schonebaum and Tina Liu (New York: Modern Languages Association of America, 2012): 236–258.

Yu, Anthony. "Cao Xueqin's *Hongloumeng* (*Story of the Stone* or *Dream of the Red Chamber*)." In *Masterworks of Asian Literature in Comparative Perspective: A Guide for Teaching*. Edited by Barbara Stoler Miller (Armonk, New York: Sharpe, 1994): 285–298.

Zhang, Xinzhi. "*Honglou meng dufa* (How to Read the *Honglou meng*)." Translated by Andrew Plaks, annotated by David Rolston. In *How to Read the Chinese Novel*. Edited by David Rolston (Princeton: Princeton University Press, 1990): 323–340.

Zhou, Zuyan. "*The Dream of the Red Chamber*: A Shattered Dream of Androgyny." In *Androgyny in Late Ming and Early Qing Literature* (Honolulu: University of Hawaii Press, 2003): 155–198.

Zhunshine, Lisa. "From the Social to the Literary: Approaching Cao Xueqin's *The Story of the Stone* from a Cognitive Perspective." In *The Oxford Handbook of Cognitive Literary Studies*. Edited by Lisa Zhunshine (Oxford University Press, 2015): 176–198.

Important Doctoral Dissertations

Minford, John. "The Last Forty Chapters of *The Story of the Stone*: A Literary Appraisal." Australian National University, 1980.

Scott, Mary Elizabeth. "Azure to Indigo: *Honglou meng*'s Debt to *Jing Ping Mei*." Princeton University, 1989.

Xu, Weihe. "Novel Ridens in Ming-Qing Fiction: Pathetic Humor in and of *Honglou meng*." Washington University, 1999.

Yee, Angelina C. "Sympathy, Counterpoise, and Symbolism: Aspects of Structure in *Dream of the Red Chamber*." Harvard University, 1986.

Works of Chinese Literature That Influenced Cao Xueqin

The Complete Works of Chuang Tzu. Translated by Burton Watson (New York: Columbia University Press, 1968).

Holzman, Donald. *Poetry and Politics: The Life and Works of Juan Chi* (AD 210–262) (Cambridge: Cambridge University Press, 1976).

Lu, Guanzhong. *Three Kingdoms*. Three volumes. Translated by Moss Roberts (Beijing and Berkeley: Foreign Languages Press and University of California Press, 1994).

Mowry, Hua-yuan Li. *Chinese Love Stories from "Ch'ing-shih"* (Hamden, Connecticut: Archon Books, 1983).

The Plum in the Golden Vase or, Chin P'ing Mei. Five volumes. Translated by David Tod Roy (Princeton: Princeton University Press, 1993–2013).

The Poems of Du Fu. Six volumes. Translated by Stephen Owen (Berlin: Gruyter, 2015).

Pu, Songling. *Strange Tales from a Chinese Studio*. Translated by John Minford (New York: Penguin Books, 2006).

Qu, Yuan. "Li Sao" ("Encountering Trouble or Sorrow"). Translated by David Hawkes. In *Classical Chinese Literature: An Anthology of Translations*. Volume One: From Antiquity to the Tang Dynasty. Edited by John Minford and Joseph S.M. Lau (New York: Columbia University Press, Hong Kong: The Chinese University Press, 2000): 240–253.

Shi, Nai'an, and Luo Guangzhong. *Outlaws of the Marsh*. Three volumes. Translated by Sidney Shapiro (Beijing: Foreign Languages Press, 1980).

Ssu-Ma, Ch'ien. *Records of the Grand Historian of China*. Two volumes. Translated by Burton Watson (New York: Columbia University Press, 1961).

Tang, Xianzu. *A Dream of the Southern Bough*. Translated by Zhang Guangqian (Beijing: Foreign Languages Press, 2003).

———. *The Handan Dream*. Translated by Wang Rongpei (Beijing: Foreign Language Teaching and Research Press, 2003).

———. *The Peony Pavilion*. Second Edition. Translated by Cyril Birch (Bloomington: Indiana University Press, 2002).

Wang, Shifu. *The Story of the Western Wing*. Edited and Translated by Stephen H. West and Wilt L. Idema (Berkeley: University of California Press, 1995).

Wang, Yangming. *Instructions for Practical Living and Other Neo-Confucian Writings*. Translated with notes by Wing-tsit Chan (New York: Columbia University Press, 1963).

Wu, Cheng'en. *Journey to the West*. Three volumes. Translated by W.J.F. Jenner (Beijing: Foreign Languages Press, 1982).

Books on Everyday Life, Gender, History, Art and Cultural Practices in Late Imperial China

Bray, Francesca. *Technology and Gender: Fabrics of Power in Late Imperial China* (Berkley: University of California Press, 1997).

Crossley, Pamela K. *The Manchus* (Oxford: Blackwell Publishers, 1997).

Elliott, Mark C. *Emperor Qianlong: Son of Heaven, Man of the World* (New York: Longman, 2009).

———. *The Manchu Way: The Eight Banners and Ethnic Identity in Late Imperial China* (Stanford: Stanford University Press, 2001).

Elman, Benjamin. *A Cultural History of Civil Examinations in Late Imperial China* (Berkeley: University of California Press, 2000).

Goldman, Andrea S. *Opera and the City: The Politics of Culture in Beijing, 1770–1900* (Stanford: Stanford University Press, 2012).

Goodrich, Luther Carrington. *The Literary Inquisition of Ch'ien-Lung*. Second Edition (New York: Paragon Book Reprint Corp., 1966).

Goossaert, Vincent. *The Taoists of Peking, 1800–1949: A Social History of Urban Clerics* (Cambridge: Harvard University Asia Center, 2007).

Ho, Clara Wing-chung. (Editor). *Biographical Dictionary of Chinese Women: The Qing Period, 1644–1911* (Armonk, New York, 1998).

Hummel, Arthur W. Jr. *Eminent Chinese of*

the Ch'ing Period. Two Volumes (Washington: Government Printing Office, 1943–1944).

Idema, Walt and Beata Grant. *The Red Brush: Writing Women of Imperial China* (Cambridge: Harvard University Press, 2004).

Jia, Jun. *Beijing Courtyards* (Beijing: Tsinghua University Press, 2012).

Li, Xiaorong. *Women's Poetry of Late Imperial China: Transforming the Inner Chambers* (Seattle: University of Washington Press, 2012).

Mann, Susan. *Precious Records: Women in China's Long Eighteenth Century* (Stanford: Stanford University Press, 1997).

McDermott, Joseph P. *A Social History of the Chinese Book: Books and Literati Culture in Late Imperial China* (Hong Kong: Hong Kong University Press, 2006).

Naquin, Susan. *Peking: Temples and City Life 1400–1900* (Berkley: University of California Press, 2000).

———, and Evelyn S. Rawski. *Chinese Society in the Eighteenth Century* (New Haven: Yale University Press, 1987).

Peterson, William J. (Editor). *The Cambridge History of China*. Volume 9, Part One: *The Ch'ing Dynasty to 1800* (Cambridge: Cambridge University Press, 2002).

———. *The Cambridge History of China*. Volume 9, Part Two: *The Ch'ing Dynasty to 1800* (Cambridge: Cambridge University Press, 2016).

Rawski, Evelyn S. *The Last Emperors: A Social History of Qing Imperial Institutions* (Berkeley: University of California Press, 1998).

Ropp, Paul, Paolo Zamperini, and Harriet Zurndorfer (Editors). *Passionate Women: Female Suicide in Late Imperial China* (Leiden: Brill, 2001).

Rowe, William T. *China's Last Empire: The Great Qing* (Cambridge: Harvard University Press, 2009).

Smith, Richard J. *The Qing Dynasty and Traditional Chinese Culture* (Lanham: Rowman & Littlefield, 2015).

Sommer, Mathew H. *Sex, Law and Society in Late Imperial China* (Stanford: Stanford University Press, 2000).

Spence, Jonathan D. "Ch'ing." In *Food in Chinese Culture, Anthropological and Historical Perspective*. Edited by K.C. Chang (New Haven: Yale University Press, 1977): 259–294.

———. *Treason by the Book* (New York: Viking, 2001).

Tobert, Preston M. *The Ch'ing Household Department: A Study of its Organization and Principal Functions, 1662–1796* (Cambridge: Harvard University Press, 1977).

Tun, Li-Ch'en. *Annual Customs and Festivals in Peking*. Second edition. Translated by Derk Bodde (Hong Kong: Hong Kong University Press, 1965).

Wu, Cuncun. *Homoerotic Sensibilities in Late Imperial China* (New York: Rutledge, 2012).

Yuqun, Liao. *Traditional Chinese Medicine*. Third Edition (Cambridge: Cambridge University Press, 2011).

Overviews of Chinese Literature, Gardens, Mythology and Philosophy

Chan, Wing-tsit. *A Source Book in Chinese Philosophy* (Princeton: Princeton University Press, 1963).

Chang, Kang-I Sun and Stephen Owen. (Editors). *The Cambridge History of Chinese Literature*. Two volumes (Cambridge: Cambridge University Press, 2010).

De Bary, W.M. Theodore, Wing-tsit Chan, and Burton Watson. (Compiled by). *Sources of Chinese Tradition*. Volume One (New York: Columbia University Press, 1960).

Dongchu, Hu. *The Way of the Virtuous: The Influence of Art and Philosophy on Chinese Garden Design* (Beijing: New World Express, 1991).

Fung, Yu-Lan. *A History of Chinese Philosophy*. Two volumes. Translated by Derk Bodde (Princeton: Princeton University Press, 1952).

Ke, Yuan. *Dragons and Dynasties: An Introduction to Chinese Mythology* (New York: Penguin Books, 1991).

Keswick, Mary. *The Chinese Garden: History, Art, and Architecture* (Cambridge: Harvard University Press, 2003).

Mair, Victor. (Editor). *The Columbia Anthology of Traditional Chinese*

Literature (New York: Columbia University Press, 1994).

_____ (Editor). *The Columbia History of Chinese Literature* (New York: Columbia University Press, 2001).

Nienhauser, William H. (Editor). *The Indiana Companion to Traditional Chinese Literature*. Two Volumes (Bloomington: Indiana University Press, 1986, 1998).

Owen, Stephen. (Editor and translator). *An Anthology of Chinese Literature: Beginnings to 1911* (New York: W.W. Norton & Company, 1996).

Zhang, Dainian. *Key Concepts in Chinese Philosophy*. Translated by Edmund Ryden (New Haven: Yale University Press, 2002).

Index

Abbot Wang 23
Adamantina (Miao-yu) 23–24, 104, 108, 113, 194, 203, 204, 214, 227, 251
Approaches to Teaching the Story of the Stone 78
archery 24
Aroma (Xi-ren) 24–25, 38, 104, 155, 156, 169, 204
The Art of War 25
Aunt Xue 25
Aunt Zhao (Zhao Yiniang) 25, 154, 170

Bai, Ju-yi 213
Banana Garden Poetry Club 185
Bao, Er 26, 166
Bao, Yong 26
Bech, Lene 34
bees 26
Beijing 26–27
Big Jiao (Jiao Da) 27–28
Birch, Cyril 183
Bond of Gold and Jade 28
Bond of Stone and Flower 28–29
bondservants 29–30
Bonsall, B.S. 85
Book of Changes 30–31
Bowra, Edward Charles 82, 83
Bray, Francesca 124
Brightie (Wang-er) 31
Brightwell, Erin 231–232
Brown, Gerald Tristan 167
Buddhism 31–34
butterfly 35

Cai, Yijiang 208
Cai, Yuanpei 55
calligraphy 35
Caltrop (birthname Zhen Ying-lian, later changed to Xiang-ling) 35, 71, 73, 104, 186, 204, 229
Cao, Cao 36
Cao, Yin 13, 24, 64, 116, 233
censorship 36–37
chamber wives and concubines 37–38
Chan, Bao *see* Moonbeam
Chan, K. Hung 130, 131
Chan, Wing-tsit 42
Chang, Connie Oi Sum 87
Chang E 38
chapter endings 39
character description 39
Chen, Pauline 211
Cheng, Weiyuan 144
Chess (Siqi) 40–41, 217, 229
Chinese philosophy: characteristics and syncretism 41–43
The Classic Chinese Novel: A Critical Introduction 86
clothing 43–44
coastal defenses and disturbances 44
A Companion to the Story of the Stone 88
Confucianism 45–50
Cook Liu 103, 166
corruption 50–52
Cousin Zhen *see* Jia Zhen
Crab Flower Club 53
crab tree flowering 53–54
crabs and chrysanthemums 54
Crimson 165, 212
Crimson Pearl Flower *see* Lin Dai-yu
critical reception—Chinese 54–58
Crompton, Louis 117
Crossley, Pamela Kyle 127–128

Cui, Ying-ying 58–59, 207
cutting hair as protest 59

Dai Quan 26
Daoism *see* Zhuangzi
death by a thousand cuts 59–60
Deva Kings 60
Diagram of the Supreme Ultimate 60
ding 60
Door Gods 60–61
doubles and doubling 61–62
dragons 63
drama 64–68
Dream of the Red Chamber as encyclopedia 69–71
dreams 71–72
Drenched Blossoms Bridge and Pavilions 72–73
Drunken Diamond 138, 180
Du, Fu 73
Duck and Drake Swords 73–74
Duke of Ning-guo 93, 182, 188
Duke of Rong-guo 93, 182
Dun, Cheng 148
Dun, Min 184
Dun Brothers 15

Eber, Irene 89–90, 205, 206
education and the examination system 74–78
Edwards, Louise 87, 88, 105, 106, 195, 196, 232, 234, 235
Egan, Susan Chang 107
Eifring, Halvor 91, 92, 106, 195–196, 198, 247
Eight Stems and Branches 78–79
Elliot, Mark 11, 29–30

Index

Elman, Benjamin 75, 77
The Embroidered Jacket Raid 79–80
"Embroidered Purse with Human Figures" 80–81
Eminent Chinese of the Ch'ing Period Period 86
English critical reception and translation 81–89
enlightenment 89–90
Epstein, Maram 46, 48, 49, 127, 152, 198
eunuchs 91

face 91
faces in the novel 91–92
Fairy Disenchantment (Jing-huan) 92–93, 99, 101
Faithful (Yuan-yang) 94, 204, 217, 231
Fang, Chaoyang 86
fate 106–107
"Father-in-Law Pokes in the Ashes, Aunties Has It Off with Nevvy" 94
Feng, Menglong 196, 197, 208
Feng, Yuan 94–95
fireworks 95
first meeting/first fruits 96
the first six and other key chapters 96–102
Five Elements 102–103
Five Major Abuses 103
Fivey (Wu-er) 103
flowers 104
food 104–106
Ford of Error 106
foreshadowing 106–108
fortune sticks 109
Four Books and Five Classics 45–46, 74–75
funerals 109–111
Furth, Charlotte 234

games 111–112
Gao, E 144, 145, 146, 219, 220, 227
Gatha 112
Gazette (Peking) 112
Gem 217
Giles, Herbert 82, 83, 84
ginseng 112–113
Go 113
God of Longevity 113
Gold Kylin 113
Golden 142, 156, 217
government 114–115
Graham, A.C. 253

Grand Canal 115
Grandmother Jia (Jiamu) 13, 48, 101, 109, 110, 111, 113, 115–116, 135, 142, 159, 160, 204, 209, 221, 231, 236, 243
Grannie Liu (Liu Laolao) 24, 116, 175, 177, 179, 184, 231
Gu, Mingdong 224
Guanyin 116–117
guess fingers 117
Gutlaff, Karl 82–83

Half-Immortal Mao 30
Han, Jiaming 233
The Handan Story 65
The Handful of Snow 65
Hawkes, David 29, 84–85, 186, 208
He, San 117
The Heap of Honors 66
Hegel, Robert 39, 40, 90, 201, 221, 222
homosexuality 117–118
Hsia, C.T. 39, 80–81, 86, 97, 197, 224, 232, 247
Hu, Shi 18, 55, 56, 207, 208
Huang, Martin W. 179, 197, 198, 235
humor 118–119

Idema, Wilt 207
Immortals of the Islands 119
Imperial Household Department 119–120
incense 120–121
influences on Cao Xueqin 121–123
inner apartments 123–124
Iron Crutch Li 215

jade 124–125
Jade Emperor 125
Jia, Bao-yu 23, 24, 25, 27, 28, 35, 38, 44, 48, 54, 55, 56, 60, 61–62, 68, 65, 66, 71, 72, 74, 76, 77, 79, 90, 92 94, 95, 97, 98, 99, 101, 102, 103, 105, 106, 107, 108, 109, 111, 113, 117, 118, 120, 121, 124, 125, 132, 149, 155, 158, 163, 164, 165, 176, 177, 181, 183, 185, 188, 197, 198, 199, 203, 204, 205, 206, 207, 208, 209, 210, 213, 214, 226, 227, 232, 237, 242, 245, 246, 247, 248, 251–254
Jia, Dai-ru 129

Jia, Gui 242, 249
Jia, Huan 131
Jia, Jing 111, 131–132
Jia, Lan 132, 154
Jia, Lian 26, 111, 112, 132, 159, 182, 213
Jia, Qiang 133
Jia, Qiao-jie 132–133, 153, 204, 213, 227
Jia, Qin 168
Jia, Rong 26, 94, 110, 11, 111, 133
Jia, Rui 112, 133–134, 197, 223
Jia, She 52, 94, 100, 134
Jia, Tan-chun 53, 107, 134–135, 204, 205, 226, 227
Jia, Xi-chun 104, 113, 135, 176, 179, 204, 226, 227, 246
Jia, Ying-chun 41, 135–136, 204, 205, 226, 227
Jia, Yu-cun 52, 90, 98, 100, 112, 114, 136–137, 157, 178, 180, 192, 193, 210, 215, 249, 253
Jia, Yuan-chun 29, 108, 120, 135, 137, 189, 204, 205, 227
Jia, Yun 137–138, 177
Jia, Zhen 24, 26, 52, 94, 109, 11, 114, 138, 219, 246
Jia, Zheng 25, 27, 28. 38, 48, 51, 100, 112, 114, 115, 138–139, 164, 187, 205; literary gentlemen 139, 172
Jia, Zhu 149
Jia and Zhen 125
Jia family economics 129–131
Jiang, Yu-han (also known as Bijou) 139–140
Jin Ping Mei 69, 110, 191, 122, 224
Jinsheng, Jennie 222
Joker (Xing-er) 140
Joly, H. Bencraft 82, 83
Journey to the West 69, 96

Kalgren, Bernard 86
kang 140
Ke-qing 106
kites 140–141
Ko, Dorothy 235, 236
Koan 141
Kongkong daoren *see* Vanitas
kotow 141–142
Kuhn, Franz 84

Lady Wang (Wang Furen) 38, 112, 142, 239, 240
Lady Xing 110, 142, 240

Index

Land of Illusion 142–143
language 143–144
the last 40 chapters 144–146
Lee, Haiyan 196
Lee, Mei Hwa 97
legal system 146–147
Leng, Zi-xing 100, 148, 177
Levy, Dore 7, 28, 61–62, 176, 185, 186, 191, 193, 228, 239, 241
Lew, Albert Y. 130, 131
Leys, Simon 74
Li, Bai (also known as Li Bo) 148
Li, He 148
Li, Qiangcheng 32–33, 139, 221
Li, Wai-yee 70, 90, 143, 196, 223
Li, Wan 107, 148–149, 204, 226, 227
Li, Xiaodong 48
Li Sao and "The *Summons of the Soul*" 149
Lin, Dai-yu 25, 28, 35, 38, 44, 54, 55, 56, 65, 68, 71, 72, 73, 92, 93, 97, 100, 104, 106, 104, 106, 107, 108, 115, 116, 118, 120, 150–152, 156, 175, 181, 183, 186, 187, 194, 204, 205, 207, 214, 217, 226, 229, 236, 239, 241, 242, 243, 247, 248, 252
Lin, Yutang 85
linked verse 151
lion 151–152
Liu, Laolao *see* Grannie Liu
Liu, Tina 34, 72
Liu, Xiang-lian 73, 153–154
Liu, Xinwu 57
Liu, Zaifu 69
Lives of Noble Women 153
Lord Red Beard 154
Lu, Zaifu 69
Lucky 156

maids and other servants 154–157
Mair, Victor 163
Manchu salute 157
Mandarin's Life Preserver 157
Mann, Susan 185, 237
marriage 157–160
"The Mattress" 217
Mayers. W.F. 83
McMahon, Keith 209, 210,
medicine and the problem of doctors 160–162

melancholy and sleep 162–163
Mendelson, Edmund 69
Miller, Lucien 175, 193, 221, 223, 239
Minford, John 7, 75, 86, 193, 221
mirrors 165–166
missing bracelet 166–167
Miyazaki, Ichisada 75
money and measurements 166–167
monkey 167–168
monks, nuns, and temples 168–169
moon cake 170
Moonbeam (Bao Chan) 240
Morrison, Robert 81, 84
Mother Ma 170–171
Motsch, Monika 164
mourning periods 171
Murder in the Red Chamber 211

naming system 171–172
Nanny Li 234
Nanny Liu 234
Naquin, Susan 109
narration 172–172
narrative patterns and techniques 173–176
Nightingale (Zi-juan) 156, 176
Nivison, David 77–78
Nostalgia Studio 176
Nuwa 96, 177

Odd Tablet 16
One Plaster Wang 177
The Outlaws of the Marsh 69, 96, 208
outsiders 177–179
Owen, Stephen 184

painting 179–180
Pais, Hsien-yung 107
the Palace 180
The Palace of Eternal Youth 65
palanquins or sedan chairs 180
Parfume (Fang-guan) 103, 181
Park, Nancy 50–51
parrot 180–181
Pastereich, Emanuel 179
Patience (Ping-er) 156, 181–182, 210, 226
Patton, Chris 141

The Peony Pavilion 65, 66, 82, 182–183, 196
Plague God 184
Plaks, Andrew 65, 66, 82, 182–183, 189, 190
poetry 184–187
Pohl, Karl-Heinz 221
The Power and Guanxi of the Jia Family 187–188
Prince of Beijing (Shui Rong) 95, 180, 188
Prince of Xi-ing 188
Prospect Garden 188–191
Proverbs 191–192
Pu, Songling 51
Puett, Michael 42

Qi 192–193
Qin 193–194
Qin, Shi (Qing Ke-Qing) 16, 57, 94, 103, 108, 109–110, 129, 161, 194–195, 197, 204, 217, 227, 246
Qin, Zhong 95, 105, 118, 195, 197, 244
Qin Ke-qing *see* Qin-Shi
Qing 101, 190, 191, 195–199

Rawksi, Evelyn S. 109, 143
reading and rereading 199–201
The Records of the Grand Historian 123
red 201–202
The Red Chamber 211
Red Dust 176
Red Inkstone (Zhiyanzhai) 16, 39, 65, 110, 134, 145, 170–171, 174, 179, 189, 197, 202, 206, 223, 238, 239, 247, 248, 251
Red Pine 220
Red Plum 203
Registers 203–204
rice 204
riddles 205–206
Rolston, David 200, 221
The Romance of the Western Chamber 66, 206
Rooster of Lovers 208
Ropp, Paul 235
Rowe, William T. 76
Ruan, Ji 123, 251

Samadhi 208
Saussy, Haun 243
Scholar and Beauty Romances 208–209
The Scholars 51, 208
Schonebaum, Andrew 162

Index

Scott, Mary 110, 120, 122, 191
screen wall 209
seating arrangements and sitting style 210
sequels 210–211
Seven Sages of the Bamboo Grove 251
The Seventh Branch 66
Shi, Xiang-yun 13, 152, 186, 211–212, 227, 246
Shi, Yaohua 96, 219, 220
Shui, Rong *see* Prince of Beijing
Sima, Qian 123
Simple 212
Skybright (Qing-wen) 104, 106, 142, 156, 161, 204, 212–213, 215, 232, 236, 240
Smallpox Goddess 213
Smith, Richard 30, 38, 47, 69, 78–79, 158–159, 237
Sommer, Matthew 37
"Song of Everlasting Grief" 213
the south 214
Spence, Jonathan 105
spirit money 167
spirit writing 214–215
spiritual tablets 215
spitting at/on 215–216
the stone 92, 96, 97, 98, 99, 125, 151, 200, 209, 222, 227, 228, 249, 251, 252
Su, Dong-po 216
suicide 216–218
Sun, Shao-zu 218
supernatural 218–220
Sutras (Diamond and Heart) 220–221
swastika 221
Sychou, L. 43, 44
Sychou, V. 43, 44

Taku, Ashibe 211
Tang, Xianzu 183, 196
Tealeaf 221
Theiss, Janet 217, 218
themes and indeterminacy 221–225
Thom, Robert 82
The Three Kingdoms 121
Three Springs 226
Tong, Marian Yew Jen Wu 130, 131
Top of the List Gold Medallions 226
tortoise 226
Trinket 166
Tripitaka 226–227

Ts'ao Yin and the K'ang-hsi Emperor 86
Twelve Songs of the Suite *A Dream of Golden Days* 227
Tyrant King 227

van Gulik, R.H. 203
Vanitas (Kongkong Daoren) 97, 98, 197, 222, 227–228
Volpp, Sophie 68

Wade, Eldrida 84
Wade, Thomas Francis 84
Wagner, Marsha L. 156
Wang, Chi-chen 84
Wang, Guowei 41, 54–55
Wang, Jing 122
Wang, John 174
Wang, Ren 229
Wang, Shanbao 229
Wang, Wei 229–230
Wang, Xi-feng 25, 31, 56, 60, 94, 95, 100, 103, 107, 108, 109, 110, 112, 113, 116, 118, 129, 132, 133, 161, 180, 182, 192, 204, 216, 217, 226, 227, 230–233, 240, 244, 246
Wang, Yangming 196
Wang, Zi-teng 161
West, Stephen 207
The Western Chamber see *The Romance of the Western Chamber*
western objects 232–233
wet nurses 234
The White Serpent 65
Widmer, Ellen 122
Wilkinson, Thomas Francis 83
Wolf of Zhong-shan 218
women 235–238
The Won-done Song 238–239, 249
Wong, Kam-ming 66–67
Wu, Cuncun 67, 127
Wu, I-Hsien 68, 186
Wu, Jingzi 51
Wu, Shih-Ch'ang 18, 86, 219, 239
Wu, Yenna 121

Xia, Jin-gui 92, 240, 244
Xiang, Xiu-yan 103, 240
Xiang-lian *see* Caltrop
Xiao, Chi 247
Xi-ren *see* Aroma
Xu, Ma 49, 93, 198

Xue, Bao-chai 28, 35, 66, 68, 93, 103, 104, 107, 109, 112, 119, 156, 158, 164, 185, 175, 182, 186, 187, 204, 205, 207, 214, 227, 236, 237, 240–242, 245
Xue, Bao-qin 60, 102, 203, 206, 233, 236, 242–242
Xue, Ke 52, 240, 243–244
Xue, Pan 25, 100, 35, 73, 118, 244
Xue, Weihe 119, 242
Xun, Lu 86

Yama 244
Yamen 244
Yan, Qu 123
Yang, Gui-fei 245
Yang, Michael 172
Yao and Shun 245
Yee, Angelina 174–175
Yeo, Kang-shua 47
Yim, Chi-hung 107
Yin and *Yang* 102, 245
You, Er-jie *see* You Sisters
You, San-jie *see* You Sisters
You Shi 30, 107, 246
You Sisters (You Er-jie, You San-jie) 73, 111, 153, 161, 196, 217, 246–247
Yu, Anthony 29, 32, 70, 87, 88, 98, 152, 153, 183, 198, 201, 207, 221
Yu, Pingbo 56, 159, 219, 210, 220, 223
Yu, Ying-shu 143, 190

Zamperini, Paula 82
Zhang, Dainian 42
Zhang, Yiquan 18
Zhao, Xiaohuan 147
Zhen, Bao-yu 61, 62, 201, 247–248
Zhen, Shi-yin 35, 90, 98, 99, 196, 238, 239, 248–249
Zhen, Ying-lian *see* Caltrop
Zhen family 248
Zhou, Rui 167
Zhou, Ruchang 2–6, 8, 34, 55, 56, 73, 123, 145, 179, 193, 199, 202, 208, 224, 230, 237–238
Zhou, Yiqun 168, 169
Zhou, Zuyan 33, 88, 104, 137, 249, 251, 253, 254
Zhu, Xi 75
Zhuangzi 123, 238, 249–254

www.ingramcontent.com/pod-product-compliance
Ingram Content Group UK Ltd.
Pitfield, Milton Keynes, MK11 3LW, UK
UKHW041930140426
5217IPUK00014B/408